WESTERN CAVALIERS:

EMBRACING THE HISTORY OF

THE METHODIST EPISCOPAL CHURCH IN KENTUCKY FROM 1832 TO 1844.

By A. H. REDFORD, D.D.,

Author of "The History of Methodism in Kentucky," "The History of the Organization of the Methodist Episcopal Church, South," and "Fred Brenning."

NASHVILLE, TENN.:
SOUTHERN METHODIST PUBLISHING HOUSE.
1876.

STEREOTYPED AND PRINTED AT THE SOUTHERN METHODIST PUBLISHING HOUSE, NASHVILLE, TENN.

DEDICATION.

To the Rev. Thomas Osmond Summers, D.D., LL.D.

DEAR SIR:—The first time I remember to have seen you was in the month of May, 1850, during the session of the General Conference of the Methodist Episcopal Church, South, held in the city of St. Louis. In 1854, at the General Conference which convened that year in the city of Columbus, Georgia, I had the pleasure of renewing your acquaintance; and in 1858, during the meeting of the same body in the city of Nashville, I met you again. The respective fields we occupied were too remote from each other to permit, for the time being, any farther acquaintance; hence, eight years passed away before we were thrown together again; for the most part, they were years of sacrifice, of sadness, of suffering. During this period a civil war had swept over our country, desolating the homes of our people, deluging the nation with the blood of brothers, and threatening the existence of our Church. It was in 1866, when the noise of war had been hushed in the stillness of peace, that the General Conference convened in the city of New Orleans. Although time had dealt gently with you, yet its foot-prints were seen upon your brow. At this session of the Conference, your election as Editor of Books and of the *Christian Advocate*, and mine as the General Book Agent of the Methodist Episcopal Church, South, brought us into close and intimate relations to each other. For nearly ten years we have had almost daily intercourse, and have shared each other's confidence and affections. During this time no discord has disturbed our harmony, nor has any difference of opinion chilled our friendship. In the performance of the difficult duties with which I have been charged by the Church, you have always been a judicious and faithful counselor. Amid the cares that have oppressed me, and the anxiety I have felt to meet the expectations of my brethren, the sympathy you have always expressed and the hand of a brother held out to me at all times have contributed much to the advancement and progress of the interest confided to my care. Indebted, as I am, to your generosity and kindness, it is not surprising that for you I cherish a feeling of more than friendship. I therefore beg permission to dedicate this volume to you.

With many of the stirring events recorded in this volume I am not only familiar, but was personally identified. Acquainted with most of the preachers of the Methodist Church in Kentucky from my childhood, entering the Church the year subsequent to the date at which this volume opens, and admitted on trial into the Conference four years later, I had every opportunity not only of watching its onward march, but the obstacles that confronted it in its advance. Its rapid progress, adding an hundred-fold to its membership in the short space of twelve years, commands the admiration and excites the wonder of all who are familiar with the difficulties by which it was opposed.

For more than twenty years it has been my purpose to prepare this work and offer it to the Church. During this time I have availed myself of every opportunity to gather and preserve such facts and incidents as might contribute to its interest. It covers twelve years, embracing a most brilliant period of the history of the Church in Kentucky, containing brief sketches of many of the preachers, and recounting revivals of extraordinary influence and power, the mention of which is sufficient to enliven the zeal and kindle afresh the ardor of younger men in the ministry. Incidents, too, of thrilling interest have been carefully preserved, and will contribute to the adornment of these pages.

With sincere prayers that your valuable life may long be spared to the Church, and that when you pass away you may enter upon eternal life,

I am, truly, your brother in Christ,

A. H. REDFORD.

NASHVILLE, TENN., January 1, 1876.

CONTENTS.

CHAPTER I.

FROM THE SESSION OF THE KENTUCKY CONFERENCE OF 1832 TO THE CONFERENCE OF 1833.

PAGE
The first cavalier.......................... 17
Conference at Harrodsburg.......... 18
The veterans................................ 19
The chief officers......................... 19
The recruits.................................. 19
John Emory.................................. 20
Death of Franklin Davis.............. 22
Examination of character............ 23
Benjamin Ogden.......................... 24
Barnabas McHenry...................... 25
Augusta College........................... 28
Science Hill Female Academy...... 28
Bardstown Female Academy........ 28
Bishop McKendree...................... 28
The appointments........................ 29
Asiatic cholera............................ 31
Revivals.. 33
Cholera in Louisville, Shelbyville, and Cynthiana........................... 35
Jackson's Purchase..................... 36
Hezekiah Holland........................ 36
Lewis Garrett............................... 36
Hickman Circuit.......................... 37
Sandy River Circuit..................... 37
Tennessee Mission....................... 38
Clarke's River Circuit.................. 38
Thomas A. Morris........................ 38
Interesting sketch........................ 38
Thomas Smith.............................. 43
George W. D. Harris.................... 48
Alexander L. P. Green.................. 48
Wadesboro Circuit........................ 50
Charles T. Ramsey....................... 51
Arthur Davis................................ 52
Revival in Hickman Circuit......... 58
Camp-meetings............................ 59
Thomas L. Boswell....................... 60
Calvin Thompson........................ 60
Revival in the Wadesboro Circuit.. 62
Methodism in Paducah................ 62
Support of superannuated preachers, widows, and orphans......... 63
Increase in membership............... 63
Missionary collections................. 64
Support of the preachers.............. 65
The first missionary collection..... 68
The Book Concern........................ 68
American Colonization Society..... 71
Death of Joseph B. Power............ 72
Death of Barnabas McHenry........ 73
Death of Marcus Lindsey............ 73

CHAPTER II.

FROM THE SESSION OF THE KENTUCKY CONFERENCE OF 1833 TO THE CONFERENCE OF 1834.

Conference in Greensburg............ 74
Robert Richford Roberts.............. 74
A Bishop's salary......................... 76
The *Western Christian Advocate*...... 79
Augusta College........................... 81
Roberts professorship of mathematics.. 82
A financial system........................ 83
The temperance question............ 84
The subject of dress..................... 85
Henry B. Bascom......................... 86
George C. Light........................... 87
Admissions on trial...................... 88
Locations..................................... 89
Superannuated preachers............ 89
Revival in Lexington.................... 91
Revival in Port William Circuit.... 92
Revival in Newport and Covington 92
Revival in Germantown Circuit.... 92
Revival in Fleming Circuit........... 92
Revival in Lewis Circuit.............. 93
Revival in Big Sandy Circuit........ 93
Revival in Mount Vernon Circuit.. 93
Revival in Cumberland Circuit..... 93
George W. Brush.......................... 95
Revival in Shelbyville.................. 99
William B. Landrum.................... 102
Foster H. Blades.......................... 105
Revival in Hartford Circuit.......... 106
Revival in Jefferson Circuit......... 106
Revival in Breckinridge Circuit... 107
Revival in Yellow Banks Circuit... 107
Revival in Logan Circuit.............. 107
Revival in Glasgow Circuit........... 108
Opposition to Methodism............. 108
Revival in Wadesboro Circuit...... 109
Revival in Hickman Circuit......... 109

PAGE
Increase in membership ... 109
Death of Thomas P. Vance ... 109
Death of William P. McKnight ... 109

CHAPTER III.

FROM THE SESSION OF THE KENTUCKY CONFERENCE OF 1834 TO THE CONFERENCE OF 1835.

Conference at Mount Sterling ... 111
Joshua Soule ... 111
Debts due the Book Concern ... 118
Itinerant system to be guarded ... 120
Missionary collections ... 123
Organization of the Kentucky Conference Missionary Society .. 123
Agent for the Missionary Society .. 124
The Colonization Society ... 124
Preachers admitted on trial ... 125
Locations ... 125
Revival in Frankfort ... 129
Revival in Falmouth Circuit ... 129
Decrease in Lexington District ... 129
Revival in Hinckstone Circuit ... 130
Revival in Little Sandy Circuit ... 130
Revival in Big Sandy Circuit ... 130
Revival in Germantown Circuit ... 130
Decrease in Augusta District ... 130
Decrease in Harrodsburg District 130
Revival in Mount Sterling Station .. 130
Revival in Mount Vernon Circuit .. 130
Revival in Cumberland Mission ... 131
Increase in Louisville District ... 131
Decrease in Hopkinsville District .. 132
Revival in Greenville Circuit ... 133
Revival in Hopkinsville Station ... 133
Decrease in Greensburg District .. 133
Decrease in membership ... 133
George W. D. Harris leaves Kentucky ... 134
His sermon at Mobley's Campground ... 134
Death of Benjamin Ogden ... 137
Death of Francis Landrum ... 137
Death of Samuel Harrison ... 137
Death of William Adams ... 137
Death of Minor M. Cosby ... 137
Death of William Outten ... 138

CHAPTER IV.

FROM THE SESSION OF THE KENTUCKY CONFERENCE OF 1835 TO THE CONFERENCE OF 1836.

Conference in Shelbyville ... 140
James Osgood Andrew ... 140
His first sermon in Shelbyville ... 143
A resolution to extend the circulation of the *Western Christian Advocate* ... 146
Methodist Magazine ... 147
Quarterly Review ... 147
The subject of temperance ... 147
Abolition and colonization ... 148
Delegates to General Conference of 1836 ... 150
Sermon by Thomas N. Ralston ... 150
Sermon by Henry B. Bascom ... 151
Sermon by Bishop Andrew ... 153
Missionary sermon by Bishop Andrew ... 155
Admissions on trial ... 157
Locations ... 157
Henry J. Evans ... 157
Thomas P. Farmer ... 158
Barboursville District formed ... 160
Decrease in membership ... 161
Revival in Yellow Banks Circuit ... 161
Revival in Newcastle Circuit ... 161
Revival in Falmouth Circuit ... 162
Revival in Port William Circuit ... 162
Revival in Augusta ... 162
Camp-meeting near Perryville ... 162
Revival in Bowling Green Circuit .. 163
Emigration from Kentucky ... 163
Thomas Joyner ... 165
Paducah Circuit formed ... 165
Death of Bishop McKendree ... 166

CHAPTER V.

FROM THE SESSION OF THE KENTUCKY CONFERENCE OF 1836 TO THE CONFERENCE OF 1837.

Conference in Louisville ... 167
Bishop Soule presided ... 168
Admissions on trial ... 168
Locations ... 169
William S. Evans ... 169
John Redman ... 170
Herrington Stevens ... 170
Death of Henry S. Duke ... 170
Death of John Littlejohn ... 170
Death of William Phillips ... 171
Revival in Dover ... 174
Revival in Bardstown ... 174
Revivav in Washington ... 174
Revival in Wayne Circuit ... 175
Revival in Madison Circuit ... 175
Revival in Campbellsville ... 175
Revival in Greensburg Circuit ... 175
John Newland Maffitt ... 176
Revival in Lexington ... 181
Revival in Danville ... 188
Revival in Harrodsburg ... 189
Joseph D. Barnett ... 189
Revival in Lebanon Circuit ... 191
Revival in Burksville Circuit ... 191
Revival in Germantown Circuit ... 191
Camp-meeting near Carlisle ... 192
Revival in Mount Sterling Circuit .. 192
Revival in Danville Circuit ... 192
Revival in Somerset Circuit ... 192
Revival in Richmond ... 193
Camp-meeting at Pleasant Grove, Yellow Banks Circuit ... 193
Camp-meeting at No Creek, Hartford Circuit ... 193
Revival at Bell's Chapel ... 194
Revival in La Fayette Circuit ... 194
Revival in Madisonville Circuit ... 194
Revival in Maysville ... 194

PAGE
Methodism in Jackson's Purchase 195
Adam Goodwin 195
Findley Bynum 195
Revival in Paducah Circuit 196
Increase in membership 197

CHAPTER VI.

FROM THE SESSION OF THE KENTUCKY CONFERENCE OF 1837 TO THE CONFERENCE OF 1838.

Conference at Frankfort 198
Bishop Roberts 198
Resolution guarding the itinerant system 199
Proposal to transfer Hubbard H. Kavanaugh to the Missouri Conference 200
The Conference protests 201
Thomas Lasley and slavery 202
Resolution in reference to special sermons 203
John Newland Maffitt 206
Sermons in the penitentiary 206
Admissions on trial 206
Superannuated preachers 207
Locations 207
Death of Hooper Evans 207
Missionary collections 207
Revival in Frankfort 208
Revival in Louisville, at Fourth-street 209
Francis A. Dighton 209
Revival in Louisville, at Brook-street 211
Letter from Benjamin T. Crouch 213
Revival in Hardinsburg Circuit 214
Revival in Brandenburg 214
Richard Deering 214
Revival in Hartford Circuit 220
Joseph G. Ward 220
Revival in Georgetown 225
Revivals in Covington 225
Revival in Falmouth Circuit 227
Revival at Salem Church, Cynthiana Circuit 228
James C. Crow 228
Revival in Fleming Circuit 232
Revival in Augusta 232
Revival in Maysville 233
Revival in Millersburg Circuit 233
Revival in Greenupsburg Circuit 233
Revival in Little Sandy Circuit 233
Revival in Madison Circuit 234
Revival in Danville 234
Revival in Winchester Circuit 234
Revival in Somerset Circuit 235
Revival in Bowling Green Circuit 237
Revivals in Hopkinsville Circuit 237
Revival in Princeton Circuit 238
The unwelcome preacher 238
The trials of a young preacher 238
Revivals in Greensburg District 243
Revivals in Barboursville District 245
The young preacher and Mr. L— 246
Methodism in Jackson's Purchase 255

CHAPTER VII.

FROM THE SESSION OF THE KENTUCKY CONFERENCE OF 1838 TO THE CONFERENCE OF 1839.

PAGE
Conference in Danville 256
Bishops Waugh and Morris 256
Sketch of Bishop Waugh 256
Address on Education 259
Sermon on Missions 259
Resolutions from the New England Conference 268
Bishop Waugh on the resolution 269
The *Christian Apologist* 270
William Nast 270
Missionary collections 271
Admissions on trial 273
Locations 273
Death of Thomas H. Gibbons 273
Bishop Waugh's sermon 274
Bishop Morris's sermon 275
Missionary meeting 275
A pleasant incident 275
Revival in Mount Sterling Circuit 277
Revival in Burlington Circuit 278
Revival in Fleming Circuit 278
Revival in Newport 278
Revival in Louisville 279
Revival in Hardinsburg Circuit 281
Revival at Big Spring 281
Revival at Union Star 282
Revival at Hardinsburg 282
Revival at Mount Zion 282
Revival at Head of Rough Creek 282
Revival at Liberty Camp-ground 282
Revival in Newcastle Circuit 283
James D. Holding 283
Moses Levi 285
Revival in Westport 287
Revival in Hartford Circuit 288
Richard Holding 288
Revival in Owensboro 291
Revival in Hawesville 291
Revival at New Chapel 291
Revival at Pleasant Camp-ground 291
Interesting letter from Benjamin T. Crouch 292
Revival in Shelbyville 293
Revivals in Shelbyville District 293
Revival in Greensburg Circuit 294
Peter Taylor 294
Revival in Greenville Circuit 296
Revival in Hopkinsville Circuit 296
Revival in Madisonville Circuit 296
Revivals in Barboursville District 297
Jackson's Purchase 297

CHAPTER VIII.

FROM THE SESSION OF THE KENTUCKY CONFERENCE OF 1839 TO THE CONFERENCE OF 1840.

Conference in Russellville 299
Bishop Soule 299
Appointment of Committee on the Centenary of Methodism 300

PAGE
Resolution in reference to the course of study... 301
Resolution on temperance... 302
Resolution in reference to the Western Historical Society... 303
Resolution on intemperance... 304
Delegates elected to the General Conference... 305
Bishop Soule's sermon... 306
An exciting scene... 306
Missionary anniversary... 307
Admissions on trial... 307
Locations... 307
Superannuated preachers... 307
Death of Absalom D. Fox... 307
Missionary collections... 308
Revival in Augusta... 311
John H. Linn... 311
Daniel S. Barksdale... 320
Revival in Lewis Circuit... 321
Robert Y. McReynolds... 322
Revival in Cynthiana... 323
Revivals in Lexington District... 324
Revival in Versailles Circuit... 325
John Newland Maffitt leaves Kentucky... 325
Farther account of his life... 326
He dies of a broken heart... 329
Revival at Hughes' Camp-ground, near Louisville... 332
Gilby Kelly... 333
Seraiah S. Deering... 334
Sermons on baptism, in Owensboro, by Benjamin T. Crouch... 335
John L. Waller... 335
Revivals in Shelbyville District... 336
Revivals in Bowling Green District 338
Revival in Princeton Circuit... 338
Revival in Barboursville District... 339
John P. Stanfield... 339
Revival in Paducah Circuit... 339
Daniel Mooney... 340
Revival in Wadesboro Circuit... 340
Increase in membership... 340

CHAPTER IX.

FROM THE SESSION OF THE KENTUCKY CONFERENCE OF 1840 TO THE CONFERENCE OF 1841.

Conference in Bardstown... 341
Bishop Morris... 341
Distinguished visitors... 342
A communication from Bishop Smith... 343
Moses M. Henkle... 343
The "Blue Pill"... 345
Excellent sermons... 347
The License Law... 347
Missionary collections... 348
Preachers' Aid Society... 348
Sermon by William H. Anderson... 349
Sermon by Edwin Roberts... 349
Admissions on trial... 349
Locations... 350
Death of George McNelly... 350

PAGE
Death of Elijah M. Bosley... 352
Joseph Marsee... 356
Thomas W. Chandler... 357
Andrew Peace... 357
Interesting letter from a young preacher... 358
Revivals in Maysville District... 366
Revival in Covington... 367
Revival in Newport... 367
Aaron Moore... 367
George W. Merritt... 368
Revival in Versailles Circuit... 370
Revival in Winchester Circuit... 370
John W. Riggin... 371
Thomas Bottomley... 372
William Holman... 373
Peter Schmucker... 375
Alanson C. Dewitt... 375
Revival in Hodgenville Circuit... 377
Revival in Litchfield Circuit... 377
Revival in Danville Circuit... 377
John C. C. Thompson... 378
Matthew N. Lasley... 379
Revival in Glasgow Circuit... 383
Joel Peak... 383
Revival in Russellville... 384
Revivals in Barboursville District 384
Revival in Paducah Circuit... 385
Camp-meeting in Wadesboro Circuit... 385
Revivals in Hickman Circuit... 386
Increase in membership... 387

CHAPTER X.

FROM THE SESSION OF THE KENTUCKY CONFERENCE OF 1841 TO THE CONFERENCE OF 1842.

Conference in Maysville... 388
No Bishop present... 388
Jonathan Stamper elected President... 388
The temperance question... 389
Communication from Bishop Andrew... 390
Committee on Augusta College... 390
A plan for the improvement of the ministry... 390
Preachers' Aid Society... 392
Science Hill Female Academy... 392
Resolution requiring preachers to furnish a statement of the date and place of their birth, conversion, and admission on trial... 396
Resolution of thanks to Thomas N. Ralston... 396
Resolutions in reference to Augusta College... 397
American Colonization Society... 398
Resolution in reference to a book of memoirs... 398
Transylvania University tendered to the Kentucky Conference... 400
American Bible Society... 406
Edmund W. Sehon... 407
Admissions on trial... 409

PAGE
Locations... 409
Death of Absalom Hunt... 410
Death of Alexander Robinson... 410
Death of Henry N. Vandyke... 411
Death of William D. Minga... 413
Missionary collections... 414
Jonathan Stamper... 414
William M. Grubbs... 414
Henry E. Pilcher... 423
Walter Shearer... 425
William C. Atmore... 425
William M. Crawford... 428
Revival in Shannon Circuit... 430
Revival in Covington... 430
Revival in Mount Carmel, Paris Circuit... 430
Letter from John James... 430
Letter from Benjamin T. Crouch... 431
Revivals in Lexington District... 435
John Collins Hardy... 435
Revival in Mount Sterling Circuit... 435
Drummond Welburn... 436
Revival in Athens Circuit... 439
Thomas Demoss... 440
Revival in La Grange Circuit... 442
Revival in Jefferson Circuit... 442
Dorsey's Camp-ground... 442
Hartwell J. Perry... 443
Revival in Shelby Circuit... 447
Nathanael H. Lee... 448
John Sandusky... 456
Revival in Madison Circuit... 458
Old Providence... 459
Eli B. Crain... 460
Revival in Russellville... 462
John B. Perry... 462
Warren M. Pitts... 464
Campbellism... 465
The Baptist Church... 465
Revival in Elkton... 465
A Campbellite preacher... 466
Sermons on baptism... 466
Elder Robert Williams... 467
A challenge... 467
A debate... 467
Jackson's Purchase... 468
Revival in Paducah... 468
Hickman, Paducah, and Wadesboro Circuits... 469
Increase in membership... 470

CHAPTER XI.

FROM THE SESSION OF THE KENTUCKY CONFERENCE OF 1842 TO THE CONFERENCE OF 1843.

Conference in Lexington... 471
Bishop Waugh present... 471
Albery L. Alderson... 472
George S. Savage... 474
Revival at Shannon Church... 478
Revival at Sardis... 479
Missionary collections... 479
Death of Peter O. Meeks... 479
Death of Edwin Roberts... 479
Revival in Morganfield Circuit... 482
Revival in Versailles Circuit... 482
Journal of Edwin Roberts... 483
German Mission formed... 486
Revivals in Maysville District... 486
Revival in Germantown Circuit... 487
Revival in Big Sandy Circuit... 487
Revival in Flemingsburg Circuit... 487
Revival at Covington... 487
Revival at Cynthiana... 488
John Miller... 488
Revival in Millersburg Circuit... 489
John G. Bruce... 489
Revivals in Lexington District... 489
Revival in Versailles Circuit... 490
Camp-meeting near Nicholasville. 490
Revival in Georgetown... 491
Revival in Athens Circuit... 491
Revivals in Burlington Circuit... 491
Revivals in Louisville... 491
Charles B. Parsons... 492
Revival in Shepherdsville Circuit... 495
Revival in La Grange Circuit... 495
Samuel D. Baldwin... 495
Samuel L. Robertson... 496
Revival in Owensboro... 497
Revival at Burks's... 497
Revival at Pleasant Grove... 497
Seraiah S. Deering... 497
Napoleon B. Lewis... 498
Revivals in Somerset Circuit... 502
Ransom Lancaster... 502
Revival at Richmond... 502
Revival in Madison Circuit... 503
Robinson E. Sidebottom... 503
Elkanah Johnson... 504
Revival at Bowling Green... 505
Revival in Scottsville Circuit... 505
Revivals in Hopkinsville District... 505
Revival at Ash Spring camp-meeting, Logan Circuit... 505
Revival at Pleasant Grove... 506
Revival in Hopkinsville Circuit... 507
Revivals in Barboursville District... 507
Jackson's Purchase... 507
Mayfield Circuit formed... 507
Decrease in membership in Jackson's Purchase... 508
Increase in membership... 508

CHAPTER XII.

FROM THE SESSION OF THE KENTUCKY CONFERENCE OF 1843 TO THE CONFERENCE OF 1844.

Conference at Louisville... 509
Bishop Morris... 509
Distinguished visitors... 509
The American Bible Society... 510
The *Western Christian Advocate*... 510
Resolution to promote interests of the Western Book Concern... 510
The Agent and delinquent debtors 511
The temperance question... 511
The slavery question... 512
Delegates elected to the General Conference of 1844... 512

PAGE
Resolution in reference to a history of Methodism in Kentucky.. 512
Admissions on trial.......... 513
Locations.......... 513
Superannuated preachers.......... 513
Thomas N. Ralston.......... 513
Revivals in Mount Sterling Circuit.. 515
Camp-meeting near Perryville...... 515
A convincing argument.......... 516
Affecting incident.......... 517
Death of Richard Corwine.......... 518
Death of John Denham.......... 518
Death of Elihu Green.......... 518
Missionary collections.......... 519
John Christian Harrison.......... 520
Revival at Maysville.......... 527
George B. Poage.......... 527
Revival at Mount Zion.......... 528
Campbellism in Brooksville.......... 529
Exciting scene.......... 529
Revival in Brooksville.......... 530
Remarkable conversion.......... 530
Revival in Augusta.......... 532
Revival at Minerva.......... 532
An enraged husband.......... 532
Revival at Dover.......... 533
Revival in Germantown Circuit..... 533
Revivals in Shannon Circuit.......... 533
Revival at Nelson Asbury's.......... 533
Revival in Covington.......... 534
Revival in Falmouth Circuit.......... 534

PAGE
The Lexington District.......... 534
Transylvania University.......... 534
Burr H. McCown.......... 535
William H. Anderson.......... 536
Revivals in Louisville District...... 538
George W. Crumbaugh.......... 538
George S. Gatewood.......... 539
Revival at Hardinsburg.......... 540
Revival in Hawesville Circuit.......... 540
Revival in Hartford Circuit.......... 540
Revival in Big Spring Circuit.......... 540
Morganfield District formed.......... 541
Learner B. Davison.......... 541
Revival in Henderson Circuit....... 542
Revival at Smithland.......... 542
Revival at Eddyville.......... 542
Revivals in Princeton Circuit.......... 543
Revivals in Russellville District... 543
Robert Fisk.......... 543
Revivals in Bowling Green District 544
Timothy C. Frogge.......... 545
John S. Magee.......... 545
Robert G. Gardner.......... 545
Revivals in Barboursville Circuit.. 546
Jackson's Purchase.......... 547
Revival in Hickman Circuit.......... 547
Revival in Mayfield Circuit.......... 547
Revivals in Paducah and Wadesboro Circuits.......... 547
Decrease in membership.......... 547
Review.......... 547

Western Cavaliers.

WESTERN CAVALIERS.

CHAPTER I.

FROM THE SESSION OF THE KENTUCKY CONFERENCE OF 1832 TO THE CONFERENCE OF 1833.

Tranquil amid alarms,
  It found him on the field,
A vet'ran, slumb'ring on his arms,
  Beneath his red-cross shield.
His sword was in his hand,
  Still warm with recent fight,
Ready that moment, at command,
  Through rock and steel to smite.

IT was Wednesday morning, October the seventeenth, one thousand eight hundred and thirty-two. The first Western cavalier* still lived. The privations he had suffered, the hardships he had encountered, and the labor he had performed, in the service to which he had pledged his life, had so far

* Benjamin Ogden.

impaired his once robust constitution that he was unable longer to lead to victory, or to mingle in the din of battle. His comrades-in-arms, who had caught the inspiration of his ardor, and followed his fortunes amid the rains of summer, the frosts of autumn, and the snows of winter, on many a hard-fought field, were sleeping their last sleep in the bivouac of the dead, or were patiently awaiting the summons that would release them from a conflict in which they could not be active participants. He was a brave cavalier. For forty years he had been in the thickest of the fight, the gallant leader of a band of men as valiant as ever unsheathed the sword of truth; but for five years his name had stood on the retired list, honored for deeds of chivalry and daring. His keen Jerusalem blade still hung at his side. "I wish to die," he said, "having the whole armor on, contending like a good soldier for the prize." The frosts of nearly seventy winters had bleached his brow, and his trembling and unsteady step indicated, too plainly, that he must soon receive his furlough, and enter upon eternal rest. His zeal, however, was unabated; and the abiding interest he felt in the cause for which he had battled so long evinced itself in the fire that flashed from his eye whenever his fellow-soldiers buckled on their armor for the fight, or returned from the ensanguined field laden with the spoils of victory.

To arrange for a year's campaign, more than one hundred men had met in the beautiful village of Harrodsburg, in the State of Kentucky. Some of them were veterans. For many years they had bared their bosoms to the storm, and been familiar with the shock of battle. They had often felt the clash of arms, and joined in the shouts of victory. They knew what privations meant. Ever true to the ensign beneath whose folds they fought, they shunned no danger, and avoided no suffering. Their names were Benjamin Ogden, John Littlejohn, James Ward, Barnabas McHenry, Clement L. Clifton, John Ray, Zadok B. Thaxton, Henry McDaniel, Esau Simmons, Blatchley C. Wood, Luke P. Allen, William Atherton, Samuel Helms, Joseph B. Power, Moses Clampit, and Absalom Hunt. William Gunn, Richard Corwine, George W. Taylor, Benjamin T. Crouch, John Johnson, and Marcus Lindsey were also present. They were in the prime of life. Their prowess, their faithful service, their aptitude and devotion to the cause which had been ennobled by their valor, had suggested them as persons well qualified to lead to battle and to victory.

In this company there were younger men. They, too, were inured to hardship. On some of them might have been seen the scars received on many a hard-fought field—on all, the marks of faithful service. "They counted not their lives dear," so that they might be good soldiers of the cross, and achieve success. They were the rank and file.

There were those, too, who had come to enter the ranks. They were twelve in number. Their names were Lorenzo D. Parker, John Nevius, Joseph W. Shultz, Richard Deering, William G. Bowman, Thomas S. Davis, Foster H. Blades, Herrington

Stevens, Richard Holding, James H. Brooking, William McMahon, and Gilby Kelly. They were in the rosy morn of life. Some of them had already encountered hardships, while others had never confronted danger. One of them was a smooth-faced boy, and more than one had not reached the years of manhood.

The life upon which these young men were entering was not one of pleasure or of ease. They were not to tread the path that leads to fortune or to fame. If roses bloomed along their route, they had no time to gather them. They were to face opposition, and to become accustomed to hardship; or, if unequal to the privations, sacrifices, and duties incident to the life of toil that lay before them, they must retire from the struggle. Others were present, whose names will adorn these pages, whose deeds of chivalry and daring shook the empire of darkness to its center, and who, under God, recovered from the grasp of Satan many who became valiant soldiers of the cross.

John Emory was a gallant leader—as prompt in action as he was wise in counsel. To him had been assigned the command of the Western division of the work. His presence at the Harrodsburg Conference contributed much to the advancement of the cause to which these men had pledged their energies and their lives. Not only in his private counsels, but in his public ministrations, he won upon the hearts and the affections of all. His sound judgment, his polished manner, his commanding presence, his thorough qualification for the duties that devolved upon him, inspired a confidence which was the harbinger of success.*

The business which had called these men together was of no ordinary importance. Their cause was a common one. They had met to examine, with the most scrutinizing care, into the conduct of each cavalier during the year which was closing, to bestow the proper meed of praise on those who had been good and true, and to censure any who had not come up to the full measure of duty. They had assembled to recount their sufferings, to tell of their conflicts, to rejoice in the victories they had achieved, and to devise plans for future conquests and successes.

A few years before and Kentucky was a wilder-

* Bishop Emory entered the itinerant ministry in 1810, in the Philadelphia Conference. Devoted to the work to which he was divinely called, and favored with an intellect of the highest order, he soon attained to eminence in the Church. In 1820 he was chosen by the General Conference to visit the British Conference as the representative of the Methodist Episcopal Church in the United States. In 1824 he was elected Assistant Agent, and in 1828 he was chosen by the suffrages of his brethren as the Senior Agent, of the Book Concern in New York. On the 22d of May, 1832, James O. Andrew and John Emory were elected to the office of Bishop—the former having received, on the first ballot, one hundred and forty votes, and the latter one hundred and thirty-five—two hundred and twenty-three votes having been cast. The career of Mr. Emory as a Bishop was brief. On Wednesday, the 16th of December, 1835, he left his home in the morning to go to Baltimore, on business connected with the Church. On his way he was thrown from his carriage, and received a wound in his head, of which he died about seven o'clock in the evening of the same day.

ness, wrapped in moral night, on which fell scarcely a single ray of hope. Through privations, suffering, and want, brave cavaliers had toiled and battled until the powers of darkness trembled, and victory was perching on the standard of the cross. Much, however, was yet to be achieved. Sin, in hideous forms, walked with high and proud steps through the land; infidelity, with its brazen front, defied the power of truth. The strongholds of vice must be attacked, its very citadel must be demolished, and light, and truth, and happiness must pervade this grand Commonwealth, until the wilderness and solitary place shall be glad, and the desert shall rejoice and blossom as the rose.

To accomplish the task for which they had convened on this occasion required wisdom and prudence, no less than skill and courage. Bishop Emory was in the chair, and William Adams was Secretary. The roll was called, and all responded to their names, with the exception of Franklin Davis, who had fallen during the year.*

To institute a rigid examination into the labors and conduct of these men for the previous year was one of the first duties to be performed. The task was a delicate one. On one hand, it was important that no cavalier should be charged unjustly with either a want of promptness or fidelity in the per-

*At the session of the Kentucky Conference of 1830, Franklin Davis was admitted on trial, and appointed to the Cynthiana Circuit; in 1831 he was the junior preacher on Breckinridge Circuit, and died during the year. No memoir of him was furnished.

formance of the duties assigned him; and on the other, that the cause for which they were battling should not suffer from either the inefficiency or negligence of those to whom it had been intrusted.*

In the examination of character it was necessary to ascertain whether any who had been on the retired list, from either the infirmities of age or sickness, were able to reënter the effective service. We have already mentioned the names of

* The Kentucky Conference, at this time, was divided into six Districts, each one under the supervision of a Presiding Elder. The Districts embraced ten or twelve stations, each of which was occupied by from one to three preachers. No body of preachers in the world passes through an ordeal so rigid as do Methodist itinerant preachers in the examination of their characters, which takes place once a year. Not only the propriety, but the importance, of this will be apparent when it is known that our preachers are appointed to fields of labor where they are strangers, the people to whom they are sent not knowing any thing of them only that they have been indorsed by the Annual Conference. When the name of a District is called, the question is asked by the Bishop whether there is any thing against the Presiding Elder. This question embraces not only his moral character, but his efficiency and the faithful performance of the duties of his office. The preachers of his District are expected faithfully to represent him, when, after the approval on the part of the Conference of his character and administration, the name of each preacher in his District is called, and his character examined. The following were the names of the Districts and of the Presiding Elders at this time: Kentucky District, William Gunn; Augusta District, Richard Corwine; Rockcastle District, George W. Taylor; Ohio District, Benjamin T. Crouch; Green River District, John Johnson; Cumberland District, Marcus Lindsey.

those who had been excused from labor the previous year.

The name of Benjamin Ogden was first called. There is nothing more trying to a soldier, whose courage never has been called in question, than to listen to strains of martial music inviting his comrades to arms and to duty, and he not be able to engage in the strife. To hear the sound of the fife and drum, and to see the ensign beneath whose folds he had fought and conquered thrown to the breeze, and yet not to be allowed to buckle on his armor, is a position that no brave man can envy. The name of Benjamin Ogden was the synonym of courage and of suffering. No cavalier had preceded him in the West. He had alone traversed its wilds, had swum its rivers, had encountered difficulty and danger, and had met and conquered many a foe; and then on the green-carpeted earth had laid him down to rest and sleep, with no covering save the deep blue sky. When, in 1786, just forty-six years before, he came to the West, but few rallied to his standard; the sound of his bugle-horn arrested here and there a solitary wanderer. He was young, active, and strong, capable of endurance, and willing to perform the arduous duties assigned him. Old age, however, had crept upon him, until he could only watch the camp-fires, and join in the shout of victory; still there is much to gladden his heart, and cheer his declining years. One hundred and thirteen brave and gallant men are contending for the truth where he had stood alone, while twenty-six thousand nine hundred and eighty-seven men and women adhered to the cause to which his life had been devoted.

"Nothing against Benjamin Ogden," was the prompt response of the officer in charge of the District in which he resided. "For many years he has gone in and out among us, occupying the front ranks, and leading to battle and to victory. Although no longer able to perform effective service, yet his devotion to the cause and his bright example are exerting an influence little less than did the heroic labors he performed in the strength of his manhood," was the testimony in his favor. His character was passed.

Another name was called. "Is there any thing against Barnabas McHenry?" Mr. McHenry came to the West in 1789, three years later than Mr. Ogden. At the time he entered the service in Kentucky there were only five cavaliers besides himself to occupy the entire State—Francis Poythress, James Haw, Wilson Lee, and Peter Massie, had preceded him, while the name of Stephen Brooks appears at the same time with his own.

Among the noble men who battled for the cause of God at this early day in the West, no one bore himself more gallantly than did Barnabas McHenry. Panoplied with the truth as it is in Jesus, familiar with the doctrines of which he was a fearless and able advocate, his sword gleamed in the sunlight on almost every hill-top and in every valley in Central Kentucky. The days of his active service, however, had been numbered; yet, unwilling to repose amid the trophies he had won, or the laurels he had gathered on so many hard-fought fields, we find him contributing his remaining energies to the advancement and progress of the cause which had been the cherished object of his life. "He can no longer bear the exposure of the field, nor even stand on guard; but there beats no truer heart than his," was the answer of the officer in charge.

The names of John Littlejohn, James Ward, John Ray, Zadoc B. Thaxton, Henry McDaniel, Samuel Helms, Absalom Hunt, Blatchley C. Wood, Esau Simmons, Luke P. Allen, Clement L. Clifton, William Atherton, Moses B. Clampit, and Joseph B. Power were called, and their characters approved.

Not one of these tried veterans was able to reënter the service. The repose from labor that had been granted them during the previous year had failed to restore their impaired health or to prepare them to engage in the campaign for the coming season.

As the name of each cavalier was called, his character passed in review before his fellow-soldiers, meeting with approval. Of the number who had gone out one year before, with "sword in hand and armor on," not one had deserted his post or dishonored his flag. Whether in the crowded city or in the solitary waste, amid mountain fastnesses or in miasmatic swamps, in palaces of wealth or the cabins of the poor, none had betrayed the noble cause, or been untrue to the colors beneath which he had enrolled. Amid snow, and hail, and storm, they had held aloft their banner, bearing the inspiring inscription, "Behold the Lamb of God!" They had thrown its folds to the breeze, and many a wayfarer, attracted by the shelter it offered from the storm, sought beneath it a haven and a rest. It is true that four other names were placed on the retired list because of failing health, and six withdrew from the cavalry service to enter another department,* but no want of fidelity stained the escutcheon of a single cavalier.

The Conference of 1832 was in several respects of greater importance than any of its predecessors. A more decided stand was taken against the use of all intoxicating liquors as a beverage; the Bible, Tract, and Sunday-school societies received a stronger indorsement than ever before; a resolution was passed looking to the inauguration of the Missionary Society of the Kentucky Conference;† and a more stringent rule was adopted in reference to

*At this Conference Thomas G. Reese, James L. Greenup, Wilson S. McMurry, Elijah Knox, Alexander H. Stemmons, and John W. F. Tevis located.

† The following resolution was adopted by the Conference: "*Resolved, by the Kentucky Annual Conference,* That the Presiding Elder and stationed preacher of Louisville Station be directed to use their influence to form a Conference Missionary Society in that place, auxiliary to the Missionary Society of the M. E. Church at New York, and the Presiding Elders and preachers in charge be required to use their utmost efforts to form societies auxiliary to said Conference Society; and that, as soon as said society shall have been formed, it shall be the duty of the Presiding Elder or preacher in charge to furnish the same for publication in *The Christian Advocate and Journal.*"

the support of the superannuated preachers, and widows and orphans.

The question of education also occupied a prominent place in the deliberations of the Conference. Not only Augusta College, at that time under the joint supervision and patronage of the Kentucky and Ohio Conferences, but Science Hill Female Academy, at Shelbyville, with Mrs. Julia A. Tevis at its head, and the Bardstown Female Academy, at Bardstown, received special consideration. An Agent was also appointed in behalf of the Colonization Society.

On Saturday morning, the fourth day of the Conference, the venerable Bishop McKendree appeared in the Conference-room. His once erect form was bending beneath the weight of labor and of years. He made an impressive address to the Conference, recommending that no departure from the old landmarks of Methodism be entertained for a moment, and that constant attention to the doctrines and discipline of the Church be observed. He then prayed with the brethren, after which he bade them an affectionate farewell. It was his valedictory.

The entire session was distinguished by the most perfect harmony, each endeavoring to promote the happiness of all others.

It was late on Tuesday evening, the 23d, when the Conference adjourned.

After an appropriate address by Bishop Emory, the following appointments for the Conference-year were announced:

LEXINGTON DISTRICT.
William Gunn, P. E.

Lexington, J. James.
Lexington Circuit, S. Veach, W. Philips.
Frankfort, H. H. Kavanaugh.
Cynthiana, G. W. Brush.
Cynthiana Circuit, A. Woolliscroft, L. D. Parker.
Burlington, J. C. Crow.
Port William, J. King.
Newport and Covington, W. P. McKnight.
Falmouth, J. Whitaker.
G. C. Light, Agent for American Colonization Society.

AUGUSTA DISTRICT.
Richard Tydings, P. E.

Maysville, M. L. Eades.
Germantown, F. Landrum, one to be supplied.
Fleming, R. Corwine, R. Deering.
Hinckstone, D. H. Tevis, G. Kelly.
Lewis, T. Waring.
Little Sandy, R. Bird, J. H. Brooking.
Big Sandy, W. S. Evans, J. D. Barnet.
Highland, W. Cundiff.
J. Tomlinson, President of the Augusta College.
H. B. Bascom and B. H. McCown, Professors in Augusta College.

HARRODSBURG DISTRICT.
William Adams, P. E.

Mount Sterling, H. S. Duke.
Mount Sterling Circuit, J. F. Young, one to be supplied.
Madison, J. Beatty, R. Holding.
Danville and Harrodsburg, W. Holman.
Mount Vernon, R. J. Dungan.
Cumberland, C. Babbit, one to be supplied.
Winchester, C. M. Holliday, J. Nevius.
Danville Circuit, M. Jamieson, M. M. Cosby.

LOUISVILLE DISTRICT.
Benjamin T. Crouch, P. E.

Shelby, S. Harrison, T. P. Farmer.
Shelbyville and Brick Chapel, M. Lindsey.
Taylorsville, J. Williams.
Jefferson, I. Collard, J. W. Schultz.
Louisville, E. Stevenson, J. Stamper.
Breckinridge, W. Helm, F. H. Blades.
Yellow Banks, T. P. Vance.
Hartford, R. Y. McReynolds, S. Harber, sup.
Newcastle, J. Marsee, L. Campbell.
J. Tevis, Superintendent of Shelbyville Female Academy.

HOPKINSVILLE DISTRICT.
John Johnson, P. E.

Bowling Green, T. H. Cropper.
Bowling Green Circuit, J. G. Ward, R. F. Turner.
Russellville, H. J. Evans.
Logan, D. S. Capell, H. Stevens.
Hopkinsville, T. W. Chandler.
Christian, N. G. Berryman, J. Redman.
Greenville, I. Malone, E. Sutton.
Livingston, W. B. Landrum, one to be supplied.
Henderson, A. Long, B. Farris.

GREENSBURG DISTRICT
George W. Taylor, P. E.

Glasgow, T. H. Gibbons, W. McMahon.
Elizabeth, B. Henry, W. G. Bowman.
Bardstown and Elizabethtown, W. Fagg.
Salt River, S. Lee, H. Evans.
Lebanon, J. Sandusky, T. Hall.
Green River, H. Crews, H. J. Perry, T. Lasley, sup.
Wayne, J. Sutton, one to be supplied.
Somerset, J. C. Harrison, T. S. Davis.
W. M. McReynolds, Superintendent of Bardstown Female Academy.

In a Conference of Methodist preachers there is a degree of moral heroism nowhere else to be found. A body of ministers, whose wives and children are to them dearer than life, voluntarily surrendering their right to select their fields of ministerial labor, referring the whole question of their appointments to the Bishop and his council, and cheerfully going wherever they are sent, whether to city or country —nearly always among strangers, and often with a poor prospect of support—affords a sublime "spectacle unto the world, and to angels, and to men."

It will be seen from the above list that the Kentucky Conference contained at this date six Districts, embracing fifty-seven separate charges, to which eighty-four preachers were appointed.* Besides these, George C. Light was appointed Agent for the American Colonization Society; John Tevis, Superintendent of Shelbyville Female Academy; William M. McReynolds, Superintendent of Bardstown Female Academy; and Joseph S. Tomlinson, Henry B. Bascom, and Burr H. McCown, the first as President, and the other two as Professors, in Augusta College—making a total of ninety preachers in the effective work, including Thomas Lasley and Stephen Harber, who were supernumeraries. In addition to these, there were nineteen preachers on the superannuated list, making a grand total of one hundred and nine.

At this early period the Kentucky Conference could boast of a constellation of great men in the ministry whose peers have seldom been found in

* The six Districts are embraced in this calculation.

any body—their superiors, never. In charge of the Districts were the strong-minded Gunn, the sweet-spirited Tydings, the unostentatious Adams, Crouch the logician, the eccentric yet gifted Johnson, and the plain, pure-hearted Taylor; while Bascom, Tomlinson, McCown, Kavanaugh, Light, Eades, Landrum, Corwine, Duke, Holliday, Lindsey, Jamieson, Collard, Stevenson, Stamper, and Tevis, would have adorned any pulpit in any age.

On Wednesday morning, October the 24th, the members of the Conference took leave of the families where they had been hospitably entertained, and, mounting their horses, started to their new fields of labor. How diversified the stations to which they were appointed! Some were sent to the crowded city, some to the pleasant village, some to beautiful rural districts, some to large and laborious circuits, and some to poor and humble mountaineers—but all where sinners lived, to whom the tidings of a Redeemer's love must be proclaimed.

The appearance of Asiatic cholera in the Old World excited fearful apprehensions in the minds of thousands in this country, and, as it made its advances toward the United States, the stories of the desolation that marked its path made many a face turn pale. In the autumn of 1832 it reached the city of Louisville, and, while the Conference was still in session, bore hundreds to the grave. This sad reality made a profound impression on the minds of the members of the Conference, and they recognized it by the passage of a suitable preamble and resolutions,* observed the Saturday of their session as a day of humiliation and prayer, and appointed Jonathan Stamper to deliver a sermon on the occasion.†

In taking leave of each other, many felt that they would not all meet again on this side the last river, but contemplated a happier meeting in a world of light, and love, and joy.

The year upon which these men were entering was destined to be a year of suffering and of toil.

---

*Whereas, the Asiatic cholera has at length visited our borders, and is now carrying forward the work of death in one of our most populous cities, as well as in other important sections of our work; and whereas, we regard it as a dispensation of Divine justice in consequence of our national and individual sins; and believing it to be our duty, in all such visitations, to humble ourselves before the Most High, therefore,

Resolved, by the Kentucky Annual Conference, That we will observe Saturday, the 19th inst., as a day of humiliation and prayer, and that Brother Stamper be requested to deliver a discourse on the occasion, at three o'clock, in the M. E. Church in this place.

And be it farther resolved, That we set apart, as a day of solemn fasting and prayer throughout the bounds of this Conference, the first Friday in November next, and that the members of this Conference be directed to use their utmost efforts to have the above resolution carried into effect in their respective circuits and stations.

†At this Conference Bishop Emory proposed to send Marcus Lindsey to Louisville. Mr. Lindsey expressed a preference for Shelbyville, and offered as the reason that he had strange apprehension in reference to the cholera, and that Shelbyville had not been, and probably would not be, visited by it. Shelbyville was terribly scourged in 1833.

The fearful cholera, whose presence had created so much alarm, and was still carrying desolation to many a home, might subside, but in tenfold fury it would return the following season, and shroud in gloom hamlet, village, and city; Churches in many places would be more than decimated, and men who for years had led the Israel of God to victory would fall victims to the scourge. At no Conference had brethren separated with sadder hearts.

This year, however, so replete with suffering and loss, would be crowned with extraordinary revivals of religion, without a parallel in the annals of the past.

In entering upon a new field of ministerial labor a Methodist preacher enjoys an advantage unknown to the pastorate of any other Church. Indorsed by the Conference of which he is a member, it is but seldom that he meets with other than a kind reception among the people whom he is appointed to serve. He may be young and without experience, or he may be a stranger, yet he finds a warm place in the hearts of the people of his charge; and hence he is at once prepared to devise plans for success in his high and holy calling.

The first round of quarterly meetings in the several Districts evinced more than an ordinary concern on the subject of religion. An awakening was felt in several sections of the work, and in some of the charges the gentle shower which precedes the full rain had fallen upon the Church. In the Lexington District, the Church in Lexington was considerably revived under the ministry of John

James, a zealous preacher of the gospel, while the Church in Frankfort, of which Hubbard H. Kavanaugh was pastor, enjoyed some refreshing showers of grace. In the Augusta District, the Church in Maysville had some prosperity, through the labors of Martin L. Eades, while Mount Sterling and Harrodsburg, in the Harrodsburg District—the former with Henry S. Duke in charge, and the latter served by William Holman—were favored with interesting revivals of religion.

The Church in Louisville, in the Louisville District, to which Edward Stevenson and Jonathan Stamper had been appointed, realized times of refreshing from the presence of the Lord, while, in the Hopkinsville District, the labors of Henry J. Evans, the faithful pastor at Russellville, were greatly blessed.

Besides these, occasional showers of grace were falling upon the Church in different places—indices of a wide-spread revival of the work of God. The spring of 1833 opened favorably. All along the line the Presiding Elders had sounded the tocsin, and every man was at his post. Men and women in every community were reflecting seriously upon the subject of religion, and the impression obtained that there would be, throughout the Commonwealth, a general revival of the work of God. In the several Districts revivals broke out so nearly at the same time that it would be difficult to decide where the work began. In the Lexington, Cynthiana, and Port William Circuits, in the Lexington District; in the Germantown, Hinckstone, Fleming, and Little Sandy Circuits, in the Augusta District; in the Madison, Danville, Cumberland, Winchester, and Mount Sterling Circuits, in the Harrodsburg District; in the Breckinridge and Newcastle Circuits, in the Louisville District; in the Henderson, Christian, Logan, and Bowling Green Circuits, in the Hopkinsville District; and in the Glasgow, Salt River, Lebanon, and Green River Circuits, in the Greensburg District, the work began early in the spring, and continued throughout the summer.

In several other charges, although favored with no general revival of religion, sinners were awakened and converted to God. Late in the spring of 1833 the cholera reäppeared, and in the most malignant form visited many portions of the State. Louisville, Shelbyville, Cynthiana, and many other towns, were almost depopulated by this fearful scourge. It swept through the country, and many a home, in the morning cheerful and happy, was clad in mourning before the stars shone out.

In Cynthiana, several of the best members of the Church were stricken down, yet, under the pastoral care of George W. Brush, a young preacher, the membership increased.

In the Big Sandy Circuit, in the Augusta District; in the Greenville and Livingston Circuits, and Bowling Green Station, in the Hopkinsville District; and in the Wayne and Somerset Circuits, in the Greensburg District, many were added to the Church. Indeed, so general were the revivals during this year that only seven charges in the Conference failed to report an increase in the membership

—the Mount Vernon Circuit, in the Harrodsburg District; the Shelby, the Yellow Banks, and the Hartford Circuits, in the Louisville District; the Hopkinsville Station, in the Hopkinsville District; and the Elizabeth Circuit, in the Greensburg District. From the Shelbyville and Brick Chapel Station no change is reported in the membership from the previous year.*

It is proper to state that as early as 1820 missionaries were appointed from the Tennessee Conference to that portion of Kentucky known as Jackson's Purchase. Hezekiah Holland and Lewis Garrett, men distinguished for their piety and zeal, were the first Methodist preachers to bear the tidings of a Redeemer's love to that section of the State. Mr. Holland remained in the itinerant ranks but a short time. The exposure and arduous duties of his office were more than equal to his strength; hence, in 1822, he located. During the brief period of his ministry he was not only faithful, but eminently successful. Lewis Garrett had preceded his colleague in the Conference two years. He had been identified with the fortunes of Methodism in Kentucky at an earlier period, having been appointed to the Cumberland Circuit, where he remained for two years. In entering upon their work in the Purchase, difficulties such as are common in new and sparsely-settled communities confronted them. Without church-edifices of even the plainest

*The pastor of the Church died during the year, and, no report having been furnished the Conference, the statistics of the former year were recorded.

structure, they carried the gospel to the homes of the people, and reported at the ensuing Conference *one hundred and forty-two* white and *three* colored members.

In this new and interesting field, in which Methodism was destined to act so prominent a part, these faithful men were succeeded by William B. Carpenter, a young man just admitted on trial, who was appointed to the Hickman, and Benjamin T. Crouch and Lewis Parker to the Sandy River Circuit, lying partly in Kentucky and partly in Tennessee—Mr. Garrett presiding over the District. Considerable success crowned the labors of Mr. Carpenter; while on the Sandy River Circuit, under the ministry of Benjamin T. Crouch and Lewis Parker, many were converted and added to the Church.*

John Kesterson became an itinerant in 1818, and traveled that year the Tuskaloosa Circuit, with the gifted Thomas D. Porter as his Presiding Elder. In 1819 his field of labor was the Lee Circuit, on the waters of the Holston; in 1820 he was appointed to the Sequatchie Valley Circuit, under the leadership of the eccentric Axley; and in 1821, with John Tevis as his Presiding Elder, he traveled the Ashe Circuit, in the Holston District. Faithful in these several fields of labor, in 1822, with Nathan L. Norvall for his colleague, he was sent to the

---

* In his diary, in possession of the author, Mr. Crouch says, referring to the year he spent on Sandy River Circuit: "Several new Societies were organized, classes established the previous year revived and increased, two large circuits formed, and the whole work left in a prosperous condition."

Hickman Circuit. His colleague, Mr. Norvall, had been an itinerant but one year, and had traveled the Richland Circuit. At the following Conference we have no report from the Hickman Circuit, hence we are unable to give the result of the labors of these men.

At the Conference of 1823 the name of the Hickman Circuit disappears from the roll, having probably been connected with some other charge.

In 1824, the veteran Ogden was appointed from the Kentucky Conference to the Tennessee Mission, which embraced the most, if not all, of Jackson's Purchase, in both Tennessee and Kentucky. At the close of the year Mr. Ogden reported *one hundred and seventy-five* white and *five* colored members. At the session of the Kentucky Conference in 1825 Green River District included Jackson's Purchase. At the same time the name of the Tennessee Mission disappears from the list, and is substituted by the Clarke's River Circuit. Thomas A. Morris, afterward Bishop Morris, had charge of the District, and John S. Barger and James L. Greenup were the preachers. At the Conference of 1826 *two hundred and eighty-eight* white and *six* colored members were reported. Bishop Morris* says:

"In 1825 my District embraced that part of Kentucky west of the Tennessee River, which was then all in one circuit, called Clarke's River, of which John S. Barger was preacher in charge. We were not the first on that ground after the Indians left. Brothers Crouch and Parker had been there form-

* "Miscellany," pp. 241–244.

ing a circuit the year previous; and if they would speak out they could relate scenes of suffering sufficient to cause the ears of some readers to tingle. Still, when they went, the settlements were 'few and far between,' and frequently without any road, or even path, from one to the other. When we wished to visit a neighborhood fifteen or twenty miles distant, we ascertained as near as we could the general course, and struck off through the woods without road or guide. If the sun was visible, we steered by him, and if not, by a pocket-compass; and if a creek—too deep to ford—obstructed our course, we had our choice to swim or stay on our own side, having neither boat, bridge, nor canoe. Of the manner of overcoming these obstructions I will here furnish an example or two.

"At the close of a camp quarterly-meeting in Clarke's River Circuit, July, 1826, the small streams were much swollen by reason of heavy rains. Soon after leaving the camp we had to encounter a small stream, which was usually some three rods wide, but at that time spread over the banks and much of the adjoining low ground. However, we were told that by going to the Shallow Ford, above the forks, we could probably ride across without losing bottom; but, where we expected a shallow ford, we found a sheet of water about a hundred yards wide, it having overflowed its banks, with a rapid current in the middle. Our company consisted of George Richardson, John S. Barger, Alexander H. Stemmons, another young preacher whose name I have forgotten, and the writer. We were all sound, except myself. I was sick, had been so for five or six days, and was much more fit to be in bed than on horseback. In consequence of this circumstance the company objected to my swimming, lest the wetting, after taking medicine, might prove injurious; but, by riding in mid-sides to the horse, I gained the large end of a great tree, which had been cut down so as to fall across the main channel just above the ford, for a temporary foot-bridge. Here they deposited me and the baggage till they should swim the horses over. In the meantime, others came up from the meeting, forming a company of some fifteen in all. The coming-out place lay rather up stream from us, and just below it, we were told, the bank, then under water, was too steep for the horses to rise when they should strike bottom. To avoid this, and procure a sloping bank to rise on, they selected a place below, where the bluff changed sides; so that after riding in till the horse was nearly covered, and arriving at the main channel, he suddenly and unexpectedly to himself, though not to his rider, stepped over a precipice, perhaps ten feet high, into a sweeping current, where horse and rider were violently immerged, but soon emerged some distance from where they first disappeared, and presently made safe landing. In this way the young brethren conveyed their own horsès over, after which Richardson and Stemmons rode for the whole company, securing one horse and swimming back for another, making several trips each. This done, Richardson led me over the channel on the log; and leaving still between us and the dry ground a sheet of water some thirty yards wide, and three feet deep, he deliberately stepped in, took me upon his shoulder, and, notwithstanding much brush and drift-wood were on the way, placed me safely on solid ground. The whole was accomplished in a few minutes. Here we parted with all but our own company, with whom we first started from camp; and, leaving the *Shallow Ford*, our way was clear before us to the next branch of the same stream, only a few miles distant.

"Our second crossing was like to prove more difficult than the first, having an equally rapid stream, without the advantage of any log. Having appointments ahead, it was important to get on somehow or other; and, after a short consultation, it was thought best, on account of my condition, to head the stream, or at least go far enough up to ford. This being agreed on, we made the attempt, but were so much embarrassed by quicksand, especially where the ground had been overflowed, that we soon became weary of it, and determined to cross, if possible. Finding a place where the banks were dry on both sides, the water being there confined within its usual channel, we dismounted, and were consulting about the mode of crossing, when Stemmons concluded it was time to execute as well as plan. Fixing his large, laughing, blue eye on a tall, slim hickory, growing on our side of the creek, he deliberately began to ascend, which he did almost as easily and rapidly as a wild bear would climb a chestnut-tree in search of nuts. When he had left the ground about forty feet below him, and arrived where the sapling had scarce strength to support him, he turned on the side next to the stream, held on with his hands, letting his feet swing clear, and his weight brought the top down on the other side, and, with the assistance of another, who swam over to his relief, tied the limbs fast to the root of a tree. This bent sapling formed an arched bridge about forty feet long, six inches wide, and elevated in the center about twelve or fifteen feet over the deepest of the turbid stream, on which we crossed—*astride*—safely, pushing our baggage before us, and resumed our journey, leaving the *hickory bridge* for the accommodation of the public.

"Such were our facilities for crossing in those days, when we had help; but, when alone, there was often no alternative but to make the horse swim with his rider and baggage, and trust to Providence to get safely through. And such were the difficulties to which we were accustomed in carrying the gospel to the poor, in the new countries, then; and the same are, doubtless, realized now by many of our traveling preachers on the frontiers of the work. Now, for such work as this I would rather have a half a dozen such young preachers as those above named than twenty graduates of any theological seminary in the United States. A. H. Stemmons has gone to his reward, and John S. Barger and George Richardson are still in their Master's work, though the latter has been for many years much disabled by hemorrhage from the lungs. Peace be with them!"

William Crain and William Cundiff succeeded

Barger and Greenup the following year. They were zealous young men, and devoted to their work. Their labors were greatly blessed. Revivals crowned their ministry, and at the close of the year *three hundred and eighty-five* white and *six* colored members were reported by them to the Conference.

In 1827, William Brown was sent alone to the Clarke's River Circuit. The Minutes of 1828 report a small decrease in the white membership, but an increase in the colored.

At the General Conference of 1828 all that portion of Kentucky embraced in Jackson's Purchase was transferred to the Tennessee Conference; hence, in the autumn of that year, we find the Clarke's River Circuit in the Forked Deer District, over which Thomas Smith presided. Mr. Smith was in many respects a remarkable man. Dr. Rivers* says:

"It was in the year 1828 that I met for the first time with Thomas Smith, Presiding Elder of the Forked Deer District, Tennessee Conference. I was but a boy. My father had but recently removed from Franklin county, Tennessee, and had settled in Hardeman, a few miles west of the town of Bolivar, and not far from Ebenezer Church, of which he became a member. It was in this Church that I first heard a sermon from the lips of Thomas Smith. He was a man of robust frame, florid complexion, and with hair thinly scattered over a large, round head. At the time of which I write, Ebenezer Church was torn with dissensions. It was during

* Letter to the author.

the controversy which resulted in the formation of the Methodist Protestant Church. The *Mutual Rights*, a most bitter partisan sheet, assailed the Old Church with every sort of weapon known to ecclesiastical warfare. The Bishops were at once the butt of ridicule and the objects of vituperation; the itinerant ministry came in for a large share of obloquy; the entire Constitution of the Church must be changed, the Bishops disrobed, and the lay element be admitted into the Conferences, both Annual and General. In order to carry out these radical measures, a Union Society had been formed in Ebenezer Church. Some of the most prominent members of the Church belonged to it; they were men of talents, piety, and wealth. Under the direction of Mr. Smith, these members were charged with sowing dissensions, speaking evil of ministers, etc., and were expelled the Church. He brought the whole force of his character, and all the power of his administration, against those whom he regarded as enemies to the peace of the Church. He did nothing by piecemeal. He carried on a most relentless war, and did not rest until the offending members were cut off and the Church purified. As he thought of this heresy, with him compromise was cowardice, and cowardice was disaster and disgrace. His loyalty to the Church was undoubted, his courage universally admitted, and his character as a warrior was fully established. He determined to crush out the rebellion, and he did it by driving from the fold some of his best members. In all this he was thoroughly conscientious, and was fully convinced that the glory of God and the good of the Church were promoted by throwing overboard from the good old Methodist ship these rebellious members.

"In the meantime, he did not forget his great work of saving souls. His District extended from Florence, Alabama, to Memphis, Tennessee, and from La Grange, Tennessee, to Paducah, Kentucky. It included the whole of the present Memphis Conference, together with several counties in Middle Tennessee and North Alabama. It required him to be absent from home more than four-fifths of his time. The country was new and rough; the roads were in many places impassable, except to a brave cavalier. Alone on horseback he passed through deep and gloomy swamps, and across frightful creeks, muddy sloughs, and dangerous bayous. He never hesitated; he never murmured. He was appalled by no dangers, and he shrank from no obstacles. His frame was stalwart, his health perfect, his constitution of iron. His spirits were elastic, and his adventures were often full of romance. He seldom failed to be at his appointment. He was happy in the hut of the backwoodsman, and loved to preach the gospel in the log-cabin of the hunter, or beneath the shade of some grand old forest. With a powerful physical frame, great capacity for endurance, a stentorian voice that sounded like the peals of a clarion, and could be distinctly heard by thousands, he was a splendid representative of the pioneer Methodist preacher. His early education had been almost entirely neglected. He read badly, and his orthography was wretched; he could not have taught a common school of the lowest order. This captain of the hosts of Israel could not have been a champion in the most common orthographical tournament; and yet he was a man of vigorous intellect, and often preached with great power. He was great at a camp-meeting; he was here a general marshaling his forces. He kept all the elements in order; he ruled with an iron will and a steady hand; he preached with great pathos and power. His appeals to the unconverted were earnest, and his unstudied eloquence often stirred the multitudes, and brought many a penitent to the altar. I have known him to have more than a hundred conversions at one camp-meeting. In the pulpit, in the altar, in the tent, and in the grove, he was a worker. His voice always clear, his faith ever strong, and his heart always in the work, he was just such a leader as the enthusiastic young men delighted to follow.

"I have said that his spirits were elastic; they were sometimes too exuberant, bordering on levity. In the pulpit, he was grave and dignified; out of it, he was full of mirth, and loved a hearty, ringing laugh. This was sometimes spoken against by those whose displeasure he happened to incur. For four years, with a salary of one hundred dollars for himself, and the same for his estimable wife, and a pittance for each child, he traveled over this extensive District, preaching the unsearchable riches of Christ. He took great interest in spreading Methodist literature, and was active in the sale of our standard books. He never went with empty saddle-bags. He felt that this was part of his great calling, and, though a Presiding Elder, was not above selling our books; and while his voice responded to the ax of the woodman and the rifle of the hunter, his richly-laden saddle-bags offered the writings of Wesley and Clarke to all that were able to purchase. After awhile he did what he never intended to do: he located, studied law, and joined the Methodist Protestant Church. After this I lost sight of him. He, however, returned to his first love, and died in peace many years ago."

The Clarke's River Circuit was served by Nathan Johnson. Under his ministry the Church was greatly blessed. At the next Conference he reported *four hundred and forty-two* white and *seventeen* colored members.

In 1829 William M. Smith, who had traveled two years, and William W. Phillips, a young man just admitted on trial, were appointed to Clarke's River Circuit. Under their ministry the membership continued to increase. At the ensuing Conference they reported *four hundred and eighty-nine* white and *fourteen* colored members.

In 1830 we find Thomas Smith, who had traveled the Forked Deer District the previous year, returned to the same field, and three preachers sent to Clarke's River Circuit. The appointment of so many men to a field occupied the year previous by a solitary preacher plainly indicated the importance of the work to be accomplished.

This section of the State of Kentucky was, just at this period, inviting more than ordinary attention. Families from the more densely populated sections of the State, as well as from other States, attracted thither by the fertility and cheapness of the lands, were seeking homes in this portion of Kentucky. The Presiding Elder, aware of the importance of meeting the growing demands of his work, asked for the appointment of Moses S. Morris, Harris G. Joplin, and Duncan McFarlin to this inviting field. Moses S. Morris had been in the itinerancy two years; his previous appointments were the Winchester and Wolfe Circuits. Harris G. Joplin had entered the Conference the preceding year, and had traveled the Gibson Circuit; while Duncan McFarlin had just become an itinerant. Entering upon their work in the spirit of the Master, these faithful ministers of Christ resolved to succeed. The gospel was preached by them with commendable zeal, and with great simplicity, winning many souls to Christ. At the close of the year the white membership had increased to *six hundred and fifty-five*, although only *four* colored members were reported.

In 1824 two of the most remarkable men of American Methodism were admitted on trial into the Tennessee Conference—George W. D. Harris and Alexander L. P. Green. Without the advantages of early education, both soon attained to eminence, and became giants in the ranks, and for nearly half a century were leaders, the one in the Memphis and the other in the Tennessee Conference.

George W. D. Harris was born in Montgomery county, North Carolina, January 25, 1797. He spent his youth and early manhood as a prodigal from God, wandering far away on the wastes of folly and of sin. The impressions, however, made upon his mind and heart by the teachings of his mother, a woman eminent for piety, and a Methodist, were never effaced.* All along the pathway of vice her instructions, like faithful monitors, rose before him, telling him of a better life and a happier destiny. In 1821 he attended a camp-meeting at Norvill's old camp-ground, in Bedford county, Tennessee, where, under the faithful preaching of Benjamin Sewell, he was powerfully awakened. Mourners were invited to the altar for the prayers of the Church, and Mr. Harris was among the first to accept the invitation. There, while pleading for mercy, he was soundly converted to God.†

Impressed with the conviction that he was divinely called to the work of the ministry, in 1824 he received license to preach, and was admitted on trial into the Tennessee Conference. In 1831 Mr. Harris was placed in charge of the Paris District, which embraced the Wadesboro and Hickman Circuits, formed from the Clarke's River Circuit, lying in Kentucky. He had traveled the Pond Springs, the Bedford, the Winchester, the Lincoln, the Stone's River, and the Nashville Circuits—the last-named two years.

To the office of Presiding Elder Mr. Harris

* His father did not join the Church until after his son did.

† Mr. Harris was married at the time. His wife had been brought up by Baptist parents, but had joined the Methodist Church.

brought not only a ripe experience, gathered from seven years of arduous toil and privation on large and laborious circuits, but a commanding presence, a robust constitution, capable of much endurance, an herculean intellect, richly stored with gems of religious truth, a heart sanctified to God, and energy and zeal which scarcely knew any bounds. No man in the Tennessee Conference was better qualified to be a leader than George W. D. Harris. Entering upon the work of his extensive District, he soon became familiar with every portion of it, and everywhere his presence and his power were felt. In the pulpit, in the Quarterly Conference, in the family and social circles, he exerted an influence extending not only to the preachers among whom he was a leader, but to all the people.

To the Wadesboro Circuit Robert L. Andrews and Drury Womack were appointed, and Uriah Williams and Elias R. Porter to the Hickman.

Robert L. Andrews had been a traveling preacher for three years, having entered the Conference in 1828. Before he was sent to Kentucky he traveled the Duck River, the Dickson, and the Red River Circuits. His colleague was admitted on trial in 1829, and appointed to the Cypress Circuit. His name, however, does not appear in the Minutes again until 1831, when we find him the junior preacher on the Wadesboro Circuit.

The name of Uriah Williams first appears on the roll of traveling preachers in 1829. His first appointment was to the Cypress Circuit, with James McFerrin as his Presiding Elder. In 1830 he was sent to Caney Fork, and in 1831 he came into Kentucky. Elias R. Porter had just been admitted on trial. The foundations of Methodism had been laid by faithful men who had preceded them—classes had been formed and Churches organized; but under their ministry the Church attained an influence in the "Purchase" it had not known before. At the close of the Conference-year *three hundred and sixty-one* white and *thirteen* colored members were reported from the Wadesboro Circuit, and *four hundred and five* white and *five* colored from the Hickman.

This brings us up to the period where this volume opens.

In the Tennessee Conference, the gifted and indefatigable Harris was returned to the Paris District, which still embraced the Hickman and Wadesboro Circuits, in Kentucky; Charles T. Ramsey and Arthur Davis were appointed to the Hickman Circuit, and Hiram M. Glass and Calvin Thompson to the Wadesboro Circuit.

Charles T. Ramsey was born in North Carolina in 1794, but, before he attained to manhood, he removed with his parents to East Tennessee. At a later period he settled in Missouri, where, in the twenty-seventh year of his age, he became awakened to a sense of his condition as a sinner through the instrumentality of the Methodist ministry. He joined the Church, was soundly converted, and soon afterward removed to the Western District of Tennessee, where, in the autumn of 1829, he became a traveling preacher. His fields of labor before he entered Kentucky were the Beach, the Hatchie, and the Gibson Circuits.* In these several charges he had been highly acceptable as a preacher, as well as successful in winning souls to Christ.

Arthur Davis† was born in Stewart county, Ten-

*At the close of his year on the Hickman Circuit, Mr. Ramsey was transferred to the Missouri Conference, which then embraced the State of Arkansas, and was appointed to the Mount Prairie Circuit, where he was eminently useful. His next field of labor was the Little Rock District, which he filled two years with great acceptability. He was appointed the third year to the Little Rock District, but was taken sick during the session of the Conference in Batesville, and died November 10, 1836. His end was triumphant.

†In the *Western Methodist*, several years ago, Dr. Rivers, after giving a sketch of James O. Williams, a gifted young preacher, thus speaks of Arthur Davis: "Altogether unlike Williams was Arthur Davis. Williams had the eloquence of intellect and of imagination, Davis the eloquence of passion. Both were young and zealous, and commenced preaching about the same time. Williams was much the more highly cultivated intellectually; Davis had much deeper communion with his own heart and with his God. Davis stirred the people by his deep earnestness, his gushing tears, and his intense feeling. He sought to win souls; he had no ambition for fame. He was deeply, painfully conscious of his defects of education, and want of mental training; but he could not turn aside from his great work. His humility, his prayerfulness, his sincere and earnest piety, and his vehemence of passion, carried all before him. 'Ah!' said he to me, 'I have shed a bushel of tears this year on the Hatchie Circuit.' And so he had. He literally went forth weeping, bearing precious seed. He will come again, bringing his sheaves with him. I heard Williams preach, and his sermon was followed by such stunning applause as I had never heard bestowed upon a young man; I heard Davis, and his sermon was followed by a hundred mourners in the altar."

nessee, February 17, 1811. He was brought up under Baptist influence, but took but little, if any, interest in the subject of religion until he was well-nigh grown, when he was awakened under the faithful ministry of Richard Hudson. On the 16th of August, 1830, he was converted at Manly's Chapel, and was received into the Methodist Church by Mr. Hudson on the following day. He was licensed to preach by Thomas Smith in 1831, and entered the traveling connection in the autumn of the same year. His first appointment was to the Hatchie Circuit, where he was eminently useful. The Hickman Circuit, to which he was next appointed, as the colleague of Mr. Ramsey, was large, embracing Hickman and a portion of Graves county, in the State of Kentucky, and extending into Obion and Weakley counties, in Tennessee.

The first round of appointments was filled by Mr. Davis. What is now known as the pleasant village of Hickman at that time bore the name of Mills's Point. Although Mills's Point was on the plan of the circuit as a preaching-place, Christianity had exerted but a feeble influence in the community, and on more than one occasion the preacher had met with rude treatment.

The first appointment for this place was at night. Having preached in the morning a few miles from the village, a brother, who was a class-leader, familiar with the unkind reception and rough treatment which preachers had generally met in Mills's Point, endeavored to dissuade Mr. Davis from filling his appointment, and from incurring the hazard of personal violence. Arthur Davis was not the man to be alarmed. He had been commissioned to preach the gospel of Christ, and the constituted authorities of the Church had embraced this village in his field of labor, and no amount of opposition could deter him from the performance of what he believed to be his duty. Without the polish of education—but possessed of a masterly intellect, an indomitable energy, a burning desire to save sinners, and with a courage that knew no fear—dressed in plainest homespun, he made his appearance in the village that afternoon. Alighting from his horse at the tavern where he stopped, he was invited into the bar-room, where he found a motley crowd of wicked men — some playing fiddles, some dancing, some swearing, some gambling, and all under the influence of ardent spirits. Taking his seat among them, he could not do otherwise than listen to their obscene jests and ribaldry—the Church and the preachers being freely denounced.

Learning that in the community there was *one* family friendly to Methodism, at whose house there had been occasional preaching, Mr. Davis called at the house and inquired for the gentleman. Being told that he was not at home, he asked the lady whether preaching was expected at her house that evening. The rough exterior of the preacher was repellant to her ideas of the "cloth," and she promptly replied in the negative. He then asked her whether there was an appointment for preaching anywhere in town. Her reply was, "*Not that I know of.*" "Do the people want preaching?"

was the next inquiry made by Mr. Davis. "I do not know," was the hasty reply. "It makes no difference with me; the gospel I preach is not on the beg," was the answer of Arthur Davis. He bade her good evening, and although she called to him several times, as he retreated from the house and yard, he heeded her not, but returned as rapidly as he could walk to the tavern, and was once more in the midst of the drunken crowd.

At the announcement of supper all went into the dining-room, where Mr. Davis had still to hear the rough language of these ungodly men. A few moments later found them in the bar-room, engaged in almost every kind of vice, uttering the most horrid oaths, and occasionally walking to the door and looking for the preacher, whom they were expecting, and with whom they contemplated "some fun."

In the meantime, the gentleman at whose house Arthur Davis had called had returned home; and, being informed by his wife that the preacher had been to his house, and of what had occurred, he sent a servant to the tavern to invite him to his house. The landlord declared that no preacher was there, and swore that he had "not seen a preacher for a long time." A deep concern was at once expressed by the vulgar crowd, who declared that no preacher would dare venture into the village, and if one should do so they would like to see him. Quiet and calm, Mr. Davis did not move from his seat. The servant was persistent. "There is a preacher here," he replied; "he has been to our house, but did not find my master at home. He has, however, come home, and prepared seats for preaching; had sent word to the people in town that there would be preaching at his house that night, and a good many persons are there now waiting for him." In the most profane manner, the landlord and his crowd swore again that no preacher had stopped at his house.

Thinking it time to stop the discussion, Arthur Davis arose from his seat, and, calling for his saddle-bags, took out his Bible, and, holding it up before them, said: "I am the preacher; I am the man you want to see so badly." Speaking with the authority of a brave man, he commanded them to follow him. Unable to resist the presence of such a man, or attracted by the boldness with which he confronted them, without uttering a word they obeyed his command, and went with him to the place of preaching. The house was already well filled, but Mr. Davis determined to provide for that part of the congregation by whom he was accompanied, who, although unable to obtain seats, found comfortable places to stand.

A small table for a pulpit, on which were placed a hymn-book and Bible, indicated the place to be occupied by the preacher. Without taking a seat, he opened the hymn-book, read two lines and sang them, and knelt in prayer. The prayer was brief; before the congregation could kneel, the preacher said "Amen."

It was late in November, and the evenings were quite uncomfortable. After announcing his text, he said: "I am quite comfortably situated myself, and on this occasion I will preach the best I can. I do not know how long I may preach, but shall not quit until I get ready. If any of you get tired, you are at liberty to leave at any time; it will not disturb me."

For more than an hour Arthur Davis preached to that audience. They were spell-bound. Not a whisper disturbed the silence. It was the simple story of the cross; it was salvation by faith in the atoning merits of Jesus Christ; it was the witness of the Spirit bearing witness with ours that we are the children of God; it was an escape from the damnation of hell, and the abundant entrance into heaven, and the enjoyment of its resplendent glories, told in a plain and simple manner, by a sincere preacher of the gospel, that so entranced them.

If a desire was expressed by the gentleman and his wife at whose house Mr. Davis had preached that another appointment be left for preaching, the entire congregation participated in it, none of whom were warmer in their expressions than the crowd from the tavern, some of whom had heard the gospel for the first time in many years.

After announcing an appointment for Mr. Ramsey, the preacher in charge, and another for himself, he pronounced the benediction, with as little ceremony as he had entered upon the service.

Mr. Ramsey had preached, but the people looked forward to the next appointment of Mr. Davis with peculiar interest. He had arrested the attention of a community where all others had failed. He had reached the hearts of men addicted to every species of vice, and in a single sermon impressed upon them the importance of religion; and, in the hands of God, he was to be the instrument in organizing the Church and in taking into its fold many who had been wanderers from Christ. His reception on his second appearance was a warm one. All were glad to see him. He preached; his congregation was large, and at the close of the sermon he organized a Church consisting of twelve persons.

From this period to the close of the Conference-year the Hickman Circuit was in a blaze. Every appointment was on fire. The cries of awakened sinners and the shouts of souls converted to God were heard wherever the gospel was preached and the tidings of a Redeemer's love proclaimed. At the quarterly and camp-meetings the gifted Harris delivered his message of life — of death — "in thoughts that breathe, and words that burn," * while throughout the circuit, ever at their post, the zealous Ramsey, the most powerful exhorter in the Conference, as well as a model preacher, and the plain, unostentatious, but strong-minded Davis, with such local preachers as Joshua Cole and Fletcher Sullivan, fearlessly warned sinners to flee the wrath to come.†

---

*There were three camp-meetings during this year in the Hickman Circuit—one at Oliver's Camp-ground, and two at Mobley's. At the Oliver camp-meeting on Sunday, at eleven o'clock, Mr. Harris preached the funeral-sermon of a Brother Atterbury, an excellent man. His text was, "That as sin hath reigned unto death, even so might grace reign through righteousness unto eternal life by Jesus Christ our Lord." The sermon was one of great power, and left a lasting impression on the community.

†At one of the camp-meetings at Mobley's, on Sunday, at

At the camp-meeting at Oliver's Camp-ground many were born to God; and at the first camp-meeting for this year at Mobley's more than one hundred souls were converted. At the ensuing Conference *seven hundred and six* white and *forty-three* colored members were reported, increasing the membership nearly one hundred per cent.

We are not surprised at these results when we consider the energy, the zeal, and the untiring devotion of these faithful men.*

three o'clock, while Calvin Thompson was preaching, a man, wild in appearance, and remarkable for his muscular power and fighting qualities, only half clad, and bare-headed, came running into the camp-ground, making tremendous bounds, and screaming, at every leap, "The devil is after me!" He jumped over the heads of several ladies, and landed in the middle of the altar, falling on one of his shoulders and dislocating it. He was immediately removed to the preachers' tent, and the disjointed limb was reset by Dr. Nichols. Somewhat relieved from pain and quieted in mind, he was asked for an explanation of his strange conduct, when he stated that, being under conviction, he had retired to the woods to pray, whereupon the devil confronted him in person, and that, having been hitherto accustomed to fight his way through the world, he made a heavy pass at his antagonist. The devil, he affirmed, gathered him by the hair of his head, and shook him as though he had been an infant, and when let loose he started for the altar as a place of refuge.

*In a letter to the author from the Rev. T. L. Boswell, D.D., of the Memphis Conference, he says: "I remember being at one of the camp-meetings held on the Hickman Circuit, at Mobley's Camp-ground, when Brothers Ramsey and Davis were the preachers. It was a time of the greatest religious excitement it has ever been my privilege to witness. The exercises of the meeting, like the employment of the hosts of heaven, never ceased day nor night during my stay. The

We have already referred to the appointment of Hiram M. Glass and Calvin Thompson to the Wadesboro Circuit. Hiram M. Glass became a traveling preacher in 1829. Before his appointment to Kentucky he had traveled the Stone's River, Jackson, and Neely's Grove Circuits. This, however, was Mr. Thompson's first year in the Conference.

Mr. Glass remained on the Wadesboro Circuit but a short time. One of the preachers appointed to Sandy Circuit, from the failure of his health, was unable to continue in the work. The Presiding Elder deemed it proper to transfer Mr. Glass to that circuit, and employ Thomas L. Boswell, a youth only seventeen years of age, to assist Mr. Thompson, whom he placed in charge of the work.

Calvin Thompson was an excellent young man, deeply pious, and distinguished for his zeal and his usefulness.*

Young Boswell reached the circuit in the month of February. Converted to God in his childhood, he had been divinely called to the work of the Christian ministry, and entered upon its sacred duties when a beardless boy, only seventeen years of age. He met from the people a kind welcome in every portion of his circuit, and with commendable zeal labored to do good and to save sinners.

The Wadesboro Circuit was large, embracing the

---

altar exercises would suspend at the sound of the trumpet long enough for preaching, and then commence afresh."

* He remained in the traveling connection until 1839, when he located.

counties of Calloway, Graves, and McCracken, extending as low down as "The Iron Works." It contained twenty-four regular appointments, to be filled every four weeks, besides many occasional ones. The rides were long and lonesome, and the privations such as are incident to a recently settled country.

The large area embraced in this circuit, and the great number of preaching-places, deprived these young men almost entirely of each other's society. They met but seldom during the year, only at the quarterly and camp-meetings.

The inexperience of Thompson and Boswell was in a great measure supplied by several excellent local preachers, who resided in the bounds of their work. Robert Whitnel, C. A. Waterfield, Caleb Cole, and William Holyfield enjoyed, in the fullest sense, the confidence of the people among whom they lived, were distinguished for their piety and zeal, and were eminently useful.

It would be a pleasant task to follow these faithful and zealous preachers of the gospel throughout the year—to listen to the invitations, the appeals, the warnings, that fell from their lips; to see them as they held up the cross, "all stained with hallowed blood," as the only refuge for a lost and ruined world; and to hear the cries of awakened sinners, and the shouts of converted souls brought to Christ through their ministry.

Young Boswell did not know much of books; but with "the one Book," which reveals the plan by which sinners may be saved, he was familiar. The cardinal doctrines of the word of God—the depravity of man's nature, the atonement, justification by faith, the witness of the Spirit, and the sanctification of the soul—were great truths which had been written upon his own heart, and which he impressed upon the hearts of others.

If the Hickman Circuit was blessed with extensive revivals, they were not confined to that field. Revivals also crowned the labors of these young men in every part of the Wadesboro Circuit. The interest on the subject of religion was so great that two camp-meetings were held during the summer at the Wadesboro Camp-ground, and hundreds were converted to God.

It was during this year that Methodism was introduced into Paducah, at that time a small village, in McCracken county.

A few members of the Methodist Church had settled at that point, among whom was Joseph Cole, a brother to the preacher we have mentioned, and a Mrs. Smith, by whom the preachers were entertained (her husband, although friendly to the Church, not being a member); yet no Church had been organized.

A small vacant store-room stood on the banks of the beautiful Ohio, in which Calvin Thompson and Thomas L. Boswell preached the gospel of Christ, and where they organized a Church whose influence would be felt in the coming years.

Pleasant as was the year through which young Boswell had passed, he was not exempt from privations. We have already referred to the large extent of territory over which his circuit spread. The country was new, the traveling difficult, and many of the people uncultivated, and opposed to the advances which were being made by the Church.* His extreme youthfulness, however, often protected him from insult. He had counted the cost, had consecrated his life to the service of the Church, and nothing could deter him from the faithful performance of duty.

It has been intimated already that this would be a year of unparalleled success. The Minutes show a net increase in the Kentucky Conference, at the close of the year, of *three thousand five hundred and seventy-five* white and *one thousand and fifty-eight* colored members.

In the Wadesboro Circuit an increase of *two hundred and twenty-seven* white and *twenty-seven* colored members was reported, and in the Hickman Circuit the increase was *three hundred and one* white and *thirty-eight* colored, making the total increase *four thousand five hundred and five* white members, and *eleven hundred and four* colored.

By referring to the Minutes of 1832, it will be observed that for the first time the following questions were asked:

"What amounts are necessary for the superannuated preachers, and widows and orphans of preachers, and to make up the deficiencies of those who have not obtained their regular allowance on the circuits?

*A crowd of ruffians on one occasion invited Calvin Thompson to drink with them from a jug they had. Upon his refusal, they tried to force him to drink, but failed.

"What has been collected on the foregoing accounts, and how has it been applied?

"What has been contributed for the support of missions, and what for the publication of Bibles, tracts, and Sunday-school books?"

In answer to the first question, it was stated that the deficiency was four thousand one hundred and fifty-five dollars and fifty-seven cents. To meet this deficiency, seven hundred and thirty-seven dollars and eight cents was collected, four hundred dollars of which was received from the Book Concern, and seventy-five from the Chartered Fund, making the collections from the several stations and circuits only two hundred and sixty-two dollars and thirty-eight cents.

The largest contribution (twenty-one dollars) was sent from Georgetown Circuit. The Shelbyville Female Academy and Mount Sterling Circuit sent each twenty dollars, Lexington Station eighteen dollars and sixty cents, the Lexington Circuit eighteen dollars and fifty cents, Jefferson Circuit fifteen dollars and eighty-seven cents, the city of Louisville fifteen dollars and twenty-five cents, Shelbyville and Brick Chapel fourteen dollars and eighty-seven cents, Cynthiana eleven dollars and seventy-five cents, and Maysville eleven dollars. The remaining contributions were in smaller amounts, only twenty charges sending up any collection at all.

Out of the amount collected there was paid to Bishop McKendree $10 71, to Bishop Roberts $14 48, to Bishop Soule $17 76, to Bishop Hedding $15 48, to Bishop Emory $18 52, to Bishop Andrew $18 52

—total, $96 47. After deducting this amount, only $640 91 was left to be divided between the superannuated preachers, and the widows and orphans of preachers, and to make up the deficiencies of those who had not obtained their regular allowance on the circuits and stations.

When we consider the small salaries allowed the preachers at this period—one hundred dollars for a preacher, one hundred dollars for his wife, sixteen dollars for each child under seven years of age, and twenty-four dollars from seven to fourteen years of age, after which no allowance was made for the children, with but seldom any allowance whatever for table expenses *—and then remember that this meager salary was scarcely ever half paid, we pause to inquire, How was it possible for these men to continue in the work? †

Many of them, indeed, were compelled to retire. At this very Conference six men—active, energetic, and zealous—located. ‡

There is no plainer duty laid down in the Bible than that "those who preach the gospel shall live of the gospel," and no Church can prosper to its full extent that fails in this respect. In places where no Societies have been organized preachers must be supported by contributions from Churches

---

* The first money for table expenses ever paid to Benjamin T. Crouch was in 1840, and was collected by the author on the Yellow Banks Circuit. The amount was *twenty-six dollars*.

† Fifty-one preachers report a deficiency at this Conference.

‡ Thomas G. Reese, James L. Greenup, Wilson S. McMurrey, Elijah Knox, A. H. Stemmons, and John W. F. Tevis.

already established; but in Kentucky, at this time, Churches were fully organized almost everywhere.

That the support of the ministry was willfully neglected will not be gainsaid, and that a fearful responsibility rests upon the Church of that period for the neglect will scarcely be denied. It may be that the preachers, too, were to blame. A feeling of delicacy prevented them from presenting their claims to the people they served, and hence the people in many instances were not instructed as they should have been in the duty of supporting their preachers.*

*The author was once holding a class-meeting, and asked a wealthy brother to relate his Christian experience. After referring to his conversion, and the conversion of his wife and eight children, he added: "And I owe it all, under God, to Methodist preachers." Knowing that he paid very little for the support of the Church, I asked him how much he gave annually for missions. "Not a cent," he promptly replied. I then inquired, "How much do you pay to aid in the support of your preachers?" "I pay FIFTY CENTS a year," was the answer. I said to him: "Brother, it seems to me, from your statement, that on the one hand you have been greatly blessed by the Church, and on the other you have been criminally negligent in reference to your obligations and duty. The small amount you pay toward supporting your preachers, and the fact that you pay nothing for missions, is an insult to God. Cannot you do better?" "Perhaps I can," he answered. "How much better?" I demanded. "I can possibly double the amount for the preachers, and give as much for other purposes." "Too little," I rejoined. "How much would you have me pay?" he asked. Thinking it better not to press him very hard at first, I replied: "Not less than twenty dollars for the support of the preachers, and at

The support of the superannuated preachers, and the widows and orphans of preachers who had fallen in the work, was far below the necessities of the claimants, as well as the ability of the Church. Benjamin Ogden and Barnabas McHenry, to whom the Church in Kentucky was so greatly indebted, received *thirty-six dollars and thirty-seven cents;* James Ward, whose health had broken down under the labor and exposure of arduous campaigns, received *forty-eight dollars*, and the other superannuated preachers in the same proportion; while Mrs. Finley and her children received, to support them one year, *thirty-one dollars and twenty-five cents*, and Mrs. Dill's children, whose father had fallen at his post, beloved and honored, and whose mother, too, had died, were paid *fourteen dollars and fifty cents*, and Atterbury's children, doubly orphaned, *seven dollars and twenty-five cents.*

It certainly required no little zeal and devotion to the cause which these men were laboring to advance—with such a support, and such prospects before them in old age, and before their families, if they should die—to continue in the work. Their trust, however, was in God, who had called them to the ministry. He had fed the ravens, and watched the falling sparrow, and had promised to be with them in every trial, and they were willing to trust to his promise.

---

least half that sum for missions." He accepted my suggestion, and became a very liberal man. The members of the Church, too, where this interview occurred contributed that year more than twice as much as they had ever given before.

The Missionary Society of the Methodist Episcopal Church in the United States was organized in 1819. Very little, however, had been done for the cause of missions anywhere in the Church. In the Kentucky Conference no interest had been awakened, or, if so, it had passed away without any active demonstrations.

At the Conference of 1832 *forty-four dollars and fifty cents* was reported for missions—the first report for this cause we have on record in Kentucky. The resolution adopted by the body at this session, to which we have already alluded, indicated that a new feeling had been imparted to the Church on the question—that it would be impossible for the Church at home to succeed if it took no interest in the extension of the kingdom of Christ. The results of the year in this direction, although far below what might have been expected from the action of the Conference, showed an upward tendency. At the Conference of 1833 *seventy-nine dollars and seventy-five cents* was collected for missions.

Another question of grave importance—the publishing interests of the Church—had been freely discussed in several previous Conferences, and suitable resolutions concurred in.

In the Conference of 1831 the following resolutions were adopted:

"*Resolved, by the Kentucky Annual Conference, unanimously—First,* That we view the Book Concern of the M. E. Church as an important auxiliary in the great work in which we are engaged, both as a means of spreading religious knowledge and as a source of relief and support to an itinerant ministry, particularly to the worn-out preachers and their families, as well as to the widows and orphans of those who have fallen in the work.

"*Second*, That we view with regret and disgust the ungenerous efforts of certain individuals to undermine and ruin the Concern, evidently from motives of private interest, in publishing and vending such books as have hitherto been published exclusively by our Concern, and in endeavoring to impose spurious publications on the public as the genuine and standard publications of our Church.

"*Third*, That we, as a body and as individuals, will use our best exertions to secure the interests of our Concern by recommending and promoting the sale of those books and publications which are issued from our presses, and that we will have no agency whatever in the sale of those books and publications which are published by others with the evident view of supplanting or injuring our own establishment."

The importance of the circulation of religious books of our own publication among the people was felt by every preacher in the Conference. Other denominations of Christians were sending out all over the country books advocating their peculiar tenets and doctrines; and if Methodism would keep pace with them, it must have not only an efficient ministry, but an efficient colportage. The difficulty of procuring books was great compared with that which a preacher now encounters. Express trains and railroads were unknown in the West, and yet it was difficult to find a preacher anywhere from whom the standard works of the Church might not be purchased. They carried them in their saddle-bags on horseback to their meetings, to the homes of the rich, and to the cabins of the poor. Our books were thus scattered everywhere. A Methodist family could rarely be found without the works of Wesley, Fletcher, and Watson, and the biographies of sainted men and women.* Under such training the characters of our people were formed; and at this period some of the brightest examples ever known among the membership in Kentucky shone with undiminished luster, while the ministry, in many instances, could scarcely boast abler defenders of the doctrines held by the Church than were to be found in the laity.

Another benefit accruing from the circulation of books was, it supplemented the salary (or, rather, the allowance, for the amount was not dignified with the name of *salary*) of the preacher. The profits on the sales were small, it is true, but still many a preacher was enabled to remain in the itinerant field by the revenue received from this source.

In addition to the circulation of books on the plan we have stated, public collections were ordered in the several congregations for the publication of Bibles, tracts, and Sunday-school books. At the

---

* Two of the best Methodist libraries I have ever met with were to be found in the bounds of the Manchester Mission, which was my first appointment. They were owned by the Rev. George Stivers, a worthy local preacher, and Thomas Bowman, a layman.

Conference of 1832—the first at which we find any account of funds raised for this purpose—*twenty-seven dollars and sixty cents* were reported, which amount was increased the following year to *forty-two dollars and twenty-five cents.*

The subject of Colonization was not only agitating the mind of the Church at this time in Kentucky, but the popular feeling was strongly enlisted in its favor. There were in the State many free persons of color who desired to emigrate to Liberia, where a colony had been established, and was at that time in a prosperous condition.

The object of the American Colonization Society was not only to provide means for transporting such as might choose to go to Liberia, but to make provision for their support in that distant land until they should be able to take care of themselves.

At the Conference of 1831 George C. Light, one of the most gifted men in the Conference, having been solicited by the Society to become their Agent in Kentucky, requested to be appointed to this interesting work. He had served the Society from the Conference of 1831 to the Conference of 1832, when he was reäppointed to that important field. By his eloquence, his power, and his zeal, he had invested the scheme with an interest it had not previously known. Communities that had looked upon the enterprise with indifference and doubt were awakened, and became its earnest advocates.

The Kentucky Conference adopted the following preämble and resolution:

"Whereas, in the opinion of this Conference, the

Colony of Liberia presents an asylum for the free people of color of these United States, where liberty in the popular sense of the word may be enjoyed; and whereas, the scheme of African colonization is considered as the most likely means, and well calculated to extend the blessings of civilization and the light of the gospel of the grace of God to the benighted regions of Africa; and whereas, the Colonization Society has manifested a laudable zeal, and spirit of benevolence, and virtuous enterprise in performing much with very limited means in promoting the interests of the colony, which is said to be in a flourishing condition; therefore,

"*Resolved, by the Kentucky Annual Conference,* That we highly approve of the scheme of African Colonization, and that we will recommend it to the attention of the people of our charges, and to the community in general, as a cause worthy their patronage and united coöperation."

During the year three cavaliers were called from labor to reward—Joseph B. Power, Barnabas McHenry, and Marcus Lindsey.

Joseph B. Power and Barnabas McHenry were both on the list of superannuates.

Mr. Power was born in Montgomery county, Kentucky, September 15, 1802, and had entered the ministry in 1826, when twenty-four years of age. For four years he had faithfully performed the arduous duties of an itinerant preacher. The failure of his health compelled him to retire from active service, which he was never afterward able to resume. He died July 23, 1833. His end was peaceful and happy.

For forty-six years the name of Barnabas McHenry had been favorably known in the West. No one of the early preachers had labored with greater devotion to the cause of truth than had this venerable man. Gifted beyond many of his contemporaries, he presented the doctrines of the Church with a clearness, and defended them with an ability, that distinguished but few men. His life was a comment on the religion he professed. He enjoyed the blessing of sanctification, and died of cholera, in triumph, on the 16th of June, 1833.

When Marcus Lindsey fell, a hero and a warrior passed away. He died of cholera in Washington county, Kentucky, July 27, 1833. He had entered the ministry in 1810, and from that period until his death he had performed the duties assigned him with a fidelity that commanded the admiration of his friends and challenged the criticism of the enemies of the cause he had espoused. With an intellect of the highest order, as a bold and fearless advocate of the doctrines he had accepted as the teachings of the Bible, he had no peer in the West. From the time he became a cavalier until he fell on the field of battle, his sword had never been permitted to rust, nor his armor to be sullied. He was brave and chivalrous in life, and in death triumphant.*

* For a fuller sketch of the life, labors, and death of Joseph B. Power, Barnabas McHenry, and Marcus Lindsey, see "History of Methodism in Kentucky."

CHAPTER II.

FROM THE SESSION OF THE KENTUCKY CONFERENCE OF 1833 TO THE CONFERENCE OF 1834.

What troubles have we seen!
  What conflicts have we past!
Fightings without and fears within,
  Since we assembled last;
But out of all the Lord
  Hath brought us by his love,
And still he doth his aid afford,
  And hides our life above.

THE labors of the year were completed, and brave cavaliers who had taken leave of each other nearly twelve months before met in the village of Greensburg. The meeting was pleasant, yet mingled with sadness; for Power, McHenry, and Lindsey were not present to answer to the roll-call. They had been summoned from labor to reward.

The session of the Conference opened on the 11th of September, and was presided over by Robert Richford Roberts. Mr. Roberts was born in Frederick county, Maryland, August 2, 1778. When only fifteen years of age he became a member of the Methodist Episcopal Church, having previously been converted. A youth of more than ordinary promise, and of fervent piety, from the time he made a profession of religion the impression rested on the mind of the Church that God would call him to preach the gospel. Believing himself to be divinely chosen to this sacred work, he yielded to his convictions, and preached his first sermon about Christmas, 1801. In the spring of 1802 he was admitted on trial into the Baltimore Conference, and appointed to the Carlisle Circuit, with the sweet-spirited Wilson Lee as his Presiding Elder. His subsequent fields of labor, in the Baltimore Conference, were the Montgomery, the Frederick, the Chenango, and Erie Circuits, and the Pittsburgh, West Wheeling, Baltimore, Fell's Point, Alexandria, and Georgetown Stations. In 1813 we find him in the Philadelphia Conference, and, with William Hunter, Thomas Boring, John Emory, and Manning Force, stationed in the city of Philadelphia, with the celebrated Henry Boehm as his Presiding Elder. He remained in Philadelphia two years, when he was placed in charge of the Schuylkill District, where we find him in May, 1816, when the General Conference met in the city of Baltimore.

The death of Bishop Asbury, which had occurred on the 31st of March preceding the General Conference, devolved the duties of the episcopal office on Bishop McKendree, the only surviving Bishop. There were nine Annual Conferences, embracing the United States of America, requiring the supervision of this remarkable man. The immense labors he had performed had so far impaired his health as to render him unequal to the duties his office demanded; hence, the Committee on Episcopacy recommended the election of two additional Bishops. On Tuesday, the 14th of May, Enoch George and Robert Richford Roberts were elected to this office.

The responsibilities of the Episcopacy are such as no man should covet. If the duties of the office at the present period demand greater sacrifices and more heavy responsibilities than any other department of ministerial labor, they were certainly not less at the time Bishop Roberts was elevated to this position. Besides his long and wearisome travel on horseback, his constant exposure, his sacrifice and toil, the support he received was inadequate to the demands of his family, and often left him embarrassed, if not penniless. Until 1824 there was no provision in the Discipline for a Bishop's family, and he consequently received, for the eight years preceding that date, only two hundred dollars a year and his traveling expenses.*

Bishop Roberts had previously, on several occasions, visited the West. In the autumn of 1816 he attended the Ohio Conference, which embraced the northern portion of Kentucky, and met in Louisville; in 1817 he was again present at the session of the Ohio Conference, and the same year presided

---

*On the 25th day of May, 1824, the General Conference adopted the following resolution:

"*Resolved,* That the Book Agents and Book Committee in New York shall be a committee to estimate the amount necessary to meet the family expenses of the Bishops, which shall be annually paid by the Book Agents out of the funds of the Book Concern; and that the above resolution be incorporated into our Discipline."

over the Tennessee Conference, which included Southern Kentucky.* In 1818 he was again present at the Ohio Conference, with Bishops McKendree and George. In 1821 we find him at the Kentucky Conference, which met in Lexington,† and in 1823 at the session in Maysville. From this period until 1830 he attended every session of the Kentucky Conference, which met, respectively, in Shelbyville, Russellville, Louisville, Versailles, Shelbyville, and Lexington. Again we meet him at the session in Louisville in 1831.

No Bishop in the Church could have received a more cordial welcome than did Bishop Roberts when he attended the Conference of 1833. He was not only familiar with the work in Kentucky, and the demands of the Church, but he was intimately acquainted with many of the preachers, and shared in the affections of all.

If he did not bring to the holy office he so acceptably and usefully filled pulpit talents of the highest order, yet we find him a clear and forcible preacher, with a mind richly stored with gems of gospel truth. If he did not rise to the loftiest heights of oratory, yet strains of impassioned eloquence often fell from his lips. He was a workman who needeth not to be ashamed. Throughout the West were to be found

* It was either at this or a subsequent session of the Tennessee Conference that he reached the session the day after it opened. On taking the chair he proposed to explain to the Conference the cause of his delay: "I started from home one day later than I should have done," was the only explanation he gave.

† The Kentucky Conference was organized in 1820.

his living epistles, known and read of all men. In all the walks of life pious men and women, brought to Christ through his instrumentality, adorned the circles in which they moved, and called him blessed.

William Adams was appointed Secretary; the preliminary business occupied the first day of the session; the Committees on Public Worship, on the Book Concern, Finance, and on Memoirs, were appointed. In addition to these, a special committee looking to the publication of a weekly paper in the West was appointed. This committee consisted of George C. Light, William P. McKnight, Henry B. Bascom, Jonathan Stamper, and Benjamin T. Crouch.

Up to this period the West had depended chiefly, if not entirely, on the *Christian Advocate and Journal*, published in the city of New York, for Church intelligence. Without the advantages of railroads, the mails were tardy in reaching their destination, and hence weeks would sometimes elapse before information of importance could be received. Five large Conferences had already been organized in the West, to say nothing of the Tennessee, Holston, and the Conferences farther South. The Western States were rapidly filling up, and the Methodist Church was keeping pace with the population. To the Kentucky Conference, as well as to others equally interested, the establishment of a paper west of the Alleghany Mountains seemed essential to the growing demands of the Church. On the 17th day of the month the following report was submitted by the committee, and adopted:

"In answer to the interrogatories proposed by the Agents at New York, respecting the publication of a weekly religious paper, kindred in character with the *Christian Advocate and Journal*, to be issued at the Book-room, Cincinnati, your committee give it as their opinion, briefly:

"*First*, That the establishment of such a paper is not only expedient, but important to the interests of the Church in the West.

"*Secondly*, That the Agents and Book Committee at New York have the undoubted and constitutional right to establish such a paper.

"*Thirdly*, That the power to appoint the editor belongs to the Agents and Book Committee, and grows naturally out of their right to establish a paper.

"*Fourthly*, It is the opinion of your committee that, in making the appointment of editor, the Agents and Book Committee will be expected to consult the Western Conferences most interested in the paper proposed."

The first number of the paper, with Thomas A. Morris as editor, under the title of *Western Christian Advocate*, was issued in the following April.

At this session of the Conference a communication from H. W. Rogers and John Saunders was read, proposing to publish a newspaper in the interest of the Church, in Kentucky, and asking for the patronage of the Conference.

The Conference, believing that their allegiance was to the Church rather than to sustain an individual enterprise, promptly declined the proposition.* They felt that if a paper were established in the West, worthy of the Church and capable of exerting an influence that would be felt, the Kentucky Conference must coöperate with other Conferences in sustaining it, and not fritter away their power to do good by giving any countenance to an enterprise by which individual prosperity, and not the weal of the Church, would be promoted.

While in the Kentucky Conference, at this period, there were men of high literary attainments, yet the majority of the body had not enjoyed the advantages of a first-class education. The subject of education had, however, always been a popular one with both the ministry and laymen of the Methodist Church in Kentucky. Augusta College—the first Methodist institution of learning in this country—belonged conjointly to the Ohio and Kentucky Conferences, and both were pledged for its support.

A deputation from Augusta was present, to represent the interests of that institution. The Conference appointed a committee, consisting of John Tevis, Jonathan Stamper, George C. Light, William Gunn, and Hubbard H. Kavanaugh, to confer with the deputation from the College, to take its interests into consideration, and "jointly report to the Conference as soon as convenient."

---

* The following resolution was adopted:

"*Resolved*, That the writers of this communication be informed by Brother Kavanaugh that, in the opinion of this Conference, it is inexpedient to attempt the establishment of a paper, as contemplated by said communication."

On the fourth day of the session the following report was submitted:

"The committee appointed to confer with the deputation from Augusta College, having performed the duty assigned them, unite with said deputation in submitting to the Conference the following resolutions—unanimously—as their report:

"*Resolved, first,* That the plan submitted to the Board of Trustees of Augusta College, for the endowment of professorships in said institution, and which has received the sanction of the Board, duly, and upon the basis of which the Ohio Annual Conference has recently endowed the 'McKendree Professorship of Moral Science' in the Augusta College, is every way worthy of confidence, and obviously calculated to secure the prosperity and permanence of the institution.

"*Resolved, second,* That this Conference adopt the plan proposed, and that we proceed immediately to the endowment of another professorship in the College.

"*Resolved, third,* That we select for this purpose the Professorship of Mathematics, and that we give some suitable honorary designation, as suggested in the plan of endowment.

"*Resolved, fourth,* That this Conference will promptly and perseveringly imitate the noble example of the Ohio Conference in creating the necessary fund for the endowment of the professorship selected."

During the reading of these resolutions Bishop Roberts was in the chair. As soon as they were adopted, he was courteously invited to vacate it, and George C. Light was called upon to occupy it, when the following resolution was submitted and unanimously adopted:

"*Resolved,* That the professorship selected for endowment by the Kentucky Conference be denominated the 'Roberts Professorship of Mathematics,' in consideration of the untiring zeal and persevering fidelity, and to perpetuate the memory of the ministerial worth and almost unexampled efforts, of the Rev. Robert R. Roberts, Bishop of the Methodist Episcopal Church, especially in the large amount of labor contributed by him in the West, in building up and extending the limits and influence of the Church, and thus effectually increasing its ability in the extension of benevolent enterprise, and the enlargement of its field of operation; and also in view of the fostering regard and paternal solicitude which he has uniformly evinced in behalf of the Institution, as originating in Western enterprise, and the first of Methodist origin in the United States, on which account it is believed there is obvious and high moral fitness in the honorary designation of the professorship agreed upon by the Kentucky Annual Conference in the adoption of this resolution."

After properly acknowledging the courtesy shown him by the Conference, the Bishop resumed the chair.

The appropriateness of the resolution will commend itself to every one. No minister, no Bishop, not even the devoted McKendree, had done more for the advancement of the Church in the West than had Bishop Roberts. He had presided over the Kentucky Conference at almost every session since its organization, and his wisdom had safely guided them through difficulties on more than one occasion.

The subject of ministerial support was still a very embarrassing one. Whether the preachers were successful or poor financiers was a question that admitted of controversy. If receiving a less support than any other body of men, and living on it, was evidence of financial skill, then the premium should certainly be awarded them; but if the ability to induce liberality on the part of the people is necessary to entitle them to this distinction, they must abandon the claim; for surely the contributions of the Church were neither adequate to the support of the preachers nor equal to the ability of the Church.

At this session of the Conference a committee of five was appointed, consisting of George C. Light, Edward Stevenson, William Holman, Henry B. Bascom, and Jonathan Stamper, to draft a financial system.

The subject of temperance, in the following resolution, came before the Conference:

"*Resolved*, That this Conference, before its adjournment, form itself into a Temperance Society."

Thomas Lasley, Hooper Crews, and George W. Taylor were appointed a committee to draft a Constitution for a Temperance Society, and to report on the following day. When the report was read, some objections were made to it, and it was recommitted. This was just on the eve of final adjournment; and, as the committee could not possibly revise their report before the close of the session, the Conference adopted the following resolution:

"*Resolved, by the Kentucky Annual Conference,* That we will, in our several fields of labor, do what we can to promote the temperance enterprise now going forward in our country."

Intemperance, like a sirocco, was sweeping over the land, and spreading ruin through every community. Along its path were blighted homes, ruined fortunes, and blasted characters. The tears of wives, mothers, and sisters, and the penury, and want, and grief of widows and orphans—made such by the tremendous curse—appealed to the popular heart to stay the dreadful evil. The appeal was irresistible. A grand movement for reform in this regard had been inaugurated, and the cause of temperance was commanding public attention as it had never done before. It was certainly proper for the Church to lead the van in this great moral reform. The Methodist Church in Kentucky was fully abreast with the spirit of the times, and at this early period took a proud position, from which sophistry, ridicule, and abuse have never been able to drive them. "Wine is a mocker, strong drink is raging: and whosoever is deceived thereby is not wise." They believed that the man who professes Christianity, and makes, vends, or uses ardent spirits as a beverage, does not "abstain from every appearance of evil," but plainly violates the teachings of the word of God, and deserves not a place in the Church of Christ.*

An address from "certain brethren," of the Greenville Circuit, on the subject of dress, was read on Tuesday morning, the 17th of September, and laid on the table. At an afternoon session on the same day it was called up, and the consideration of the subject postponed until the ensuing Annual Conference.

The address of these brethren recommended uniformity in the style of dress, on the part of the members of the Conference. The Conference, however, adopted the following resolution:

"We, the members of the Kentucky Conference, being convinced of the propriety of uniformity in dress, therefore,

"*Resolved*, That we will endeavor to return to old Methodism on this subject."

We are not prepared to define the views of the brethren as to what "old Methodism on this subject" was. At this period we had never looked upon a Conference of Methodist preachers. Two years later, however, we enjoyed this pleasure, and were

---

* The author was once at a fashionable dining, given him in an Eastern city, with several others. On the table were many bottles of wine, of which all partook except himself. One of the party, after drinking a glass of wine, handed him his glass, and requested him to pass it for replenishing. He placed the glass in front of his plate, when he repeated, "Will you pass my glass for more wine?" "I will not," was the reply; "I have never passed any man's glass for wine, and never will." The host immediately took every bottle from the table, saying, at the same time, "I accept the reproof."

struck with the absence of all uniformity in the style of their dress. The ordinary frock-coat was the style generally worn, the round and straight-breasted the exceptions.

On the first day of the Conference it was resolved to observe the following Friday "as a day of fasting, or abstinence, and prayer to God for his blessings on" themselves and the work with which they might be intrusted. The members of the several Churches in Greensburg were invited to unite with them in this service.

Quite a number of local preachers were elected to deacon's orders, among whom were Edward L. Southgate, Daniel Ruark, Joseph Sewell, John F. Strother, Thomas M. Smith, Harmon Bailey, Thomas H. Lyle, Garland Moore, Elijah Covington, Benjamin Hill, and Stephen Rogers.

George Stivers, John Brown, James Weaver, and Thomas Brooks were elected to elder's orders.

Among these names are some who took high rank in the ministry, and through more than a generation exerted an influence for good. Some of them yet live to bless the Church and the world.

The preaching during the session was remarkable not only for the clear and forcible manner in which the great truths of the gospel were presented, but for the unction and power that attended it.

On Sunday, at eleven o'clock, Bishop Roberts preached in the Methodist Church, and was followed by William Adams, at three o'clock. At night Henry B. Bascom, Professor of Moral Science in Augusta College, and the most eloquent preacher in America, then in the full vigor of manhood, also preached in the Methodist Church. The house was densely crowded, and hundreds stood at the doors and windows on the outside. For two hours, or longer, the immense multitude hung in breathless silence on his lips, while he told them of a Saviour's love, of a Redeemer crucified, of the sweet comforts of religion, of the joys of the blessed, and the horrors of the damned. The effect was wonderful. On Monday morning, in an appropriate resolution, signed by John James, Edward Stevenson, and William P. McKnight, he was requested to furnish a copy of the sermon for publication—the first request of the kind that had ever been made by the Kentucky Conference.

George C. Light was requested to preach the sermon in memory of Barnabas McHenry, Marcus Lindsey, and Joseph B. Power, and Tuesday afternoon, at two o'clock, was fixed as the time for this service. The occasion was one long to be remembered. Joseph B. Power had been called away in early manhood, before he had fully developed as a minister of Christ; for twenty-four years the name of Marcus Lindsey had been familiar to the Church, and for nearly all that period he had been a gallant leader; while Barnabas McHenry had planted the standard of the cross in the West nearly half a century before. To portray the lives and labors of these excellent men—to follow them amid the varied scenes through which they had passed—to listen to the words of comfort, of exhortation, and of cheer which they had proclaimed—to contemplate the thousands brought to Christ through their ministry —to catch the strains of more than mortal music as they fell from their dying lips, and then to accompany them to the great beyond, and hear the notes of welcome as they entered upon eternal life—was the privilege of the preacher on this occasion. Many were incited to higher aims and nobler purposes as they contemplated the characters of these cavaliers.

At this session *seventy-nine dollars and seventy-five cents* was reported for missions, and *forty-two dollars and twenty-five cents* for Publishing Fund, which, although small, was a handsome increase over that of the previous year. The preachers were still poorly supported, receiving less than for the previous year, while only *one hundred and twenty-six dollars and forty-five cents* was contributed by the Church, in the Conference, to make up the deficiencies and to support nineteen superannuated preachers and the widows and orphans of deceased preachers. The Conference was also authorized to draw on the Book Concern for *four hundred dollars*, and on the Charter Fund for *seventy-five dollars*.

Edward L. Southgate, William Outten, Claiborne Pirtle, John W. Riggin, John Carr Harrison, Daniel Sherwood, Thomas E. Thompson, Elijah M. Bosley, Eli B. Crane, Alberry L. Alderson, and Moses Evans this year entered the list of cavaliers.

Among those who, the year before, had joined their fortunes with this band of noble men, only one proposed to retire from the ranks—Joseph W. Shultz was discontinued, at his own request.

Robert F. Turner, Isaac Malone, Samuel Hellums, Daniel H. Tevis, Moses Clampit, and William McReynolds, located.

It is difficult for a faithful minister of the gospel to retire from the pastoral work. Called to preach the unsearchable riches of Christ, and having taken upon himself the vows of ordination, which bind him to devote his life to exhorting sinners to repentance, the consent of his mind to abandon a work to which he was pledged by every motive of happiness and of duty is not easily obtained. If health fails, or if the health of his family demands it, he may retire until the obstruction is removed; but nothing less than this can justify the surrender of duty.

Robert F. Turner, Isaac Malone, Samuel Hellums, and Moses Clampit were unable, because of feeble health, to prosecute the duties of itinerant work. We have no information as to the motive which influenced the location of William McReynolds. He was a good and true man. Daniel H. Tevis had failed to attend to his work, and was located by the Conference.

Of those who the previous year were on the list of the superannuated, only John Denham and Littleton Fowler were placed on the effective list, the latter having been transferred to the Tennessee Conference. We have already referred to the location of Samuel Hellums and Moses Clampit, and the death of Barnabas McHenry and Joseph B. Power.

To the list of the superannuated for this year are added the names of Richard Corwine, Thomas

Waring, Milton Jamieson, Edward Stevenson, John Johnson, and Samuel Harrison.

The appointments at the present Conference show that but few preachers were returned to the fields of labor they had occupied one year before. William Gunn, the sweet singer, was still the leader of the hosts in the Lexington District; Richard Tydings, in the Augusta; William Adams, in the Harrodsburg; Benjamin T. Crouch, in the Louisville; and George W. Taylor, in the Greensburg. The only change that was made in the presiding eldership was the appointment of Isaac Collard, a good and true man, to the Hopkinsville District, in the place of John Johnson, whose health had failed, and who had been placed on the list of the superannuated.

The Burlington Circuit was still served by James C. Crow, a most exemplary young preacher, while the eccentric Josiah Whitaker was returned to the Falmouth Circuit. On the Germantown Circuit we again see the popular and zealous Francis Landrum, and on the Little Sandy the plain and unostentatious James H. Brooking. The Church in Mount Sterling had requested the reäppointment of Henry S. Duke, and the Bishop had complied with their wishes; and Lewell Campbell, the sledge-hammer of the Conference, was permitted to remain on the Newcastle Circuit. With these exceptions, the preachers were sent to new charges.

Before the lapse of a month every cavalier had entered fully upon the work to which he had been assigned. The revivals, which during the previous year had swept over the State, had somewhat abated, yet a deep religious feeling pervaded almost every community, and impressions had been made in favor of Methodism that would never be effaced.

A more zealous band of men had never entered the itinerant ranks than those composing the Kentucky Conference at this period. Controlled by a single desire—the salvation of the souls of the people—there was no sacrifice they were unwilling to make, and no hardship which they would not cheerfully encounter. Others might travel the paths that lead to wealth, to pleasure, to fame; but, influenced by duty, they regarded no danger too great to be braved, and no obstacle a serious hinderance to their progress. To build up the Church, to repair the waste places of Zion, and to persuade sinners to be reconciled to God, were the aim and only business of their lives. They desired success, and their desire was fulfilled.

The winter of 1833 and 1834 passed away with no special demonstration of Divine power. In the several Districts, however, some were added to the Church and converted to God. In the city of Lexington, under the faithful ministry of Hubbard H. Kavanaugh, there was a gracious revival, which commenced on the 5th of January, 1834, at which one hundred and eighty-one persons joined the Church; while in the Lexington Circuit, whose preachers were the zealous Absalom Woolliscroft and the gifted William Phillips, more than three hundred persons were converted and became members of the Church. Lorenzo D. Parker, a son of consolation, and one of the sweetest-spirited preachers we ever knew, had charge of the Port William Circuit, which included the present town of Carrollton (then called Port William), at the mouth of the Kentucky River. Feeble in health, he prosecuted his work with a zeal which even his failing strength could not dampen, and success crowned his labors. In the early part of the year his circuit was blessed with some revival influence, which gradually deepened and widened until three hundred and thirteen souls "passed from death unto life." At Newport and Covington, where Joseph Marsee proclaimed the tidings of a Redeemer's love, at the third quarterly-meeting, commencing on the 2d of May, in the city of Covington, thirty persons asked for membership in the Church, and on the following Tuesday evening, at a love-feast held in Newport, six others availed themselves of the same privilege.

Passing to the Augusta District, we see Richard Tydings, the beloved disciple, leading to battle and to victory. In every part of his large District his influence is seen and his power felt. In the Germantown Circuit, under the ministry of Francis Landrum and Richard Deering—the latter a mere youth, just admitted on trial, but who had traveled the previous year on the Hinckstone Circuit, under the appointment of the Presiding Elder—God graciously revived his work. Early in the month of May the good work began, and before the frosts of autumn more than one hundred persons embraced religion. The Fleming Circuit enjoyed a richer display of Divine power. Under the indefatigable labors of Richard Bird and John W. Riggin more than two hundred persons cast in their lot with the people of God. The Lewis and Big Sandy Circuits—the former with the energetic Martin L. Eades, and the latter with the simple-hearted Thomas Hall and the young and promising Gilby Kelly, as the pastors—enjoyed times of refreshing from the presence of the Lord. In the Lewis Circuit there were nearly two hundred additions to the Church, and in the Big Sandy more than half that number became followers of the meek and lowly Jesus.

In the Harrodsburg District the revival influence seemed to be confined to its more rugged portions. John Williams and Richard Holding—the latter one of the purest men we ever knew—traveled the Mount Vernon Circuit, and Carlisle Babbit, Elijah Sutton, and Moses Evans, the Cumberland Mission. In the Mount Vernon Circuit about fifty persons were added to the Church, and in the Cumberland Mission more than two hundred.*

---

*In the *Western Christian Advocate* of June 11, 1834, Mr. Babbit writes: "This Mission is in the wilderness of Kentucky, almost surrounded by high and rugged mountains, including three or four hundred miles of boundary, located on the head-waters of Cumberland River. Since September we have extended our labors and taken in eighteen preaching-stands on the head of Kentucky River. In some parts of this country Methodism has never been known, and the religion of Jesus is an entire stranger. Numbers that have come to years of maturity had never heard a gospel-sermon, nor attended Divine service, previous to our arrival, as I have been credibly informed. Add to this, as near as I have been able to learn, a majority of the rising generation cannot read

The Louisville District shows a large increase in the membership during this year. The Shelby and the Taylorsville Circuits show a small decrease, but in every other charge in the District there were extensive revivals of religion. No cavalier was more devoted to his work, and none knew better how to marshal his forces, than Benjamin T. Crouch. Either in a defense or an attack, he had but few peers. His example impressed those associated with him with the importance of punctuality and promptness, and inspired them with a confidence that no difficulties could dampen.*

For several months previous to the Conference of 1833 the Shelbyville and Brick Chapel Station was left without a pastor, in consequence of the death of Marcus Lindsey. The names of the most distinguished preachers in the State were mentioned in connection with that station for the ensuing year. Shelbyville had been served by such men as Tevis, Stevenson, Light, Stamper, and Lindsey, and the Church, comprising a membership distinguished for their intelligence and culture no less than for their enlightened piety, had a right to expect a preacher of experience to be sent to them.

A young man had entered the Conference in 1828, and for two consecutive years had traveled

---

or spell, and you know there is something more than pulpit exertion to be attended to in cases of this kind. One hundred and forty-five have joined the Church since Conference."

* For three years Mr. Crouch was our Presiding Elder. During this period he was never absent from a quarterly-meeting in our work, and never reached one too late.

the Breckinridge Circuit; in 1830 he was stationed in Bowling Green; in 1831 he was appointed to the Germantown Circuit, and in 1832 to the Cynthiana Station. In these several fields of labor he had accomplished good, and left behind him the savor of a good name; yet beyond these charges he was scarcely known. In 1833 he was sent to Shelbyville and Brick Chapel, to succeed the gifted and sainted Lindsey.

George W. Brush was born in Rockbridge county, Virginia, October 28, 1805. His mother, whose maiden name was Nancy Caven, was born in the North of Ireland; his grandmother on his mother's side—Elizabeth McCaw—was reared in Scotland, and belonged to the Kirk. Rockbridge county, Virginia, had been the home of his paternal ancestry for several generations. His father—John Brush—and Blakeley Brush, his grandfather, were born in that county, and also his great-grandfather, who was killed by the Indians. John Brush removed to Kentucky in November, 1806, and settled in Shelby county, where his son remained until 1824, when we find him in Bullitt county, teaching a small country school. His parents were prominent and zealous members of the Presbyterian Church; and, although their son was distinguished rather for his wildness than for any adaptation to the pulpit, it was their earnest desire that he should become a minister in their Church. With but little or no inclination toward a religious life, he, however, attended preaching at the Church of his parents, occasionally visiting a Baptist or a Methodist meeting, when there was no preaching in their Church. His mother, although prejudiced against the Methodists, was a woman whose piety was deep and uniform. On one occasion she attended a Methodist camp-meeting on a week-day, hardly thinking it proper for a Christian woman to be found at such a place on the Sabbath; and, in an account of the meeting she gave in her family, she said: "Some of the people were cooking, some talking, some coming, some going, and quite a number about the stand, where they were singing, praying, shouting, and, after awhile, preaching;" and she added: "But the one we heard spoke well, indeed, and seemed to be a good man, and well acquainted with the Scriptures."

Young Brush had heard one or two local preachers in the Methodist Church, under whose ministry he had been made to feel uneasy; and under a sermon preached by Dr. Clelland he had been greatly alarmed, and in the church cried aloud for mercy. His religious impressions, however, were soon effaced, and in the society of wild associates he drowned the voice of conscience, and forgot the teachings of childhood. The first traveling preacher with whom he ever met was Benjamin T. Crouch, for whom he entertained feelings of the highest regard.

In the autumn of 1826 Richard D. Neale, distinguished for his zeal, was appointed to the Jefferson Circuit, which included Bullitt county, in which George W. Brush resided. Sociable in his disposition and courteous in his manner, the zealous preacher soon won upon the affections of the young schoolmaster, who, through his instrumentality, was brought into the Methodist Church, and soundly converted to God. Feeling that he was called to preach the gospel, he reluctantly yielded to his convictions, and on the 6th of October, 1828, he was licensed to preach by Marcus Lindsey, and at once entered the itinerant ranks.

The appointment of George W. Brush to the Shelbyville and Brick Chapel Station was unexpected alike to the preacher and the congregation. The Church, however, received him kindly, and in the spirit of the Master he entered upon his work. He reached his new field in due time, and preached at eleven o'clock, on the first Sunday, at the Brick Chapel, to a crowded audience, several of whom resided in Shelbyville. At night his appointment was in the town, and not only the Methodists, but the members of other Churches, were present to give him a welcome. The church was densely packed. The good John Tevis was sitting in the pulpit, and the pious William Atherton in the altar. A slender young man, with a pleasant countenance, nearly six feet high, weighing about one hundred and fifty pounds, with grayish-blue eyes and jet-black hair, entered the church, and walked into the pulpit. *It was George W. Brush, the new preacher.** He read his hymn, after which the congregation sang; he then prayed, and another hymn was read and sung. "Therefore let no man glory in men: for all things are yours; whether Paul, or Apollos, or Cephas, or

* We resided in Shelbyville, and had just joined the Church, and were present on this occasion.

the world, or life, or death, or things present, or things to come; all are yours; and ye are Christ's; and Christ is God's," was announced as the text. The sermon was brief, delivered in a plain, conversational style. In it there was nothing great, according to the estimation of the world; there was no rhetorical display, no burst of eloquence, no flash of lightning, no peal of thunder; it was the message of life and salvation, delivered not in "enticing words of man's wisdom," but in the simplicity of gospel truth.

If in the pulpit Mr. Brush made a favorable impression upon the Church he was appointed to serve, in his social intercourse he made friends in every circle. Sociable in his disposition, and pleasant in his intercourse with the community, he won the hearts of the people in other Communions as well as in his own. As a preacher he was not considered great, yet crowds waited upon his ministry, and each person left the house of God, after hearing him, resolved to be better than ever before. His preaching was peculiar. No one preached as he did, and he copied from no other person. Short, pointed, practical sermons, from week to week, fell from his lips, and urged his congregation to a better, a holier, and a higher life. Under his ministry a Bible-class was formed, of which he was the leader; the Sunday-school prospered; the prayer-meetings were well attended; the class-room was crowded, and prospects for a revival were more promising than they had been for many years. Everybody knew the preacher, and everybody loved him. He visited the homes of wealth and influence, and was the companion of the poor and the humble; his prayers went up from every family altar, and from the bedside of the sick and the dying.

The winter was over; gentle spring, with its sunshine and flowers, came and passed away. On the 3d of June the third quarterly-meeting commenced. The Church had been looking to this occasion with prayerful interest. In the class-room the quarterly-meeting was talked of, and prayers were offered for a revival of the work of God. On the street members of the Church conversed freely on the subject of religion, and not only expressed the hope that souls would be converted during the meeting, but that much good would be done. From the commencement of the meeting the signs of the times were favorable for a general outpouring of the Spirit upon the people. The first night penitents were invited to the altar, and several persons presented themselves for the prayers of the Church, and two or three professed faith in Christ. As the meeting progressed the interest increased, and before a week had elapsed the altar was crowded with persons anxiously inquiring the way of life and salvation, and many had "passed from death unto life."* In the *Western Christian Advocate* of June 20 a letter from the pastor of the Church was published, dated June 11, in which he says: "Our third quarterly-meeting commenced eight days since, and we are holding it still. Fifty-eight whites and twenty-eight

* Messrs. Crouch, Gunn, Stamper, Tevis, Atherton, Rice, and other preachers, were present and assisted at this meeting.

colored joined; fifty converted; meeting yet going on."

As the meeting was protracted from day to day, and from week to week, its influence permeated the entire community, extending to every class of society, awakening the young and the old, embracing many heads of families—men and women of influence—and reaching to those who had hitherto been impervious to the claims of religion.* Some who up to this time had discarded Christianity altogether, and were distinguished for their wickedness, recognized the claims of religion, bowed to the scepter of Christ, and became burning and shining lights in the Church of God, while many remembered "their Creator in the days of their youth," some of whom are yet living to adorn the profession they made.†

During the entire meeting commendable zeal was displayed by the membership of the Church, who contributed largely to its success. They visited and conversed freely on the subject of religion with such as were serious, and bore an active part in the

---

* The author's father and mother, also his uncle—Samuel Wise Topping, by whose charity he was brought up and educated—joined the Church at this time.

† During the progress of the meeting Mr. Brush met on the street Thomas P. Wilson, an eminent lawyer, and Judge of the Circuit Court, and said to him: "Judge Wilson, what would you think of me if I were to remain here a year, and say nothing to you about saving your soul?" "I would regard you as a very unfaithful preacher," was the reply. "What does Mrs. Wilson think on this subject?" he then asked. "Call and see her, and inquire for yourself," replied the judge. On the Friday following this conversation Judge Wilson, with his wife, and son, and sister-in-law, joined the Church.

exercises of the altar. Among them no one contributed more to the interest than Mrs. Amanda McGrath,* a young and accomplished widow, deeply pious and devoted to the Church. Gifted in prayer, her appeals before the throne of grace not only reached the ear of Jehovah, but melted many an obdurate heart.†

The entire community was aroused, and not only the village, but the surrounding country, was in a blaze. From the rural districts the people came several miles to church, and many who were prompted to attend these meetings through curiosity became awakened, and returned to their homes "clothed and in their right mind." Indeed, so great was the influence excited that a holy atmosphere seemed to surround the place of worship.‡ When the meeting closed nearly two hundred persons had been converted.§

While the Methodist Church in Shelbyville was

---

* Mrs. McGrath became the wife of the Rev. Richard Deering, and is the mother of the Rev. John R. Deering, of the Kentucky Conference.

† Her father, John McGaughey, Esq., was brought into the Church, at this meeting, through her instrumentality.

‡ A gentleman said to the author, several years after this meeting, that when he entered the church-yard, during its progress, he felt a religious influence he could not express.

§ A young man professed religion during this meeting, and joined the Methodist Church. His uncle and guardian, who was a prominent member of the Campbellite Church, was dissatisfied with this step on the part of his nephew, and required him to withdraw from the Methodist Church and to join the Campbellite Church. This compulsion unsettled him in his religious character, and he soon became a wreck in his morals, being so greatly blessed other denominations of Christians received valuable accessions to their Churches.

The influence of this extraordinary revival did not stop with the close of the meeting. Two months later a camp-meeting was held at Cardwell's Camp-ground, three miles east of Shelbyville, and in the vicinity of the Brick Chapel. The meeting was one of great power. On one occasion during its progress the heavens became black with angry clouds, fierce lightnings leaped along the sky, and thunder muttered solemn peals. The audience retired to the tents. The rain fell in torrents—it was eleven o'clock in the forenoon—and at nightfall there was no abatement; the stars were still concealed, and the elements appeared to be engaged in angry strife. Peace and joy, however, reigned within the tents. Preaching, exhortation, singing, prayer, followed in quick succession; cries for mercy rent the air; shouts of converted souls pierced the heavens; the Church partook of the joy. On that memorable night about forty souls were converted.* Nearly one hundred persons professed religion at that camp-meeting.

William B. Landrum was born in Fluvanna county, Virginia, May 14, 1803. He entered the Conference the same year with George W. Brush. The great-grandfather of Mr. Landrum was a Scotchman, but emigrated to America at an early day, and settled in Virginia. His grandfather—

*The author's mother, who had joined the Church in June preceding, as a seeker of religion, was converted that night.

Francis Landrum—who was born in Essex county, Virginia, September 19, 1739, became a Methodist preacher, and was identified with Asbury, Waters, Drumgoole, Poythress, and others, who laid the foundation of Methodism in that State, a hundred years ago.

From the introduction of Methodism into this country, the family of William B. Landrum had been identified with the Methodist Church. At the knees of his mother he was early taught the principles of religion, and before the removal of his parents to Kentucky, which occurred in the autumn of 1810, his impressions on the subject were deep and abiding. They spent the first winter after their removal to Kentucky at Boonsboro, in Madison county; but in the following spring they removed to Clarke county, where they settled permanently. A "meeting-house"—a rude log building, with dirt floor, situated on the land of Thomas Landrum—belonging to the Hinckstone Circuit, was the "temple" where the Landrum family attended circuit preaching. The pulpit from which the preacher dispensed the word of life had a puncheon floor, and two forks driven into the ground, with a cross-piece, for a hand-board. Although the circuit was large, embracing several counties, every two weeks the gospel was preached in this neighborhood. Such men as Nelson, Rhoton, McMahon, Lakin, Stamper, and Hunt traveled this circuit, and under their ministry, with the instructions of a pious home, the religious character of William B. Landrum was formed.

In the summer of 1821, while reading "Baxter's Call to the Unconverted," he was powerfully awakened to a sense of his condition as a sinner, and on the 26th of August he joined the Church as a seeker of religion. It was not, however, until the spring of 1822 that he obtained the forgiveness of his sins. Soon after his conversion he was placed in the responsible position of class-leader. In 1827 he was licensed to exhort, and in 1828 to preach.

At the Conference of 1828 he was admitted on trial, and appointed to the Little River Circuit, with William Cundiff. In 1829 we find him on the Somerset Circuit, with Elijah Knox as his colleague. In 1830 his field of labor is the Henry Circuit, with William Helm, and in 1831 he travels the Lewis Circuit alone. At the Conference of 1832 his name appears in connection with the Livingston Circuit, in the Hopkinsville District, having Napoleon B. Lewis, who was employed by the Presiding Elder, as his colleague.

At his first quarterly-meeting on the Little River Circuit, Mr. Landrum received FIFTY CENTS quarterage, and TWENTY-FIVE CENTS to meet his expenses for traveling from Shelbyville, the seat of the Conference, to Christian county, a distance of about two hundred miles. Thirty-five dollars was paid him for the entire year.

On the Somerset Circuit, which embraced the counties of Wayne, Pulaski, Russell, Adair, and Casey, he received thirty-three dollars during the year. On the Henry Circuit his receipts were fifty dollars, and on the Lewis sixty dollars. In all these fields of labor Mr. Landrum was a useful minister of Jesus Christ. Notwithstanding his meager support, no murmur falls from his lips, but in his Autobiography, now before me, he dwells upon the kindness of the people. Hundreds of miles frequently separated him from his parents, but, with true filial affection, he never failed to visit them twice a year.

At the Conference of 1833, with Foster H. Blades—the smooth-faced boy to whom we alluded in Chapter I.—as his colleague, he was appointed to the Hartford Circuit, which was embraced in the Louisville District.

The Hartford Circuit was one of the oldest in the Conference, appearing in the Minutes as early as 1804. In this circuit Mr. Landrum was thrown among a people where Methodism had been long established, and where a field of usefulness presented itself, upon which he entered with energy and zeal.

His colleague had joined the ministry one year before, when only sixteen years of age. He had attended a camp-meeting in Shelby county when but fifteen years old—a wild, uneducated boy. Fond of music, he had purchased a fiddle, and carried it with him to the camp-ground, for the purpose of amusement. Hardly, however, had he reached the inclosure before the Holy Spirit arrested him, and cries for mercy fell from his penitent lips. He was converted; and believing that he was called of God to preach the gospel, and yet without the first rudiments of education, he applied to a lady who was teaching a small country school in his neighborhood for admission into her school, and was kindly received, although unable at the time to pay her a farthing.* At the close of eight months, being only sixteen years of age, he was licensed to preach, and recommended to the Kentucky Conference. The Conference admitted him, and he was appointed by the Bishop to the Breckinridge Circuit, as the colleague of William Helm. He was tall and slender, with light hair and deep blue eyes. Remarkably sprightly and earnest in the work to which he was called, he at once took rank among the young men of promise in the Conference.

In speaking of Mr. Blades, Mr. Landrum says "he was a nice young man, with considerable preaching ability."

No two preachers, on any charge in the Conference, labored more earnestly than did these. Their circuit was soon in a flame, and revivals visited every portion of their work.

In the Jefferson Circuit, Charles M. Holliday and Hooper Evans, both in the prime of manhood, and distinguished for their zeal, were eminently useful. From the time they entered upon their labors until the 3d of June one hundred and thirty-seven persons had joined the Church, and nearly all of them had been converted. On the 4th of September Mr. Holliday writes to the *Western Christian Advocate:* "At our last quarterly-meeting a camp-meeting was held at Hughes's Camp-ground, commencing Au-

*At his first quarterly-meeting, on the Breckinridge Circuit, he sent her eight dollars—which was all he received at the time—the amount he owed for eight months' schooling.

gust 8th, and closing the 12th. Twenty-one were converted, and twenty-four joined the Church. Thirty-two joined at Cane Run, in September. Two hundred and thirty-three joined during the year."

In the Breckinridge Circuit, whose preachers were Stephen Harber and William G. Bowman—the former remarkable for the neatness of his apparel, and the latter for the earnestness with which he delivered his message—there were extensive revivals of religion. The Yellow Banks Circuit included not only the beautiful town of Owensboro, but all of Davis and Hancock counties, and portions of Ohio and Muhlenberg. To this immense field Thomas W. Chandler was appointed. When he first entered the ministry it was said of him by an intelligent gentleman of another Communion, who heard him preach, "Dress a fence-rail in the clothes of a Methodist preacher, and he can surpass any of our college graduates." During the year there was great prosperity, and at the camp-meeting at Pleasant Grove, which commenced July 18, "many found peace."

Thomas B. Farmer, a plain gospel-preacher, and Lewell Campbell, a son of thunder, traveled the Newcastle Circuit, and reported large accessions to the Church.

Turning to the Hopkinsville District, a considerable decrease in the membership appears in the Minutes. In the Logan Circuit, however, under the ministry of Thomas Wallace and William S. Evans, both of whom were faithful ministers of Christ, there were times of refreshing from the presence of the Lord. Mr. Wallace writes, May

28, to the *Western Christian Advocate:* "More than one hundred have been added to the Church since Conference." There was also considerable prosperity in the Livingston Circuit, whose preachers were Abram Long—who for several years had been an itinerant—and Joseph D. Barnett, a young cavalier, full of daring as well as energy and zeal.

In every other charge in this District there was a falling off in the membership, the largest decrease being in the Henderson Circuit, amounting to one hundred white and five colored.

The Greensburg District presented a less favorable report. The decrease in this District was two hundred in the white membership, and forty-six in the colored. In every charge, with the exception of the Glasgow Circuit, the membership was smaller than at the previous Conference. Jesse Sutton, a preacher of more than ordinary ability—with Eli B. Crain, a promising young man, for his colleague—traveled this circuit. On the 3d of July Mr. Crain wrote: "Our Church is now in a flourishing state. Many have been added to the Church." * Under the ministry of G. M. Campbell there was a gracious revival of religion in Glasgow, resulting in the conversion of many souls to God.

It frequently occurs that revivals of religion excite opposition to the Church of Christ on the part of those who are unfavorable to any demonstration on this subject. It was so in Glasgow. The Campbellite Church, under the leadership of Joseph Davis, made an attack on Methodism, which re-

* *Western Christian Advocate,* July 18, 1834.

sulted in a controversy between Mr. Davis and Milton Jamieson, of the Kentucky Conference. Mr. Jamieson was an able and experienced debater, and familiar with the points at issue. His triumph was complete, leaving his opponents to regret the folly and madness of the attack they had made.

It is gratifying, however, while we lament any falling off in the membership of a single District, to be able to record an increase in the entire Conference of *six hundred and sixty* white members, although there was a decrease in the colored of *one hundred and seventeen.*

Turning to the Wadesboro and Hickman Circuits, in the Tennessee Conference, we still find George W. D. Harris the Presiding Elder, while George W. Martin and George W. Casey are the preachers on the Wadesboro Circuit, and Wilie B. Edwards and Thos. L. Boswell on the Hickman. In both of these fields of labor there were extensive revivals of religion, although in the Hickman Circuit the General Minutes show a decrease in both the white and colored membership—in the former *seventy-nine,* and in the latter *twenty-nine.* In the Wadesboro Circuit the increase was *one hundred and forty-three* in the white membership, and *two* in the colored—making the total increase in Kentucky *seven hundred and thirty-two* in the white membership, and a decrease in the colored of *one hundred and forty-four.*

Two preachers had fallen during the year; but they fell at their posts. Thomas P. Vance and William P. McKnight had entered the itinerant field together, in 1829, and closed their careers within the same Conference-year—the former having died on the 6th of October, 1833, and the latter on the 30th day of the following June. Both passed away in triumph.*

* For fuller sketches of Thomas P. Vance and William P. McKnight see the "History of Methodism in Kentucky," vol. iii., pp. 454, 458.

CHAPTER III.

FROM THE SESSION OF THE KENTUCKY CONFERENCE OF 1834 TO THE CONFERENCE OF 1835.

Although the vine its fruit deny,
  Although the olive yield no oil,
The with'ring fig-tree droop and die,
  The field illude the tiller's toil,
The empty stall no herd afford,
  And perish all the bleating race—
Yet will I triumph in the Lord,
  The God of my salvation praise.

THE session of the Kentucky Conference for 1834 was held in Mount Sterling, commencing on the 10th day of September. Bishop Soule presided, and William Adams was chosen Secretary.

"Joshua Soule* was born in Bristol, Maine—then a province belonging to Massachusetts—August 1, 1781. He was the fifth son of Joshua and Mary Soule. His father was the eldest son of Joseph Soule, a descendant of George Soule, one of the Pilgrim Fathers who came to New England in the "Mayflower." His father was captain of a merchant-vessel and a whaler, and would have con-

* Bishop McTyeire, in Nashville *Christian Advocate*, March 14, 1867.

tinued in a sea-faring life but for the loss of his vessels during the Revolutionary War. After this he devoted himself to the pursuit of agriculture. At the time of the birth of their son Joshua, they belonged to a Scotch Presbyterian congregation, under the pastorate of the Rev. Mr. McLain. After their removal to the country their house was a home for all ministers, who preached in it, but organized no Church.

"The first Methodist preacher who came into their neighborhood was Jesse Lee. This apostle of New England Methodism was the first Methodist minister Joshua ever heard. This was about 1793. He joined the Methodist Episcopal Church in the spring of 1797—two preachers having been sent on a circuit which embraced his home. His parents and friends were violently opposed to his becoming a Methodist, and he joined the Church under full expectation of being banished from his father's house. Before taking this step he conferred with his parents in reference to it. He challenged them to adduce an instance in which he had ever disobeyed them. He assured them that it would afford him the greatest pleasure in life to join the Methodist Church with their consent; but join it he must. His mother was almost distracted. His father, however, never prohibited him from going to meeting. On one occasion he asked his father to accompany him to hear one of his ministers—the Rev. Mr. Stebbins. He said, 'No; they are all alike.' Joshua expressed the hope that his father's law judged no man before he was heard. After dinner his father ordered two horses, and accompanied his son to the meeting. Mr. Stebbins preached a powerful sermon. After the service Joshua introduced his father to Mr. Stebbins, who, on invitation, went home with Captain Soule. Joshua told Mr. Stebbins about his father, and advertised him that he might expect controversy. Accordingly, after supper they entered the lists—not without some apprehension on the part of Joshua, as his father was strong on the dogmas in question. But Mr. Stebbins got the better in the argument, and Captain Soule felt it. After breakfast the next morning he invited Mr. Stebbins to preach in his house. This he did the next round, to a large congregation—two or three Baptist ministers being present. The sermon was a powerful one—on the vision of the dry bones, in Ezekiel. From that time Captain Soule's house was a regular preaching-place. In less than six months after Joshua joined the Methodist Episcopal Church, his father, mother, two brothers, and two sisters joined it, also. Some years after, his parents died in the communion of the Church, and in holy triumph.

"Joshua Soule was never an exhorter or a local preacher. He received license to preach, and recommendation to the itinerancy, from a Quarterly Conference, in the latter part of the year 1798; he traveled under the Presiding Elder until the session of the Annual Conference in June, 1799. He was admitted on trial by the New England Conference at that session, and was appointed to Portland Circuit, in Maine—Timothy Merritt being the preacher in charge, and Joshua Taylor the Presiding Elder. It was a four weeks' circuit, five hundred miles in circumference, and comprising twenty-seven appointments.

"In 1800 he was sent to Union River, the lowest circuit in Maine, embracing the Penobscot, and extending to the British lines. That year he had no colleague.

"In 1801 he was sent to the Sandwich Circuit, near Cape Cod, without a colleague.

"In 1802 he was sent to Needham Circuit, with Thomas Percy as an assistant.

"At the close of his second year he started to Conference, at Boston, by sea, but did not reach there until after the close of the session; he was, however, admitted into full connection, and elected deacon. At the close of his third year he was ordained deacon, at Cranston, Rhode Island, by Bishop Whatcoat; and at the close of his fourth year he was ordained elder by the same Bishop.

"In 1803 he received his fifth appointment, which was to Nantucket, without a colleague. This year he was married to Miss Sarah Allen, an orphan, in Providence, Rhode Island. With her he lived in connubial felicity for fifty-four years. We shall never forget his look of sorrow and hope when, in May, 1857, we consigned her remains to the tomb.

"In 1805 and 1806 he was Presiding Elder of a District which embraced the entire territory of Maine, twelve hundred miles in circumference, comprising twelve circuits and one station. He visited the remotest settlements, and lodged in wretched cabins, frequently covered with snow, which beat in upon him. Sometimes, indeed, he had to sleep out in the frost, having the snow for his bed and the sky for his covering. He swam streams and encountered many other hardships. During the two years that he was on that District, and counting every day that he spent at home, he was only three weeks with his young wife. This, he assured us, he never could have done if she had not been an extraordinary woman, and encouraged him in his arduous and self-denying work.

"In 1806 and 1807, the District being divided, he traveled the lower part, known as the Kennebeck District. Bishop Asbury said, when he made the appointment, that he gave Joshua Soule the eastern section, which was much harder than the other, as he feared that Oliver Beale, who was appointed to the upper portion, would break down on the lower. During these two years he performed a vast amount of laborious service. The next four years he was Presiding Elder on the lower, or Portland, District.

"In 1808 he attended the General Conference, in Baltimore. At that session the plan of a delegated General Conference was adopted, and the grave responsibility was devolved upon him to draw up the Constitution as it now appears in the Book of Discipline.

"In 1812 he was stationed in Lynn. That year he attended the session of the General Conference held in New York. The next three years he traveled the Kennebeck District.

"He was a member of the General Conference of 1816, at which he was elected Book Agent and editor of the *Methodist Magazine*. For four years he performed the arduous and apparently incompatible duties of these offices with great fidelity. His position as Book Agent was at first singularly embarrassing. The Book Concern was insolvent; it could not get discount for five hundred dollars. The stock was old and comparatively valueless. His predecessor, Daniel Hitt, was a good and faithful man, but did not possess the requisite business qualifications for an undertaking so difficult and responsible. Mr. Soule immediately opened new books; and as a loan of money was indispensable, he procured it from the Mechanics' Bank, in Baltimore—his friends, Philip Littig and John Bryce, indorsing for him. The Book Concern prospered under his administration. He had no difficulty afterward in getting all the money he wanted, even during the tremendous financial crisis which occurred while he was in the agency. He made the *Magazine* a useful and interesting miscellany—the more so as this was before the era of *Christian Advocates*. But we have frequently heard him decry his own editorial capacity, pleasantly observing that the editing of the *Magazine* was a work of darkness, as it was performed chiefly at night, after the daily duties of his agency were closed.

"In 1820 he was succeeded, as Agent and editor, by Dr. Bangs, being himself elected to the Episcopate. He, however, respectfully declined consecration, in view of what is known as the Presiding Elder question. He never would consent to execute the office of Bishop if the Presiding Elders were elected by the Annual Conference. He always considered that act as one of great importance; and Bishop Waugh told him, in after years, that by his firmness on that occasion he saved the Church. That year he was stationed in the city of New York.

"In 1821 he was stationed in New York, as preacher in charge.

"In 1822 and 1823 he was preacher in charge of the Churches in Baltimore City Station. Here he was greatly beloved and admired. When, some years after, we followed him as junior preacher in the same station, we found that his name was as ointment poured forth.

"The session of the Baltimore Conference for 1824 was held in Winchester, Virginia. Although strong opposition was made to him, because of his decided stand on the Presiding Elder question, yet he was elected to the General Conference, and his name stood first in the list of delegates. His opponents—Messrs. Emory, Waugh, Griffith, and Morgan—were all left out. In after years they all saw their error, and made honorable apologies to Bishop Soule for the course they had pursued. At the General Conference, which was held that year in Baltimore, he was reëlected to the Episcopate, and was ordained by Bishops McKendree, George, and Roberts. From that time until he was forced by the weight of years and increasing infirmities to retire from active service, he was abundant in labors, scorning ease and self-indulgence, consecrating all his powers to the difficult and responsible work which had been assigned him by the Church."

Bishop Soule was first present at the Kentucky Conference which was held in Shelbyville in 1824, when Bishops McKendree and Roberts were also in attendance. In 1826, with Bishop Roberts, he attended the session of the Conference in Louisville, and in 1827 at Versailles, with Bishops McKendree and Roberts. In 1828, with Bishop Roberts, he was again present in Shelbyville, and in 1830 he presided alone over the Conference in Russellville. His presence at the session of 1834 was peculiarly gratifying to the body over which he presided.

Among the resolutions adopted by the Conference on the first day of the session, the following deserves a prominent place:

"*Resolved*, That the members of this Conference will in future be more diligent in the observance of the rule of Discipline which is as follows: 'Every Presiding Elder, minister, and preacher shall do every thing in his power to recover all debts due the Book Concern.'"*

It was the policy of the Agents in charge of the Book Concern, at this early day, under the instructions of the General Conference, to place the publications of the Church on sale at eligible points, or, what was almost as disastrous, to sell them to the preachers *on time.* Many of the preachers traveled on circuits which failed to meet their expenses for the year, yet had promised to do so. The preacher, believing that his claims would be fully met before the close of the year, and not being required to pay for his books until the Conference, did not deem it

*See Discipline for 1834, Part II., sec. 8, page 156.

improper to use the money received for books, expecting to replace the amount from his *quarterage* receipts. The Church, however, was unmindful of its obligations, and in too many instances the faithful pastor had to leave his charge, to whom he had ministered "in season and out of season," only half paid, and frequently his receipts fell below one-half. The result was obvious: his account with the Book Concern must go unpaid. In other instances preachers largely in debt to the Book Concern would die, and the limited means left by them for the support of their families could not well be spared to meet an obligation in this direction.

Another evil growing out of the credit system was that the preachers were disposed to supply the people with their books on the same terms which had been granted themselves—that is, to be paid for before the close of the year. Thus, fifty or one hundred dollars' worth of books, in small amounts, were scattered over a large circuit, embracing several counties. Under the most favorable circumstances, to collect all these debts would be impossible; besides, frequently a purchaser *might* forget that he owed the preacher, and the preacher would be too diffident to present the account. We have known some preachers who have become financially bankrupt by adopting this policy, while others, because they had been unable to collect the money due them on their circuits and stations, declined selling books in future.

If the policy of the Book Concern had been different—if the business from the commencement had been conducted on a *cash* basis—all parties would have been better satisfied.

On the credit system, in Kentucky a large debt was due the Book Concern, a considerable portion of which was against the preachers themselves. The success and interest of an institution dear to the Church demanded that these obligations be met, and be met at once. Indeed, many of the preachers indebted to the Concern felt that to impress upon the people they served the duty of promptitude, while they seemingly lacked this virtue themselves, would be worse than useless; and hence they resolved to meet their responsibilities in this matter, at whatever cost on the score of economy.

While some of the preachers became involved by the failure of their people to pay them for books, there were others in the Conference who supplemented their salaries from this department of their work. They felt it to be their duty to circulate the literature of the Church, but deemed it proper that those whom they served should pay them for the books they purchased. We have known preachers who realized the larger portion of their support from the energy they displayed in the sale and circulation of books; and there is perhaps no preacher who may not derive valuable aid from this source, if he gives it proper attention.*

Apprehensions were entertained by the Conference at this period that the itinerant system was

* We know a preacher who from the profits realized on the sale of books in his circuit supported a widowed mother, and aided in the education of two brothers and two sisters, and

likely to be impaired by the formation of so many stations, as distinct from circuits. In the Kentucky Conference there were at this time, besides the six Districts, fifty-three separate charges, twelve of which were stations.

In order to correct a tendency which they deemed subversive of a system which had operated so successfully in "spreading scriptural holiness" throughout the country, the following resolution was submitted on the first afternoon of the session:

"*Resolved, by the Kentucky Annual Conference of the Methodist Episcopal Church*, That the Bishop and Presiding Elders, in the arrangement of circuits and stations within the bounds of this Conference, be respectfully requested to connect with each station a sufficient number of appointments to constitute them circuits, or, where that is impracticable, to connect them with the adjacent circuits."

A motion was made to lay this resolution on the table, which was, however, withdrawn. The resotion was then referred to a committee of seven, to be appointed by the Bishop, and George C. Light, Henry B. Bascom, John Tevis, Joseph S. Tomlinson, Edward Stevenson, Milton Jamieson, and Jonathan Stamper were appointed the committee.

If we do not concur in the sentiment that the formation of stations imperiled the itinerant system, to which we were attached in our youth, in our early manhood, and to which we are still de-

---

purchased and owns handsome property. He has sold many thousands of dollars' worth, and never lost but one debt, which was *four dollars.*

voted, yet we cannot but admire the vigilance of our fathers over it—a vigilance that would not allow the least encroachment.

On Friday morning the committee submitted the following report, which was adopted:

"*Resolved, by the Kentucky Annual Conference of the Methodist Episcopal Church,* That the Bishop and Presiding Elders, in the arrangement and supply of the circuits and stations within the bounds of this Conference, be respectfully requested to connect with each station, as early as practicable, a sufficient number of appointments to constitute them, in fact, circuits, to be formed of places not previously occupied, or of such appointments, belonging to contiguous circuits, as may be agreed upon by the parties interested, in accordance with the provisions of the Discipline."

That there was a disposition to disconnect from the circuits, in many instances, small towns, and form them into separate charges, will be obvious to any one who will examine the history of the Church at this period. Very frequently, by such an arrangement, a good circuit was greatly weakened, and a small station was formed without sufficient strength to support a married preacher, and, with one destitute of experience, was unable to compete with other pulpits.

At the Conference of 1832 the question "What has been contributed for missions?" was asked for the first time, and it was repeated at the two sessions following. No steps, however, had been taken to form the Conference into a Missionary Society until the session of 1834.

On the second day of the session the amount contributed during the year for missions was reported, and found to be only $269.30, which, although an improvement on the receipts of the previous year, was inadequate to the demands, as well as a reflection upon the liberality, of the Church.

Without an organization and unity of purpose and effort but little improvement could be expected. Here and there might be found a solitary preacher, abreast with the spirit of the times, who would commend the missionary enterprise to the people he served; but the majority of them would fail to present or advocate the cause. The preachers needed instruction, in most instances, no less than the people they were commissioned to teach.

Immediately after the report was read it was proposed that the Conference form itself into a Missionary Society, auxiliary to the Parent Society of the Methodist Episcopal Church, located in the city of New York. A constitution was adopted for present purposes, and Milton Jamieson, Henry B. Bascom, and John Tevis were appointed a committee to revise it, and report at the ensuing session. The following officers were elected: President, the presiding Bishop; First Vice-president, Jonathan Stamper; Second Vice-president, Henry B. Bascom; Treasurer, Hubbard H. Kavanaugh; Corresponding Secretary, William Adams; Recording Secretary, John Tevis. Managers: Joseph S. Tomlinson, Richard Tydings, William Phillips, Benjamin T. Crouch, Isaac Collard, John James, Henry McDaniel, George W. Brush, George W. Taylor,

Henry S. Duke, Joseph Marsee. James Ward was appointed one of the Vice-presidents of the Parent Society. An Agent was also appointed for the Missionary Society, whose duty it should be to travel through the Conference, deliver sermons on the subject, form societies, take up collections, and awaken, as far as possible, general interest in behalf of the enterprise. This pleasant duty was intrusted to Milton Jamieson.

For several sessions the subject of Colonization had occupied a prominent place in the discussions of the Conference, and Agents had been appointed for the advancement of the scheme.

The Kentucky Colonization Society had sent to Liberia Joseph Jones, a man of color, and of more than ordinary intelligence and undoubted piety, for the purpose of ascertaining all that was requisite in reference to the Colony in Africa—the soil, climate, and productions. He had returned from his tour of observation, and was present at the session of the Kentucky Conference. The Kentucky Conference had no sympathy with Abolitionists. They believed the principles advocated by them to have been born in fanaticism, and fraught with mischief to society, and subversive of the American Union; and hence they repudiated alike the doctrines they taught and those who taught them. They, however, believed that the shores of Africa offered an asylum and a home for the free man of color, where he might build for himself a government, and be useful and happy; hence, at all times, they favored the measures by which their colonization might be effected, and on this occasion appointed Richard Corwine—a man who enjoyed the confidence of all who knew him—as the Agent for this Society.

Twenty-two preachers were admitted on trial at this session: Ezekiel Mobley, Henry Edmundson, Peter Taylor, Reuben W. Landrum, Robert Fisk, James M. Buchanan, Daniel S. Barksdale, Robinson E. Sidebottom, Solomon Pope, Alexander Robinson, Clinton Kelly, Thomas Rankin, James D. Holding, Henry N. Vandyke, John C. Niblack, George W. Merritt, George W. Simcoe, William M. Grubbs, George Switzer, Albert Kelly, Napoleon B. Lewis, and Matthew N. Lasley.

Of those who entered the itinerant field one year before, the names of Claiborne Pirtle and Daniel Sherwood disappear from the Minutes. Unable to perform the duties of traveling preachers, because of feeble health, they retire from the work.

Daniel S. Capell, Thomas H. Gibbons, George W. Fagg, Thomas C. Cropper, Joseph G. Ward, and John Sandusky enter the local ranks, but at a later period are found in the Conference again.

The names of Richard Corwine, Milton Jamieson, and Edward Stevenson, who had been on the superannuated list, appear in the effective ranks, while Samuel Harrison is found among the supernumeraries.

Hooper Evans is the only preacher whose health failed during the Conference-year. He becomes superannuated.

In the Methodist Church the preacher surrenders the privilege of selecting his own field of labor, while at the same time the Church yields its right to call a pastor, each vesting the authority in the Bishop. Nothing can be more interesting or exciting than the closing scene of an Annual Conference, when the appointments are announced, fixing the home of each member for a year. Several congregations may desire the services of the same preacher, and several preachers may wish to be appointed to the same charge. It is inevitable that some of them must be disappointed, and not unfrequently the expectations of none of them are realized. A preacher has traveled on a District or circuit, or filled a station, for a single year, and to his mind there is no reason why he should not be returned to the same field; or the Church which has had his services may deem his reäppointment important to the advancement and success of the cause of God. An interchange of opinion, however, among those in whom is vested the authority to make the appointments may develop reasons why a change should be made, which must surely be obvious to all.

The appointing of a single preacher, or the supplying of a solitary pulpit, would be an easy task; but the responsibility, as well as the difficulty, increases a hundred fold when a hundred men, embracing every variety of talent, are to be provided for, and a hundred Churches to be supplied.

It is not uncommon for a preacher to entertain the opinion that he should be appointed to a certain place, or for a Church to believe that it is entitled to a certain preacher. Their views would be well founded if no counter-claims were presented. It is not surprising, then, that both preachers and people are sometimes disappointed.*

*A preacher in the Louisville Conference was at one time appointed to —— District. His first quarterly-meeting in the District was to be held in the most prominent charge in his work. On arriving at the place a leading member of the Church called to see him, and informed him that his appointment was both unexpected and unsatisfactory to the people; that they desired their pastor for the previous year to be their Presiding Elder; and that even if he had not been their first choice, they preferred some other preacher to himself. The Presiding Elder made no reply at the time, but felt considerably embarrassed. He preached on Saturday, both morning and evening. On Sunday, after preaching at eleven o'clock to a crowded audience, he availed himself of the opportunity to refer to what had been said to him. He remarked that he was not surprised that the Church at that place desired the appointment of their former pastor to the District; that he would be very much astonished if any congregation, after having been favored with his ministry, should not desire to retain him; nor was he surprised that he was not their second choice. "But," said he, "there are two sides to this question. I was stationed last year among a Christian and intelligent people, where I seemed to be useful, to whom I was greatly and sincerely attached, and by whom I was beloved. I wished to serve them another year, and they unanimously requested my reäppointment; but I was taken from them, and your pastor was sent to fill my place. They are greatly dissatisfied, and I have just spent several days with them, trying to reconcile them. Besides, if I had expected to be removed, I would not have chosen your District. I think I deserve a better place and a more appreciative people. But I am your Presiding Elder, and you are a portion of my District, and I propose that we bury the tomahawk to-day, and for one year try and be a mutual blessing to each other." At the fourth quarterly-meeting in this charge he announced, in the Quarterly Conference, his purpose to decline a reäppointment to the District,

In the appointments for this year we find William Adams on the Lexington District, in the place of William Gunn, who had traveled it the year before. The Augusta District is still supplied with Richard Tydings. On the Harrodsburg District, John James succeeds William Adams. Benjamin T. Crouch, Isaac Collard, and George W. Taylor are returned to the same Districts they traveled the previous year. In the Lexington District, Hubbard H. Kavanaugh was returned to Lexington. In the Augusta District, John W. Riggin was reäppointed to the Fleming Circuit. We find Jonathan Stamper again at Danville and Harrodsburg, in the Harrodsburg District. George W. Brush, in the Louisville District, was again stationed in Shelbyville, and William Holman in Louisville. In the Hopkinsville District, Newton G. Berryman was returned to Bowling Green, and Buford Henry to the Green River Circuit; in the Greensburg District, Jesse Sutton to Glasgow, and John Denham to the Lebanon Circuit.

To record the growth and advancement of Methodism in the State of Kentucky is always a pleasant task. Identified, as we have been, for the past forty-two years with the Methodist Church, and for thirty-eight years with the fortunes of the Methodist ministry, we would be untrue to every generous and noble impulse if, in the midst of duties in other sections of the Church, our thoughts did not revert with feelings of pleasure to the home of our child-

at which they demurred, and appointed a committee to attend the Conference and protest against any change. He remained in this District four years.

hood and the scenes of our first religious impressions and early ministry. To follow in the path of those who preceded us, and to watch the struggling cause to which so many valiant lives were pledged, and in which so many were sacrificed, and to see it as from year to year it became more commanding and powerful, has ever been a fondly-cherished pleasure.

The year which followed the Conference of 1834, although "times of refreshing from the presence of the Lord" were realized in several sections of the Conference, was not distinguished by any extraordinary outpourings of the Holy Spirit. Valuable accessions to the Church cheered the hearts of the disciples of Christ in some portions of the work; but, with these exceptions, the Church was quiet and calm.

In the Burlington Circuit, in the Lexington District—to which John Carr Harrison and Henry N. Vandyke were appointed—there was some increase in the membership, but in every other charge in that District the membership decreased. It is true that in the city of Frankfort, under the ministry of Thomas W. Chandler, there was a revival of religion, in which a few persons were converted and added to the Church; but even in this station there was a falling off in both the white and colored membership. In the Falmouth Circuit, also, one hundred and fifty-seven persons were added to the Church; yet the Minutes report fifty white and twenty-five colored less than the previous year. In the entire District there was a decrease of four hundred and ninety-two in the white membership, and two hundred and eight in the colored.

If we look over the Augusta District we find but little more to cheer us than in the Lexington. In the Hinckstone, the Little Sandy, and the Big Sandy Circuits the revivals were extensive, and many were brought to Christ. In the Hinckstone Circuit, through the instrumentality of the quaint Josiah Whitaker and the young and zealous Robinson E. Sidebottom, many were converted. Lorenzo D. Parker—distinguished for his success in "winning souls to Christ"—and Peter Taylor, plain and pure-hearted, were eminently useful on the Little Sandy, and under their ministry two hundred persons became members of the Church; while, on the Big Sandy Circuit, John Nevius and Daniel S. Barksdale were equally successful. In the Germantown Circuit, whose preachers were Absalom Woolliscroft and George W. Simcoe, one hundred and fifty persons joined the Church, and yet a decrease in the membership was reported. In this District there were three hundred and eighteen white members less than the year before, while in the colored membership there was an increase of ninety-four.

The Harrodsburg District also reported a decrease of one hundred and eighty-seven in the white membership, and of one hundred and nine in the colored. The Mount Sterling Station and Mount Vernon Circuit—the former under the pastoral charge of Edward Stevenson, a preacher of a high order of talent and uncompromising zeal, and the latter under the leadership of Elijah Sutton and Reuben W.

Landrum, indefatigable young men—were greatly blessed during the year. Revivals crowned the labors of these faithful men, and an increase was reported in both of these charges.

In the Cumberland Mission—which embraced a vast extent of territory, covering the head-waters of the Cumberland and Kentucky Rivers, amid the mountains of South-eastern Kentucky—between fifty and sixty persons had been brought into the Church. Richard Holding, a pure and simple-hearted preacher of the gospel, and Napoleon B. Lewis—a young man of extraordinary pulpit ability, and with a zeal that knew no bounds save his wasting strength—had charge of this work. Thirty-three preaching-places had been established in this rugged field, at each of which these young evangelists preached every four weeks. Their ministry was greatly blessed, although a small decrease at the close of the year appears in the Minutes. In the other charges in the District the decrease was greater.

It is pleasant to turn from such barren scenes as those through which we have just passed to the contemplation of a more productive field—the Louisville District. Although the increase in this District was small, being only sixty in the white and thirty in the colored membership, yet it is gratifying to know that amid the religious dearth so prevalent in Kentucky during this year the Louisville District maintained the ground previously occupied. In the city of Louisville there was a falling off in the membership, and also in the Newcastle Circuit—

both of these charges being under the pastoral care of men who were distinguished for the success that usually crowned their labors. The other appointments in the District not only maintained their former strength, but made some progress.

The Shelby Circuit, with William Gunn and James D. Holding—the former the sweet singer, and the latter the weeping prophet, of the Conference—had a small increase in the white membership, but reported a falling off in the colored. Shelbyville—still under the leadership of George W. Brush—continued to advance in numbers and in influence. The Taylorsville Circuit, with John Christian Harrison* as the preacher, enjoyed prosperity, while Francis Landrum and Robert Y. McReynolds were eminently useful on the Jefferson. The Breckinridge Circuit was favored with the ministry of Thomas P. Farmer and John Beatty—the former large and robust, the latter small and lean, but both devoted to their work, and their ministry acknowledged in a large ingathering into the fold of Christ. The Yellow Banks Circuit, under the ministry of the modest Robert F. Turner, was greatly blessed; while the Hartford Circuit, with Thomas S. Davis as the preacher, enjoyed many gracious seasons.

For two years the Hopkinsville District declined

* John C. Harrison was appointed to the Yellow Banks Circuit, and Robert F. Turner to the Taylorsville. The Rev. Samuel Harrison, the father of John C. Harrison, died soon after Conference, which rendered it necessary that he should travel near the residence of his mother; hence the change between him and Mr. Turner.

in membership. Two hundred and ninety-two white and thirty-three colored members less than at the previous Conference are reported in the Minutes for this year, the Hopkinsville Station and the Greenville Circuit being the only charges where an increase is reported. In the Greenville Circuit, James H. Brooking and Henry Edmundson accomplished great good. Revivals in several Societies blessed their ministry, and at the close of the year they reported a net increase of eighty-nine white and three colored members. In the Hopkinsville Station, under the ministry of William S. Evans, the popular and zealous pastor, the white membership was nearly doubled. In the remaining charges a decrease was reported, with the exception of Bowling Green, where no change appears in the Minutes.

In the Greensburg District we are confronted with losses in every charge except the Salt River Circuit—where the veteran Denham and the beardless Blades traveled and preached—and the Bardstown Station, under the pastoral care of the eloquent Silas Lee, where one white member less and one colored more than for the previous year are reported. The total loss in this District was four hundred and twenty-seven white and forty-five colored members.

In Jackson's Purchase we find an increase reported in the Hickman Circuit, to which Thomas Lloyd and H. B. McCord had been sent; while in the Wadesboro Circuit a small decrease is reported.

The entire loss in Kentucky for this year was

sixteen hundred and sixty-six white and *two hundred and fifty-nine* colored members.

The ministry of George W. D. Harris in Kentucky closes with the present year. We regret to part with him. We first met him in the autumn of 1831, in charge of the Paris District, which included the Wadesboro and Hickman Circuits. During the four years in which he presided over this District his ministry in Kentucky was greatly blessed. Faithful in every department of his work, he exerted an influence for good which was felt from the center to the circumference of the vast field he occupied. As a preacher he ranked with the first pulpit men in the West, and was instrumental in bringing hundreds into the fold of Christ. His sermons, always replete with instruction, were often attended with remarkable power, and under his masterly arguments and earnest appeals many a sinner was led to abandon a life of vice, and to fly for refuge to the hope set before him in the gospel.

In the summer of 1832 he was present at the camp-meeting held at Mobley's Camp-ground, in Graves county, Kentucky, and preached on Sunday, at eleven o'clock. The crowd was immense, eagerly catching the words of life as they fell from the lips of the preacher. A feeling of awe pervaded the assembly as he portrayed the life and final doom of the sinner. Pausing in the midst of the sermon, he exclaimed: "I will give the process by which a Deist may be converted." In the audience was Major Collins, a refined and polished gentleman, who had rejected the claims of Christianity and embraced

Deism. Attracted by the statement of Mr. Harris, his attention became riveted on the speaker. He watched him as he progressed in the argument until he saw himself a sinner before God, standing on the threshold of ruin, a yawning gulf, without bank or bottom, beneath him, and above a frowning Judge. Despair, with raven wings, hovered over him, and, rising from his seat, he pressed his way to the altar, crying aloud, "Lost, *lost*, LOST!" No, not lost. Just then a ray of golden light pierced the gloom, bringing hope to the despairing soul. The bow of mercy spanned the heavens, and threw its mellow radiance over a sorrowing heart. God was gracious, and in a few moments peace and joy filled the soul of the repentant sinner. The Major joined the Church that day, and was baptized by Mr. Harris.*

It would be a pleasant task to follow this faithful man through the long period of his ministry, and to record the success that crowned his labors for nearly half a century; but another will perform this duty. He died in Dyersburg, Tennessee, December 9, 1872.†

---

*At the session of the Memphis Conference in 1867, Dr. Harris related the above incident to the author. Major Collins was then living, a pious member of the Church.

†Bishop McTyeire, in the Nashville *Christian Advocate*, of December 28, 1872, says:

"G. W. D. Harris was no common man. Of strong will, clear perceptions, and deep convictions, of high and consecrated purpose, consistent and blameless in life, and capable of zeal in a good cause, he combined all the qualities that make a leader among men; and such he was. The natural sternness of his elements was relieved by the tenderness of love and a vein of chastened humor. Even down to old age he was a most agreeable companion to persons of every class—full of striking sentiment, incisive remark, and of pertinent, instructive anecdote and interesting reminiscences. It is significant of his character that he was titled and habitually spoken of by his younger brethren not as 'Doctor Harris,' but as 'Uncle George.' The doctrines and morals of Christianity were firmly grasped and perspicuously enunciated by him. Often a great unction rested upon his preaching and his prayers. Our ecclesiastical polity he understood and loved, and was a model Presiding Elder, which high office he adorned and magnified for more than half of his ministerial years. He might have been, by the strength of his mind, the force of his character, the power of his speech, and the opportunities of his times—yes, he might have been rich and great in the world's esteem. But what were these to him? He kept to the lot God assigned him: he fulfilled his life-work as a Methodist preacher, without turning aside to the right hand or the left. How many preachers has he recruited into the Master's service? how many members has he added to the Church? how many souls have been quickened and converted under his ministry? The annals of time may not yet answer these questions. A pioneer in these broad fields, he endured the burden and heat of the day. We have entered into his labors, and he into his rest.

"When the Memphis Conference was constituted, in November, 1840, G. W. D. Harris naturally found his place at the head of it, and his brethren have had the wisdom and the grace to keep him there. Unavoidably and fortunately he has impressed himself upon that large and valuable body of ministers and members. His decision, his practical wisdom, his love of the Church's welfare, and jealousy for its honor, commanded for his opinions marked deference. 'Unto him men gave ear, and waited, and kept silence at his counsel.' Grand old man! When shall we see his like again? We thank God for having given him to the Church, and permitted him to continue with us so long. Many, very many, of his sons in the gospel and spiritual children have gone before him to paradise; others, faint, yet pursuing, are following on.

The itinerant ranks were thinned this year by the death of several preachers. Benjamin Ogden, Francis Landrum, Samuel Harrison, William Adams, Minor M. Cosby, and William Outten passed from labor to reward.

The names of Ogden, Landrum, Harrison, and Adams had for many years been familiar not only to the Methodists in Kentucky, but to other Christian denominations. Shoulder to shoulder they had toiled and labored, sacrificed and suffered, and together had passed away and entered upon eternal life.*

Of the time and place of the birth of Minor M. Cosby we have no record. He was about twenty-one years of age when he embraced religion, and two years later was admitted on trial into the Kentucky Conference. His first appointment was to the Greenville Circuit, as the colleague of Thomas G. Reece. In 1832 he traveled the Danville Circuit

---

"After he grew to manhood he knew no second childhood. The outward senses were dulled and decayed toward the last, but his mental faculties were firm and his faith clear. The long shadows of life's closing day fell upon him still at work. He attends his forty-eighth Annual Conference, and answers to his name at roll-call; his farewell sermon is preached, his 'character passes,' and he goes home to die. This, indeed, is the itinerant's much-coveted *euthanasia*. As the aged servant utters *Nunc dimittis*, and retires from the field, we join all his brethren in saying, 'Servant of God, well done!' You leave the world better for having lived in it."

* For sketches of Benjamin Ogden, Francis Landrum, Samuel Harrison, and William Adams, see "History of Methodism in Kentucky."

with Milton Jamieson, and in 1833, as the colleague of John James, he performs the duties of an itinerant on the Winchester Circuit. At the Conference of 1834 he was appointed to the Henderson Circuit, where he closed his labors with his life.

No young man in the Conference promised greater usefulness to the Church than did Minor M. Cosby. Although his talents were not of the highest order, yet his pulpit abilities were far above mediocrity, while his deportment out of the pulpit exerted no ordinary influence for good. During the four years of his itinerant service he was eminently useful and greatly beloved in the several fields in which he labored. He died of congestive fever, on the 5th of September, 1835, five days preceding the opening of the Conference. His last sufferings were severe, but were borne with firmness and resignation. In his dying moments he bore testimony to the saving power of the religion he had preached so successfully.

William Outten was a native of Fayette county, Kentucky, and was brought up in the city of Lexington, where he joined the Church when quite young, and was converted to God. From the time he became a member of the Church his piety was uniform and consistent. Active in all the enterprises of the Church, he devoted himself to its interests with laudable zeal. Feeling that God had called him to preach the gospel, he applied himself to study with true diligence, and gave promise of great usefulness in the Church. At the Conference of 1833 he offered himself for the itinerant work, and was accepted, and appointed to the Burksville Circuit. At the Conference of 1834 he was continued on trial, and appointed to the Green River Circuit, with Bluford Henry. He, however, had scarcely entered upon his work when a malignant fever fastened upon his system, and bore him to the grave. During his illness he suffered acutely, but not a murmur fell from his lips. He died in great triumph, December 24, 1834, at twelve o'clock M., at the house of Mr. Porter, a member of the Church.

CHAPTER IV.

FROM THE SESSION OF THE KENTUCKY CONFERENCE OF 1835 TO THE CONFERENCE OF 1836.

Sow in the morn thy seed,
  At eve hold not thy hand;
To doubt and fear give thou no heed—
  Broad-cast it o'er the land.
Beside all waters sow,
  The highway furrows stock,
Drop it where thorns and thistles grow,
  Scatter it on the rock.

THE Kentucky Conference for 1835 met in Shelbyville, on the 16th of September. Here, for the first time, we saw Bishop Andrew. It was his first visit to Kentucky.

James Osgood Andrew was born in Wilkes county, Georgia, May 3, 1794. His father, the Rev. John Andrew, was for three years a traveling preacher, but in 1792—two years previous to the birth of his son—retired to the local ranks, in which sphere he was distinguished for his zeal and usefulness.

Not only favored with a Christian father, but also with a mother remarkable for her superior intellect and fervent piety, young Andrew grew up in the bosom of the Church, developing traits of character which would render him useful in the time to come. When only a child he was often taken by his mother to her place of private prayer, where, with her soft hand upon his head, she would commend him to God, and pray that he might become a Methodist preacher. When only thirteen years of age he was admitted to the communion of the Church, and at eighteen was licensed to preach.

Denied the advantages of a classical education, he was led by his fondness for study to his father's library, where he improved his time in reading the books thus placed in his way.

A congregation of colored people was the first to hear him proclaim the words of eternal truth; and to the negroes of Georgia his ministry was signally blessed through the long years of his life. His first appearance in the pulpit, in the presence of his neighbors and friends, elicited from a prominent member of the Church the remark, "Well, *Jeemes*, I voted the other day for you to be a preacher; but if I had heard that sermon first, I never would have done it." His recommendation to the Annual Conference was presented by his Presiding Elder—Dr. Lovick Pierce—at the session of the South Carolina Conference which met in Charleston, December 12, 1812, at which time he became an itinerant preacher.

The first field of ministerial labor to which Mr. Andrew was assigned was the Saltketcher Circuit, as the junior preacher. The second year of his ministry was spent in charge of the Bladen Circuit. At the Conference of 1814 he was sent to the Warren Circuit, and the following year he was stationed in

Charleston. We next find him lifting the standard of the cross in Wilmington, North Carolina, where he remained for two years. From Wilmington we follow him to Augusta, Georgia, and thence to Savannah, serving two years in each city.

No man in so short a period had risen more rapidly to eminence in the Church than this faithful minister of Jesus Christ. The plainness and simplicity with which he delivered his message, the zeal which distinguished his pulpit efforts, the power that attended his sermons, his success in winning souls to Christ, together with his abundant labors and his uncompromising devotion to the work to which he had been divinely called, betokened the high position he was destined to occupy in the Church of Christ.

In 1824 he became the leader on the Edisto District, and in 1825 and 1826 on the Charleston. He returned to the city of Charleston in 1827, where, twelve years before, when a young man, he had proclaimed the tidings of salvation. For two years he remained in Charleston, whence he was appointed to Athens and Greensboro, in the State of Georgia, and in 1830 to Greensboro and Madison. In 1831 he was again stationed in Augusta—the Georgia Conference having been organized that year—and in January of the following year was returned to the same city.

At this period no minister in the State of Georgia occupied so prominent a place in the public thought as James O. Andrew. Pure as the crystal drops as they fall from the clouds, with an intellect broad and massive, with a zeal commensurate with the wants and woes of mankind, and with a heart warmed by the fires of eternal love, he delivered, in burning words, the mighty truths of the gospel to saint and to sinner. From the time he became an itinerant until his elevation to the Episcopacy, in 1832, he had labored with fidelity and success, winning hundreds of souls to Christ.

He entered upon the duties of a Bishop in the full vigor of manhood, bringing to the office not only commanding talents, but the fervor and zeal which had distinguished his ministry in the Carolinas and in Georgia.

He reached Shelbyville several days previous to the opening of the session. On Sabbath, at eleven o'clock A.M., he preached in the Methodist Church. His fame had preceded him, and an immense audience, for a full hour, hung in breathless silence on his lips. His text, like the sermon, was a plain one: "Now when John had heard in the prison the works of Christ, he sent two of his disciples, and said unto him, Art thou he that should come, or do we look for another? Jesus answered and said unto them, Go and shew John again those things which ye do hear and see: the blind receive their sight, and the lame walk, the lepers are cleansed, and the deaf hear, the dead are raised up, and the poor have the gospel preached to them. And blessed is he whosoever shall not be offended in me." *

The sermon was one of great simplicity and power. John the Baptist was confined in a lonely prison,

* Matt. xi. 2–6.

from which he would soon be led to execution. The precursor of the Messiah, to him it was a matter of surprise that His arm had not interposed in his behalf, and broken the fetters that bound him. Tempted to call in question the claims of Christ to the Messiahship, yet unwilling to yield to the siren voice of the tempter, he sends two of his disciples to the Master, to ask him whether he was the Messiah or not. How simple the reply! In the crowd which had assembled before him every malady was represented. There stood the man blind from his birth, who had heard of the fame of the Nazarene, and had come to ask for sight; there, too, the lame man, unable to support his tottering frame, was pleading for relief; the leper, whose life was blighted by the most loathsome of all the maladies that ever cursed the human family, in piteous tones was begging for compassion; the deaf man, too, who in childhood had never heard the sound of the lullaby from a mother's lips, and upon whose ears musical strains had never fallen, was seeking to be cured; close by where he stood the place of graves spread out before the view of the assembled multitude; while the poor and the outcast, for whose souls no man seemed to care, with countenances on which despair had been written, were catching here and there a word of hope. He speaks—and the scales fall from the eyes of the blind, and earth, with all its scenes of grandeur and beauty, and sky, with all its loveliness and brightness, greet the astonished vision; the lame man throws away his crutches, and, forgetful of all the sorrows of the past, leaps for joy; the leper, scorned and hated, and driven into solitude, returns to the bosom of society, blessing and being blessed; the deaf, no longer insensible to the voice of melody and of song, are enraptured with strains far surpassing the grandest conceptions of the mind; but, look! mausoleums are crumbling, graves are opening, and the dead are starting from their beds of dust, and mingling with the living throng; and the poor, whose homes have been in the highways and hedges, and to whose ears no sweet invitation to be saved had ever come, are included in the plan of mercy, and have the gospel preached to them. Go, and tell your master what you have heard and seen, and then, if he can, let him doubt.

We have given scarcely an outline of the introduction to this remarkable sermon. During its delivery the audience was often moved to tears.

William Phillips was appointed Secretary of the Conference, in the place of William Adams, who had for many years previous to his death occupied that position.

The usual committees were appointed, after which Henry B. Bascom offered a resolution expressive of the deep sorrow of the Conference over the loss sustained by the inroads of death during the year which had just closed, and suggesting the appointment of some one to preach a sermon commemorative of those who had died.

During no previous year had the Church sustained so heavy a loss by the death of its ministers. The greater number of the deceased were cavaliers whose names were familiar to the Church, because of the long service they had rendered, and who had led the victorious charge in many a stirring conflict. They had fought their last battle, and entered upon "the rest that remaineth to the people of God."

In an appropriate resolution, Henry B. Bascom was "requested" to preach a sermon in memory of the departed ministers.

Among the items of business transacted by the Conference during this session the resolution proposing that "a committee of five be appointed to prepare an address to the members and friends of the Methodist Church on the subject of patronizing the *Western Christian Advocate*, for the purpose of extending its circulation within the bounds of the Kentucky Conference," deserves a prominent place.

The *Western Christian Advocate*, established in the city of Cincinnati, was intended to meet a want which was deeply felt in the West. No Conference, not even the Ohio, was more deeply interested in its success than the Kentucky. The information it contained from week to week was important to the Church, not only making known its progress and growth, but awakening an interest in behalf of all its enterprises. Up to this period the circulation of the paper in Kentucky was not equal either to the wants of the Church or the expectations of its friends. It is true that in some of the charges the subscription-list was all that could be reasonably expected, and in these charges the Church prospered and all its undertakings were successful; in others, however, it scarcely found its way to a solitary home, and a corresponding indifference was shown in reference to every interest of the Church. While many of the preachers felt that the *Christian Advocate* was a potent auxiliary in the accomplishment of good, and presented its claims to the patronage of their people, there were others who gave no thought to the subject, and almost reluctantly received the names of subscribers when offered to them. To support a Church-paper then, as now, was no easy task; it required the coöperation of all the patronizing Conferences to insure its success. Something more than mere Conference resolutions, however, was necessary to consummate this object, and the design of the action of the body was not only to awaken an interest in the minds of those preachers who had hitherto made no effort to place the *Advocate* in the families they visited, but to call the attention of the Church to the benefit to be derived from such a visitor to every Christian family.*

Resolutions recommending the *Methodist Magazine* and *Quarterly Review* were also adopted.

The subject of Temperance came before the Conference at this session, as it had done for several years preceding. The General Conference, which was to meet the following May, was memorialized "to restore Mr. Wesley's rule on the subject of ardent spirits."† It is certainly gratifying to know

*No preacher is true either to himself or the people he serves if he allows a family in his charge to be without their Church-paper, and no family will feel the same interest in the Church, deprived of this blessing, as if they enjoyed it.

†The rule is as follows: "Drunkenness; buying and selling spirituous liquors, or drinking them, unless in cases of extreme necessity."

that the resolution embodying this petition to the General Conference received the unanimous vote of the body, with a single exception. The Journal of the Conference declines to furnish the name of the preacher who voted in the negative.

The Friday before the ensuing Christmas was set apart "as a day of fasting and prayer for the peace and prosperity of Zion, and that the great Head of the Church would send forth more laborers into his vineyard."

Resolutions were adopted, urging more active efforts in behalf of education, and expressing opposition to the policy of Abolitionists on the subject of slavery.

The questions of Abolition and Colonization had been referred to a large and able committee, consisting of Henry B. Bascom, Jonathan Stamper, John Littlejohn, Joseph S. Tomlinson, Hubbard H. Kavanaugh, Richard Corwine, John Tevis, and John Beatty. They submitted the following report, which was unanimously adopted by the Conference:

"1. *Resolved, by the Kentucky Annual Conference,* That we strictly adhere to the principles of our Church on the subject of slavery, and that it is our purpose to persevere in the course hitherto pursued, without any alliance whatever with men or measures whose object may be an interference with the question of slavery, uncalled for by the common good, and productive of mischievous rather than beneficial results.

"2. *Resolved,* That, in the judgment of this Conference, the interference of Abolitionists and antislavery associations, in the North and elsewhere, by which the peace and quiet of a large portion of the nation are disturbed, and their common interest, laws, and safety placed in jeopardy, should be looked upon as an unwarrantable assumption of claim and an abuse of the rights of citizenship.

"3. *Resolved*, That, in the opinion of this Conference, whenever such interference with the rights of American citizens is attempted by foreign emissaries, whether as lecturers, ecclesiastics, or otherwise, all lawful means should be promptly resorted to, to arrest at once the mischievous tendency of their seditious intermeddling and officious insolence.

"4. *Resolved*, That, without presuming to decide, we would respectfully suggest that it is a dangerous maxim to be adopted by American citizens in the present crisis, that we may appreciate as pure and correct the motives of men whose measures and movements tend directly to subvert the Constitution and dissolve the Government.

"5. *Resolved*, That it is not considered by this body allowable for any minister or member of the Methodist Episcopal Church, within the limits of this Conference, or, as we conceive, elsewhere, to resort to any extra-judicial means whatever for the purpose of interfering with the question of slavery.

"6. *Resolved*, That we continue to repose entire confidence in the rectitude, policy, and operations of the American Colonization Society, and that we commend it to all who are likely to regard our opinions as any way worthy their approval and patronage."

The Kentucky Conference plainly foresaw the results of the policy of Abolitionists upon the Church as well as the State, and deemed it proper to place itself right before the people of Kentucky and before the nation.

On Monday, the fifth day of the session, Henry B. Bascom, Benjamin T. Crouch, Edward Stevenson, Jonathan Stamper, Hubbard H. Kavanaugh, and George W. Taylor were elected delegates to the General Conference, and John Christian Harrison and Josiah Whitaker were elected reserve delegates.

Under the administration of Bishop Andrew the business was rapidly dispatched, and from the commencement to the close of the Conference the most perfect harmony prevailed.

The preaching during the session was of a very high order. It was the first Conference on which we had ever looked, and we listened to every sermon that was preached in the Methodist Church. We were too young, perhaps, to be able to form an accurate judgment in reference to the pulpit ability of the distinguished preachers who were present, yet accustomed, as the citizens of Shelbyville were, to listening to the ablest ministers of all denominations, it was the commonly expressed opinion that on no former occasion had that community been so greatly favored in this regard. Although forty years have intervened since that meeting, we remember with distinctness several of the sermons which were preached, and the impressions they made on our mind.

The sermon delivered by Thomas N. Ralston—

then a young man—from the text "Return unto thy rest, O my soul; for the Lord hath dealt bountifully with thee,"* was not only a masterpiece of composition, but produced a wonderful effect. We have since often listened, with thrilling interest, to the same distinguished divine, but on no occasion have we heard him excel the sermon he preached at that time. The soul—its immortality and its capacity for suffering or for bliss—a wanderer from God, its only source of rest—the exhortation to return, and the rich provision made through the atonement of Jesus Christ for its happiness here and hereafter—were the themes on which the preacher dwelt. In a whisper soft as the evening zephyr he portrayed the sufferings of Christ for the sins of mankind, and the rich inheritance provided for the world by the death of the Son of God. He dipped his pencil in living light to paint the agonies that Jesus bore, and to unfold the glittering splendors of the heavenly state in which the soul should bask forever and ever. Then, rising to the loftiest heights of oratory, he pointed to the realms of night—unending night—where the soul, invested with immortality, should roam amid darkness and gloom, through eternal ages—lost, lost, forever lost!

Tuesday morning, September 22d, at half-past ten o'clock, was fixed as the time for the service in memory of deceased ministers of the Conference—Mr. Bascom to preach the sermon, according to appointment. The veteran Ogden, the quaint and devoted Harrison, the mild and gentle Adams, the

* Psalm cxvi. 7.

zealous Landrum, the youthful Cosby and Outten, had fought their last battle, and received their discharge. The interest of the occasion, as well as the fame of the preacher, attracted to the house of worship an immense assembly. It was a solemn time. Mr. B. read his text: "O death, where is thy sting? O grave, where is thy victory? The sting of death is sin; and the strength of sin is the law. But thanks be to God, which giveth us the victory through our Lord Jesus Christ." *

Sin had introduced death into the world, and death was the enemy of mankind. He passes over the world, and through the generations destroys the human race; he brings desolation and sorrow to every hearth and to every heart; none can escape his grasp. The home of poverty and the abode of wealth are alike invaded, and, without distinction, all fall a prey to his prowess and his power. The world is a vast grave-yard, and all are hurrying to the goal. Is there no hope for the human family? Is there no relief from the terrible doom from whose threatenings all would flee? Where shall man look for help? The heavens above are dark; the cloud of Divine wrath rolls up heavy from the horizon, until it covers our spiritual sky with sackcloth and gloom; it hangs about the world silent, dark, and terrible. The sleeping thunderbolt is ready at every moment to leap from its stormy home, and explode on the very hearthstone of our planet. Every human system is impotent to avert the awful catastrophe. It was then that the Son of

* 1 Cor. xv. 55–57.

God, with an arm omnipotent, disarmed the cloud of its wrath, until its darkness dissolved in purple and gold, and the rainbow came out and stood, like an angel of peace, on its glittering folds. "It is finished!" falls from the dying lips of the Man of Sorrows, and rolls with inexpressible sweetness to the skies; and Death, powerless in his own dominions—no longer a conqueror—yields to Him who broke his massive bars and "brought life and immortality to light."

We will not, however, attempt even a synopsis of this sermon.

On Sunday of the Conference, at eleven o'clock, Bishop Andrew preached previous to the ordination of the deacons. His text was "Preach the word; be instant in season, out of season."* No man was better qualified to preach at an hour like this than Bishop Andrew. Soundly converted, and divinely called to the work of the Christian ministry, and by experience familiar with every variety of appointment, and devoted to the cause in which he was spending his noble life, he was well prepared to utter words of cheer to younger men who had entered upon this service. With him a divine call to the work of the Christian ministry was essential. "No man taketh this honor to himself, but he that is called of God." "The harvest truly is plenteous, but the laborers are few; pray ye therefore the Lord of the harvest that he will send forth laborers into his harvest." No man, however brilliant his talents—however anxious he may be to build up

*2 Tim. iv. 2.

the Church, or to accomplish good—has the right to become a preacher unless God calls him to the work. In God, and in him alone, is vested the authority to call men into this high and holy office; nor has the man whom he chooses any right to refuse. No plea for declining to enter upon the work can avail. A man may be destitute of commanding abilities, or he may not be fluent in speech—outward circumstances may be all unfavorable—yet, if God calls him to preach the gospel, the call is imperative. He discussed the itinerant system of the Methodist Church, and advocated it as the apostolic plan, adopted by Jesus Christ himself, and as the only plan by which the highways and hedges can be visited and the poor have the gospel preached to them. By this system, Methodism—younger by far than any other leading branch of the Church in America—has surpassed and distanced all others in the achievement of good. To-day it stands without a rival not only in the energy it displays, but in the thousands who worship at its altars. Its votaries are everywhere—in the crowded city and in the home of the humble mountaineer—brought into the Church and to Christ through the instrumentality of the itinerant system. It is God's plan. Now and then a restless spirit may be found, who would blot itinerancy from the map of Methodism, because he is unwilling to participate in its sacrifices. The life of a traveling Methodist preacher is not a life of ease; it is not the road to pleasure, to fortune, or to fame. If influenced by any of these considerations, abandon at once a work which makes no such promises and offers no such rewards. He urged upon the preachers the fact that in entering the itinerant ministry they had no right to break the rules, or to inveigh against the system; that they had entered it voluntarily, and could retire from it whenever it might please them to do so.

We shall never forget his earnest appeal to the preachers, not only to go to the fields of labor assigned them, promptly, but to be faithful in their work. "Never neglect an appointment," he said, "if possible to meet it. Let neither sunshine nor storm, rain nor snow, keep you from meeting your appointments; *you may be water-bound, but never weather-bound.*"

It was two years later when we joined the Conference; but the impressions made on our mind by this sermon have never been effaced. The admonitions of that hour contributed largely to the formation of our character as a Methodist preacher, and are still among the most fondly-cherished memories of our heart.

It was at this Conference that the first annual report of the Kentucky Conference Missionary Society was read. The missionary meeting was held on Monday afternoon, September 21st. Bishop Andrew was invited to preach a sermon on the occasion. His text was "Say not ye, There are yet four months, and then cometh harvest? behold, I say unto you, Lift up your eyes, and look on the fields; for they are white already to harvest." *

Three years had elapsed since the first missionary

* John iv. 35.

money had been reported by the Kentucky Conference, and the amounts previously collected were chiefly, if not entirely, contributed by the preachers themselves. Little, however, had been done in this direction. An apathy pervaded the Church, or rather but little interest had ever been awakened, in reference to missionary enterprise; and both the preachers and people needed to be aroused. The whole field demanding Christian effort was surveyed by Bishop Andrew. *The world belonged to God*, having been purchased by the sufferings and death of his Son Jesus Christ. They had revolted from their rightful Sovereign, and sought for bliss in other objects, but had sought in vain. The pagan world, becoming disgusted with idol-worship, passed in review before the audience—with uplifted hands, appealing for help, and with the cry upon their lips, "Who will show us any good?" No friendly hand had reached out to save them; no ear had listened to their plaintive appeal; their cries, their tears, their prayers, had been unheeded; and nation after nation had fallen into hell, while Christians, with folded arms, satisfied their consciences with the convenient plea, "Charity begins at home." For more than an hour he pleaded, as a man pleads for his life, the cause of those "who sit in darkness and in the valley of the shadow of death." The sermon gave a fresh impulse to the preachers; the entire assembly was stirred; tears flowed freely down the faces of men unused to weep, and resolutions were formed never to be broken.* The collection, at

*The Rev. John Netherton, a Baptist preacher, was occu-

the close of this very effective sermon, amounted to $1,684.50.

Seven preachers were admitted on trial—viz.: Thomas Demoss, William M. Crawford, George S. Savage, Thomas R. Malone, John C. C. Thompson, William Burns, and Alexander Kessinger.

Of those who had entered the Conference one year before, Ezekiel Mobley, George W. Simcoe, and John C. Niblack were discontinued—the first because of inability, on account of feeble health, to perform the duties of an itinerant, and the latter two because they had failed to attend to the work assigned them.

On the superannuated list we find but ten names. The names of Herrington Stevens and George W. Taylor appear on this list for the first time.

William Cundiff, Henry J. Evans, Richard I. Dungan, Thomas P. Farmer, Newton G. Berryman, Bluford Henry, John Johnson, Clement L. Clifton, Blachley C. Wood, and George Richardson, located.

William Cundiff had been an itinerant since 1826. His fields of ministerial labor were the Clarke River, Livingston, Little River, Big Sandy, Little Sandy, Highland, Little Sandy, and Lewis Circuits. In all these charges he had been faithful and useful.

Henry J. Evans was admitted on trial into the Virginia Conference in February, 1827, and was

---

pying the same seat with the author. During the sermon, overcome by the powerful appeals of the Bishop, he thrust his hand into his pocket and, taking out his pocket-book, exclaimed aloud: "I am crazy to give! I wish he would quit, and give me an opportunity to do so."

appointed to the Banister Circuit. In 1828 we find him on the Haw River Circuit, and in 1829 on the Elizabeth. At the Conference of 1830 he was appointed to the Straits Circuit, in North Carolina, and in 1831 to the Cumberland Circuit, as supernumerary. In the autumn of 1831 we find him stationed in Hopkinsville, Kentucky, to which Conference he was regularly transferred from the Virginia Conference, at the session held in the city of Norfolk, in February, 1832. His second appointment in Kentucky was to the Russellville Station. In 1833 he was appointed to Mount Sterling Circuit, and in 1834 to the Winchester. During the year he traveled the Winchester Circuit his health became feeble, and at the ensuing Conference he asked for a location. Mr. Evans was an excellent man, and a preacher of more than ordinary promise, and was rising rapidly in the Conference. While he traveled he was eminently useful. His location was greatly regretted by his brethren. In a local sphere he was successful and beloved.

Thomas P. Farmer was admitted on trial into the Conference of 1829. His appointments were the Fleming, Breckinridge, Yellow Banks, Shelby, Newcastle, and Breckinridge Circuits. He was greatly beloved by the people he served, and won many souls to Christ. As a preacher his talents were not of a high order, but his sermons were plain and practical.*

---

* Thomas P. Farmer lived less than a year after he located. He joined the Methodist Church and embraced religion in 1824, when only twelve years of age, and entered the ministry

Bluford Henry entered the Conference the same year with Thomas P. Farmer. His appointments were the Mount Vernon, Big Sandy, Hartford, Elizabeth, and Green River (two years) Circuits. He was a good and true man.

John Johnson had entered the itinerant ranks in 1808, Blachley C. Wood in 1820, George Richardson and Clement L. Clifton in 1823. They were useful and true ministers of Jesus Christ.*

We also find the names of Richard I. Dungan and Newton G. Berryman among those who located at this Conference. At a later period, however, we see them again in the itinerant ranks, prosecuting their ministry with undiminished zeal.

The Kentucky Conference, at this period, embraced seventy appointments, to which ninety-seven preachers were sent. Henry S. Duke was placed in charge of the Lexington District, as successor to the lamented Adams, who had fallen at his post.

---

in his eighteenth year. He located for the purpose of visiting friends who had removed West, and to examine the country, intending to reënter the Conference the following year. He possessed a fine constitution, and was deeply pious. He died July 24, 1836, of bilious fever. During his sickness, which lasted eleven days, he exhorted all who came to see him to meet him in heaven. While dying, he said: "O that I had strength and language to describe the glorious scene before me! I am so happy—had I strength, I would shout the high praise of God." His last words were, "Tell the preachers to be faithful."

* For sketches of John Johnson, Blachley C. Wood, George Richardson, and Clement L. Clifton, see "Methodism in Kentucky."

The eloquent Jonathan Stamper follows Richard Tydings, whose term had expired, on the Augusta District. John James is returned to the Harrodsburg District, and William Gunn, who the previous year had traveled the Shelby Circuit, becomes the leader of the hosts in the Louisville District, in the place of Benjamin T. Crouch, who is sent to Shelbyville, Brick Chapel, and Christiansburg. On the Hopkinsville District we still find Isaac Collard, while the name of Thomas Lasley appears on the Greensburg, instead of that of George W. Taylor, who is placed among the superannuated.

In the South-eastern portion of the State, the Cumberland and Kentucky Missions—embracing a vast extent of territory—had been included in the Harrodsburg District. Under this arrangement it was impossible for the work in the mountains to receive such attention from the Presiding Elder as the interests of the Church in that region demanded. To this rugged field young preachers, not only without experience, but without ordination, were usually sent, and there were not ordained local preachers sufficient to administer baptism. It was deemed advisable at this Conference to form a mountain District, to be called the Barboursville District, and appoint to it a Presiding Elder whose entire time would be spent in that field; hence we find another District, with Thomas W. Chandler as Presiding Elder, and with six separate charges, instead of two as before, supplied with nine preachers, where the previous year four had been appointed.

Last year we reported a large decrease in the

membership in Kentucky; we regret that we are compelled to do so again. The decrease in the Kentucky Conference this year is *one thousand six hundred and twenty-eight* in the white membership, and *three hundred and seventy* in the colored. In every District except the Barboursville a decrease in the white membership is reported, and the Louisville District alone shows an increase in the colored membership.

The transfer of the Cumberland and Kentucky Missions from the Harrodsburg to the Barboursville District will more than cover the decrease reported in the former. In the Lexington District there is a falling off in every charge, and in the Maysville District the Lewis Circuit—to which Lorenzo D. Parker had been appointed—is the only charge where any increase is reported. In the Harrodsburg District, the Danville and Harrodsburg Station, under the ministry of William Helm, reports a small increase. The Yellow Banks and Newcastle Circuits, in the Louisville District—the former in charge of the indefatigable Richard D. Neale, and the latter served by Joseph G. Ward and Eli B. Crain, both of whom were zealous young men—enjoyed prosperity. In the Hopkinsville District, the Russellville Station, with Richard Deering as pastor, and the Livingston Circuit, under the charge of Robert F. Turner and Henry Edmondson, both of whom were devoted to their work, reported many additions to the Church. In the Greensburg District, an increase is reported in the Wayne Circuit, whose preacher was Joseph D. Barnet; in the

Glasgow Circuit, where Clinton Kelley and John C. C. Thompson were the preachers; in the Elizabeth Circuit, served by the good John Denham; in the Bardstown Station, to which John Beatty had been appointed; and in the Burksville Circuit, whose preacher was the sweet-spirited Elijah M. Bosley. In all the other charges in the Conference a decrease is reported. However, revivals occurred in several of the charges that were numerically weakened. In the Burlington Circuit, in the Lexington District, whose preachers were Thomas Rankin and William M. Crawford, sixty persons were received into the Church; and the Falmouth and Port William Circuits, in the same District, enjoyed revivals. In the former, under the ministry of James C. Crow, twenty-five were admitted to membership, and in the latter, served by John Carr Harrison, many were converted. In the city of Maysville, in the Maysville District, the labors of Thomas Waring were greatly blessed; while in the same District, in the pleasant village of Augusta, there were nearly one hundred conversions and additions to the Church—one-fifth of them students in the college; and at Dover seventy additions to the Church, under the ministry of John W. Riggin and Peter Taylor. The Danville Circuit, in the Harrodsburg District—Gilby Kelley and Robinson E. Sidebottom, pastors in charge, both gifted and zealous—was aroused, and at a single camp-meeting, held on Ridgeway's land, two miles from Perryville, between ninety and one hundred were converted. In the Hopkinsville District, there was an extensive revival in the Bowling Green Circuit, under the ministry of William S. Evans and Daniel Barksdale.

We may properly pause, and inquire into the cause of so great a declension in the membership in Kentucky during the past two years. In several of the charges where extensive revivals were reported a decrease occurs. For the two previous years there had been a large ingathering into the Church; many hundreds had professed saving faith in Christ, and had become identified with his followers. That a dearth in religion sometimes succeeds a great outpouring of the Holy Spirit is familiar to all who have watched the signs of the times; and that many become connected with the Church during a period of religious excitement who, when the interest and ardor of the hour pass away, turn back to the world will scarcely be denied. It was so in the apostolic age of the Church, and will be so to the end of time. While this fact may account, in part, for the losses to Methodism in Kentucky during the two past years, there is another reason to which we may allude. The lands in many sections of the State of Kentucky had reached figures that were almost fabulous, while the cheap lands of Missouri, Illinois, and Indiana invited emigration from older and more populous settlements. For several years preachers from Kentucky had been transferred to these new and flourishing States. As early as 1830 William H. Askins, John Sinclair, and Samuel Julian were transferred to the Illinois Conference, and John K. Lacey to the Missouri; in 1831 William A. H. Spratt, Andrew Peace, John S. Barger, and Learner B.

Stateler left Kentucky, and identified themselves with the Missouri Conference; in 1832 the gifted and popular Peter Akers was transferred to the Illinois Conference; in 1834 John F. Young and Thomas Wallace were left without appointments "in view of a transfer to the Missouri Conference;" in the same year George C. Light was transferred to Missouri, Richard Bird to Illinois, and Charles M. Holliday to the Indiana Conference. The majority of these preachers had attained to eminence in Kentucky, and the most, if not all, of them were well known throughout the State. Pleased with the reception extended them in their new homes, in corresponding with the people they had formerly served and, in many instances, brought into the Church, they gave flattering accounts of the healthful climate and fertile soil of these new States. Hundreds were thus induced to sell their homes in Kentucky, and go farther West. It was not unfrequently the case that the membership of a single Society was thereby reduced one-half, and sometimes entirely broken up. The cause, however, was a common one. What was lost in Kentucky was gained elsewhere. While Kentucky reported such a decline in membership in the Conference of 1835, the Missouri Conference reported an increase of nine hundred and twenty-eight white and one hundred and twenty-eight colored members, the Illinois Conference an increase of two hundred and thirty white and nine colored members, and the Indiana Conference an increase of two hundred and fifty-two white and eleven colored—making a total increase in these new Conferences of fourteen hundred and thirteen white and one hundred and forty-eight colored members. In 1836 the Missouri Conference reported an increase of nine hundred and seventy-two white and one hundred and twenty-four colored, the Illinois Conference seventeen hundred and twenty white, and the Indiana Conference two thousand four hundred and forty-nine white and one hundred and sixty-seven colored. Much of the decrease in Kentucky may be traced to emigration to these new States.

On the Paris District, in the Tennessee Conference, Thomas Joyner succeeded George W. D. Harris, and on the Hickman Circuit we find Nathan L. Norvell and Edmund J. Williams, and on the Wadesboro Circuit John D. Neale and John H. Mann. At the Tennessee Conference of 1835 the Paducah Circuit was formed, and Garrett W. Martin and Jacob Custer appointed to it. Mr. Joyner had previously preached the gospel of Christ in other portions of Kentucky, and made for himself a good name wherever he had labored. He had left the State in 1824, when almost a youth, and we are gratified to record that in the full zenith of his manhood his name again appears in the list of preachers in Kentucky. He was no ordinary man, and no preacher in the Conference was better qualified to follow the gifted Harris on the Paris District.

Notwithstanding the preachers were earnest and zealous in their labors, the membership in Jackson's Purchase decreased one hundred and fourteen in the white and thirty-five in the colored—making a total decrease in the State, for the year, of *seventeen hundred and seventy* white, and *three hundred and six* colored.

This year the Church was called to mourn the loss of Bishop McKendree. He died in great triumph, March 5, 1835.

CHAPTER V.

FROM THE SESSION OF THE KENTUCKY CONFERENCE OF 1836 TO THE CONFERENCE OF 1837.

Soldiers of Christ, arise!
  And put your armor on,
Strong in the strength which God supplies
  Through his Eternal Son:
Strong in the Lord of hosts,
  And in his mighty power,
Who in the strength of Jesus trusts
  Is more than conqueror.

THE Conference of 1836 met in Louisville, on the 19th of October. The weather was remarkably cold for the season of the year. On Monday night, before the session opened, considerable snow fell, which rendered the traveling of the preachers—performed chiefly on horseback—quite unpleasant. The attendance was full, scarcely a member of the body being absent.

Bishop Soule, to whom Kentucky was assigned in the plan of episcopal visitation, had not reached the city when the Conference opened. Jonathan Stamper was elected President, and George McNelly and Richard D. Neale were elected Secretaries.

During the morning session the several committees—on Public Worship, on Finance, and on Memoirs—were appointed, after which the Conference adjourned until three o'clock P.M.

In the meantime Bishop Soule arrived, and was present at the afternoon session, and took the chair.

The report of the Book Agents at New York was submitted and referred to an appropriate committee, and a committee was also appointed to "draw up and report a proper course of study for candidates for the ministry."

The greater portion of the session was taken up with the examination of the characters of the preachers, and the election of traveling and local preachers to the offices of deacon and elder.

The subject of Education and the interest of Augusta College received more consideration than any thing else. Resolutions were adopted, calculated to enlist in behalf of the college the sympathies and patronage of the Church and the active efforts of the members of the Conference. Too little had been done in this direction. A few of the preachers had used every means within their reach to promote the success of this institution of learning, while others seemed scarcely to give it a serious thought. To rally the Conference to its support and to awaken the Church throughout the State to the good that might be accomplished through its instrumentality were the objects of the resolutions adopted.

Besides what we have mentioned, nothing unusual took place during the session.

Thirteen preachers were admitted on trial at this

session of the Conference: Andrew J. McLaughlin, Greenup Barker, William B. Maxey, Edwin Roberts, John J. Harrison, George S. Gatewood, Theophilus Powell, John Waring, Seybourn Crutchfield, Robert G. Gardner, William James, Alanson C. Dewitt, Aaron H. Rice.

The names of William Burns and Alexander Kessinger disappear from the list of those admitted the previous year. The circumstances of Mr. Kessinger were such that he could not devote himself exclusively to the work of the ministry. Mr. Burns's itinerant career was brief. He had scarcely entered the Conference when death summoned him away. He was appointed to the Prestonsburg Circuit, as the colleague of Foster H. Blades, and entered upon his work with the zeal of a true disciple of Christ. His ministry among the people was greatly blessed; but in the midst of his usefulness he was called from labor to reward.

The name of John Tevis appears on the superannuated list, while the names of George W. Taylor and George McNelly are again restored to the effective roll.

James G. Leach, William S. Evans, John Redman, and Herrington Stevens, located.

The name of James G. Leach first appears in the Minutes in 1810. After traveling a few months he retired voluntarily from the itinerant ranks, but reentered the same in 1815, and labored in this service until 1823, when he located.*

William S. Evans became a traveling preacher in

* For a sketch, see "Methodism in Kentucky."

1830. His appointments were the Livingston, Christian, Big Sandy, and Logan Circuits, Hopkinsville Station, and Bowling Green Circuit. After his location he settled in Logan county, where, by his exemplary life and earnest zeal, he did much good. At a later period he reëntered the Conference, but, after preaching a few years, again located.

John Redman commenced his career as a traveling preacher on the Livingston Circuit, in 1826. His subsequent fields of labor were the Liberty, Yellow Banks, Logan and Gasper, Christian, Greenville, Bowling Green, and Hartford Circuits. As a preacher he did much good.

Herrington Stevens was admitted on trial in 1832. His first appointment was to the Logan Circuit, after which he traveled the Bowling Green and the Livingston Circuits. In 1835 he was placed on the superannuated list, and located at the Conference of 1836. He settled in Livingston county, where he practiced medicine, and preached as often as his health would allow. He was a good man and useful preacher.

Henry S. Duke, the Presiding Elder on the Lexington District, and John Littlejohn* died during the year which had just closed. By a resolution of the Conference, Mr. Bascom was requested to preach a sermon in memory of these ministers. One of them had fallen from the walls of Zion in the midst of a career of usefulness and success, and before he had reached the meridian of life; the other had been

*For sketches of these ministers, the reader is referred to the "History of Methodism in Kentucky."

identified with the Methodist ministry since 1777. Both were good and true men, and passed away in holy triumph.

The death of William Phillips had also occurred since the previous Conference. He joined the ministry, in Kentucky, in 1831, and had risen rapidly to eminence and distinction. By the General Conference of 1836, while stationed at Newport and Covington, he was elected one of the editors of the *Western Christian Advocate*. Hardly had he entered upon the duties of his office when God called him. He died August 4, 1836.*

The question, "What amounts are necessary for the superannuated preachers, and the widows and orphans of preachers, and to make up the deficiencies of those who have not obtained their regular allowance on the circuits?" was asked, and the answer given was "$6,109.97." For the purposes stated the following amounts were collected: From circuits and stations, $864.45; Book Concern, $400; Chartered Fund, $75; collection at Conference, $33.50; total, $1,372.95. From this amount the Bishops were paid $77.50; the remainder was applied as the question indicates. For missions there was collected $1,492.02. For the benefit of the Book Concern $237.58 was collected—of which amount the Church in Shelbyville contributed $170, Christian Circuit $20, and Shelby Circuit $47.58.

During the two years preceding the Conference of 1836 the Lexington District had lost two Presiding

* A sketch of William Phillips may be found in the "History of Methodism in Kentucky."

Elders—Adams and Duke. The name of Richard Tydings appears in the Lexington District, as the successor of Duke. Jonathan Stamper was returned to the Augusta District, and John James to the Harrodsburg. William Gunn, Isaac Collard, Thomas Lasley, and Thomas W. Chandler occupy the same fields they had cultivated the previous year.

During the session of the Conference frequent interviews were held between the members on the subject of the losses sustained in the membership of the Church during the previous two years. While the causes that we have assigned were accepted as the reasons for the decrease, yet not a single cavalier felt willing that a similar decline should mark the annals of another year. Buckling on their armor afresh, they more determinately resolved to push the battle to the gates of the enemy, and, through their Captain, to conquer or perish in the struggle. Thus nobly impelled, each warrior marched to his new field of duty.

Edward Stevenson was returned to the city of Lexington, where he had labored the previous year under discouragements which well-nigh dampened his ardor. In every other charge in this District the pastor was changed.

In the Augusta District, Stephen Harber, who had been appointed as a supernumerary on the Lewis Circuit the year before, is reäppointed to this work, in an effective relation.

In the Harrodsburg District, Robinson E. Sidebottom was returned to the Danville Circuit as junior preacher—the position he held during the former campaign.

William Holman, in the Louisville District, is again sent to Louisville, while Absalom D. Fox still travels the Jefferson Circuit.

In the Hopkinsville District no preacher was returned to his former appointment; while, in the Greensburg District, James King was again sent to Columbia.

Solomon Pope, in the Barboursville District, was reäppointed to the Mount Pleasant Mission.

Several new Circuits appear in the list of appointments. The Cynthiana Station, which had been thrown into the Circuit, is restored as a separate charge, in the Lexington District; while, in the Augusta District, the Minerva Circuit appears for the first time. In the Harrodsburg District, Ebenezer and Athens is made an independent charge, Bowling Green disconnected from the circuit and made a station; while, at the same time, the Hopkinsville Station again falls into the Hopkinsville Circuit. The La Fayette and Princeton Circuits, in the same District, appear in the Minutes, while the name of the Henderson Circuit is lost in that of Morganfield. No change occurs in the Greensburg District. In the Barboursville District, the change is the addition of Paintville to Prestonsburg, and the formation of the Louisa Circuit.

Near the close of the Conference-session Mr. Bascom offered a resolution to "observe the Friday before the 25th of December as a day of fasting and prayer for the prosperity of the Church," and the preachers were requested to invite the membership to unite with them in this service.

The Conference closed, and without any unnecessary delay the preachers were at their posts. During the winter an apathy pervaded the Church throughout the State, and under able sermons and powerful appeals the people seemed unmoved. The autumn passed, the cold months of winter followed, and were just dying away, when a note of triumph was heard on the banks of the beautiful Ohio. Martin L. Eads and George S. Savage—the former in his eighth year in the itinerant ministry, and the latter a young and zealous preacher in his second year—had been sent to the Minerva Circuit, in the Augusta District, which embraced the village of Dover. Early in February the Church at that point was blessed with seventy additions to the membership, and about the same number were converted.

In the Greensburg District, during the following month, the Church in Bardstown—which enjoyed the ministry of Hubbard H. Kavanaugh, the faithful pastor—was greatly blessed. Under Mr. Kavanaugh's preaching a gracious revival began, and it swept through the community, reaching the Presbyterian Church, which was blessed equally with his own. Seventy persons professed religion, thirty-five joining the Methodist Church and the same number the Presbyterian.

Returning to the Augusta District, in April the town of Washington—an appointment in the Germantown Circuit—was favored with a revival of religion. The meeting continued for two weeks, under the supervision of Joseph Marsee and William M. Grubbs, both of whom were useful and zealous. The interest of the occasion was greatly augmented by the presence of John Collins, a veteran, who preached and labored during the meeting. About fifty professed religion.

While the revival was in progress in Washington, a note of triumph was again heard from the Greensburg District. In the Wayne Circuit, under the faithful labors of Elijah M. Bosley and William B. Maxey, twenty persons were converted, and the work of grace was spreading all over their extensive circuit.

In the month of May the work commenced in the Madison Circuit, in the Harrodsburg District, whose preachers were Absalom Woolliscroft and George S. Gatewood, both of whom were styled revivalists, and more than one hundred persons were happily converted to God.

In the village of Campbellsville, in the Greensburg District, under the ministry of Matthew N. Lasley, a good and true man, seventy-three persons "passed from death unto life," about the same time that Woolliscroft and Gatewood were rejoicing over the trophies they had won to their Master's cause. In the Greensburg Circuit—where the plain and unostentatious George W. Taylor had charge—in a neighorhood five miles from Greensburg, at a single meeting, in the month of July, forty persons received "the peace of God, which passeth all understanding." At this meeting James King, a true evangelist, and Stephen Rogers, a faithful local preacher, were present, and labored shoulder to shoulder with the pious pastor.

About this time a remarkable man appeared in Kentucky; he was an Irishman by birth. John Newland Maffitt was born in the city of Dublin, Ireland, December 28, 1794. His father was a member of the Methodist Society, and endeavored to impress upon his son the principles of true religion. Death, however, deprived him of his paternal parent, leaving him in childhood to the sole guidance of his mother, who was a member of another Communion. Frivolous and gay, he passed through his youth forgetful of the instructions of his sainted father and the oft-given advice of his mother, engaging in every species of amusement where God and heaven are forgotten.

At the age of nineteen he was arrested by the Holy Spirit, was powerfully awakened to a sense of his condition as a sinner before God, and, deeply penitent, pleaded for mercy, poising between hope and despair. The struggle was severe, and was protracted through several days and nights; but the joy that succeeded was "unspeakable and full of glory." From his early childhood he had entertained the impression that he would be a preacher; yet after his conversion we see him reluctant to yield to the conviction of his heart, or to listen to the voice which appealed to his conscience: "Woe is unto me, if I preach not the gospel!" Only a few weeks elapse, however, until we find him praying in public, exhorting sinners to repent, and making an appointment to preach, but failed in the attempt.

Discouraged and depressed, he resolved to abandon all thought of the pulpit, when a revival in the city of Dublin, under the ministry of a soldier-preacher, opened the way for him to exercise his gifts; and we soon behold him offering hope to the despairing, salvation to the lost, and life to the dead. From time to time, without official authority from the Church, he continued to preach the unsearchable riches of Christ. His earnest appeals arrested the ungodly, aroused the Church, and brought much fruitage to his Master. Ungenerous criticism and opposition determined him again to decline a work to which he believed himself to be divinely called, when Arthur Noble, the friend and colleague of Gideon Ouseley, the famous Irish missionary, invited him to meet him in Ballymena, and travel with him on his missionary route. Handsome in person, graceful in his manners, tender in his address, and endowed with a powerful and persuasive eloquence, he soon occupied a place in the popular thought that could be claimed perhaps by no man of his age in the Emerald Isle.

Early in life he was married to a young and very beautiful girl, who joined her influence with that of his mother to dissuade him from being a preacher. Added to this, pecuniary misfortunes overtook him, and determined him to emigrate to America. On the 21st of April, 1819, he landed in the city of New York, being in the twenty-fifth year of his age.

In 1822 he offered himself as an itinerant preacher to the New England Conference, and was admitted on trial. His first appointment was with the celebrated George Pickering, as a Conference missionary. In 1823 he was appointed to Fairhaven and New Bedford, and the following year he was the junior preacher on the Barnstable Circuit. In 1825 he was stationed in Dover, and in 1826 in Dover and Somersworth. At the Conference of 1827 he was sent to the city of Boston, and in 1828 to Portsmouth, where he continued for two years. In 1830 he was returned to the city of Boston, and the following year was left without an appointment, to give him the opportunity of settling his temporal affairs, which had become somewhat embarrassed. In 1832 he located.

During the ten years that Mr. Maffitt traveled as a preacher he performed the duties of an itinerant with energy and zeal, and in the several fields he occupied success crowned his labors. Whether as a missionary, carrying the tidings of a Redeemer's love to the poor and the humble throughout the New England Conference, or lifting the standard of the cross in the rural districts, or unfurling its crimsoned banner in the capital of Massachusetts, we find him not only faithful, but beloved by the people he served, and everywhere gathering stars to deck the crown of his rejoicing in the hereafter.

It is to be regretted that Mr. Maffitt turned away from the itinerant work, to which he was so well adapted; yet it is cause for gratitude that, in retiring to the local ranks, he lost none of the fire that had so often flashed from his eye as he presented the glories of the cross, nor the zeal that had distinguished him as an itinerant preacher, nor an iota of the purpose he had formed to devote his energies and his life to the service of the Church.

In 1833, in connection with Lewis Garrett, he issued, in the city of Nashville, Tennessee, the first number of the *Western Methodist*, a religious weekly paper, which from that period has continued under various names, as the *South-western Christian Advocate*, *Nashville Christian Advocate*, *Nashville and Louisville Christian Advocate*, and is at present the *Christian Advocate*, the central organ of the Methodist Episcopal Church, South.

His fame had preceded him to the West, and wherever he preached vast assemblies thronged to hear him, eager to catch the words of life as they fell from his lips. As an orator he had taken rank with the first preachers of the age, and in the horizon of public esteem occupied a commanding eminence. It was not merely the fire that lit his eye, nor the flashes of genius that sparkled through every portion of his mighty appeals, nor his lofty flights of oratory, that won for him a reputation and a name scarcely equaled in the history of the pulpit: it was the burning zeal that was consuming him; it was his fervent piety; and, above all, it was the brilliant success, which threw its full-orbed light along his path. Thousands came to hear him, and thousands, through his instrumentality, were converted to God and added to the Church.

In the autumn of 1833 he entered the Tennessee Conference, and, with Littleton Fowler as his colleague, was appointed Agent for La Grange College, of which Robert Paine was President. In 1834 he was elected to the chair of Elocution in that college, which position he occupied for two years. At the session of the Tennessee Conference of 1836 he requested and obtained a location, and never afterward reëntered the itinerant field. His mode of warfare in the ministry was that of a guerrilla—outside the regular method employed by the itinerant preachers.

It was in the summer of 1837 that Mr. Maffitt made his appearance in Kentucky. His earliest trophies in the State were won in the village of Glasgow. Passing on to the city of Lexington, which he pronounces "one of the most beautiful cities west of the mountains," he entered at once upon the great business of his life. Edward Stevenson was the pastor. The stay of Mr. Maffitt in Lexington was protracted upward of two months, during which time he preached almost every day and night. On his first appearance in the pulpit, in that city, every pew in the Church was filled, the aisles were crowded to their utmost capacity, and the occasion was distinguished by a quickened religious interest in the popular mind. On the corners of the streets, in the marts of trade, in places of business, the fame of the preacher was on every lip, while many were anxiously inquiring the way of life and salvation. The city press teemed with his praise, and the entire community listened to his earnest sermons, coming from his great, warm, Irish heart. From the very commencement the interest increased, and during his protracted stay in the city there was no abatement. Bishop Morris was present, and preached a few sermons; but the public eye was turned to Mr. Maffitt, who had won so largely upon the hearts of the people. In the *Western Christian Advocate*, of August 18, Mr. Stevenson writes: "*Eighty-four persons have been converted, and our meeting is still in progress.*" At a later period Mr. Maffitt writes to Mr. Stringfield, editor of the *South-western Christian Advocate:* "About *one hundred and sixty*, as nearly as I can remember, were the fruits of the revival in Lexington, and over *one hundred and thirty* became members of the M. E. Church, most of whom, if not all, were, in the judgment of charity, soundly converted to God. May we all be so happy as to meet one another around the burning throne, to dwell with God and the holy angels, in sweet companionship, forever!" *

The preaching of Mr. Maffitt was peculiar, and difficult to describe. We have heard ministers who were more profound in research and more logical in argument than he was; but we have seldom, indeed, listened to any one who excelled in so many departments of ministerial work as did John Newland Maffitt. We have heard him when his voice was persuasive and soft as the harp of Æolus, and we have sat beneath his ministry when like thunderbolts it fell upon the ear. His prototype was the great apostle of the Gentiles, whose life and character he loved to portray. Of St. Paul he presented the following beautiful portrait:

"As he had received his commission direct from heaven, he counted all worldly honor but dross when

* *South-western Christian Advocate,* January 25, 1838.

compared to the excellency of the sacred treasure given him by the Lord Jesus. The glittering charms of time and sense he despised, rejecting, like holy Moses, the splendid trophies of aspiring fame. It was the excellency of the religion of Jesus, disclosed to his mind by the power of the Holy Ghost, that won his great soul, and spurred him on to victory and conquest.

"He therefore laid aside every weight and hinderance that might encumber him in his arduous work, suffered himself to be stripped for the race and harnessed for the battle, and, girding up his loins, resolved, in the strength of Israel's God, to tread in the footsteps of that same Jesus he once persecuted to death in the person of his followers. Throwing himself on the resources of his own mind, buoyed up by the spirit of the holy prophets, which had fallen on him at his first introduction to the holy office, he moved forward through danger and suffering, not anxious to avoid either if in the path of duty, tampering not with sin, nor trimming between God and the world for gain or ease.

"He expressed cheerfulness and joy under suffering. 'We are troubled,' says he, 'on every side, yet not distressed; we are perplexed, but not in despair; persecuted, but not forsaken; cast down, but not destroyed.' 'I take pleasure in infirmities, in reproaches, in necessities, in persecutions, in distresses for Christ's sake.' His language at Ephesus, on taking leave of his brethren, was expressive of the elevated state of his mind: 'And now, behold, I go bound in the spirit unto Jerusalem, not knowing the things that shall befall me there: save that the Holy Ghost witnesseth in every city, saying that bonds and afflictions abide me. But none of these things move me, neither count I my life dear unto myself, so that I might finish my course with joy.' And when passing through Cesarea he appeared in the same interesting light. 'What mean ye,' says he, 'to weep and to break mine heart? for I am ready not to be bound only, but also to die at Jerusalem for the name of the Lord Jesus.'

"*He was gloriously successful to the end of his course, because the hand of the Lord was with him.* This is evident from the repeated assurances which God gave of almighty strength, support, and guidance. In visions of the night angels appeared to strengthen his mind against the assaults of every enemy, bidding him be of good cheer. The divine agency rendered him invincible, as well as patient and resigned, under suffering, strengthened with all might by the Spirit in the inner man. What or whom should he fear?

"For he had wings that neither sickness, pain,
Nor penury could cripple or confine;
No nook so narrow but he spread them there
With ease and was at large. The oppressor held
His body bound, but knew not what a range
His spirit took, unconscious of a chain,
And that to bind him was a vain attempt,
Whom Heaven approved.

"*He was gloriously successful to the end of his course.* The arm of God was stretched out in his behalf, and signs and wonders were wrought by his word. For upward of thirty years he had labored incessantly in the Lord's vineyard, extending the savor of divine love to every spot he visited, or to which he sent his writings—encompassing sea and land, traveling over a vast portion of the then known world, and extending the Redeemer's kingdom from the east to the uttermost bounds of the west. He marched forth into the thickest ranks of the enemy, vexing them with his incursions. Equipped with armor of divine proof, his only weapon the word of God, which is the sword of the Spirit, he rushed on his most puissant foes, assaulting them in all their strongholds. As he advanced, the temples of the gods were forsaken, the walls of superstition tottered, and the spreading glories of the cross illumined the palaces of kings. His weapon prevailed against the potentates of the earth, the wisdom of the greatest philosophers, and on the ruins of barbaric pride and pontific luxury he placed the simple majesty of the religion of the Galilean peasant.

"Behold this champion of the cross, after he had fought a good fight! See him coming in at the close of the glorious warfare. With what calmness and grandeur he looks down upon suffering and death! Truly they move him not. The cross glitters on his bosom; his hand firmly grasps the sword of the Lord; a halo of glory encircles his brow; the sunshine of eternity gleams upon his countenance.

"Happy Paul! thy sun is going down in brightness, growing larger as it sinks, like that luminary, throwing its golden splendors far and wide over distant lands when itself is no longer visible to the eye. Thus departed this prince of apostles from the field of missionary enterprise, crowned with the laurels of victory and glory, to reap an eternal reward in the Church triumphant above."

If Mr. Maffitt spoke of the temptation in Paradise, you would imagine yourself in the garden of Eden, surrounded with all its charms, or reposing amid its flowers, where all was joy, and innocence, and love, listening to strains of gratitude and praise breaking forth from hearts pure and holy; you would see the tempter insidiously entering this delightful retreat, and hear his siren voice as he reasoned with the woman, guileless and beautiful, and fresh from the creative touch of the almighty hand; you would feel the increasing danger to which she was exposed, as the coils of the serpent were gradually fastening upon her, until the triumph of the enemy was complete, and all was lost. If the redemption of the world was his theme, he would carry you to the lofty mount of prophecy, and then bid you accompany him down the corridors of time, leaving generations behind you, to the period when angels announced to the astonished shepherds on Bethlehem's star-lit plains the birth of the Son of God; with Simeon, you would take the Babe in your arms, and watch the Nazarene as he passed from infancy to youth, and from youth to manhood; the entrance of Christ upon his public ministry would take place in your presence, and you would see him at his baptism, when the Holy Spirit in the likeness of a dove descended and abode upon him; you would follow him, while here and there he gathered a solitary disciple, and be entranced by the strange doctrines he preached in his Sermon on the Mount; you would mingle with the astonished multitudes while the blind were being restored to sight, the deaf to hearing, the dumb to speech, and would see the leper, scorned and hated, and exiled from society, cleansed, and again received into its bosom; in your presence the lame man would throw away his crutch, and leap for joy; and the tear would be wiped from the cheek of sorrow as Jairus received his daughter again to life, as the son of the widow of Nain was restored to his mother, and as Lazarus returned from the grave where he had been buried to his sisters at Bethany. If he describes the crucifixion, you stand by the cross, and see the nails as they pierce his hands and feet; you are touched with the compassion that floats in the dim and languid eyes of the illustrious Sufferer, and are startled as the words of agony, "My God, my God, why hast thou forsaken me?" fall from his expiring lips; the heavens are shrouded in blackness, fierce lightnings leap from cloud to cloud, and thunders peal their notes of sorrow, as the God-man cries, "It is finished!" If the resurrection of Christ is the topic on which he preaches, the descending angel, the alarmed chivalry of the Roman army, the risen Lord, stand out with prominence; and if the subject is the ascension of the Redeemer, your eye follows the falling cloud until it rests on the side of Olivet; you behold the Saviour as he steps upon it, and then you watch it as it ascends higher and higher, until it is lost to sight in the immeasurable distance, and still your eye lingers in that direction until you hear the joyous acclaim: "Lift up your heads, O ye gates; and be ye lifted up, ye everlasting doors; and the King of glory shall come in." Then a hush like the stillness of the sepulcher passes over the audience, lasting but for a moment, when once more from the celestial parapets a voice is heard, "Who is this King of glory?" The reply rolls back to heaven: "The Lord strong and mighty, the Lord mighty in battle. Lift up your heads, O ye gates; even lift them up, ye everlasting doors; and the King of glory shall come in." Then he passes through the portals.

We have heard him describe the horrors of the damned until we almost gazed upon the burning flame, and seemed to listen to the rattling of the chains of the lost, and hear their groans of anguish, and see them as they writhed in their agony and woe. We have listened to him as he spoke of heaven and portrayed its joys, until the jeweled gates rolled back, and walls of jasper and streets of burnished gold met our vision, and an innumerable multitude, with palms and crowns, were reposing beneath the boughs of the tree of life, or wandering along the banks of the beautiful river that makes glad the city of God; and we seemed to hear their songs of victory and shouts of triumph, as they exclaimed: "Unto him that loved us, and washed us from our sins in his own blood, and hath made us kings and priests unto God and his Father; to him be glory and dominion forever and ever."

We heard him once as he talked of the Judgment,

and the scenes of the last day appeared full in view: the heavens, black with angry clouds, canopied the world; the lightnings flashed along the sky; thunders pealed forth in every direction, till distant worlds reëchoed the direful clangor of the last agonies of dissolving nature. Then he cried: "Behold a rising world, and see demons and spirits damned coming up from realms of blackest night, and see the Judge coming down the vaulted sky, attended by all the hosts of heaven, and all the redeemed from earth who had entered upon eternal life. *See him, as he comes!*" The vast assembly that sat before him with one accord rose from their seats and looked upward, expecting to behold Him who would judge the world, with all his shining retinue surrounding him.

We repeat, we have heard preachers who in some respects excelled Mr. Maffitt, but we have never met with one who exercised such power over an audience as he did.

From Lexington we follow him to Danville, where, about the 1st of September, he commenced a series of meetings. As in Lexington, he preached to crowded audiences, day and night, for several weeks. Under his ministry the Church was revived, backsliders were reclaimed, and sinners awakened and converted to God. The gospel preached by him was mighty, through God, to the "pulling down of strongholds;" it was the "power of God unto salvation." Day after day eager throngs came to the house of God to be instructed in the way of life, and night after night the altar was crowded with sincere penitents, inquiring, "What must we do to be saved?" In the pulpit, in the altar, in the social circle, on the street, he pleaded the cause of his Divine Master, and never seemed to be weary. "God forbid that I should glory save in the cross of our Lord Jesus Christ" was the feeling which animated and inspired him in the grand and noble work to which he had consecrated his energies and his life.

From Danville we accompany him to Harrodsburg, where the same results attended his labors. Noble man! stars gathered on these fields deck thy crown to-day. At Danville and Harrodsburg one hundred and thirty joined the Methodist Church, under his ministry, while more than that number were converted.

We here take leave of Mr. Maffitt, but will soon meet him in other fields, prosecuting with untiring energy his high and holy calling.

The name of Joseph D. Barnett first appears in the Minutes of 1831, at which time he was admitted on trial into the Kentucky Conference. He was born in Jefferson county, Kentucky, July 21, 1811. His parents were worthy and pious members of the Baptist Church, and they brought him up in the "nurture and admonition of the Lord." Under the Methodist ministry Mr. Barnett was effectually awakened and soundly converted to God, when only sixteen years of age. He at once became a member of the Methodist Church, through whose instrumentality he had been brought to Christ.

His first experience as an itinerant was along the

waters of the Little Sandy, as the colleague of Isaac Malone. In 1832 he was appointed to the Big Sandy Circuit, with William S. Evans in charge. At the Conference of 1833, with Abram Long as the senior preacher, we meet with him on the Livingston Circuit, in South-eastern Kentucky, and the following year we find him in charge of the Burksville Circuit, with the genial and warm-hearted Matthew N. Lasley as his colleague. From the Conference of 1835 we follow him to the Wayne Circuit, which he travels alone. It will be seen that much of the experience of young Barnett, up to this period, had been in rugged portions of the State. In all these fields his ministry had been greatly blessed in the conversion of souls. As a preacher he was plain and unostentatious; but in his manner and style there was a peculiarity that enabled him to reach the hearts of the people, and persuade them to be reconciled to God. Along the turbid waters of the Big Sandy and Little Sandy, on the banks of the Ohio and Cumberland, and amid the hospitable homes of Cumberland and Wayne counties, he had successfully borne the banner of the cross, and proved himself "a workman that needed not to be ashamed."

In 1836, with Alanson C. Dewitt as his colleague, he was appointed to the Elizabeth Circuit, in the Greensburg District, then embracing a large extent of territory. On this circuit he developed tact and skill, as a field-officer, for which he had never before been distinguished. If he found a circuit in a lukewarm condition, through his energy, zeal, and management it soon became quickened into life Revivals of religion had crowned his labors in other fields, and he entered upon his work here, determined to succeed. The circuit was soon in a flame of fire. All around it revivals of religion took place, and under the labors of these faithful men hundreds were brought into the Church.*

About the same time the Lebanon Circuit—in the same District—was enjoying extraordinary revivals of religion. Under the ministry of Matthew N Lasley hundreds were awakened and converted, many of whom had been Roman Catholics. One hundred and fifty persons joined the Methodist Church, while the work extended to other Communions.

In the Burksville Circuit, too, with that noble veteran John Denham at its head, the battle was steadily pushed to the gate. Sixty souls were converted at a meeting in the village of Edmunton, and eight in Burksville, to be stars in the crown of his rejoicing.

The Wayne Circuit, in which during the early part of the year there had been indications of good, was greatly blessed in the summer and autumn—one hundred persons having been added to the Church.

We have already alluded to the revival which occurred in the town of Washington, an appointment in the Germantown Circuit, in the Augusta District. This was only the precursor of a general outpouring

*In a class-meeting, on one occasion, nineteen persons were converted.

of the Holy Spirit throughout the circuit. At the close of the year two hundred additions to the Church were reported. The Minerva Circuit, which adjoined the Germantown, also enjoyed great prosperity.

The most extraordinary meeting held during the year in this District was a camp-meeting in the Carlisle Circuit, six miles from the village of Carlisle. Carlisle Babbit and Theophilus Powell were the preachers. The meeting commenced on the 25th of August. In different portions of the circuit showers of grace had fallen upon the people, and many had passed from darkness to light. At the camp-meeting, however, the work was more extensive. On Monday night, after a powerful exhortation, more than two hundred persons presented themselves at the altar, asking an interest in the prayers of the Church. The occasion was a sublime one. The night was calm—its stillness broken only by the songs of Zion, the sobs and cries of penitents, and the shouts of new-born souls. Fifty persons were converted that night, and nearly one hundred during the meeting.

In the Harrodsburg District, in addition to the revivals in Danville and Harrodsburg to which we have alluded, there were revivals in the Mount Sterling, the Danville, and the Somerset Circuits. The zealous James traveled over his large District, preaching the gospel and weeping over the people. In the Mount Sterling Circuit forty persons, who had been strangers to God, became his followers; while, under the faithful ministry of George W.

Merritt and William McMahon, many more were converted. The work which began early in this year in the Madison Circuit continued to spread until more than three hundred souls passed into the liberty of the children of God. In the town of Richmond, at a single meeting, seventy persons were converted.

In the Louisville District, the Yellow Banks and Hartford Circuits were both greatly blessed—the former under the pastoral charge of Richard Holding, and the latter under that of James D. Holding. The preachers were brothers, and useful ministers of Christ. Neither of them possessed talents of a high order, but both were instrumental in winning many souls to Christ. Faithful in the discharge of the duties devolving upon them, the Church prospered under their ministry, and many, through their instrumentality, were brought to Christ. In each of these circuits a camp-meeting was held in August. In the Yellow Banks Circuit the camp-meeting was held at Pleasant Grove, and for the Hartford at Noe Creek. We were traveling with Mr. Gunn, the Presiding Elder, and were present at each of these meetings. Both were times of refreshing, and many were added to the Church. At the meeting at Pleasant Grove, besides William Gunn, the Presiding Elder, there were present James Gunn, his father—a local preacher from Tennessee—James D. Holding, and John Daveiss, John Pinkstone, John Phipps, and Joe Miller, who were among the best local preachers we ever knew. At the meeting at Noe Creek Richard Holding was present, and the same local preachers, with the exception of James Gunn.

In the Hopkinsville District, the labors of James H. Brooking and Edwin Roberts resulted successfully. At a meeting at Bell's Chapel thirty-three persons were added to the Church, and more than twice that number in the circuit. Elijah Sutton, in charge of the La Fayette Circuit, witnessed, under his ministry, a gracious revival of religion; while, in the Madisonville Circuit, Alberry L. Alderson and Foster H. Blades met with extraordinary success. More than one hundred persons in each of these charges became members of the Church.

Other fields of labor besides those we have mentioned shared in the showers of grace which had fallen on the Church in Kentucky.

In the Lexington District, on the Port William and Falmouth Circuits, many were converted and brought into the Church. In the Maysville District, the Church in Maysville, under the ministry of George W. Brush, enjoyed great prosperity. In the Louisville District, in the city of Louisville, there were "times of refreshing from the presence of the Lord." The Taylorsville and Newcastle Circuits were also highly prosperous. The Columbia Circuit, in the Greensburg District, increased in numbers, in influence, and in piety. In the mountain District, while there were no extensive revivals at any point, there was a steady increase in nearly every charge.

The total increase in the Kentucky Conference, for this year, was *fourteen hundred and ninety-four* in the white membership, while there was a decrease of one hundred and eighty-one in the colored.

In Jackson's Purchase, we still find Thomas Joyner in charge of the Paris District, while Matthew F. Mitchell and Spencer Waters are appointed to the Hickman Circuit, Adam Goodwin and Robert W. Cole to the Wadesboro, and Findley Bynum and George W. Kelso to the Paducah.

Matthew F. Mitchell and Spencer Waters were both admitted on trial at the session of the Tennessee Conference of 1836, and, without any experience as itinerant preachers, were sent to the Hickman Circuit. The Minutes show that they were eminently useful. At the close of the year they reported an increase of one hundred and forty-seven in the white membership, and one in the colored. At the fourth quarterly-meeting, held near Feliciana, thirty five persons professed religion.

Adam Goodwin had entered the Conference in 1834, and was appointed to the Shoal Circuit, in the Florence District, as junior preacher. In 1835 we find him on Mill Creek Circuit, in the Nashville District. When he came to Kentucky, in 1836, he brought with him the experience of two years in the itinerant work. His colleague, Robert W. Cole, had just been admitted on trial. The report of the membership on the Wadesboro Circuit, at the close of the year, shows but little increase—five in the white and six in the colored membership.

Findley Bynum was a North Carolinian by birth, having been born in Chatham county, North Carolina, May 14, 1814. In August, 1830, he attended a camp-meeting held at Mobley's Camp-ground, where he was awakened and soundly converted to God. He was licensed to preach the gospel by George W. D. Harris, September 13, 1834, at Oliver's Camp-ground. At the session of the Tennessee Conference of 1834 he was admitted on trial, and appointed to the Dickson Circuit, in the Nashville District, with Thomas L. Douglass as his Presiding Elder. In 1835 he was sent to the Forked Deer Circuit, as the colleague of John B. Summers, and in 1836 we find him in charge of the Paducah Circuit, with George W. Kelso—who had traveled one year as junior preacher on the Franklin Circuit—as his colleague. Under the ministry of these faithful men the Paducah Circuit increased largely in membership; revivals crowned their labors at several points, and many were added to the Church. Near the close of the year a camp-meeting was held for the Paducah Circuit, near Milburn, which resulted in the conversion of many souls. Such a general outpouring of the Holy Spirit had but seldom been realized in that section of country. Speaking of this meeting, Messrs. Bynum and Kelso, the preachers, in a letter to the *South-western Christian Advocate*, say: "Believers were refreshed, mourners crowded to the altar, the most wicked fell on the borders of the congregation, and the groves and tents resounded with the exultation of new-born souls. Indeed, the last several days of the camp-meeting the work became so powerful that of those who were accustomed to attend, almost without exception, they had to leave the place or yield. Some who went off could neither work nor sleep, and had to return; others, who came merely to revile or to disturb, were made the happy subjects of converting grace. The tenters moved home on Wednesday morning; but the meeting was continued, more or less, every day but one, until Sabbath night following. It had to be discontinued mostly for want of materials to work upon, for scarcely a sinner was left in the attending congregation; not one man remained in the adjacent town who did not set out for heaven, and few persons in the neighborhood. Seventy joined the Church, and upward of eighty professed religion. The work is running through the circuit, and souls are converted."* The net increase in this circuit was seventy-one white and four colored members—making a total increase, in Kentucky, of *seventeen hundred and seventeen* in the white membership, and a decrease of *one hundred and seventy* in the colored.

---

* *South-western Christian Advocate*, September 28, 1837.

CHAPTER VI.

FROM THE SESSION OF THE KENTUCKY CONFERENCE OF 1837 TO THE CONFERENCE OF 1838.

My talents, gifts, and graces, Lord,
  Into thy blessed hands receive;
And let me live to preach thy word,
  And let me to thy glory live;
My every sacred moment spend
In publishing the sinner's Friend.

THE Kentucky Conference of 1837 met in the Representatives' Hall, in the city of Frankfort, October 18. Bishop Roberts presided, and George W. McNelly and George W. Brush were elected Secretaries.

After the appointment of the Committees on Public Worship, on Finance, on Books and Periodicals, and on Memoirs, a communication from the Book Agents at New York and Cincinnati, together with an exhibit of the affairs of the Book Concern, was read and referred to the appropriate committee.

A resolution was offered, but not adopted, suggesting the appointment of a committee to inquire into "the expediency and necessity of publishing the Minutes of the Conference, for the use and benefit of the members within its bounds."

A committee, consisting of Edward Stevenson, Joseph S. Tomlinson, Lewell Campbell, Henry B. Bascom, and Richard Tydings, was appointed to write a Pastoral Letter to the Church throughout the bounds of the Conference.

In a former chapter we made mention of the vigilance with which the Kentucky Conference guarded the itinerant system, and of the dissatisfaction which was felt at the least departure from the old landmarks of Methodism. At this session of the Conference the following resolution was offered:

"Whereas, many evils arise from the present state of our work; and whereas, a change would be of great advantage; therefore,

"*Resolved*, That we respectfully request the Bishop, or a committee that he may appoint, so to change the work as to dissolve all the stations (the cities excepted), and in their stead to form small circuits, consisting of from ten to twelve appointments, and that some principal town be at the head of every such circuit, and that one or two preachers be appointed to all such circuits, as their demands may require."

This resolution was signed by Jonathan Stamper, Richard Tydings, and Thomas W. Chandler, all of whom were Presiding Elders. It was referred to a committee of seven, consisting of the Presiding Elders, who were instructed to report on it as early as practicable.

There was an increasing tendency on the part of

the Churches, in small towns where they were not sufficiently strong to support a preacher, to become disconnected from the circuits in which they were the principal appointments, and form themselves into stations. This policy was certainly disastrous to both the towns and rural districts. The stations thus formed would be too weak to command the talents and experience necessary to their success, while the circuits, disconnected from thriving villages, were also weakened by the change, to an extent that greatly impaired their influence. The object of the resolution was to correct the tendency in this direction, and, as far as possible, to equalize the several charges in the Conference; and the report of the committee looked to this result.

The Conference for several years had suffered from the loss of many of its ablest preachers, not only by death, but by transfer to other Conferences. Within a few years McHenry, Lindsey, Powers, Vance, McKnight, Ogden, Landrum, Harrison, Outten, Adams, Cosby, Duke, and Littlejohn had died, and within the same time McCown, Young, Wallace, Light, Bird, Holliday, Evans, and Frazee had been transferred to other Conferences. It would be difficult for any Conference to sustain itself under such a draught upon its members. It was proposed, however, to make a farther invasion upon its ranks by the transfer of Hubbard H. Kavanaugh to the Missouri Conference, for the purpose of stationing him in the city of St. Louis. Unwilling to interfere with the episcopal prerogative, the Conference, nevertheless, deemed it not improper to request the

Bishop not to transfer Mr. Kavanaugh. The following resolution was offered by Benjamin T. Crouch and Henry B. Bascom:

"Whereas, it has been represented to many members of this Conference that some steps have been taken to remove Brother Hubbard H. Kavanaugh from the ranks of this Conference by transfer; and whereas, this Conference is already very much impoverished in the older portion of its membership, by removals, deaths, and otherwise; therefore,

"*Resolved*, That we *respectfully request* Bishop Roberts to give Brother Kavanaugh an appointment in this Conference."

The removal of Mr. Kavanaugh from Kentucky at this period would have been a serious misfortune to the Church in the State. No preacher in the Conference more fully enjoyed the confidence of the public, or held a warmer place in the affections of the Church, than did Mr. Kavanaugh. For many years he had occupied the most important fields, and his ministry was sought everywhere throughout the commonwealth. Endowed with intellect of a high order, with powers of oratory rarely equaled, and with zeal and devotion to the Church that no one could challenge, he exerted an influence that was felt not only in the walks of Methodism, but in other Communions. He was no common man, and the Kentucky Conference felt that if his ministry was needed elsewhere, for the very same reason it was required in Kentucky; besides, he had grown up among them. He had entered the Kentucky Conference in 1823, and for fourteen years their fortunes and his had been one, and they felt unwilling that a separation between him and them should occur. Their petition to the Bishop was respectful; Mr. Kavanaugh was not transferred.

Thomas Lasley, a prominent and influential member of the Conference, had become connected with slavery by the will of his deceased father. A committee was appointed to "consider and report on this and all kindred cases which may be referred to them." After a thorough investigation of the entire question, the following report was adopted:

"The committee find Brother Lasley in possession of eight negro slaves—one a woman aged eighty years, and consequently infirm; a man aged sixty, and his wife aged fifty; a young man and his wife, son and daughter-in-law of the two preceding—all of whom have recently fallen into his hands under the provisions of the will of his deceased father, and three boys aged, respectively, twelve, fourteen, and sixteen years, who were born his property. The committee have availed themselves of all the advantages of a full and frank interview with Brother Lasley. Your committee are determined that, so far as they are concerned, there shall be no essential infringement of the excellent rule of our Discipline on this subject; yet, in view of all the circumstances of this case, and former usages of this Conference in similar cases, your committee are induced to recommend to the Conference the adoption of the following resolutions:

"*Resolved*, *first*, That, as soon after the adjournment of this Conference as practicable, Brother

Lasley be required to execute a will securing the emancipation of the *young* man and his wife aforesaid, providing expressly that their emancipation shall take effect upon the death of their parents.

"*Resolved, second,* That he be required to provide, by a bill of manumission, for the liberation of the three boys before named, specifying that they shall all go free so soon as the youngest shall have attained the age of twenty-five years."

This report, which was adopted, was signed by Joseph S. Tomlinson, Joseph Marsee, Lewell Campbell, William Holman, and Robert Y. McReynolds.

The following resolution was adopted:

"*Resolved,* That the Conference, at its present session, proceed to appoint, by ballot or otherwise, or request the Bishop of the Conference to do so, three members of its body, whose duty it shall be, at the next session of the Conference, to preach, or deliver addresses, before the Conference and audiences which may be in attendance, on the following subjects: 1. The nature, dignity and duties of the Christian ministry; 2. On the moral fitness and probable results of missionary effort; 3. *On the nature and claims of literary education,* viewed as a general interest, and especially viewed in connection with the foregoing subjects. And that this arrangement be considered as permanent, and be annually attended to by the Conference in future, as probable means, among others, of accomplishing the great object we have in view, as a component part of the Methodist Episcopal Church."

This resolution was signed by Henry B. Bascom,

Jonathan Stamper, Joseph S. Tomlinson, and Benjamin T. Crouch. The Bishop appointed Mr. Bascom to deliver the sermon on the Ministry, Mr. Stamper on Missions, and Mr. Tomlinson on Education.

Although the health of Bishop Roberts was feeble during the Conference, he gave full satisfaction in the chair, in the cabinet, and in the pulpit. He not only presided with the dignity becoming the high and holy office he had so long filled with signal ability, but exhibited throughout the session that calmness and patience for which he was distinguished. In the cabinet, where the most difficult and delicate portion of the work of a Bishop is performed, he gave due consideration to the opinions of those with whom he counseled, and made himself well acquainted with the gifts and peculiarities of the preachers, as well as with the nature of the work to be supplied; while in the pulpit he proved himself to be a true apostle—"a workman that needed not to be ashamed."

We were present at the Conference in Shelbyville two years before, a youth, looking to the ministry; but now we were in attendance to identify our fortunes for life, for weal or woe, whether in prosperity or adversity, with this body of tried and faithful ministers of Jesus Christ. In the proceedings of the Conference we felt the liveliest interest, and of much that occurred during the session we still cherish the fondest recollection. We remember the bending form of James Ward, and were impressed by the unpretentious Josiah Whitaker; we recollect how we trembled and feared when Mr. Bascom examined us, previous to our admission on trial,* and we recall the soft and pleasant voice of Mr. Tomlinson; we have not forgotten the open and happy countenance of John James, nor the tears that we saw fall from the face of Edward Stevenson while he besought sinners to repent and turn to God; the keen, dark eye of Isaac Collard and the pleasant shake of the hand of Thomas Lasley are with us yet; we had seen Hubbard H. Kavanaugh, Jonathan Stamper, Benjamin T. Crouch, Richard Corwine, and William Gunn, before. The first sermon we remember to have heard was preached by Mr. Kavanaugh; Mr. Stamper had baptized us in childhood; Mr. Crouch had received us into the Church; Mr. Corwine had licensed us to exhort, and Mr. Gunn to preach; but these faithful men never looked so commanding as when we saw them in their places in the Conference. Other preachers were present whom we knew, and to whom we owe

*On taking our place in the class, Mr. Bascom inquired if we had studied English grammar. We answered, "No." He then asked if we had studied geography. We gave the same reply. Lastly, he asked, "What English branches have you studied?" The answer was, "None." He said: "Then, my brother, Dr. Bascom (who lived a few doors from my father), has misinformed me; he told me that you had received a classical education." Embarrassed beyond expression, we could only say: "Brother Bascom, please pass me at present; and when I am composed, perhaps I can answer your questions." With the kindness which ever distinguished him, he offered us words of encouragement, and then passed on until he reached us again, when we were able to give an affirmative response to his interrogatories.

much. There was John Tevis, who had found us in childhood with bad associates, and had kindly taken us by the hand and led us to the Sunday-school; and there, too, we met George W. Brush, our first pastor, whom we had not seen for two years, and Richard D. Neale, with his cheerful and smiling face; and others, whose memory is with us yet.

The preaching during the Conference was not only instructive, but attended with great power. John Newland Maffitt was there a short time during the session, and preached in the Methodist Church, to a large and admiring audience. Many wept during the sermon. We heard the sermons of Richard Deering and Thomas H. Gibbons, preached to the prisoners in the State Prison; tears flowed copiously. Thoughts of childhood, in its innocence, and of home with all its pleasures, of a father's advice and a mother's love, crowded upon our mind as we listened to the words of eternal life, delivered by faithful men to these unfortunate ones. Some of them had been reared in ease, and all, perhaps, had known a mother's love. How sad the hour when, influenced by evil associates, they for the first time desecrated the holy Sabbath, or took the name of the Lord in vain, or drank from the accursed bowl! Having taken the first step in sin, the second was not so difficult; and thus step by step they had progressed in vice, until they were immured in prison-walls, disgraced and ruined.

Joel Peak, William McD. Abbett, Wright Merrick, Edmund M. Johnson, John C. Hardy, Wesley G. Montgomery, Williams B. Kavanaugh, Walter

Shearer, Moses Levi, Albert H. Redford, John B. Perry, William D. Matting, Lorenzo D. Harland, Jesse P. Murrell, Jedidiah Foster, and Calvin W. Lewis were admitted on trial.

Of those who were received on trial at the previous Conference, Greenup Barker, John J. Harrison, Theophilus Powell, and Seybourn Crutchfield retired from the itinerant ranks.

The names of William Atherton, Milton Jamieson, John Denham, and James H. Brooking were added to the list of the superannuated.

Thomas Lasley, Stephen Harber, Elijah Sutton, and George W. Fagg, located.

The death of Hooper Evans, a good and true man, had occurred during the year just closed.*

The support of the preachers was still far below their actual necessities, although the state of the finances showed a slight improvement over the preceding year. The collections to meet deficiencies were small, but more generally distributed throughout the Conference than they had been in the past. The missionary collections amounted to *two thousand and eighty-three dollars and six cents*, which was a large advance on that of former years.

The revivals which had blessed the Church during the previous year, and which had spread through the State, in some sections had not abated when the Conference met. It was, therefore, the privilege of many of the preachers in entering upon their work to find it in a blaze.

---

* For a sketch of Hooper Evans see "History of Methodism in Kentucky."

Henry N. Vandyke, a young man of more than ordinary promise, was stationed in Frankfort, where the Conference had been held. We have already alluded to the presence of Mr. Maffitt in Frankfort during the session of the Conference. He left the city before the adjournment, but returned after a few days, and entered upon an active campaign. On the 26th of December Mr. Vandyke addressed a letter to Mr. Stringfield, editor of the *South-western Christian Advocate*, in which he says: "Permit me to say through your paper, to the friends of Zion, that there has been a most gracious outpouring of the Holy Spirit upon Frankfort. We have had a protracted-meeting of about nine weeks. It commenced with the session of the Annual Conference, which was held in this place, and which closed October 25. Just at its close our beloved Brother Maffitt, of your place, visited us, and preached every day, and frequently twice a day, for about six weeks, the Lord blessing his labors greatly. There have been about one hundred and thirty conversions; one hundred and twenty have joined the Methodist E. Church, about fifteen the Baptist, and several the Presbyterian. The work still goes on in a most interesting manner. I have had the pleasure of being in and witnessing several revivals, but I do not know that I ever saw a more genuine revival in all my life. What is remarkable about it is a large majority of the converts are men, principally young men. There were, however, some gray-headed fathers, and some of middle age. A decided victory has turned upon the side of Israel; but we are still praying and looking for more. Our hope is that the glory of God may fill the whole city, and his praise be sung by every tongue. Doubtless many will rejoice through eternity that Brother Maffitt visited Frankfort. They think of him with emotions of deepest gratitude; and certainly no man deserves more applause than he, for his perseverance and zeal. The salvation of souls seems to be his only object; hence, he labors most indefatigably, day and night, amidst discouragements, difficulties, and persecutions. May God long preserve his life, that he may prove a blessing to thousands more!"*

While hundreds were listening to the appeals of Mr. Maffitt in the city of Frankfort, Francis A. Dighton, of the Erie Conference, Agent for the American Bible Society, was proclaiming salvation to the vast assemblies that waited upon his ministry, in the Fourth-street Church, in Louisville.

Mr. Dighton was born in Erie county, Pennsylvania, October 7, 1812. On the 24th of June, 1827, he experienced religion, at a camp-meeting held in the town of Villenova, New York. In 1833 he was admitted on trial, in the traveling connection, into the Pittsburgh Conference, and appointed to the Westfield Circuit, in the State of New York, and the following year to the St. Clairsville Circuit, in Ohio. In 1835 he was stationed in Cleveland, where he remained two years. In 1837 he traveled as Agent for the American Bible Society. The duties of the agency which he had accepted, and which he was faithfully prosecuting, brought Mr. Dighton

*_South-western Christian Advocate_, January 4, 1838.

to the city of Louisville, where he was destined to gather many stars to deck the crown of his rejoicing. Consumption, that sure destroyer, had fastened its fangs in his system, and he was rapidly hastening to the grave. He had a message, however, from God to mankind, and he was delivering it with an energy and ardor to which his wasting strength was not equal. Easy in his manners, agreeable in conversation, eloquent in the pulpit, and fervent in his work, he was beloved wherever known. His labors in Louisville were greatly blessed. Mr. Tydings, stationed at Fourth and Eighth streets, with John Christian Harrison as his colleague, writes from Louisville: "With great pleasure I would inform you that the great Head of the Church has, in the abundance of his mercy, visited this place. As hard, and dark, and wicked as it has been, the Lord has made known his power and saving grace to many precious souls, in a most wonderful manner. Between *seventy and eighty* were received into the Church on probation, in about two weeks after the work commenced, the most of whom profess to be happily converted to God; and one of the best omens that I have noticed is that a considerable number are children from ten to fifteen years of age, the most of whom have been carefully nursed in the precious—*yes, precious—Sabbath-school.* Such was the rapidity and glory of the work that as many as twenty or upward professed to be converted in one night. Glory to God for his unspeakable goodness! and let all the Church shout aloud, Amen! And 'what shall be done unto the man whom the king delighteth to honor?' and what can be greater honor than to be made instrumental in bringing souls to God? Surely, this is the greatest ever conferred upon man. Then, it can be no harm to say, on the present occasion, that the principal, if not sole, agent in this good work here was our well-beloved Brother Francis A. Dighton, Agent for the American Bible Society, who was on a visit to this place. He labored constantly and faithfully, day and night, for about the space of two weeks, and great and glorious success attended his word. Many here, no doubt, shall rise up in the great day and call him blessed; and we would, as we should, give all the glory to His abounding grace, and at the same time thank Him, also, for sending such an instrument of good among us. May God bless our dear young brother, and make him still more abundantly successful! The good work has not altogether subsided, and we hope it will continue until all shall be brought home to God."*

Mr. Dighton had come to Louisville a stranger, almost unknown; he left the city with the blessing of hundreds.†

The notes of triumph at Fourth-street had not died away before the Brook-street Church, in the same city, also experienced a revival, which had no parallel in Louisville in the past. The meeting commenced about the first of January, under the ministry of George W. Brush, the pastor of the

---

* *Western Christian Advocate*, December 29, 1837.

† Mr. Dighton's health rapidly declined after he left Louisville. He died December 26, 1838.

Church, and soon showed indications of a good work. After it had been in progress for five weeks, without any cessation, Mr. Brush writes: "There is now going forward in the Methodist Church, on Brook street, one of the most powerful revivals of the work of God that has ever been seen here. It is now five weeks since it began, but for seven days past it has swept all before it. The crowd is so great every evening that few pretend to keep their seats, and unless the mourners take their place in the altar before preaching, it is fruitless to attempt making their way thither after the crowd has convened. We regularly dismiss the people at ten o'clock, but they do not leave until twelve and one o'clock. We are unable to give the number of converts; we kept count for awhile, but the battle grew so warm that no one could tell who or how many were blessed. There were mourners in every part of the house. One hundred and twenty-seven have given in their names to join the Church. A great many—perhaps seventy-five—have been converted; and yet, on last evening, more than sixty were at the altar for prayer and instruction. Among all the converts, we know of only three or four who did not join the Church before they found the blessing. The character of those who have joined gives good ground to hope that this will prove to have been a sound and genuine work of God. We have had comparatively but little preaching. The sermons preached have seldom been more than thirty minutes long, and often we exhort and call the mourners at once. The members of the Church were a little slow at first to go into the work; but when once they made a break, they threw their whole souls into it. Many of the sisters, too, have been 'our helpers in Christ Jesus.'" *

The meeting was still in progress when the above letter was written. The interest continued to increase, reaching in its influence every portion of the city. At a later period another letter is published, from the pen of the pastor, announcing that two hundred and twenty persons had joined the Church, and about the same number had been converted to God.† The meeting continued forty days, and before its close *four hundred* persons joined the Church.

A letter from Benjamin T. Crouch, the Presiding Elder of the Louisville District, dated Frankfort, Kentucky, March 14, to the *Western Christian Advocate*, says: "We have gracious times in Louisville. Nearly *four hundred* have been added to the Methodist Episcopal Church, in that city, during the last three months. Conversions have been numerous and powerful. Glory to God for his saving influence! Our Baptist and Presbyterian friends have also been much refreshed. The work is very general in the city, and is still progressing. God is reviving his work elsewhere in this District."

During this year the white membership of the Church in Louisville was almost doubled, and the colored membership increased thirty-three per cent. Mr. Crouch, in his letter, refers to revivals in other portions of his District. In almost every charge

* *Western Christian Advocate,* March 9, 1838. † *Western Christian Advocate,* March 23, 1838.

there were "times of refreshing from the presence of the Lord," and in some extraordinary outpourings of the Holy Spirit. The Hardinsburg Circuit was greatly blessed. The preachers were Daniel S. Barksdale and Moses Levi—the former a young man of great worth, who had been in the Conference since 1834, and the latter a converted Jew who, although fifty years of age, had just been admitted on trial. In the month of February a meeting was commenced in the village of Brandenburg—a small town on the Ohio River—and was continued through several weeks, at which one hundred and two persons joined the Church, and more than that number made a profession of religion. It rained almost constantly during the meeting, and the church was unfavorably located for the community; yet, day and night, the people, with scarcely a sidewalk in any part of the town, walked through the deep mud to the house of God. The church was constantly crowded, and the result was glorious. As the year progressed other portions of the circuit were equally favored, until over three hundred persons were added to the Church.

The Jefferson Circuit—to which Richard Deering and Williams B. Kavanaugh were appointed—enjoyed much prosperity. Mr. Kavanaugh joined the Conference at its previous session, but Mr. Deering had been an itinerant since 1832. He was born in Greenup county, Kentucky, August 25, 1811. In the month of June, 1828, before he was seventeen years old, at Dement's Chapel, in the same county, he was received into the Church as a seeker of religion, by Nehemiah A. Cravens. A year passed—a year of doubts, and fears, and struggle—before he realized a sense of the pardoning love of Christ. During this time his father had removed to Missouri. It was June, 1829, when he was converted. Almost despairing of the mercy of God, which he had so long and so earnestly sought, he retired to a pine-forest, on the bank of Current River, in Wayne county, Missouri, where, in agony and prayer, he poured out his soul to God. At this time and place he was powerfully converted. Returning to Kentucky, he met with Thomas Waring, the junior preacher on the Little Sandy and Highland Circuit, who not only invited but urged him to accompany him around the circuit. Impressed with the conviction that he ought to preach the gospel of Christ, he pleaded every excuse rather than enter on the responsible work. His youth, his inexperience, his want of qualifications for the duties of an itinerant preacher, were offered as arguments; but "Woe is unto me if I preach not the gospel!" confronted him by day and by night. On his tour with Mr. Waring he exhorted a few times, and finally attempted to preach, and afterward preached several times before Mr. Waring left the circuit. Unwilling to enter the Conference, Mr. Corwine, the Presiding Elder, kindly proposed to reserve a place for him on the Hinckstone Circuit, as junior preacher, if he would promise to fill it. He conferred with his father, who gave his consent, and with older members of the Church, who encouraged him to take up the cross. On the 9th of November, 1831, he bade adieu to his parents, and brothers and sisters, and started for his field of labor. On his way thither he stopped at the home of Mr. Corwine, who resided in Flemingsburg, and on the following day, in company with the Presiding Elder, continued his journey to his charge. He reached the circuit in time for the first quarterly-meeting, which was held in Millersburg. Martin L. Eades was the preacher in charge, and to him was committed the care of young Deering. The circuit included more than twenty preaching-places, one of which was in Paris, where his itinerant ministry commenced. He continued to preach with varied success until the second quarterly-meeting, which began May 12, 1832. At this time he was made a licentiate, having exercised his gifts up to this period under the authority of the Presiding Elder—preaching nearly one year before he was licensed.

William B. Landrum traveled the Lewis Circuit this year. The fourth quarterly-meeting on his circuit was a camp-meeting, and was held at Bethel. Among the preachers who were present on that occasion, and preached, Mr. Landrum, in his Autobiography, mentions Richard Deering. He says: "I have often thought of a sermon he preached at that meeting. His text was, 'I have a message from God unto thee.' He declared his message in such a manner as to have a wonderful effect on the congregation." The year spent by Mr. Deering on the Hinckstone Circuit was profitable to him as well as a blessing to the Church. He had entered fully into the labors of an itinerant preacher, and "the pleasure of the Lord had prospered in his hands." In every portion of the circuit he had gathered souls into the Church, and witnessed gracious revivals of religion.

At the fourth quarterly-meeting, September 1, 1832, he was recommended to the Kentucky Annual Conference, and was duly received. Richard Corwine, the Presiding Elder, under whose auspices he had entered the itinerant field, was sent to the Fleming Circuit, and we are not surprised that he requested the appointment of Richard Deering as his colleague. The year was one of great prosperity. Revivals of religion occurred throughout the circuit, and hundreds were brought to Christ and added to the Church. The Asiatic cholera was sweeping through that section of the State, spreading consternation along its path, and carrying hundreds to the grave. Before its appearance the minds and hearts of the people were turned toward religion, and amid its ravages there was no abatement of interest on this great question. So intense was the feeling of the people on the subject of religion, and so wide-spread was the revival influence, that the Quarterly Conference requested that Mr. Deering be allowed to remain on the circuit during the session of the Conference, and carry on the work, aided by Benjamin Northcott and other local preachers.

At the Conference of 1833 Richard Deering was sent to the Germantown Circuit, as the colleague of Francis Landrum. In this field, as in those he had previously occupied, he was eminently useful. The preacher in charge was distinguished for his great zeal and abundant success. Following in the lead of this great revivalist, the young preacher, like a flame of fire, passed through his work, preaching the gospel and exhorting sinners to be reconciled to God. The circuit was in a blaze: the cries of penitents pleading for mercy, and the shouts of new-born souls, were heard everywhere.

At the following Conference we find him in Louisville, as the colleague of William Holman. William P. McKnight, of precious memory, had preceded him in that city, and had fallen soon after entering upon his work. The labors of Mr. Deering hitherto had been in the rural districts, although in the most inviting fields in the Conference. The duties of a city pastor differ materially from those of a preacher on a circuit: the labor is much more onerous, presenting at the same time much less variety. In this new and interesting sphere the young preacher not only sustained himself, but was instrumental in the accomplishment of much good.

It was during the pastorate of Mr. Deering in the city of Louisville that we first met him. Late in the spring of 1835 he visited Shelbyville for the purpose of aiding George W. Brush in a meeting. Youthful in appearance, courteous in his manners, and withal modest and unassuming in his deportment, and able and interesting in the pulpit, he won upon the hearts of the people, not only in the Church, but throughout the community, as few men had done. His voice was the most melodious we had ever heard, and the words of life, as they fell warm from his lips, penetrated every heart. He was a favorite of the young, the middle-aged admired and loved him, while the old regarded him with favor and affection. With timidity we approached him as he was leaving the pulpit, the first evening he preached, and offered him our hand. Looking us steadily in the face, he said, "Young man, God has work for you to do." He had never seen us before, and did not ask our name, yet he gave utterance to a sentiment from which we were endeavoring to escape.

At a later period in the year he attended a camp-meeting at Cardwell's Camp-ground, three miles east of Shelbyville, where he preached with great power and success. His singing, too, was sweeter than any we had ever heard. That beautiful hymn of Kirke White's was his favorite:

When, marshaled on the nightly plain,
  The glitt'ring host bestud the sky,
One star alone of all the train
  Can fix the sinner's wand'ring eye.
Hark! hark! to God the chorus breaks,
  From every host, from every gem;
But one alone the Saviour speaks,
  It is the Star of Bethlehem.

At the close of the year, in Louisville, he was married to Mrs. Amanda McGrath, a young widow of deep piety and of rare accomplishments.

From Louisville we follow him to the Russellville Station, and thence to the Newcastle Circuit—in both of which charges he was beloved and useful. His next appointment was the Jefferson Circuit, where we find him the present year. Although the ministry of Mr. Deering on the Jefferson Circuit was not so signally blessed as on other fields where he had labored, yet through his instrumentality the Church was built up, and many were brought "from darkness to light." During the year fifty persons were added to the Church.

Early in the summer the Hartford Circuit—the extreme appointment in the Louisville District—was blessed with extraordinary revivals. The preacher was Joseph G. Ward. Mr. Ward was the son of the Rev. James Ward, whose name had been for many years a household word in the Methodist families of Kentucky. He was born in Botetourt county, Virginia, August 29, 1805, and was brought up in Jefferson county, Kentucky, where his father settled in 1807. Although the son of a Methodist preacher, he did not embrace religion, nor become a member of the Church, until he attained his majority. At a camp-meeting at Shrader's Camp-ground, in 1826, he was powerfully awakened under the ministry of Richard D. Neale, and at the same meeting was converted and joined the Church. Believing himself to be divinely called to preach the gospel, he was licensed by Marcus Lindsey, by order of the Quarterly Conference of Jefferson Circuit, October 6, 1828, and at the same time recommended to the Kentucky Conference for admission on trial.

The first appointment of Mr. Ward was to the Cumberland Circuit, with James C. Crow in charge. The circuit to which he was sent embraced portions of Rockcastle and Pulaski counties, and the counties of Laurel, Clay, Knox, and Harlan, and spread over the most rugged portion of the State. Although there was no general revival on the work, yet sixty-eight persons were added to the Church, and about the same number professed to find the forgiveness of sins. At the Conference of 1829 he was sent to the Madison Circuit, with the saintly Samuel Harrison. Notwithstanding the fidelity with which these preachers performed the duties assigned them, there was no ingathering into the Church on this work. Here and there a solitary individual became identified with the people of God; yet no remarkable demonstrations of divine power were seen or felt. In 1830 his appointment was to the Lewis Circuit, with Francis Landrum. The preacher in charge from some cause failing to go to the circuit, Mr. Ward was placed in charge, and John W. Riggin—then a local preacher—employed to assist him. The year was one of great prosperity. At a camp-meeting in Lewis county, held in the summer of 1831, on Cabin Creek, many precious souls were awakened and converted. The following year we find him on Germantown Circuit, with George W. Brush. The removal of Mr. Brush to the pastoral charge of the Church in Maysville, in the early part of the year, left Mr. Ward alone on the circuit, where, through his instrumentality, many were gathered into the fold of Christ. From the Germantown Circuit we follow him to Bowling Green—a circuit with twenty-eight appointments, to be filled every four weeks. Successful as Mr. Ward had been on other fields, in this his success was of eclipsing superiority. At almost every appointment sinners were awakened and penitents converted. Near the close of the year, at a camp-meeting held at Drake's Camp-ground, in Warren county, the revival bore down every thing before its mighty power. Hundreds were awakened and cried for mercy, and at this meeting about seventy persons found the pearl of great price. The pastor of the Church in Bowling Green—Thomas H. Cropper—having left his work because of affliction, late in the winter, the station was added to the circuit, and formed a part of Mr. Ward's field of labor. We have more than once alluded to the appearance of cholera during the spring and summer of 1833. The interior of the State was suffering to an alarming extent, and the epidemic was making rapid progress in its march toward Southern Kentucky. In Bowling Green—at that time a comparatively small village—a conference was held by the ministers of the several Communions, and a day of fasting and prayer appointed for the purpose of averting the threatening scourge, and to ask God to revive his work among the people. At the appointed time the Christians of all denominations met together in the Baptist Church, and many and fervent prayers were offered up to God. A few days later a meeting commenced in the Baptist Church, under the ministry of Mr. Chapman, a Cumberland Presbyterian, and other ministers of that denomination, in which all the Churches united, and at which about two hundred persons "tasted" for the first time "the good word of God and the powers of the world to come." Bowling Green was not only blessed with this great revival, but no case of cholera occurred there during the season.

In 1833 we find Mr. Ward on the Shelby Circuit, with William Helm. He only remained on the Shelby Circuit until the following spring, when the business of his father rendered it necessary for him to return home, and at the ensuing Conference to ask for a location. He continued in a local relation but one year, during which time he preached almost as constantly as he had done in an itinerant capacity.

While sustaining the position of a local preacher, in the summer of 1835, he united with Mr. Remley, a Presbyterian minister, in a meeting in Middletown, and here their labors were greatly blessed. Many persons turned "from darkness to light." As the result of this meeting, twenty-five persons joined the Presbyterian Church, and fifty the Methodist, and a subscription was taken up to build a house of worship for each denomination.

Eager to devote his life to the one work of doing good, in 1835 we find his name again in the Minutes, and on the Newcastle Circuit. Without any general revival, the Church enjoyed "times of refreshing from the presence of the Lord." In 1836 his name appears in connection with the Breckinridge Circuit, where he found much to discourage him, and met with but little success.

At the Conference of 1837 he was sent alone to the Hartford Circuit, where we meet with him faithfully prosecuting his work as a minister of Jesus Christ. Early in the spring, at a meeting held three miles from Hartford, at Goshen Meeting-house, thirty persons were converted in a single week. The third quarterly-meeting, which was held in Hartford, commenced May 19, and was protracted for two weeks. At this meeting between ninety and one hundred professed religion, and eighty-one joined the Methodist Church. The labors of Mr. Ward, during the continuance of the meeting in Hartford, were very arduous. The duties of the Presiding Elder forbade his remaining only a few days at the meeting, and the claims of other portions of the circuit, which was a large one, required the pastor to be absent a large portion of the time. Unwilling to abandon a work that promised so much blessing to the Church, Mr. Ward would leave Hartford in the morning, and attend his appointments in the country, and return at night and preach in the village. At the close of the year more than *two hundred* persons had been added to the Church.

As a preacher Mr. Ward took high rank with the young men of promise in the Conference.

The net increase in the Louisville District was *five hundred and ninety* white and *one hundred and seventy-seven* colored members.

We have already referred to the revival in Frankfort, in the Lexington District, under the ministry of Mr. Maffitt. The interest of the meeting did not terminate with the labors of this distinguished preacher. Throughout the year a lively concern was manifested on the subject of religion, which extended to the State Prison—more than thirty of the unfortunate inmates of that institution entering upon a better life.*

We follow Mr. Maffitt from Frankfort to Georgetown, where sixty persons, under his ministry, are brought to a saving knowledge of the truth, as it is in Jesus. The interest awakened by his labors in this beautiful village can scarcely be expressed. All classes of society went to hear him, and a deep religious impression rested on every mind and heart.

While the Church at Georgetown was receiving valuable accessions, the labors of Henry E. Pilcher, stationed at Newport and Covington, were proving successful. At a meeting, commencing near the first of February, in the city of Covington—where Mr. Pilcher, the pastor, was aided by Messrs. Hamline and Swormstedt—one hundred and ten persons became members of the Church. Mr. Pilcher, in a letter to the *Western Christian Advocate*, says: "I am happy to say that the work of God is still progressing in this station, and in a more glorious manner than ever before witnessed. For five weeks past we have been, almost every day and night, more or less engaged in the services of the sanctuary. The set time to favor Zion surely has come, and the current of salvation is rolling over the whole city. There are but few in this place who are disposed to raise the standard of opposition, and many of those who in the incipient stages of this revival were the most violent opposers of the work of God have become the most zealous advocates of

*Henry N. Vandyke in the *Western Christian Advocate*, May 18, 1838.

the cross. I here cannot forbear mentioning one circumstance that occurred during the progress of this glorious work. At one of our meetings, whilst the saints of the Most High were exulting in the triumphs of the cross, and penitents were earnestly pleading for mercy, a lady in the congregation, who was looking on, saw with amazement two of her daughters appear deeply interested in the work. One of them, having obtained the blessing of justification the night previous, was seated in a chair, instructing her sister, who was kneeling, with her head reclining upon her lap, and sighing for redemption through the blood of Christ. This sight was appalling to the mother, who had been advised by some of her friends to take care of her daughter, or those Methodists would be the cause of her death. In the trepidation of her mind she sprang from her seat, rushed forward, and wrested her daughter from the altar, seated her on a bench, and endeavored to quiet her; but all to no purpose. The child refused to be comforted. The mother was urged to permit her daughter to seek religion. We assured her there was no danger, inasmuch as the same Power that had wounded was able to heal. She concluded the next evening that her daughter might go to the altar again; and while the child was earnestly pleading for mercy, the mother gazed upon her in sadness and silence. God soon spoke peace to the soul of her child, who proclaimed aloud the song of redemption. The mother began to quake and tremble, and exclaimed: 'That is the right kind of religion! I will know the next time whom to believe,' and immediately bowed at the altar, and began, herself, to plead for mercy. When the door of the Church was opened, the same night, she came forward and gave her name for membership, and on the next day, at a prayer-meeting, the daughters saw their mother powerfully converted to God. O how delightful to see the mother embracing her daughters, and all of them exulting in the love of God together—all of one mind and of one heart! I never saw a revival of religion progress more regularly than in this place. Conversions have been clear and powerful. Indeed, the greater portion of the whole number that have joined on probation have witnessed a good confession before God; and my prayer to God is that they may continue so to do until they may all come to Mount Zion, where they will join with all the redeemed in the chorus of the skies. Since the former accounts which I gave you of the revival in this station we have received into the Church, on probation, one hundred and ten, making an aggregate of one hundred and ninety received on probation since the work commenced. Our prayer is that the good work may still go on till all the people are converted to God. My soul is happy while I write, and I can truly say I never felt more like weathering out the storm and grasping the crown of life eternal than I do at this time. To God be all the glory!" *

In the Falmouth Circuit, where Joel Peak traveled alone, thirty persons joined the Church before the first of April; and in the Cynthiana Circuit,

* *Western Christian Advocate*, March 9, 1838.

under the ministry of James D. Holding, a revival occurred at Salem Church, in which several Sunday-school scholars professed religion and were brought into the Church. In the Cynthiana Station, the Church, under the ministry of Hartwell J. Perry, enjoyed a gracious season.

James C. Crow and Thomas R. Malone this year traveled on the Burlington Circuit. Mr. Crow was born in Adair county, Kentucky, March 1, 1802. His parents, Thomas and Nancy Crow (formerly Nancy Danley), came from Virginia to Kentucky at an early day, and settling first in Adair county, removed at a later period to the county of Jefferson. Thomas Crow was not a professor of religion, but his wife was a Christian woman and a member of the Baptist Church, and endeavored to bring up her children "in the nurture and admonition of the Lord." The triumphant death of a brother, when James C. Crow was about eighteen years of age, not only affected his heart, but turned his thoughts to the subject of religion. The funeral-sermon of his brother was preached by James Ward, and under his appeals he resolved to seek the Lord at once.

Leaving home for the purpose of learning a trade, he became an apprentice to Samuel Lyon, a local Methodist preacher, residing in Shelbyville, whose business was that of a house-joiner. Here he had the opportunity of attending Church regularly. Deeply troubled because he was a sinner before God, he attended a camp-meeting near Charleston, Indiana, where he was converted.

Speaking of this great change, Mr. Crow says: "On the 15th of August, 1820, I have reason to believe that God, for Christ's sake, pardoned my sins. I had such a clear and satisfactory view of the mercy and sufficiency of Christ to save sinners that I thought I could tell everybody just how to get religion, and under this impression I commenced directing penitents to look to Jesus, the Friend of sinners. I had the pleasure of witnessing ten or twelve conversions within a few hours after my own. It appeared to me that every person was going to be religious; for all things had become new, and all was glorious within and without."

The impression that it was his duty to call sinners to repentance alarmed him. Without the advantages of even a common education, and possessed of a natural diffidence, he was unwilling to yield to his convictions. The struggles of nearly three years so wrought upon his mind and heart that he consented to receive a license to exhort, and two years later to preach the gospel of Christ.

In 1825 he was recommended to the Kentucky Conference, and admitted on trial. His first field of labor was the Somerset Circuit, as the colleague of Thompson Holliman. Success attended the ministry of these faithful men: one hundred members were added to the Church.

In 1826 he traveled on the Madison Circuit, under the guidance of Josiah Whitaker as the senior preacher, where forty-two persons witnessed a good confession.

In the autumn of 1827 he was appointed in charge

of the Cumberland Circuit (afterward *Goose* Creek Circuit), with George W. Martin and Richard Bird as his colleagues.* One hundred and seventy-five additions to the Church were reported as one of the results of this year's labor. The following year we find him on a portion of the same circuit (yet under the same name), with Joseph G. Ward as his colleague, where his ministry was again signally blessed. During this year Mr. Crow was married to Nancy W. Whitaker—a daughter of Josiah Whitaker—a lady well qualified for the responsible position she was called to occupy.

His appointment for the following year was to the Hinckstone Circuit, with Hiram Baker. Millersburg, with fourteen other appointments, constituted the field of his operations. In this charge thirty-six persons joined the Church. At the close of this year he located, that he might provide a home for his family.

During the five years that Mr. Crow had traveled he had received three hundred and fifty-eight members into the Church, and was paid for his services *two hundred and forty-nine dollars.*

After sustaining the relation of a local preacher to the Church for two years, in which he was laborious and useful, he returned to the Conference, and was appointed to the Burlington Circuit, where he re-

*When the author, ten years later, traveled Manchester Mission, which was a portion of the old Cumberland Circuit, he frequently heard pleasant allusions to the appointment of Messrs. Crow, Martin, and Bird—all the feathered tribe of the Conference—to the *Goose* Creek Circuit.

mained for two years. Although he had labored with rare diligence during the five years which he spent as an itinerant, yet he returned to the duties of the pastorate with even a stronger purpose of accomplishing good. In the pulpit, in the altar, and in his pastoral visits, he recommended the religion he professed.

We next follow him to the Mount Sterling Circuit, with Wilson S. McMurray as his colleague, and thence to the Falmouth Circuit.

In 1836, with William B. Landrum, he traveled the Georgetown Circuit, and in 1837 his appointment is the Burlington Circuit, with Thomas R. Malone as his colleague. In these several charges the ministry of Mr. Crow was greatly blessed. On the Burlington Circuit, which he traveled for two years, *two hundred and forty-one* persons were added to the Church; on the Mount Sterling, *thirty;* on the Falmouth, *forty;* on the Georgetown, *fifteen;* and on the Burlington, where we find him this year, *one hundred and twenty-three.* He received for his support during these seven years *one thousand and eleven dollars.* No man in the Conference at this period served the Church more faithfully than did James C. Crow, and but few, if any, received a more meager support. His circuits were large, and frequently in the most rugged portions of the State, and in most instances made no provision whatever for the support of his family; and yet not a murmur fell from his lips. Almost a stranger at home, he prosecuted with fidelity the duties assigned him, and everywhere he labored gathered sheaves for his Master.

Not with enticing words of man's wisdom, but with great plainness of speech, he told the simple story of the cross, and sinners gathered to its standard. With the small support he received he managed to avoid pecuniary embarrassment, and met his financial obligations with commendable promptness.

The total increase in the Lexington District was *three hundred and eighty* white and *two hundred and eighty-eight* colored members.

Thomas W. Chandler was the Presiding Elder in the Augusta District. All over this vast field the fires of religion burned brightly on the altars of the Church. Scarcely a community could be found on which the showers of grace refused to fall. Everywhere sinners were sending their plaintive cries to Heaven for mercy, and everywhere shouts of converted souls filled the air.

In the Fleming Circuit—whose preacher was the zealous and indefatigable George W. Merritt—before the winter passed, some prosperity was enjoyed. By the first of March signs of a general revival were very apparent. Throughout the work an interest on the subject of religion was awakened, and in midsummer the good effects were manifest in every direction. In July *one hundred* persons were reported as having been added to the Church.*

In the village of Augusta—one of the principal appointments in the Minerva Circuit—at a quarterly-meeting held in March, thirty-six persons joined the Church, and fully that number "passed from death unto life." The preachers on the circuit

* *Western Christian Advocate*, July 26, 1838.

were Samuel Veach and Foster H. Blades. At the meeting in Augusta, Messrs. Bascom, Tomlinson, Trimble, and McCown, composing the Faculty in the College, preached and labored in the altar.

In Maysville, where Thomas N. Ralston was stationed, at a meeting which closed about the first of June, sixty-two persons, several of whom were heads of families, professed religion and joined the Church; while in the Germantown Circuit, under the ministry of Hiram Baker and Thomas Demoss, two hundred and fourteen persons witnessed a good confession and identified themselves with the people of God.

In the Millersburg Circuit, the labors of Carlisle Babbitt were crowned with success. The second quarterly-meeting, which was held in Millersburg, resulted in forty additions to the Church.

In the Greenupsburg Circuit, under the ministry of John Waring and Jedidiah Foster, the Church enjoyed seasons of refreshing. At Mount Zion, in that circuit, at a meeting held in April, *twenty-three* persons were added to the Church, and in the circuit during the year *three hundred and eighty-four* names were recorded.

Wesley G. Montgomery—a young man who had just entered the Conference—traveled the Little Sandy Circuit, where his ministry was owned by the Head of the Church. More than *one hundred* persons became disciples of Jesus Christ before the spring months passed away.

In the Augusta District, the net increase was *six hundred and sixty-nine* in the white membership, and *one hundred and seventy-nine* in the colored.

From the Augusta District we turn to the Harrodsburg; and although we do not meet with the success with which we have been cheered in the former, yet throughout the District we are permitted to witness gracious outpourings of the Holy Spirit.

Absalom Woolliscroft and George S. Gatewood had traveled the Madison Circuit the previous year, and had rejoiced in the full reward of their effective labors. At the Conference of 1837 they were reäppointed to this charge, and they entered upon their work with the same zeal that had distinguished their ministry the year before. Hardly had they set about the active duties of the campaign, when indications of a more extensive revival than they had hitherto witnessed appeared in the horizon. Congregations increased, the prayer and class-meetings were more largely attended, and the subject of religion occupied the popular thought. The good seed which was then sown was carefully watched. Extraordinary efforts were made to push the battle to the gates of the enemy. In January they reported five hundred souls converted to God,* and the work still progressing in every direction. John James, the Presiding Elder, about the last of March reports that "in every place there is a regular increase. In Harrodsburg and Danville Station many have been added to the Church. Danville and Winchester Circuits have been greatly blessed, and all around the District there is in progress a most glorious revival." Mr. Maffitt had again visited Har-

* *Western Christian Advocate*, January 26, 1838.

rodsburg, and was instrumental in turning many to God. On the 22d of June Edward Stevenson reports "good meetings in both places," and at the third quarterly-meeting, held late in July, in Harrodsburg, seven persons became members of the Church.

In the Somerset Circuit, Albert Kelly received into the Church more than one hundred persons.

The preachers in all parts of this District labored with unwonted zeal; but none of them displayed greater energy in their work than did Napoleon B. Lewis and William McD. Abbett. Mr. Lewis had entered the Conference in 1834, but had traveled one year earlier under the Presiding Elder. Although a young man, as a preacher of a high order of talent and as a zealous and successful evangelist, he had taken rank with the first men of his age in the Conference, and promised great usefulness to the Church. His colleague, Mr. Abbett, although in the noon-tide of life, had just entered the field. His preaching abilities were far above mediocrity, and his devotion to the Church was marked by corresponding efforts to advance the cause of the Redeemer. Many preachers are largely indebted to their wives for their success in the ministry, and no one was more obligated in this respect than Mr. Abbett. His timidity and modesty operated against him. On his pulpit ability he placed a much lower estimate than did the people he served, and frequently before preaching he alluded to his inadequacy to the work he was called to perform. He had preached on Sunday evening, in the village of

Stanford, to a large and attentive audience, and had made one of his happiest efforts. The night was dark, so that in returning from the church no one could be distinguished. The voice of a young man was recognized by a comrade on the opposite side of the street, when he cried to him, "Did you hear what 'Squire P—— said about the new preacher?" "No. What was it?" The reply was, "He said that fellow should not practice on him again," and a merry laugh rang out on the evening air. The preacher himself was too near not to hear the jest. Discouraged and depressed, he, however, prosecuted his work, meeting his appointments and faithfully delivering his message.

Spring came. The winter through which he had passed was the coldest that had been known for several years, and only a meager support had been received. Under pecuniary embarrassment, and with the impression that the work of the ministry could be better performed by some one else, Mr. Abbett resolved to abandon the itinerancy. He returned home, expecting to retire from a field which he believed himself called to occupy, and to spend the remainder of his life in a local sphere. He communicated this fact to the Presiding Elder, who used every argument to dissuade him from the purpose he had formed, urging upon him an immediate return to a work where he was so much beloved. The weeks he spent at home were weeks of inexpressible sadness. He could neither eat, nor sleep, nor work. Sympathy, tears, prayers, all failed to give him the comfort he so ardently desired.

Words of cheer, however, fell from the lips of his faithful wife, as she wept and prayed with him, and pleaded with him to return to the post he had abandoned. Unable to resist her earnest appeals, he yielded to her persuasions, and, returning to his circuit, with energy and zeal pleaded his Master's cause. A few weeks later Mrs. Abbett made a round or more on the circuit with her husband, holding up his hands in the noble work to which he had pledged anew his energies and his life. In every neighborhood she visited she made friends for herself, for her husband, and for the cause of Christ, which she so dearly loved. The ministry of Messrs. Lewis and Abbett was greatly blessed in the awakening of sinners and the conversion of penitents. Many were added to the Church.

Notwithstanding the revivals all over this District, the net increase was only *thirty-four* white and *one hundred and twenty* colored members.

In the Hopkinsville District, the reports were more encouraging. As early as January George Switzer reported an extraordinary revival in the town of Franklin, and, indeed, revivals everywhere within the bounds of the Bowling Green Circuit, of which he had charge. On the 26th of the same month Wiley B. Murphy, the junior preacher, held a meeting, at which twenty persons were added to the Church. Robert Y. McReynolds, the preacher on the Franklin Circuit, held a meeting early in March, when twenty-seven persons turned to the Lord. In the Hopkinsville Circuit, Gilby Kelly and Andrew J. McLaughlin were notably successful.

Revivals in Hopkinsville, Providence, and other parts, signalized their labors. Two hundred persons joined the Church, seventy-two of whom were received by the junior preacher after Mr. Kelly left for Conference. In the Princeton Circuit, John Nevius announced large accessions in July, and later that one hundred and eighteen had been added to the Church; while in the Greenville Circuit a "good work" was reported. The membership in the Madisonville Circuit, under the ministry of Robert G. Gardner and William James, was largely increased, and revivals blessed the Church in every portion of the District.

Among the young men in the Conference who displayed extraordinary zeal, Edwin Roberts was one of the most conspicuous. His appointment was to the Morganfield Circuit. He had entered the Conference the year before, and had been useful as junior preacher on the Hopkinsville Circuit. He was sent to Morganfield Circuit alone, and his entrance on his work was unheralded. His dress was plain: he wore a broad-brimmed white hat, and none of his apparel was of the costly kind; his face, however, was commanding, and his bearing that of a gentleman.

It was early in November when he reached his field of labor. He had traveled all day, meditating on the responsibility of the work to which he had been divinely called. The shades of night were fast gathering around him when he rode up to the gate in front of an elegant farm-house, where one of his official members resided. As he hailed, the lady of the house appeared at the front door. Mr. Roberts inquired for her husband.

"He is not at home," replied the lady; "do you wish to see him?"

"I do, madam," said the young preacher.

With that courtesy and hospitality for which the women of Kentucky are so proverbial, she invited him to alight from his horse and walk into the house, adding: "My husband is somewhere about the farm, and will be here soon."

Dismounting, and fastening his jaded horse to the rack, and throwing his well-worn and scantily-filled saddle-bags over his arm, the well-formed and fine-looking stripling entered the yard, and with wearied step approached the dwelling, conscious that he was the object of mingled curiosity and suspicion. On reaching the door he offered the lady his hand, with the remark:

"My name is Roberts. I am the new preacher for the circuit."

A clap of thunder from a clear sky would have produced no more surprise than did this announcement.

"You our new preacher!" exclaimed the lady, with evident amazement. "*You our new preacher!*" she repeated, with emphasis. "Why, young man, you must be mistaken. The Bishop usually sends us—" and here she paused, and added: "You cannot be our new preacher."

During this interview, which was brief, the young preacher stood at the door, the lady, in her surprise, having forgotten to invite him into the house. Reflecting a moment, she said: "Well, come in; my husband will return shortly, and he will see about this matter."

Entering the house, he was invited into a richly-furnished parlor, where he was left to his own reflections, and to contemplate the prospects before him in this new appointment. What those reflections must have been in the mind of a young and sensitive preacher—who had just left an affectionate home, with the kiss of mother and sisters imprinted on his cheek, and the "God bless you" of friends and loved ones, to enter with fear and trembling upon the responsibilities and trials of the itinerant ministry, for the duties of which he keenly felt his inadequacy—can only be imagined by those who have passed through the same ordeal, or whose observation has made them acquainted with the trials which beset a young preacher of tender sensibilities.

Anxious to know how he would be received by the gentleman, the "new preacher" awaited his arrival with emotions he could not describe. He did not wait long. In a few minutes he entered the house, accompanied his wife into the parlor, and was introduced to Edwin Roberts.

"Are you our preacher?" he asked, with apparent sternness.

"My name is Edwin Roberts. Bishop Roberts has sent me to the Morganfield Circuit for the present year, to preach to the people. I have been directed to your house as being one of the preachers' homes, and as convenient to my appointment on to-morrow."

While Mr. Roberts was making this plain statement the gentleman observed him closely, and, failing to be impressed by what he had said, expressed a doubt as to whether the young man had been appointed to the Morganfield Circuit. His doubts, however, were removed when Mr. Roberts, handing him a letter, said:

"Perhaps this letter may satisfy you; it is from Brother Corwine, my Presiding Elder. I left him a few days since. Before doing so, he gave me this, and requested me to call at your house on reaching the circuit, and assured me that in you I would find a friend and a brother."

"Feel perfectly at home, Brother Roberts," said the gentleman; "you shall find in me all that Brother Corwine promised you;" and then, excusing himself, he left the room.

The stranger's horse, which had been standing at the rack, was sent to the stable and properly cared for, and in a short time tea was announced; afterward family prayers were held, and then the company remained in the parlor until bed-time, spending the hours in pleasant and profitable conversation.

A history of the life of the young preacher was elicited by the family; the struggles through which he passed in entering the ministry were touchingly delineated, and anxiety expressed for success in the charge to which he was appointed.

The prejudices of the family had measurably yielded before the force of the devoted piety and sterling good sense so manifestly possessed by the guest. Nevertheless, there lingered a sense of injury to the circuit on the part of the Bishop, in sending to so important a charge a young and inexperienced man, who must be wholly inadequate to the necessities of the work.

After family prayers and breakfast, on the following morning, the young preacher retired to the woods for meditation and private prayer, but returned to the house in time to start to the church, which was not far distant. On approaching the church he found a large audience assembled, most of whom had stopped outside the house, awaiting the arrival of the preacher. He passed through the crowd, submitting to their curious gaze and their ill-suppressed wonder. He walked to the pulpit, and, kneeling down, earnestly invoked aid from the gread Head of the Church. Rising from his knees, he at once addressed himself to the work he had been sent to do. Among the last who came in were the brother and sister who had entertained him the previous night.

As he opened the service he could distinctly read upon the countenances of the people who sat before him the mingled emotions which were influencing them. Many had come to see and hear the new preacher, and to take account of his ability, and to compare him with his predecessor. "Who is he?" could not be answered, for nobody seemed to know him. "He does not look like he can preach; and, withal, he is so young."

But stop! He has read the opening hymn, and read it well; he leads the singing with a clear, musical voice; and his prayer has made its way to every willing heart, as, deep-toned, fervent, spiritual, it uprises to the mercy-seat, with its language of thanksgiving, and confession, and supplication for blessings large and full upon the congregation, the circuit, the labors of the newly-appointed pastor. Another of the songs of Zion, with a rich, beautiful chorus, has been sung, seemingly inviting and compelling all present to join in it. The text has been announced; the preacher is discussing his subject; he rises with his theme; an unction rests upon the pulpit, and reaches to the pew; a shout rolls over the assembly, and the old, the middle-aged, and the young are charmed and captivated.

To follow Edwin Roberts during the year, on the Morganfield Circuit, would afford real pleasure; to listen to him as the people are convinced by the force of his eloquent logic, or as he thunders upon them in his overpowering exhortations, or as he melts them with his pathos, or attracts them heavenward by the luster of his consistent piety—all accompanied by the demonstration and power of the Holy Spirit—would be a happiness, indeed. Everybody in the circuit loved Edwin Roberts. His ministry during the year was abundantly favored—nearly one hundred persons being converted.

The net increase in the Hopkinsville District was *seven hundred and eighty-eight* in the white membership, and *two hundred and six* in the colored.

The Greensburg District was the scene of many a hard conflict and of many a glorious triumph, this year. In this District, the Elizabeth Circuit—with Joseph D. Barnett, who had traveled it the previous year, and William D. Matting, as the preachers—sounds the initial note of triumph. The first quarterly-meeting was held in Elizabethtown, early in March, at which fifteen persons were added to the Church, and all along the year revivals crowned the labors of the preachers. In the Columbia Circuit, early in April, Elijah M. Bosley reported fifty additions. In the Greensburg Station, under the pastoral charge of George W. Taylor, the membership was quadrupled. In the Glasgow Circuit, James King and Alanson C. Dewitt had refreshing times. In the Bardstown Station, Hubbard H. Kavanaugh was eminently successful; while in the Salt River Circuit, William M. Grubbs and Jesse P. Murrell were instrumental in bringing many souls to Christ. The Lebanon Circuit, to which Matthew N. Lasley had been returned, continued to prosper under his faithful ministry; while at Burksville, Robinson E. Sidebottom and John C. C. Thompson gained many stars to deck the crown of their rejoicing. Edmund M. Johnson, the leader on the Litchfield Mission, saw the pleasure of the Lord prospering in his hands.

The net increase in the Greensburg District was *three hundred and seventy-one* white and *seventy-seven* colored members.

In the Barboursville District, the zealous and untiring Richard D. Neale was the leader. This District embraced six charges, and spread over the most rugged section of Kentucky, including the southeastern part of the State. The country was not only rough and mountainous, but sparsely settled.

Mr. Neale was a model man. He was just fifty years old, having been born in 1787. He was well formed for endurance, and possessed a fine constitution, while his snow-white hair hung loosely to his shoulders. With a countenance full of benignity, and a heart full of love for the cause of the Master, and with a burning zeal for the salvation of souls, he entered upon his work immediately after the Conference closed. His energy, which nothing could dampen, inspired the preachers of his District, and urged them on to the performance of duty.

William B. Landrum was sent to the Prestonsburg Circuit. On the last night of 1837 he commenced a meeting in Prestonsburg, at which two persons were converted. Encouraged by this success, he prosecuted his labors all around the circuit, until in every neighborhood the work of the Lord was revived.

On the Mount Pleasant Mission, the ministry of William M. Crawford was rich in blessing: nearly one hundred persons were added to the Church. Andrew Peace, on the Barboursville Mission, received into the Church about seventy members.

Albert H. Redford was the youngest preacher in the Barboursville District—indeed, the youngest in the Conference. He was appointed to the Manchester Mission. His field of labor included seventeen appointments, to be filled in three weeks, and extended from London, by the way of Manchester, to the North Fork of the Kentucky River. In entering upon his work the people received him kindly, though evidently with feelings of disappointment. On his first round he rode up to the house of a brother where preaching was expected that day. When he introduced himself as the new preacher, the old brother looked at him for a moment, and then said: "Well, jump down, my little sonny, and run into the house." The year he passed in this mission was a pleasant one, and the kindness of the people is still fondly remembered. His ministry met with but little success: only fifteen persons were added to the Church during the year.

The net increase in the Barboursville District was *one hundred and forty-two* white and *forty* colored members.

The winter months of the year had passed, but winter itself was tardy in yielding to gentle spring. At this time a young preacher was returning from a mountain mission, to visit his relations in Central Kentucky. He was riding a sorrel horse, and between the two there was a strong attachment; for together they had often endured hardships, and crossed deep and turbid streams. The rider was plainly dressed. A white blanket overcoat, which had been his only covering on many a cold and stormy night, was thrown around him, and there was nothing in his appearance to prepossess a stranger in his favor. He had just passed Mount Vernon, and was jogging along, slowly and alone, when he heard the sound of a horse's feet behind him. A stranger, riding at full speed, was overtaking him, and soon they were side by side.

The stranger was a young man, not older than the preacher, and neither had attained his majority.

He was elegantly dressed: his coat was of the finest texture and latest style; his vest was silk velvet, and his pantaloons the smoothest doeskin; his hat was silk, contrasting well with the white fur hat of the young preacher, and his polished boots covered a delicate foot; around his neck hung a gold chain, to which his watch was attached, and his horse—an elegant animal—was beautifully equipped.

"How are you, my boy?" was his salutation to the young preacher.

"Sorter middlin'," was the reply.

"Well, my boy, where do you live?" he inquired.

"In New Kaintuck" (for so the mountain region was called), the young preacher answered.

"What is your name?" was the next question.

"Fred Brenning, sir; and what mout be your name? ef I mout be so bold as to ax," rejoined the preacher.

"Mr. L——."

"Mity funny name, Mister. Do n't you think it is?"

"I do n't know; but now, Fred, tell me where you are going."

"I 'm gwine to the settlements of Old Kaintuck."

"Will you not get lost?"

"I reckon not," said the preacher. "The big road I 'm in goes there, and I 'll jest foller it."

"But sometimes the road forks. How would you know which way to go?"

"Forks! What 's that?"

"A road forks when another road shoots off from the main road, thus"—and he held up his hands so as to explain what he meant by the forks of a road.

"Yes, I see," said the preacher.

"Well, what will you do when you come to where the road forks?"

"You know, a piece of plank is nailed to a tree, p'inting the way; well, I'll go the way the plank p'ints."

"But if there are two pieces of plank, pointing in different directions, how, then, do you do?"

"I axes at the blacksmith-shop."

"Can you spell, Fred?"

"Spell? I guess I can."

"Spell 'crucifix.'"

"K-r-u-s-e-fe-i-k-s."

"That's right!" and he slapped the preacher on the shoulder. "You are a smart boy—"

"That's jest what dad allers sed; he sed I was smarter 'n enny on his children."

"Are there any other children besides you, Fred?"

"*Enny besides me!* I'd say there is—lots of 'em—three gals and five boys. *Dad says I 'm smarter 'n enny on 'em.*"

"I have no doubt that you are the smartest."

"Mr. L——, I'd like to ax you a question."

"What is it?"

"Can you spell?"

"O yes, I am a linguist."

"Spell 'baker,' 'brier,' 'cider,' 'crazy,' 'cruel.'"

He spelled each word correctly, as requested.

"Can you read, Mr. L——?"

"O certainly. I said I am a *linguist.*"

"Have you ever ben clean through the spellin'-book?"

"To be sure I have."

"You 've ben to the picturs, then?"

"Yes."

"Well, now, tell me, was n't you sorry for that little feller that was stealin' apples; you know the old feller tried to skeer him with grass, but he could n't come it; but when he picked up the dorniks he fotched him down—did n't he, Mr. L——?"

"Yes."

"Then, you know about that gal what was carryin' a ceder-pail of milk on her head, and was gwine to buy her a green gown, and the pail fell and spilt the milk—was n't you sorry for her, Mr. L——?"

"The most latent sympathies of my heart have always been awakened in her behalf."

"Mr. L——, you said awhile ago you was a thing —what was it?"

"I do not know to what you refer. What do you mean?"

"The thing you sed you was, twice."

"I have no idea to what you allude, Fred. O yes, now I know—a linguist."

"Yes, yes, a linguist. Now, tell me, who is he?"

"A Latin and Greek scholar."

"O my! Say some Latin for me."

"'*Deus creavit cœlum et terram intra sex dies. Primo die fecit firmamentum.*'"

"Can't I say that?"

"I reckon not; none but educated gentlemen can do so."

"Well, I 'm edicated. Dad allers sed I had better book larnin' 'an enny of his children."

"If you think you can repeat what I have said, suppose you try it"—Mr. L—— repeating it himself.

"'Deus coravit selorum terrorum sexes dise. Permo fermentum.'"

"Pretty well done, Fred. Try it again."

Again and again the trial was made, but with only the same success.

"Won't you say that other feller what you was?" asked the preacher.

"What do you mean?"

"You called him Greek."

"O yes. *'Apodos O katarate ta porthmia. Boa ei touto soi edion, O Charon.'*"

"Who ever heered the like? You must have mity good book larnin'."

"Yes, Fred, I am well educated."

"I'd like to ax you where you live, ef you would n't mind tellin'."

"My home is in Garrard county, in this State. It is one of the richest and best counties. My father is a gentleman of wealth, and my family one of the most influential."

"I reckoned that," said the preacher, "ef I know the meanin' of your big words. When will you get home?"

"This evening, about dark."

"Then, I 'll go home with you, and stay all night."

"No, no, you can't; there will be no place for you to sleep."

"I can sleep with you."

"Not so; my brother and I sleep together."

"Well, I can sleep in the middle."

The young gentleman peremptorily declined to take the uncouth and green mountain youth home with him, but scarcely knew how to get rid of him. They rode some distance without speaking, when the preacher said:

"How would you like to trade your overcoat for mine?"

"What boot will you give me?"

"A quarter of a dollar."

"We can't trade. My overcoat is a fine one, and cost ten times as much as yours."

"Mine is the warmest," answered the preacher.

In the midst of this pleasant conversation a rock-away appeared in front of them, in which sat a solitary traveler. As the distance between him and them was shortened, he was recognized by the preacher. It was Napoleon B. Lewis, who in turn discovered in one of the horsemen his young friend, Brenning.

"How are you, Brother Brenning?"

"How are you, Brother Lewis?"

"Now, tell me," said Mr. Lewis, "how you are getting along in your mission-field. How do you like the mountains? How are my friends in that country? How is Col. L——* and family? and where are you going?"

---

*Col. L——, to whom he alluded, was a prominent politician in the mountains. He was a special friend of Mr. Lewis, and had shown him great kindness. He was also a friend of the young preacher.

Before answering these questions Mr. L—— was introduced to Mr. Lewis by young Brenning as the nephew of the gentleman about whom and family such special inquiry had been made.

The questions were then answered as rapidly as possible, when the friends separated.

The two young men resumed their journey; but more than a mile was traveled before a word was spoken by either of them. The silence, which had become quite painful, was at length broken by Mr. L——:

"Did I understand from Mr. Lewis that you are a Methodist preacher and a missionary in the mountain region of the State?"

"I am a Methodist preacher and a missionary in the mountain region of the State."

"I think, Mr. Brenning, that you have treated me very unkindly in not telling me who you were when I first came up with you. It would have saved me from the mortification that I now must necessarily endure. I mistook you for a green mountain youth, and concluded that I would have some fun at your expense."

"And I took you for a pert young man," replied the preacher, "whose eye-teeth had not been cut, and I deemed it a kindness to cut them. I thought, too, there might be some fun, *but not at my expense.* Besides, your honored uncle, in the mountains, has shown me much kindness, and I knew of no other way of paying the debt of gratitude I owe him than by teaching his nephew a lesson that would not be easily forgotten."

"I would be glad for you to go home with me, and stay all night, Mr. Brenning."

"There is no place for me to sleep."

"You can sleep with me."

"I thought your brother sleeps with you."

"Ay, but you can sleep in the middle."

The preacher thanked him for the invitation, but declined going, as it would take him several miles out of his way. They were now within a short distance of the Crab Orchard, where they were to separate.

"My young friend," said Brenning, "we have been incidentally thrown together. We are both in the rosy morn of life, and many years may lie between us and the grave, or we may die early. The first step that a young man takes in life should be a step toward the cross. What preparation have you made for the hereafter?"

"None whatever," was the reply. "I believe in the truth of the Christian religion, and certainly intend to be a Christian; but I am young, and the world offers me many inducements to pursue its pleasures for awhile. At some future time I will turn my thoughts to this subject, and become a follower of Christ."

"So thought Felix, when he trembled under the preaching of an apostle, and answered, 'Go thy way for this time; when I have a convenient season, I will call for thee.' The convenient season, so far as we know, never came. You have no future time; the present alone is yours. You may improve the time you have, or, if unimproved, there may be to you no future when you may turn to God. Our Heavenly Father says, 'My son, give me thine heart,' and 'Seek ye first the kingdom of God and his righteousness.' Seek God, give him your heart, and in his service you will find joys that will never fade, exceeding far all that the world, with its myriad fleeting pleasures, can offer you."

The young stranger made no reply. Tears stole gently down his fair face, and his lips quivered with emotion.

"Will you be a Christian?" continued Brenning. "Without religion there is no true happiness in this life, no solace in a dying-hour, and no felicity beyond the grave. *Will you be a Christian?*" he repeated, with emphasis. "Jesus died to save you. Will you not love him?"

The young man took the preacher's hand, and said:

"Mr. Brenning, I am glad that I met with you, and thank you most sincerely for your good advice. I will try and do as you have requested. I am satisfied that there is no other path to happiness but the one you admonish me to pursue. Yours is the better life. Will you pray for me?"

As he uttered these words the tears flowed more freely down his face. The young travelers then bade each other farewell. Perhaps good seed were sown.

While Methodism was enjoying such splendid triumphs in the Kentucky Conference, there was in that portion of the State lying in Jackson's Purchase a decrease of sixty white and four colored members. The Wadesboro Circuit, under the ministry of Johnson Lewis, shows a small increase, but in the Hickman and Paducah Circuits a falling off is reported.

The increase in the Kentucky Conference was *two thousand eight hundred and seventy-four* white and *one thousand and eighty-four* colored members. After deducting the decrease in Jackson's Purchase, it leaves a net increase of *two thousand eight hundred and fourteen* white and *one thousand and seventy-nine* colored members.

CHAPTER VII.

FROM THE SESSION OF THE KENTUCKY CONFERENCE OF 1838 TO THE CONFERENCE OF 1839.

Now, then, the ceaseless shower
  Of gospel blessings send,
And let the soul-converting power
  Thy ministers attend.
On multitudes confer
  The heart-renewing love,
And by the joy of grace prepare
  For fuller joys above.

THE session of the Kentucky Conference of 1838 met in Danville, October 17. Bishops Waugh and Morris were both present.

Bishop Waugh opened the Conference by reading a portion of God's word. Singing and prayer followed, after which the Bishop addressed the Conference in reference to the work in which they were engaged.

Beverly Waugh was born in Fairfax county, Virginia, October 25, 1789. When fifteen years of age he became a member of the Methodist Episcopal Church, and was converted about the same time. The impression that it was his duty to preach the gospel of Christ was strong and abiding, and in 1809 he entered the Baltimore Conference, under the conviction that if he pursued any other calling the salvation of his soul would be imperiled.

His first appointment was to the Stafford and Fredericksburg Circuit, lying in his native State, as junior preacher. In 1810 he was placed in charge of the Greenbrier Circuit. At the Conference of 1811 he was stationed in Washington City, and in 1812 he was appointed to Stephensburg. From Stephensburg we follow him to the city of Baltimore, and from thence to the Montgomery Circuit, where he labored for two years. In 1816 he traveled on the Berkeley Circuit. In 1817 we find him again in Washington City, and in 1818 in Baltimore. In 1819 and 1820 he had charge of Fell's Point, Baltimore, and in 1821 and 1822 of Georgetown, in the District of Columbia. Frederick, Maryland, was the field of his ministry in 1823 and 1824. At the Conference of 1825 he was returned to Baltimore City Mission, where he remained two years, and in 1827 his appointment was East Baltimore. He was elected Assistant Book Agent in 1828, and in 1832 the principal Book Agent. During the eight years of his agency his name appeared in the Minutes of the New York Conference, his election consituting him a member of that body, as the rule then was. In 1836 he was elected to the office of Bishop, to the duties of which he was well adapted.

When Bishop Waugh visited Kentucky, in 1838, he was unknown to the members of the Conference, with the exception of those who had met him at the General Conference. His urbanity and his fine social qualities soon introduced him to the entire body, while his zeal and devotion to the cause of God endeared him to every heart. He presided with ease and dignity.

George McNelly was elected Secretary, and Isaac Collard Assistant Secretary.

The Committee on Public Worship consisted of John James and Edward Stevenson. John Christian Harrison, Henry N. Vandyke, and John Beatty, were appointed Stewards of the Conference.

Committees were appointed as follows: William Gunn and Thomas Waring, on Memoirs; Henry E. Pilcher, Thomas N. Ralston, and William B. Landrum, on "the business of the Eastern Book Concern;" Richard Tydings, Edward Stevenson, and Hubbard H. Kavanaugh, on "the affairs of Augusta College;" Peter Taylor, William Holman, and Robert Y. McReynolds, on "necessitous cases;" and Hubbard H. Kavanaugh, Edward Stevenson, Richard Tydings, William Holman, and George W. Taylor, to prepare "a pastoral address."

Before the close of the morning session Bishop Morris was invited to take the chair. No Bishop in the Church was so well known in Kentucky as Thomas A. Morris. Several years of his ministry were passed in the State, where he labored with fidelity and success.*

At the time Bishop Morris took the chair the Conference was engaged in the examination of the character of elders. The remainder of the morning

* For a sketch of Bishop Morris, see "Methodism in Kentucky," vol. iii., pp. 136–141.

session was occupied by this question and the adoption of a resolution, that "Friday, the 19th inst., be observed by the Conference as a day of fasting and prayer for the continued prosperity of the work of God within our bounds;" and "that the Christian community be invited to participate in this religious service."

During the remainder of the session the two Bishops occupied the chair alternately.

At the previous Conference Mr. Bascom was appointed to preach, at this session, a sermon on the Ministry. Mr. Tomlinson, at the same time, was appointed to deliver an address on Education, and Mr. Stamper a sermon on Missions.

Mr. Bascom was not present during the session of the Conference, and Mr. Kavanaugh was requested to preach the sermon on the Ministry. He, however, declined the honor, the allotted time being too short to enable him, in connection with other duties, to prepare the sermon.

The address on Education was delivered on Saturday, October 20. It was a masterly effort. For more than an hour the distinguished speaker held an immense concourse in rapt silence by his graphic treatment of the inspiring theme. On the following Tuesday the Conference requested Mr. Tomlinson to furnish a copy of his address for publication in the *Western Christian Advocate.*

The sermon on Missions, preached by Jonathan Stamper, was alike worthy of the preacher and the occasion. The revolt of the world from its rightful Sovereign, its redemption through the sufferings, death, and mediation of Jesus Christ, its conversion to God, and the final salvation of the pure and holy in heaven, were the topics on which the preacher dwelt.

God had created man holy. All the lineaments of his moral nature resembled those of his Creator. Pure, even as God is pure, he came forth from his hands, wearing his likeness and image. Placed in Eden, where every source of happiness was to be found, the expectation was a reasonable one that a corresponding obedience would mark his conduct. The insidious tempter invaded this pleasant retreat, and our globe became a prodigal in the family of worlds. Our progenitors lifted the arm of rebellion against Jehovah, and thus forfeited all claim to his favor, and all right to the paradise amid whose bowers they had found such delight. Eden had been the home of Adam; he had wandered along the banks of the river that watered its beautiful grounds; he had drunk from the purling streams that broke forth from granite lips; he had gathered from trees always pendent with delicious fruit; he had mingled with the inferior creation as their lord and sovereign; he had talked with angels, conversed with Jehovah, and reposed amid the shades of paradise, beneath the deep blue sky, when the sheen of the silvery moon and the flickering lights of the starry hosts told of a brighter world; but now he must bid adieu to all these scenes of loveliness, and go out into a world made desolate by his transgression. "Therefore the Lord God sent him forth from the garden of Eden, to till the ground from whence he was taken. *So he drove out the man:* and he placed at the east of the garden of Eden cherubims, and a flaming sword which turned every way, to keep the way of the tree of life."

Hitherto man had shown no disposition to measure arms with God; perhaps, until now he had not awakened to a consciousness of his true condition. God had, however, commanded him to leave Eden; and thoughts of its beautiful bowers, its shady groves, its crystal waters, its golden fruits, and, above all, the companionship of his Maker, rush upon his fevered brain, and he refuses to obey the command, and God *drives* him out. Perhaps, in the deep solitude into which he is *driven* he may find some relief from the bitter anguish which is crushing his guilty soul. Where shall he look for consolation? Will the serpent, whose persuasions had led to the fearful catastrophe, offer a solace? He no longer stands erect, nor speaks, as in the garden, but, crawling in the dust, responds in angry hisses, and spits his venom in the face of avenging Heaven. His wife—the woman whom God had given him—no more, with genial smile and confiding trust, leans on his stalwart arm and whispers words of cheer, but, doomed to sorrow, he sees written upon her once sweet face traces of grief and the curse of God. He turns to the animal creation, and they, no longer docile, with one accord attack him with savage cruelty, or flee from him as from a deadly foe. The earth on which he treads, just now so beautiful, is cursed, and thorns and thistles spring up in every direction. He thinks of the fruitage of Eden, that so often had chased away hunger, and which had been procured without an effort; but now he must eat of the herb of the field, and earn his bread by the sweat of his brow. As he treads upon the dust the stern decree is ever before him: "Dust thou art, and unto dust shalt thou return." He looks above, and the heavens, once so bright, are clad with the garniture of death: from the horizon to the zenith black and angry clouds spread over all the sky, while forked lightnings flash and muttering thunders peal their deafening notes. But will not the grave terminate these sorrows? No; on him is the stamp of immortality, and he cannot be blotted from existence. He looks beyond, and no voice beckons him to the skies, but an eternal night, in realms of woe, awaits him. Is he the only sufferer? Looking down the stream of time, he beholds the unborn millions of his hapless progeny involved in the common ruin with himself. Eden is yet in sight, and angels, with folded wings, are hovering over it. Once more he turns toward its pleasant shades, and fain would reënter the gate through which he had been *driven;* but there stand sentinels—the cherubim and flaming sword, placed by God himself, whose authority he dares not defy. Despair settles upon his guilty heart as he turns away; for all seems lost. But, listen! The Trinity in council has assembled and resolved on the world's recovery to God.

You would inquire into the cost of the world's redemption. We reply: "For God so loved the world that he gave his only-begotten Son, that whosoever believeth in him should not perish, but have everlasting life." The conception of the plan was the grandest that ever entered the Divine Mind. Its enunciation thrilled the heavenly legions with joy, and gladdened a world made desolate by sin.

'T was great to speak a world from naught,
'T was greater to redeem.

When announced in Eden, amid the ruins of the fall, that a redemptive scheme was provided for our race, man on earth and devils in hell were astonished; from lip to lip of the shining host, with electric flash, the inquiry passed, How can God be propitiated? and angels damned reëchoed through all the realms of night, How can God be propitiated? while, trembling and silent, our progenitors were regaled with the breezes of mercy, as their whisperings were heard amid the bowers of paradise.

Would you learn the cost of the world's redemption? See the types, and forms, and shadows, and sacrifices of the Old Testament economy; think of the immaculate Jesus—God's beloved Son—leaving the splendors of heaven, and coming down to earth to live, to suffer, and to die; think of Gethsemane—its tears, its groans, its agony; think of Calvary—its spotless Victim, his sufferings, and his death. For three dreadful hours anguish more intense than the universe had ever known is endured on the cross. The guilt and pollution of ages, past, present, and to come, are crushing his soul with all their ponderous weight. "My God, my God, why hast thou forsaken me?" falls with inexpressible sadness from his dying lips. O God, was he not thy Son? and where are thy thunderbolts? Wilt thou not come to his rescue? His Father's face is hid. "He treads the wine-press alone, and of the people there were none with him." Jehovah's arm, though omnipotent, must not interpose. Justice, stern and unpitying, with piercing eye and flaming tongue, demands the uttermost farthing. The celestial hosts stand aghast, angels droop their wings, and all the harps of heaven play mournful odes. The sun veils his face in the gloom of night, the earth trembles to its base, creation groans, and many of the graves around Jerusalem are unpeopled. O see the suffering Jesus! behold his pierced side, and on his dripping hands and on his bleeding heart read the cost of the world's redemption! The atonement is made, and God is reconciled. "It is finished!" falls from his expiring lips, and reaches heaven. The arms of a Father's love encircle a despairing world; once more angels peal their notes of joy and sweep their harps of gold; for a wandering and lost star has been restored to its orbit, a fallen planet has been recovered, a world has been redeemed, and the gospel is to be preached to all the nations of the earth.

. . . .

But has the gospel succeeded in its mission? The progress of Christianity in the apostolic age of the Church excites our wonder and challenges our admiration. "Beginning at Jerusalem," as on the wings of the wind, the gospel spread in every direction. The persecution in which Stephen lost his life resulted in the dispersion of the followers of Christ, carrying with them in their exile lives pure and spotless, as well as the unadulterated doctrines of the word of God. Added to this, the apostles, with a zeal commensurate with the woes of mankind, went everywhere, preaching the gospel of the kingdom. Not only were Judea, and Samaria, and Perea, and Galilee to listen to the story of the cross, but beyond the boundaries of Palestine the Church was commissioned to win trophies to the Redeemer. The cities and villages of the Holy Land heard the joyful sound, and all along the waters of the Mediterranean, from Berytus to Anthedon, converts were made from Judaism to Christianity. Strangers in strange lands, we find the followers of Christ scattered throughout Pontus, Galatia, Bithynia, and Cappadocia, embracing all the country between Mount Taurus and the Euxine Sea; while in the western part of Asia Minor, the cities of Laodicea, Philadelphia, Ephesus, Sardis, Smyrna, Thyatira, and Pergamos, Churches were planted and prayers and praises offered to God. Passing into Greece, Corinth bows to the scepter of Christ; while on the rivulets of Ilissus and Cephisus, in its proud capital, on Mars' Hill, in the presence of the Areopagus, and in sight of the Parthenon, and surrounded by the temples of Theseus, and of Bacchus, and of Jupiter Olympus, and the temple of Victory, and the grotto of Apollo and Pan, and hard by the prison where Socrates had been confined, and from which he was led to his tragic fate—there Paul the apostle proclaimed the gospel of Christ. Invading the Roman Empire, the apostles planted the standard of the cross on the banks of the Tiber, and found votaries to the Christian faith not only in the capital of Italy, but in the imperial household. From Jerusalem round about to Illyricum, on the eastern coast of the Adriatic Gulf, St. Paul preached the gospel. It was carried to the Parthian Empire by Peter, to Arabia by Paul and Bartholomew, and by Thomas into India. The Evangelist Mark bore its truths into Alexandria, and from thence it was taken to Cyrene. From Rome it was carried to Carthage and to Proconsular Africa. It made its appearance in Gaul, in Germany, in Britain, and in Spain. Wherever it went pagan temples were closed, oracles were struck dumb, idols were overthrown, and sinners recovered from the grasp of Satan, and placed as jewels in the crown of Christ. Like scattered lights along the sky, or like islands of beauty amid surrounding darkness, at this early period the influence of Christianity was felt and its blessings dispensed throughout the civilized world.

Mr. Stamper traced the history of the Church—its conflicts and its triumphs in the Roman Empire—through the dark ages, until Wiclif appeared, "standing out in solitary grandeur—a lone star on the brow of a long and gloomy night." He told of Luther, and Melanchthon, and Zwingle, of the full-orbed splendor of the Reformation that set all Germany ablaze, and sent its brilliant light beyond the German Confederation; the decline of religion after the death of Luther; the great revival in England,

Ireland, and Wales, under the Wesleys and Whitefield, and the conquests of the Church in the New World.

Contemplating the future of the Church, the preacher was full of hope. The Macedonian cry is heard from every direction, "Come over and help us!" Almost every nation is opening wide its doors for the reception of the gospel. The enemies of the cross, it is true, are not asleep. Paganism, in giant proportions, in the presence of her temples and her gods, has renewed her oath of eternal enmity to Christ; infidelity, with brazen front, appears in the field of battle; ritualism and sacramentalism, wearing their masquerade, are anxious to revive their waning heritage; philosophy and vain deceit are arming for the struggle; and idolatrous worship everywhere is making bare its arm against the advancing glories of the Church. Christianity, too, is awake. Fresh from conquered fields, and holding in its hands trophies gathered from every clime, with the memory of a thousand victories to inspire afresh its ardor, it enters upon the final contest. Under the command of Him who never lost a battle, before its moving columns the serried legions of sin are broken, and upon the ramparts of the enemy its ensign floats to the breeze. On, on, it presses, with unbroken front, bearing down every thing that opposes its march, its enemies bowing to its scepter, or following as captives its triumphal advance. Its success will be complete; nothing shall arrest its progress.

The preacher then called upon the Conference

and the Church to bear their part in this glorious struggle; that God would not allow them to be inactive. The world's conversion will be effected, he said, whether we assist or not; the work will go on. Shall we stand with folded arms while others are pressing to the rescue? "Curse ye Meroz, curse ye bitterly the inhabitants thereof." For what? What has Meroz done? "Because they came not to the help of the Lord, to the help of the Lord against the mighty."

The Bishop appointed Mr. Bascom to preach on Education, at the ensuing Conference, Mr. Kavanaugh on the Ministry, and Mr. Stevenson on Missions.

Bishop Waugh laid before the Conference the following resolution from the New England Conference, which he prefaced by saying that he did not admit the authority of an Annual Conference to make him the bearer of any resolution which was, in his judgment, not only not promotive of the interests of the Church at large, but injurious to its union and prosperity; but that, in the present case, as a matter of courtesy, he would present the resolution, as requested by the New England Conference, especially as he understood that his colleagues would pursue the same course. He also said that in principle and habit he was opposed to slavery, nor was he less decidedly and unequivocally opposed to Abolitionism. In submitting the resolution, he expressed the belief that its tendency was revolutionary and injurious:

"*Resolved*, That the New England Annual Conference recommend to the next General Conference, to be holden in the city of Baltimore, May, 1840, to alter our general rule on the subject of slavery, so that it shall read as follows: 'The buying, or selling, or holding men, women, or children as slaves, under any circumstances, or giving them away, unless on purpose to free them.'"

The Conference unanimously disapproved of the resolution.

The Bishop very plainly foresaw the evil tendency and disastrous results of the policy of Abolitionists; and hence, in submitting the resolution, he properly and promptly rebuked the New England Conference. He not only thought that the prosperity of the Church would be retarded by the officious intermeddling of this Conference with an institution for the existence of which New England, and not the South, was responsible, but he expressed the belief that the *union* of the Church would be imperiled.

The institution of slavery, as it existed in the South-western and Southern States—the mildest form the world had ever known—had been recognized on the part of the Church in the North as well as in the South, not only by Conference resolutions, but by the enactments of the General Conference. The restless and incendiary spirit of Abolitionism resolved that though the Church should be dismembered and broken into fragments, and the nation drenched in blood, it would persist in its policy so long as the institution existed. Not only was the harmony of the Church in the slave-holding States disturbed by those ecclesiastical agitators, but the quiet of some of the Northern Conferences was also greatly marred.

A resolution was adopted, "approving of the publication, in connection with the Western Book Concern, of the *Christian Apologist*, under the editorial supervision of the Rev. William Nast," and pledging the Conference, as far as practicable, to promote its circulation, especially among the German population in the State.

The tide of emigration from Germany had set in, and thousands were landing on our shores. While some of them were truly religious, the great majority of them were without any well-defined religious faith. The Reformation of the sixteenth century had its origin in Germany, through the instrumentality of Martin Luther, a young priest. Its splendor was soon full-orbed, but the blaze of its glory had died away, and Germany no longer held the place it once occupied on the map of Christian nations.

On reaching America these foreigners were met by Romish priests, who placed in their hands a literature that would not only poison their minds and lead them farther away from God, but would effectually close their hearts against the truth forever. The duty of Protestant Christians was obvious, and the Methodist Church—the most popular and influential Church in the United States—would be untrue to its mission if it should not lead in the effort to save the Teutonic population.

Quite a number of Germans had selected the city

of Louisville as their home, and the obligation of the Kentucky Conference to supply them with all the facilities within their power was apparent. No better method suggested itself than to place in their hands a religious weekly paper, which, by its influence and teachings, would bring them to Christ.

Mr. Nast was a German, an accomplished gentleman, a ripe scholar, and, above all, a devoted Christian. He knew the character of his countrymen, and perhaps no other man in the Methodist Church was better qualified to exert a salutary influence over this people.

In a previous chapter we referred to the impulse given to the cause of Missions by the sermon of Bishop Andrew, preached in Shelbyville in 1835. Since then the Church occupied a more elevated plane, and the collections had annually improved, reaching this year the handsome sum of $5,539.80. Of this amount William Holman collected from the Lexington Station $174, John Carr Harrison $112, from Versailles, and John Beatty, from Georgetown, $109.25. In the Augusta District, the Millersburg Circuit sent to the Conference, by Carlisle Babbitt, $500—the largest amount contributed by any charge—while its neighbor, the Paris Circuit (which was left to be supplied), paid over $321.22. Samuel Veach collected, in the Minerva Circuit, $200.; Hiram Baker, in the Germantown Circuit, $117; and John Waring $116.50, in the Greensburg Circuit. The largest amount collected in the Harrodsburg District was $190.25, and was sent from Mount Sterling by Joseph Marsee. Thomas Rankin, from

Winchester Circuit, collected $148.25, and Absalom Woolliscroft $130.50, from Madison. In the Louisville District, the Hardinsburg Circuit sent, by Daniel S. Barksdale, $200; Richard Tydings collected, from the Fourth-street Station, in Louisville, $156; and George W. Brush $118, from Brook-street. The Jefferson Circuit, where Richard Deering had charge, contributed $150.62½, while Science Hill Female Academy, in Shelbyville, sent $120. Hopkinsville Circuit, in Hopkinsville District, through Gilby Kelly, the pastor, sent to the Conference $101. In the Greensburg District, Joseph D. Barnett collected, in the Elizabeth Circuit, $411; William M. Grubbs, in the Salt River Circuit, $245.75; James King, in the Glasgow Circuit, $201; Matthew N. Lasley, in the Lebanon Circuit, $197.75; Elijah M. Bosley, in the Columbia Circuit, $173.50; Hubbard H. Kavanaugh, in Bardstown, $158.50; and George W. Taylor, in Greensburg, $102.

We have mentioned only the charges in which one hundred dollars or more was contributed to this noble cause. In adding the entire amount received, including the sums under one hundred dollars, we find the contribution by Lexington District to be $173.90; Maysville District, $1,421.59½; Harrodsburg District, $708; Louisville District, $939.37; Hopkinsville District, $281; Greensburg District, $1,638.50; Barboursville District, $77.43½. Total, $5,539.80.

Four thousand nine hundred and five dollars and sixty-nine cents was contributed toward the support of the superannuated preachers, and the widows and orphans of preachers, and to make up the deficiencies of those who had not obtained their regular allowance on the circuits.

Allen Sears, George W. Simcoe, Peter O. Meeks, Valentine C. Holding, Stephen A. Rathbun, Elihu Green, Peter Duncan, David H. Davis, William H. Anderson, Elkanah Johnson, and Nathanael H. Lee, were admitted on trial.

Of those who had entered the Conference the previous year, Wright Merrick and Jesse P. Murrell asked to be discontinued on account of ill health.

Henry McDaniel, Lorenzo D. Parker, Thomas Lasley, Foster H. Blades, Silas Lee, Hiram Baker, William Helm, and Milton Jamieson, located.

Thomas H. Gibbons had died during the year.* By a resolution of the Conference, Hubbard H. Kavanaugh was requested to preach a sermon in his memory.

We have in the Conference eight Districts, instead of seven, as the year before. Isaac Collard, who had traveled the Logan Circuit, was placed in charge of the Augusta District. Thomas W. Chandler was changed from the Augusta to the Covington District. Jonathan Stamper, whose previous field of labor was the Greensburg District, was sent to the Shelbyville District. John James, whose term of office had expired on the Harrodsburg District, became the leader in the Bowling Green District. George W. Taylor was changed from the Greensburg Circuit to the Harrodsburg District; while

*A sketch of Thomas H. Gibbons may be found in the "History of Methodism in Kentucky."

Benjamin T. Crouch, William Gunn, and Richard D. Neale, were returned to the fields they had occupied the previous year.

In looking over the appointments, we find William Holman returned to Lexington, Thomas N. Ralston to Maysville, Samuel Veach to Minerva, Carlisle Babbitt to Millersburg, John Waring to Greenupsburg, Joseph Marsee to Mount Sterling, John W. Riggin to Sharpsburg, Edward Stevenson to Danville and Harrodsburg, Richard Tydings to Fourth-street in Louisville, George W. Brush to Brook-street, Robert G. Gardner to Madisonville, Edwin Roberts to Morganfield, James King to Glasgow, and William M. Grubbs to Salt River. The preachers, with these exceptions, were changed in their appointments.

The Conference, throughout, was pleasant and harmonious, and the preaching was of a high order. Bishop Waugh, although a stranger, won upon the hearts of the preachers and the community, and Bishop Morris left Danville with increased popularity.

The pulpit in the Methodist Church was occupied, on Sunday, at eleven o'clock by Bishop Waugh, and at three o'clock by Bishop Morris. Both sermons were extraordinary. That of Bishop Waugh was addressed to the preachers, while Bishop Morris preached to the people. For one hour and fifteen minutes the former, with a power we have seldom witnessed, stirred the hearts of the preachers, urging them, by virtue of their high calling, of their responsibility to God, and of the peril of the multitudes exposed to Jehovah's wrath and journeying to the grave and to hell, to be faithful embassadors for Jesus Christ. Neither sunshine nor storm, heat nor cold, the applause of the people nor the persecutions of the world, must obstruct the path of duty. With the one purpose of doing good, he exhorted them to greater earnestness and fidelity in the work to which God had called them.

The sermon of Bishop Morris occupied about thirty minutes. His subject was the nature and importance of conversion, and it fell like the gentle dews of heaven upon the hearts of the large and attentive assembly.

The missionary meeting, held in the Presbyterian Church on Saturday evening, was a decided success. The principal speaker was Mr. Kavanaugh. The collection was a good one.

Several preachers, on their way to the Conference at Danville, stopped for dinner at a plain country house, between Salvisa and Harrodsburg. Benjamin T. Crouch was among them. The gentleman and his wife both gave them a kind reception, and entertained them with the hospitality for which the people of Kentucky have always been celebrated. Religion was the theme of conversation at the table, among the preachers, and their interchange of sentiment was listened to with silent but rapt attention by the several members of the family. Immediately on leaving the table the guests were invited to have prayers, after which the gentleman went to the stable for their horses. Before he returned to the house Mr. Crouch said he would like to know to what

Church, if any, the family belonged. One of the preachers suggested that they were Presbyterians, another that they were Baptists, and a third that they were Campbellites, while a fourth expressed the belief that they were members of the Methodist Church. A young preacher present, who had given no opinion, was asked by Mr. Crouch to tell what he thought.

"Their family Bible," he replied, "will give you the information you wish."

"How so?" asked Mr. Crouch, at the same time handing the Bible to the young preacher from the small table by which he was sitting.

The young preacher replied: "In reading the Bible, the portion of it which indicates the denominational preference of a family will be more soiled than the other parts. For example: if a man be a Campbellite, the second chapter of The Acts of the Apostles will show his religious tendency; if he be a Presbyterian, the ninth chapter of Romans is his favorite; if he be a Free-will Baptist, the damaged appearance of the eighth chapter of Acts and the sixth of Romans betrays his preference; if he be a Calvinistic Baptist, to these two chapters he adds the ninth of Romans."

"But if he be a Methodist," said Mr. Crouch, "what then?"

"If he be a Methodist," said the young preacher, "the Bible has been read regularly from Genesis to Revelation."

"Now tell us," said Mr. Crouch, "to what Church this family belongs."

The Bible was opened at the several places specified, and, after a brief examination, the young man said: "The eighth chapter of Acts and the sixth and ninth of Romans are more defaced than any other parts; the gentleman who lives here is a Hard-shell Baptist."

A moment later the host himself appeared at the door, when Mr. Crouch inquired of him, "To what Church do you and your family belong?"

"We are *Iron-jacket Baptists*," he replied. The interpretation was correct.

The extensive revivals with which the Church in Kentucky had been blessed during the two years which had just closed more than repaired the losses previously reported. The year, however, on which these cavaliers are now entering will give additional luster to their arms.

The first note of triumph, after the close of the Conference, is heard from the Mount Sterling Circuit, in the Lexington District. Joseph Marsee, who had been successful in that charge the previous year, was returned to the same field. He had scarcely entered upon the labors of his favored charge when the good work began afresh, and within a few weeks ninety-nine persons were added to the Church.

Although there were "times of refreshing" during the winter, in other portions of the same District, yet there was no general revival until the opening of spring. Albert Kelly had charge of the Burlington Circuit, with Absalom Woolliscroft—who sustained a supernumerary relation—as his colleague.

On the 17th of May they reported two hundred accessions to the Church, up to that time. A little later in the year Jeremiah Strother—a popular and useful local preacher—reported ninety conversions in the Carrollton Circuit, to which Thomas Hall had been sent.

The first revival reported from the Augusta District was in the Fleming Circuit, under the ministry of Peter O. Meeks, a young man of fine culture, of more than ordinary promise, and of deep piety. Although the work of grace in that charge was not extensive, yet profitable meetings were held all over the circuit, and up to the first of June thirty-three persons had joined the Church. The Germantown Circuit, under the ministry of John Nevius and Stephen A. Rathbun, continued to prosper, while Josiah Whitaker was instrumental in doing much good in the Lewis Circuit. The "pleasure of the Lord prospered in the hands" of the faithful Jedidiah Foster, in the Little Sandy Circuit; while the vigilant and earnest James C. Crow, on the Highland Circuit, was eminently successful in winning souls to Christ.

In the Covington District, Robert Y. McReynolds reported a gracious revival in Newport, as early as the 14th of December, at which twenty-two persons joined the Church. The interest continued all the winter, during which time sixty-six persons became the professed followers of Christ. In most of the charges in this District a decrease is reported for this year; yet, through a faithful ministry, hundreds were brought to Christ.

For three years Benjamin T. Crouch had been the leader on the Louisville District. No cavalier in the service had been more faithful, and none held a warmer place in the affections of either his brother soldiers or the people he served. In the city of Louisville, the previous year, under the ministry of George W. Brush and Richard Tydings, hundreds had been brought into the fold of Christ. Other portions of this District, as we have seen in the preceding chapter, had been favored with revivals of religion. The present year, however, in the power and extent of the work, would surpass any of the years that had gone before.

In other parts of the State the ministry of John Newland Maffitt had been greatly blessed. Indeed, wherever he had labored sinners had been awakened and penitents converted to God; in every community where he had unfurled the banner of the cross many had sought a shelter beneath its crimsoned folds. Immediately after the Conference closed Mr. Tydings invited him to Louisville, to assist him in a meeting in Fourth-street Church. He continued in Louisville several months, preaching the gospel with the fidelity and zeal for which he was distinguished. As early as the 4th of January Mr. Tydings reports more than one hundred conversions under his ministry, and on the first of February W. M. Meriwether, in a letter to the *Christian Advocate*, announces that one hundred and seventy-eight persons had witnessed a good confession. On the 22d of February a characteristic letter was written by Richard Tydings, which appeared in the same paper of March 15. He wrote: "Say to the friends of Zion that the work of the Lord is still going on in this city. The whole city, from the center to the circumference, seems to be moved by the mighty influence of divine truth. The high, the low, the rich, the poor, are coming home to Christ, by scores and hundreds. Since the revival commenced, in November last, about three hundred and sixty white and one hundred and thirty colored have been received in the Fourth-street Station, in this city, and the glorious work is still going on. Such a work for the union, peace, and comfort of the Church, reclaiming backsliders, and the awakening and ingathering of penitent believing sinners into the fold of Christ, I think I have never witnessed before during the thirty years of my labor in the traveling ministry. I have seen many glorious revivals, but this exceeds any I have ever known. Indeed, it seems to me that the long-looked-for millennium is about to blaze forth in all its splendor and glory; for the blessed work is going on in every direction around us." Such a letter is well worthy the grand old man who had given his life to this noble work. A few weeks later W. M. Meriwether writes again, and says: "Five hundred persons have been converted and added to the Church." The revival was not confined to the Fourth-street charge. The Brook-street Church, the prosperity of which exceeded that of the Fourth-street the previous year, still enjoyed the divine favor. The ministry of Mr. Brush was again very successful.

This extraordinary revival in the city of Louisville

was but the dawn of a better day for the entire District. In the Hardinsburg Circuit, in charge of Joseph D. Barnett, with Albert H. Redford as his colleague, a revival commenced at a Christmas meeting, held at Big Spring, at which nine persons professed religion. The year before Daniel S. Barksdale and Moses Levi were exceedingly successful in that field. Through their instrumentality hundreds were brought into the Church. After the Christmas meeting, besides an occasional conversion and addition to the Church, nothing remarkable occurred in the circuit during the winter. The congregations, however, were large and attentive. Whether the preachers held service during the week or on Sunday, many waited on the ministry of the word. The preacher in charge was distinguished no less for his zeal than for the skill he exhibited in the management of a meeting. Besides, he was much beloved by the Church and remarkably popular with all the people.

It was midsummer when indications of a general revival made their appearance. The third quarterly-meeting was held, and the Presiding Elder was present in the spirit of the Master. His preaching had in it more of fire than he had usually manifested. He brought encouraging reports from other portions of his District, which he said were "in a blaze of glory." His words inspired the Church with confidence. While he was preaching from the text, "Yea, doubtless, and I count all things but loss for the excellency of the knowledge of Christ Jesus my Lord," a halo of glory seemed to encircle the congregation. A mother in Israel shouted aloud the praises of God; three persons joined the Church. A few weeks later a meeting was held at Union Star, in Breckinridge county, at which forty-two persons "passed from death unto life." An old man who had lived more than four-score years was among the number. Revivals followed in quick succession in Hardinsburg, at Mount Zion, Rough Creek, Liberty Camp-ground, and at a camp-meeting held at the head of Rough Creek. The entire circuit was in a flame, and hundreds were entering upon a new and better life. At the camp-meeting at the head of Rough Creek scarcely a person who attended the meeting left it unblessed. On Monday afternoon it was proposed by Mr. Barnett that all persons who had been converted should file off to the right of the pulpit, and that those who had no evidence of acceptance with God should occupy the left. Only seven persons were to be seen on the left. They were young men, and asked an interest in the prayers of the Church. The junior preacher requested them to accompany him to an adjoining grove, where they knelt and prayed together, and six of them were powerfully converted, and the entire number joined the Church. Alberry L. Alderson was present at this camp-meeting, and preached with great power; and there, too, was John F. South, a young man of great promise, just entering the ministry, accompanied by his pious mother, whose prayers in the altar went up like sweet incense to God.

During the progress of these meetings four hundred and fifty-seven persons were converted, and more than that number added to the Church.

The morning on which the junior preacher left the circuit for Conference many friends met him at church, where they held a prayer-meeting, at which sixteen persons professed religion.

While such displays of divine power were manifested in the Hardinsburg Circuit, the Newcastle Circuit, in the upper portion of the District was sharing in the riches of grace. James D. Holding, one of the sweetest spirits that ever lived, and William H. Anderson, a young man of superior literary attainments, and of great promise to the pulpit, were the preachers. Mr. Holding had scarcely reached the meridian of life, and Mr. Anderson had just entered the ministry. Zealous in the prosecution of their Master's work, each strove to excel the other "in winning souls to Christ." Success crowned their efforts. Before the summer months had passed there was a revival of religion, which spread all over the circuit. On the 6th of September a meeting was commenced in Bedford, at which more than one hundred souls were converted, and one hundred and twelve joined the Church; and at the fourth quarterly-meeting, held at Funk's Camp-ground, thirty were converted and added to the Church. At the close of the year five hundred and twelve persons were gathered as so many witnesses to the valor, and energy, and faithfulness of these ministers of Christ.

James D. Holding was a remarkable man, and, if not distinguished for pulpit ability, was eminent for his piety and usefulness. He was born in Scott county, Kentucky, June 1, 1810. When in the fourteenth year of his age he was converted to God—the first-fruits of his mother's consistent religious life. He at once united himself with the Methodist Church, and, like Timothy, he grew rapidly in the knowledge and love of God. At an early age he was appointed to the responsible office of class-leader, which he filled with profit and acceptability. In August, 1834, he was licensed to preach, and admitted on trial into the Kentucky Conference the same year.

His first appointment was to the Shelby Circuit, as the colleague of William Gunn. In 1835 he was sent to the Kentucky Mission, in the mountain region of the State, and in 1836 to the Hartford Circuit, about four hundred miles from his former field of labor. At the Conference of 1837 we find him on the Cynthiana Circuit, in which he had been brought up, converted, and licensed to preach the gospel. In these several fields Mr. Holding had been greatly beloved and successful. Hundreds had been brought to Christ through his ministrations.

In the summer of 1837 we accompanied William Gunn, the Presiding Elder on the Louisville District, to the lower portion of his work, where we first met Mr. Holding. He was traveling on the Hartford Circuit, and his ministry there had been greatly blessed. He was tall and well formed for endurance, with dark complexion and dark eyes, and with a countenance full of benignity, which at once drew us toward him, or rather took us into his warm heart. In the autumn of 1838 he was sent to the Newcastle Circuit, where we have seen the success that followed him and his colleague.

The preaching of Mr. Holding was of the hortatory character. His sermons were chiefly appeals to sinners to be reconciled to God, and his exhortations were often powerful and overwhelming, reaching the hearts of his audience, and moving them to a higher and a better life. He literally went "forth *weeping*, bearing precious seed." Tears of grief, because men and women refused to be saved, flowed freely down his manly face. Everybody loved him.

In the Elizabeth Circuit, Alberry L. Alderson was efficient in his duties. Although no extraordinary revival occurred on his work, yet through his instrumentality many were brought to Christ. During his ministry on that circuit the Church at Grahamton was organized. It has had an active membership ever since, and from it the Conference has been supplied with several worthy and able preachers.

Amongst the preachers distinguished for their usefulness at this period, the name of Moses Levi deserves to be mentioned. He was born in Charleston, South Carolina, April 4, 1786. His parents were lineal descendants of Abraham, and claimed to be of the tribe of Levi, and brought up their son in the Jewish religion. He was converted in 1820. We have no advice as to the time he came to Kentucky. We first saw him at the Conference held in Shelbyville, in 1835, where he was a visitor, and where his sweet singing attracted much attention.

We learned that he resided in Louisville, where he was engaged in business as a merchant-tailor, and was useful as a local preacher. At the Conference of 1837 he was admitted on trial. Without the advantages of an English education, and, indeed, without being able to read, he passed a creditable examination before the committee to examine applicants for admission on trial—of which Mr. Bascom was chairman. He answered the questions submitted to him, on geography and history, with as much accuracy as though he had been a diligent student in these departments. Not a line of Blair's Rhetoric had ever been read to him, and yet his examination was highly creditable. The figures he employed, and the illustrations he used, though not the same as those used by the distinguished author, were equally forcible and expressive. On English grammar he was at fault in the theory, but passably accurate in practice. "I could never," he said to Mr. Bascom, "see the sense in going over nouns, compunctions, insurrections, and congregations." In the books on theology he was entirely at home. Orthodox in his religious belief, he was prepared to defend with signal ability the cardinal truths of the Bible. When asked by Mr. Bascom whether he had read the works of Wesley and Fletcher, his reply was: "You may report that I believe them all, with the exception of Mr. Wesley's sermon on the resurrection of the inferior animal creation." With the Bible and Hymn-book he was perfectly familiar. We have been present when he read his Lessons from the Old and New Testaments, with the Bible before him, and when he would line his hymn, although he did not recognize a letter. We have heard him when he quoted in support of his positions as many as sixty passages of Scripture, in a sermon, giving the chapter and verse, with the most perfect accuracy.

When Mr. Levi entered the itinerant ministry he was fifty-one years of age. Although his hair was silver-gray, yet his constitution was unimpaired, and he promised many years of usefulness to the Church. We have already seen the success with which his ministry was crowned on the Hardinsburg Circuit. On the La Grange Circuit, where we now find him, the churches where he preached were crowded with anxious listeners, who were attracted by the truths of the Bible as presented by this son of Abraham. With a keen, ringing voice that could be distinctly heard in the largest assemblies, he proclaimed the tidings of a Redeemer's love, and incited the Church to a higher life, and sinners to repent and turn to God. While his singing attracted hundreds, many more were aroused by his powerful exhortations.

He reached La Grange Circuit immediately after the close of the Conference, and entered upon his work with the zeal of an apostle. During the winter interesting revivals blessed his labors in different portions of his charge, and before the close of spring eighty persons had "witnessed a good confession." On the 8th of June he commenced a meeting in Westport, which continued through several weeks, and resulted in one hundred and twenty conversions. The entire circuit was in a blaze; every appointment was on fire, and before he left for the ensuing Conference four hundred and thirty-three persons had "passed from death unto life," and "were added to the Church."

In the Hartford Circuit, under the ministry of Joseph G. Ward and Seraiah S. Deering, one hundred persons were received into the Church.

The Louisville District extended, on the Ohio River, from Westport to Yellow Banks (now Owensboro), a distance of two hundred miles. At almost every appointment along the winding banks of the river "the voice of thanksgiving and praise" was heard. Westport, Louisville, Brandenburg, Hawesville, New Chapel, and Yellow Banks, joined in pæans of praise to a common Lord. In the Yellow Banks Circuit, Daniel S. Barksdale and Richard Holding witnessed the triumphs of the cross.

Richard Holding was born in Scott county, Kentucky, November 28, 1808. He professed religion and united with the Methodist Episcopal Church September 10, 1831. We have no advice as to the precise time he was licensed to preach; but in the Minutes of 1832 we find him enrolled as a traveling preacher. His first appointment was to the Madison Circuit, as the colleague of John Beatty. In 1833 he was sent, with John Williams, to the Mount Vernon Circuit. In 1834 his appointment was to the Cumberland Mission, with the gifted Napoleon B. Lewis as his colleague. There was no appointment in the Conference more difficult to travel than this. It embraced a very large extent of territory in the most mountainous region of the State, with thirty-three appointments, several of them many miles distant from each other. The duties of a missionary in this field were by no means easily performed.

On one occasion Mr. Holding was riding along a devious stream, in Harlan county, with mountains on either side, whose summits seemed to kiss the flying clouds. He was meditating on the love of God, as shown to mankind in the gift of his Son Jesus Christ, and was offering up the gratitude of his heart for His "loving-kindness and tender mercies." Every thing around him was still, save now and then the warbling of a feathered songster disturbed the silence of the hour. The road was a dreary one. A human voice on the mountain-side arrested his attention.

"Stop, *stop*, STOP!" cried a rough-looking man, armed with rifle and butcher-knife, bounding down the mountain, accompanied by two others equally rough, and armed like himself.

To escape was impossible. Anticipating an attack from ruffians, he checked his jaded horse and prepared to meet them with the boldest front he could present. As they drew nearer he asked them what they wanted.

"Do n't be *skeered*, Mr. Preacher; we would n't hurt you for the universe."

"You know me, then?" said Mr. Holding.

"I do," said the one who first accosted him. "I heern you preach yesterday, and was tellin' these fellers about you; and seein' you comin' along, I thought you would n't mind ef I 'd jest stop you a minnit and show you to 'em, as they never seed a Methodist preacher afore."

"I am glad to make your acquaintance," said the preacher, at the same time offering his hand to each of them. After conversing with them awhile on the subject of their souls' salvation, he bade them farewell.

In 1835 he traveled the Shelby Circuit, with George W. Merritt as his colleague. In all these fields of labor he gathered sinners into the fold of Christ, and left behind him the savor of a good name.

In 1836 and 1837 we find him on the Yellow Banks Circuit, still laboring with apostolic zeal. The Yellow Banks Circuit at that time extended, on the Ohio River, from Cloverport to the mouth of Green River, and from Owensboro to Rumsey, over a country which in great part was flat and marshy, with twenty-six appointments, to be filled every four weeks. The arduous labors of Mr. Holding on this circuit greatly impaired one of the finest constitutions in the Conference, and compelled him, in 1838, to ask for a supernumerary relation. It is in this relation we find him, as the colleague of Daniel S. Barksdale, the present year, on the Yellow Banks Circuit. Notwithstanding the relation he sustained to the Conference indicated that but little ministerial labor was expected of him, yet we see him in the pulpit every Sabbath, and often during the week. The preacher in charge was active and zealous, and on his former circuit was eminently successful. In the summer of 1839, under the ministry of these two faithful men, one hundred and fifty persons embraced religion in the town of Owensboro. The revival began at the quarterly-meeting, which commenced on the 25th of May. Mr. Crouch, the Presiding Elder, was present, and preached with great power and ability. Methodist preachers had for several years visited Owensboro, and preached to the people; and although a small Society had been organized, yet this was the first revival of religion that had ever occurred in that village. A few weeks later the village of Hawesville had a gracious outpouring of the Holy Spirit, through the instrumentality of the same preachers, assisted by Henry Hughes, a local preacher of considerable pulpit ability. At this meeting one hundred persons were converted and ninety-two joined the Methodist Episcopal Church. New Chapel—a country church about seven miles from Hawesville—had for several years been a preaching-place, but not a soul had ever been converted since the erection of the church. From Hawesville the revival extended to that neighborhood, embracing in its power and influence almost the entire community. A writer in the *Western Christian Advocate*, who witnessed these meetings, declared that there were "not fifteen persons in the neighborhood left unconverted." * At the camp-meeting held at Pleasant Grove in August, ninety-four persons joined the Church, and one hundred and twenty professed religion.

With the exception of the Jefferson Circuit, the entire District had been in a flame. We are not

* *Western Christian Advocate*, October 18, 1839.

surprised at the following letter from Benjamin T. Crouch, the Presiding Elder, written from his quiet home:

"HARMONY LANDING, Sept. 30, 1839.

"We have just closed the regular quarterly work of this District for the present year. We now hasten to a two-days' meeting, and then forthwith set our face toward the place of Conference, and as we go preach; for we have several appointments on the way. This has been an eventful year to us in the Louisville District—full of toils, rich in mercy, and gracious and cheering in success. The great Head of the Church has visited the District generally, and the showers of reviving grace have fallen most delightfully and copiously in many neighborhoods and Societies. Hundreds of sinners have been convinced of sin and converted to God, and happy hundreds of living Christians have been quickened, revived, and encouraged in their march to the promised land. From the Kentucky River above to the Green River below the entire length of our District has resounded with the high praises of God, especially along the margin of the beautiful Ohio. What will be our net increase cannot now be certainly determined; but the numerous admissions on probation during the year must, we think, give us an aggregate of from seventeen hundred to two thousand in the entire District. Thus has God our Saviour blessed the humble efforts of his dependent servants.

"We take pleasure in recording that some of the young men have been the most favored and efficient instruments in the revivals in this District. God grant that these zealous beginners in gospel labor may abound more and more in usefulness and holiness! 'Blessed be the name of the Lord Most High for all his goodness to the children of men.'

"Among our enjoyments we have, however, experienced none of those long intervals of rest assigned to Presiding Elders by a late communication in the *Advocate.* We know nothing, in our experience, of three or four weeks' leisure at a time, amidst the comforts of home. Indeed, from three to five days' enjoyment at home, in that many weeks, is quite a domestic treat to some of us. We well know the great pleasure of staying at home *a whole day together*, after an absence of four weeks, before we start again. But labor is rest, and pain is sweet, and even privation is pleasant, where Jesus our Lord is present. With Christ in the ship, we smile at toil and pain, and dread not the pelting storm. *This is not our rest.* O that the work of our God may still spread wider and extend farther, even to the ends of the earth!"*

The first revival in the Shelbyville District occurred in Shelbyville, under the ministry of Henry E. Pilcher. A meeting was held in January, which resulted in forty additions to the Church. After a few weeks' respite the services of the meeting were resumed and protracted through the month of March, and at its close one hundred and fourteen persons were added to the Church, and about the same number were converted. In the Salt River

* *Western Christian Advocate,* October 17, 1839.

Circuit, the labors of William M. Grubbs were still blessed, and all around that circuit there were times of prosperity. In the month of July Shelbyville was again visited by a gracious revival, under the ministry of John N. Maffitt; while, in the Hodgenville Circuit, Robinson E. Sidebottom received sixty persons into the Church. The Danville and Harrodsburg Station, with Edward Stevenson as the leader, still had refreshing times. In both the white and colored membership there was a large increase. In the Irwin and Mount Vernon Circuits—the former under the ministry of Wesley G. Montgomery, and the latter with Elihu Green as pastor—there were gracious revivals, and nearly one hundred persons in each of these charges were received into the Church. Andrew Peace, in charge of the Somerset Circuit, and Edmund M. Johnson, the preacher on Liberty Circuit, were also greatly blessed in their ministry.

In the Bowling Green District, Thomas Waring reports, early in May, thirty additions to the Church in the Greensburg Circuit, and at the close of the year two hundred and thirteen. The ministry of William B. Maxey was greatly blessed in the Wayne Circuit, and that of Robert Fisk in the Burksville Circuit was also approved by the Master.

Peter Taylor was sent this year to the Russellville Station, in the Hopkinsville District. He was born in Billings, Lancashire, England, February 28, 1809. In 1817 he came to America, and in the spring of 1830 joined the Methodist Episcopal Church. He was soon appointed to the responsible office of class-leader, in which he was useful, and then licensed to exhort, and to preach.

In 1834 he was admitted on trial into the Kentucky Conference, and appointed to the Little Sandy Circuit, with Lorenzo D. Parker; and in 1835 he was the colleague of John W. Riggin, on the Germantown Circuit. In 1836 we find him traveling the Fleming Circuit, with John Waring as the junior preacher; and in 1837 his field of labor was the Louisa Circuit. In the several fields of labor he had occupied he proved himself a workman "who needed not to be ashamed." He understood well the duties and responsibilities of the sacred office to which he was called, and discharged them with fidelity. Success crowned his ministry, and through his instrumentality many were brought to Christ. His preaching was of the tender and persuasive character. Whether he pleaded with the sinner to be reconciled to God, whether he offered comfort to the people of God, or whether he administered the consolations of religion to the bereaved or afflicted, there was a softness in his manner that rendered him dear to those whom he served. We have seen an entire audience melted to tears under his ministry, and we have heard rejoicing in the house of God while he talked of the comforts of religion and the hope of eternal life. As a Christian, he was above reproach. Soundly converted, he lived in the enjoyment of religion, and was ready on all occasions to give "a reason of the hope that was in him." Immediately after the close of the session of the Conference he entered upon his work at

Russellville, where his labors were greatly blessed. At a meeting held a few weeks after he reached his work twelve persons were converted and joined the Church.

Napoleon B. Lewis this year traveled the Greenville Circuit. No preacher in the Conference was more zealous and indefatigable than Mr. Lewis, and none more eminently successful in winning souls to Christ. In the Greenville Circuit, revivals crowned his labors everywhere, and at the close of the year more than two hundred persons had been received into the Church.

While Mr. Lewis was pushing the battle to the gates of the enemy in the Greenville Circuit, Gilby Kelly and Nathanael H. Lee—the former a preacher of several years' experience, and the latter a zealous young man who had just been admitted on trial—were making conquests for the Messiah on the Hopkinsville Circuit. Laboring shoulder to shoulder in the Master's cause, they brought into the fold of Christ many weary wanderers in search of truth. During the year one hundred and fifty joined the Church. Abram Long, at the same time, was winning trophies to the Redeemer in the La Fayette Circuit; and in the Princeton Circuit George Switzer and David H. Davis accomplished much good. Before the first of April forty-three persons professed religion and joined the Church, and one hundred and two during the year. The gifted Edwin Roberts, on the Morganfield Circuit, enjoyed another year of great prosperity; while, through the instrumentality of Robert G. Gardner, on the Madisonville Circuit—

which at that time included the town of Henderson —more than two hundred souls were converted. The Logan Circuit, with Calvin W. Lewis as the pastor, also realized the convicting power and converting grace of God.

We pass to the Barboursville District, where Richard D. Neale is found in the front of the battle. This District was supplied with efficient and enterprising preachers. On the Williamsburg Circuit, we find the zealous George S. Gatewood; on the Barboursville Circuit, the sedate John B. Perry; Andrew J. McLaughlin travels the Mount Pleasant Mission; Aaron H. Rice, the Kentucky Mission; Robert F. Turner, the Prestonsburg Circuit; William B. Landrum, the Louisa Circuit; William James, the West Liberty Mission; while the Manchester Circuit is left to be supplied.

In every charge in the mountain district there were gracious revivals of religion, while in some of them the good work was extensive. In the Mount Pleasant Mission there were one hundred and fifty, and in the Louisa Circuit fifty, additions to the Church.

From the Kentucky Conference we now turn to Jackson's Purchase, embraced in the Tennessee Conference, where we still find the Hickman, Paducah, and Wadesboro Circuits. The preachers on the Hickman Circuit for this year were James R. Walker and William T. Jones; on the Paducah Circuit, Edmund J. Williams and Edwin W. Yancey; while J. T. Sherrill traveled on the Wadesboro Circuit. In this portion of Kentucky there was a decrease of thirty-six in the white membership, and an increase of nine in the colored.

The net increase in the State of Kentucky for this year was *two thousand four hundred and thirty-four* white members, while in the colored membership there was a decrease of *one hundred and forty-three.*

CHAPTER VIII.

FROM THE SESSION OF THE KENTUCKY CONFERENCE OF 1839 TO THE CONFERENCE OF 1840.

See how great a flame aspires,
  Kindled by a spark of grace!
Jesus' love the nations fires,
  Sets the kingdoms on a blaze.
To bring fire on earth he came;
  Kindled in some hearts it is:
O that all might catch the flame,
  All partake the glorious bliss!

BISHOP SOULE presided at the Kentucky Conference of 1839, which convened in Russellville October 16. Thomas N. Ralston was elected Secretary, and William M. Grubbs Assistant Secretary.

Richard Corwine, Peter Taylor, and William Holman, were appointed a Committee on Public Worship, and George W. Brush on Memoirs.

Edward Stevenson, Henry N. Vandyke, and Robert Y. McReynolds, were appointed Stewards of the Conference.

On the first morning of the session the following resolution was adopted by the Conference:

"*Resolved*, That a committee of five be appointed,

to be called the Committee on the Centenary, to consider and report on the subject of a Kentucky Conference Centenary meeting; the propriety of uniting such meeting with the anniversary of the Kentucky Conference Missionary Society; the propriety of postponing the final Centenary day to a later period than the 25th instant; and such other matters as to them may appear suitable to act upon, that the Conference may proceed safely and expeditiously on this interesting subject."

Joseph S. Tomlinson, Benjamin T. Crouch, Jonathan Stamper, Henry B. Bascom, and Isaac Collard, were constituted the committee.

One hundred years had passed away since "eight or ten persons came to Mr. Wesley, in London, who appeared to be deeply convinced of sin, and earnestly groaning for redemption," and whose object was "that he would spend some time with them in prayer, and advise them how to 'flee from the wrath to come,' which they saw continually hanging over their heads." During this period the "United Society," of which "this was the rise," had spread not only through Europe, but through the civilized world. Methodism had become a recognized fact, and at her altars, both in Europe and America, thousands were worshiping. It was eminently proper for the leading branch of American Methodism to recognize in a suitable manner the guardian care of Jehovah over his people, as well as to offer expressions of gratitude for the prosperity which had marked the progress of the Church during the century which was just closing. It was also proper for the Kentucky Conference to participate in the centennial celebration.

The committee recommended that collections be taken up in the several circuits and stations, as a thank-offering to God, and that the amounts collected be equally divided between three great objects specified in the address of the Bishop—namely: *one-third* to missionary purposes, *one-third* to the cause of education, and *one-third* toward constituting a *fund* for the benefit of our superannuated preachers and the most necessitous cases in the Conference, and the widows and orphans of those who have died in the work.

At this session of the Conference it was

"*Resolved*, That we are as much as ever impressed with the importance of the *course of study* prescribed for our undergraduates, and that we witness with regret a remissness in attending to and enforcing an observance of it, and that in future we will insist more strictly upon the accomplishment of it on the part of all to whom it relates."

We were glad to see an advance step in this matter on the part of the Conference. The course of study prescribed for the undergraduates was not a difficult one. Any preacher with a fair amount of common sense, and with reasonable industry, could easily master it, and at the same time perform the duties of a pastor. We, however, mention with regret that undergraduates, in some instances, appeared before the Committee of Examination with but a superficial knowledge of the books in the course, and sometimes without having *read* more than one-half of them. Lenity had heretofore been extended to these delinquents. It is true that opportunities for early mental training were rare, and many young men had entered the ministry without the advantages of even the most common education. The want of early opportunities for study very frequently made an excuse for remissness in this regard. In addition to this, young men were often excused on the ground that "gaining knowledge is good, but saving souls is better"—forgetting that the gaining of knowledge, instead of being a hinderance to, will greatly facilitate, the saving of souls. Laxity could no longer be tolerated. A more rigid policy was essential to an effective ministry, and the Conference resolved to pursue it.

On the third day a communication on the subject of Temperance, from the New York Conference, and one from the New England Conference, on the subject of Slavery, were received—both of which were laid on the table, to be taken up and considered before the close of the session.

On Monday morning the communication on the subject of Temperance, sent from the New York Conference, was called up. It was as follows:

"*Resolved*, That the next General Conference be earnestly and respectfully requested and empowered so to alter the General Rules of the United Societies that the item respecting drunkenness may read as Mr. Wesley framed it, which is in the following language—viz.: 'Drunkenness, buying or selling spirituous liquors, or drinking them, unless in cases of extreme necessity.'"

The Conference concurred in this resolution by a vote of seventy-six to one.

The communication from the New England Conference, on the subject of Slavery, was the same that had been sent out the previous year. The presiding Bishop made some scathing remarks in reference to the officious intermeddling of the New England Conference with the institution of slavery—after which the Conference voted unanimously to *non-concur*.

The Conference adopted the following resolution:

"*Resolved*, That the Conference cordially approve of the organization of the Western Methodist Historical Society, in the city of Cincinnati; and that the Secretary of the Conference and the Presiding Elders of the several Districts be a committee to contribute appropriate material to that Society; and that for this purpose they shall have free access to all the books and papers belonging to this body; and that the members of the Conference, generally, be requested to contribute, as far as practicable, to the furtherance of the object of that Association."

The object of this Society was to collect and preserve past and current events and incidents of Methodist history in the Western Conferences, for the use of the future historian. Laudable as was the design of the founders of this Society, it is to be regretted that among its archives there are very few contributions from Kentucky.

No resolution was adopted during the session of more importance than the following:

"*Resolved, by the Kentucky Annual Conference*, That

all the members of this body be respectfully requested and directed to use all proper means and efforts, at a period as early as practicable, to induce the people within their respective charges, and the several divisions of their labor, to address petitions and memorials to the Legislature of Kentucky, praying for the enactment of suitable laws for the suppression of the *vice of Intemperance* within the commonwealth of Kentucky, and especially to appeal to the Legislature for a change in the existing *License Law*, as it regards the *sale of ardent spirits*."

This resolution was unanimously adopted by a rising vote. While the Secretary was reading it the feeling in the audience, as well as in the Conference, was very intense, and before the reading closed the enthusiasm was greatly increased. A young preacher, who had only been admitted on trial the previous year, and hence not entitled to a vote, became so excited that he could not remain in his seat, and when those who favored the resolution were called on to rise, he stood a head and shoulders above them all. He was the *tallest* preacher in the house.

It is gratifying to record that the Kentucky Conference, at this period, took such high and decisive ground on the subject of Temperance. Not only the resolutions, but the practice, of the Conference favored the temperance movement. The ruin of intemperance was wide-spread, and its blight was upon a thousand homes. Young men of promise, who might have adorned society, had fallen victims to the deadly curse, and hoary age was reeling to and fro on the margin of the grave. The once rosy cheek of woman—mother, wife, daughter, sister—had turned pale, while the son, husband, father, or brother, was pressing the wine-cup to his lips. The pulpit met with no obstacle to its success so dangerous and so powerful as intemperance, and every motive of duty to God and of good-will to man urged the arrest of this dreadful evil.* The Conference determined that if intemperance should not be banished from the commonwealth, the fault should not be theirs; its power should at least be broken, and its influence checked.

On Wednesday morning—the last day of the session—the following persons were elected Delegates to the General Conference: Joseph S. Tomlinson, Henry B. Bascom, Jonathan Stamper, Thomas N. Ralston, and George W. Taylor. Benjamin T. Crouch and Hubbard H. Kavanaugh were elected Reserve Delegates.

Dr. Bascom had been appointed at the previous session to deliver an address on Education, but was

---

* To those who think the temperance movement has effected but little allow us to say that at this period ardent spirits entered into every gathering. We heard a ——— minister, in 1837, preach a funeral-sermon at a private house. On the sideboard was to be seen, during the service, a gallon-bottle of whisky. When the service closed the preacher stepped forward and poured some into a glass, and drank it. In a few moments the bottle was empty. We knew a gentleman, one evening, to send to the house of a deacon in a Church for a glass of whisky for a sick servant, knowing that he kept it. He replied that he had only one gallon, and there was prayer-meeting that night at his house, and he could not spare it. Such things would not now be tolerated.

too feeble in health to perform the duty, and was excused by vote of the Conference.

The preaching during the session was excellent. The sermon by Bishop Soule, on Sunday at eleven o'clock, from the text, "For all the promises of God in him are yea, and in him Amen, unto the glory of God by us,"* was forcible and impressive.

The deacons were ordained after the close of the sermon. While the ordination-services were in progress one of the seats in the gallery was broken. The entire audience was in commotion. "The house is falling!" rang through the assembly, and the scene that ensued baffles description. A wild rush was made for the doors, some persons broke through the windows, several leaped among the excited crowd from the gallery, while others hastily passed their children from the gallery to friends on the lower floor. The strong, commanding voice of Bishop Soule was heard above the confusion, assuring the people that there was no danger, and urging them to be calm; yet the rush for the doors and windows continued until the Bishop and the preachers at the altar, with only a few others, were all that remained in the house. During the panic the ordination-services were suspended, but, as soon as the excitement subsided, were resumed.†

No sermon, however, during the session, attracted so much attention, or produced such a thrilling effect, as one preached by John H. Linn, a young preacher but recently transferred from the Baltimore Conference.

---

*2 Cor. i. 20. †The author was ordained on that occasion.

The missionary meeting, on Saturday evening, was a splendid success. One thousand dollars was collected on the occasion.

Aaron Moore, Seraiah S. Deering, Jesse Cromwell, John F. South, John Vance, John C. Baskett, Andrew M. Bailey, Samuel R. Turner, James I. George, and James J. Harrison, were admitted on trial.

Wiley B. Murphy, Samuel Veach, John Waring, Martin L. Eades, Jesse Sutton, George Switzer, James H. Brooking, and Esau Simmons, located.

George W. Fagg, Joseph G. Ward, Stephen Harber, and Elijah Sutton, were placed on the superannuated list; while the names of William Atherton and Eli B. Crain were transferred to the effective roll.

One preacher (Absalom D. Fox) had died during the year.

Absalom D. Fox was born in Pennsylvania; but we have no record of the date of his birth. He was brought up chiefly in the State of Ohio, and joined the Methodist Episcopal Church in the city of Cincinnati, in 1816. For five years he remained a local preacher, in which sphere he was laborious and useful. He was then admitted on trial into the Ohio Conference, where for ten years he was diligent and successful as a traveling preacher.

In the autumn of 1835 he was transferred to the Kentucky Conference, and appointed to the Jefferson Circuit. Here, as in the State of Ohio, his ministry was crowned with success. In 1836 he was returned to the Jefferson Circuit, where he continued to preach with acceptability and usefulness to the close of the year. Twelve years of itinerant service had greatly impaired his health, which, together with pecuniary embarrassment, induced his location in 1837.

Believing that it was his duty to devote himself exclusively to the work of the ministry, he offered himself to the Conference in 1838, and was reädmitted, and appointed to the Frankfort Station. His work, however, was done. After a severe and protracted illness, he "fell asleep in Jesus," November 2, 1838.

During the brief period in which Mr. Fox was identified with the Church in Kentucky he gathered around him a circle of friends, who appreciated him for his excellent traits of character, his fervent piety, and his pure and spotless life. As a preacher, he was always acceptable, amiable, and modest in his deportment, and as a pastor industrious and eminently qualified for the duties which lay before him. One who knew him well said of him: "Take him all in all—in his intellect and morals, his sincerity of heart and purity of life, and in the whole *contour* of his character, as a man, a Christian, and a minister—we do not hope to find, in our whole lives, a more lovely example of the union and harmony of all the Christian graces." The memorial-sermon of Mr. Fox was preached by George W. Brush, at the request of the Conference.

The missionary collections from the circuits and stations amounted to $4,581.85, one thousand dollars of which was collected at the Conference anniversary. Carlisle Babbitt, who had brought to the Conference a larger collection than did any other preacher the previous year, again stands at the head of the list. He reported, from the Versailles Circuit, $706.81.

In looking over the appointments, we find Isaac Collard, William Gunn, Benjamin T. Crouch, Jonathan Stamper, George W. Taylor, Richard Corwine, and Richard D. Neale, in charge of the same Districts they had traveled the year before. John James, who had presided over the Bowling Green District, was appointed to the Covington District, in place of Thomas W. Chandler, who was sent to the Millersburg Circuit; while James King succeeded Mr. James on the Bowling Green District. In the Augusta District, James Ward was returned to the Fleming Circuit, and Josiah Whitaker to the Lewis Circuit. In the Lexington District, Absalom Woolliscroft, who had been supernumerary on the Burlington Circuit, was returned to it in an effective relation. In the Louisville District, Clinton Kelly was returned to the Jefferson Circuit, James D. Holding to the Newcastle Circuit, while Joseph D. Barnett was sent to the Brandenburg—a new circuit formed from a portion of the Hardinsburg, which he had traveled the previous year. In the Shelbyville District, Williams B. Kavanaugh was reäppointed to the Shelby Circuit, and Robinson E. Sidebottom to the Hodgenville Circuit. Turning to the Harrodsburg District, the name of Joel Peak again appears on the Madison Circuit, and that of Andrew Peace on the Somerset Circuit. In the

Bowling Green District, Thomas Waring was again sent to Greensburg, and Robert Fisk to Burksville. In the Hopkinsville District, Abram Long again travels the La Fayette Circuit, and Napoleon B. Lewis the Greenville Circuit. In the Barboursville District, William B. Landrum was again sent to the Louisa Circuit.

The two years through which we have just passed were crowned with remarkable success. While we shall not be permitted the present year to record such extraordinary triumphs as those we have just witnessed, yet it will be our privilege to behold the Church still moving forward in the great work in which it was engaged.

Calvin W. Lewis, who was a preacher of considerable promise, was sent to the Minerva Circuit. The pleasant village of Augusta was a leading appointment in this circuit. The Augusta College—the oldest Methodist college in America—was located at this point. Joseph S. Tomlinson, Henry B. Bascom, Joseph M. Trimble, and Burr H. McCown, composed the Faculty. Methodism, not only in the village, but throughout the adjoining country, was largely indebted for the elevated position it occupied to the ministry of these faithful men. At Minerva, Dover, Germantown, and Mount Zion, from time to time, they dispensed the word of life, and through their instrumentality many were brought to Christ. In Augusta, in connection with the pastor, they labored assiduously to build up the Church and to promote the cause of God.

On the 11th of January, 1840, a meeting was commenced in Augusta, by Mr. Lewis, in which the Faculty participated, and at which one hundred persons joined the Church, twenty-two of whom were students in the college. The revival which commenced at this meeting extended to the country appointments, and before the first of March two hundred persons were added to the Church. The good work continued to spread. At Mount Zion—a popular preaching-place, four miles from Augusta—a meeting was held in May, at which Mr. Lewis was assisted by James Savage, a local preacher from Germantown, and Messrs. Trimble and McCown, where fifty-six persons joined the Church. At the close of the year the pastor reported three hundred additions.

In the spring of 1838 a young preacher made his appearance in Kentucky, who was destined to bear a prominent part in the history of the Church and to occupy a commanding eminence for more than a generation.

John H. Linn was born in Lewisburg, Virginia, February 22, 1812. From his early childhood he was impressed with the importance of religion, and was deeply convicted of his own sinful condition. Having been taught the fear of God from his infancy, it was no difficult task for him to call upon the Lord and plead for pardon. In the fourteenth year of his age he was happily converted. Brought up under Presbyterian influence, he was naturally inclined to join that Church, but, for reasons satisfactory to himself, did not do so. In the fifteenth year of his age he made the acquaintance of some

Methodist preachers, for whom he formed a warm attachment, and through their influence became a member of the Methodist Church. In 1836 he was admitted on trial into the Baltimore Conference, and was appointed, with Francis M. Mills, to the Franklin Circuit, with Norval Wilson as his Presiding Elder. In 1837 his field of labor was the Lexington Circuit (with the same Presiding Elder), as the colleague of George W. Humphreys. His wife was Ann Eliza Woodard, daughter of W. H. Woodard, of Kentucky, a lady of superior intellect, of fervent piety, and uncompromising devotion to the Church. This influenced his transfer to Kentucky, in 1838. The death of the lamented Gibbons made a vacancy on the Georgetown Circuit, and the Church was so fortunate as to secure the appointment of Mr. Linn for the remainder of the year.

He was an excellent preacher from the time he entered the ministry. When the Conference held its session in Baltimore in 1837, at the close of his first year in the itinerant ministry, he was appointed to preach in the First Presbyterian Church, then under the pastoral care of Dr. Backus, the successor of Dr. Nevins; he preached on Rom. viii. 38, 39: "For I am persuaded, that neither death, nor life, nor angels, nor principalities, nor powers, nor things present, nor things to come, nor height, nor depth, nor any other creature, shall be able to separate us from the love of God, which is in Christ Jesus our Lord." Our informant, who was present on the occasion, tells us that it was a masculine effort, and was so considered by the highly intelligent congregation to which it was delivered. It foreshadowed the high position which he was destined to occupy in the ministry.

We remember his first appearance in the Conference of 1838. He was young and buoyant—the very picture of health—and promised to the Church many years of labor and of usefulness. He came to the West asking no other favor than to be recognized as a brother and a fellow-laborer in the Master's vineyard—to work wherever the interest of the Church might demand.

During the brief period he had labored on the Georgetown Circuit he not only won golden opinions from the people, but he was successful in winning souls to Christ. His commanding presence, his piety, his zeal, his devotion to the cause of the Redeemer, together with his extraordinary talents, not only rendered him useful in a high degree, but indicated the lofty eminence he would occupy in the coming years.

At the Kentucky Conference of 1838 he was returned to the Georgetown Circuit, with George W. Simcoe as his colleague, where he spent a happy and prosperous year.

We have already alluded to the sermon he preached during the session of the Conference in Russellville. It was on Thursday evening. The Methodist Church was crowded to overflowing, while many stood at the doors and windows. We saw him as he entered the house, and watched him as he walked down the aisle, in that careless manner which has always characterized him, his large gray eye resting on the floor. He entered the pulpit and knelt for a few minutes in silent prayer. The hymn, the public prayer, the "voluntary," followed each other in rapid succession. The text was, "Gather my saints together unto me."* In the commencement of the sermon the preacher was considerably embarrassed. It was his first attempt to preach in the presence of the Kentucky Conference, and his words were tremblingly uttered. Bascom, Tomlinson, Stamper, Crouch, and Kavanaugh, who took rank with the ablest preachers in America, were present. A few introductory remarks were offered, on the life and character of the sweet singer of Israel, and then he entered into a rigid examination of the word "saint," and what constitutes a saint in the sight of God. To become a saint requires, on the part of a sinner, repentance toward God and faith toward our Lord Jesus Christ; while God, on his part, introduces him into his family by justification, regeneration, adoption, and sanctification. With great clearness he presented the difference between the justification and the regeneration of the sinner—the former merely changing the relation to God, while the latter changes his nature. Regeneration, as he understood it to be taught in the Bible, was a thorough and radical work of grace in the heart, affecting all the component parts of the moral constitution; *it was, emphatically, a new birth.* A religion that would not accomplish this fails in its grand design, and is not of God. He, moreover, affirmed that the regeneration of the penitent be-

* Psalm l. 5.

liever is accompanied by the witness of the Holy Spirit, bearing testimony with his spirit that he is born of God. "He that believeth on the Son of God hath the witness in himself." * "What is the witness?" he inquired. "Let the apostle answer: 'The Spirit itself beareth witness with our spirit, that we are the children of God.' † The necessity of such testimony cannot but be apparent to every thinking mind. Without it the Christian cannot be happy, because he cannot know whether he is in God's favor or under condemnation." In touching language he referred to the *adoption* of the regenerated person into the family of God, and then showed that Christ demands of all his followers that they "grow in grace," ‡ and that they add to their "faith virtue; and to virtue, knowledge; and to knowledge, temperance; and to temperance, patience; and to patience, godliness; and to godliness, brotherly kindness; and to brotherly kindness, charity;" § and never stop until they have fathomed every depth and ascended every height of religious life, and are sanctified of God. The life of a Christian is an active life: "For we are laborers together with God" ||—not loiterers. No Christian, for a moment, dares pause amid the conquests he has won. If success has been achieved, if victories have been won, difficulties yet confront us in the great battle of life, and we dare not rest on our arms until every foe is conquered. Then, and not until then, will our warfare be over, and our victory complete.

---

* 1 John v. 10. † Rom. viii. 16. ‡ 2 Pet. iii. 18. § 2 Pet. i. 5–7. || 1 Cor. iii. 9.

The peroration was thrilling beyond description. He had found man a sinner in the sight of God, exposed to almighty wrath; he had watched him as the Holy Spirit arrested him in his career to ruin; he had seen him as he resolved upon a better life, and when he "tasted the good word of God, and the powers of the world to come;"* he had followed him through every conflict in which he had been engaged, and beheld him when victory perched upon his banner; he watched his progress as he ascended the mountain-heights of religious life, until he was sanctified throughout spirit, and soul, and body, and become "pure even as He is pure;" and then, like a ripe shock ready to be gathered, he saw him as he entered the "valley of the shadow of death,"† and listened to strains of rapture as they came back from the borders of the spirit-world; and he contemplated, too, the joys that awaited him amid the resplendent glories of the heavenly state. Time passes on; the world becomes hoary with age, and its affairs are winding to their close; the judgment-day is at hand, and the nations are to be called from the sleep of ages, to hear their final sentence; but *where are the saints of God?* Scattered throughout the world; buried, many of them, in unknown graves, their names have perished from the page of the world's memory; no hand of friendship may plant over their graves the evergreen—the emblem of immortality—nor the rose, to throw its fragrance on the balmy air; no tears of affection may mingle with the dust that conceals them from human view;

* Heb. vi. 6. † Psalm xxiii. 4.

but the ever-watchful eye of God has kept vigils over them, and not one, however humble and lowly in life, will be overlooked or forgotten. Hark! an angel is summoned to the presence of God, and Jehovah says to him: "Go, '*gather* my saints together unto me.' Let them be the first to be raised from the dead!" "Where shall I go?" asks the angel. "Go to the cave in the field of Machpelah; call up Abraham and Sarah, Isaac and Rebecca, and Jacob and Leah. Go to Mount Nebo, and find the grave of Moses, and bid him come back to life. Go to the city of David, and find the sepulcher of the son of Jesse, whose dulcet strains have chased sorrow from ten thousand hearts, and tell him, 'I am the resurrection and the life.'* Go to the graves of the prophets who foretold the advent of the woman's conquering Seed and the splendors of his reign, and tell them, 'Because I live, ye shall live also.'† Go to the imperial city, where Paul the apostle slumbers, and awaken him from the sleep of centuries. Go to Germany, and gather Luther and Melanchthon. Go to England, and lift the stone from the grave of John Wesley, and tell him to rise and throw off the fetters of the tomb. Call Coke from his coral bed, where he has slept so long. Go to Africa, and awaken Mellville B. Cox. Go to America, and call Asbury from his tomb in the Monumental City, and McKendree from the forests of Tennessee. Wherever one of my saints sleeps, go and awake him, and 'gather him unto me.'" The angel continues his search, and from ocean and from

*John xi. 25. †John xiv. 19.

earth the saints of God are rising; from every continent, every island, and every isthmus, they are coming, in obedience to the summons of God. In his majestic flight through the world he overtakes Death, who tries to escape from his presence, and asks him whether a saint of God is confined within his empire. "No," he replies; "I have captured thousands, and carried them to my dominions, and bound them with fetters. I thought I had them secure, but they have broken the massive bars, abandoned the graves where they had slumbered long, and destroyed my power forever." He meets the prince of darkness, and inquires whether one saint can be found within his realm. "No, not one; but it is no fault of mine. I followed them through every step of life; I offered them the world, with all its pageantry, and tinsel, and glare, if they would serve me; I pledged them riches, and pleasure, and fame; but their ears were deaf to my persuasions; I confronted them with difficulties, but they overcame them; I placed snares in their path, but they shunned them; I left no means unemployed to destroy them, but they eluded my grasp. No, not one is to be found in all the regions of woe." The work is done, and the angel returns to God.

From the Conference at Russellville Mr. Linn was appointed to Maysville, one of the most pleasant stations in the Conference. He entered upon his work as early after the close of the Conference as was practicable, meeting with a cordial reception from the Church and the community. During the winter his congregations were large and attentive, and considerable interest was manifested amongst the people on the subject of religion. Early in February a meeting was commenced, in which he was assisted by Mr. Maffitt, during which one hundred and fifteen persons were added to the Church, and more than that number happily converted. The influence of this meeting extended through the entire community, leaving its benedictions on many a heart. Other Communions realized blessings from it. Under the ministry of Mr. Linn the white membership in Maysville increased from one hundred and fifty to three hundred and five, and the colored from eighty-two to one hundred and sixty.

While Mr. Linn was stationed in Maysville he made a visit to Georgetown, his former field of labor. The Church he had served so faithfully and the community in which he had lived so pleasantly were glad to see him again. He was met by them with a cordiality and warmth that thrilled him with emotions he could not conceal. Among his numerous admirers was an old colored member of the Church. The preacher had left them the autumn before, well but plainly dressed. The warm hand and generous heart of friendship, in Maysville, had dressed him handsomely. Wrapped in a fine and costly cloak, he was met by the old man on the street, and accosted with, "Well, well, you sorter looked like Brother Linn; but you gotten to be so much like a gentleman that I declare I did n't know you. I 's so glad to see you, ef you is a gentleman." We take leave of Mr. Linn here, but shall meet him before our volume closes.

In the Germantown Circuit, George S. Savage was very successful. At a meeting at the Shannon Meeting-house, in Mason county, one hundred persons joined the Church.

Daniel S. Barksdale was this year sent to the Fleming Circuit, with James Ward as his colleague. Mr. Barksdale was born May 14, 1812, in Wilson county, Tennessee. He was converted and joined the Church, under the ministry of Peter Akers, September 12, 1827, in Russellville, Kentucky. In 1834 he entered the Kentucky Conference, and was appointed, with John Nevius, to the Big Sandy Circuit. In 1835 he was sent to the Bowling Green Circuit, with William S. Evans, and in 1836 to the Kentucky Mission. At the Conference of 1837 he was placed in charge of the Hardinsburg Circuit, and was sent to the Yellow Banks Circuit in 1838. In a previous chapter we have referred to the success which followed the ministry of Mr. Barksdale on the Hardinsburg and Yellow Banks Circuits, where he received several hundred persons into the Church. We succeeded him in both these fields, and had every opportunity to witness the result of his labors. From the time he entered the Conference until he located, at the close of this year, he labored with the zeal of a true minister of Christ, and was the honored instrument in doing much good. Whether he preached along the waters of the Big Sandy or on the fertile lands of Warren county, whether he proclaimed the tidings of salvation amid the valleys and mountains of South-eastern Kentucky or along the banks of the Ohio, his trumpet gave no uncertain sound; he was beloved by the people he served, and many were brought to Christ through his labors. The fields he occupied not only extended over a large area of country, but the most of them were difficult to travel. From twenty to thirty appointments were to be filled every four weeks, besides preaching frequently at nights. These, together with long rides and the exposure incident to the life of a traveling preacher, during the period he was in the service, were too much for a delicate frame like his. The Fleming Circuit was the lightest charge he had ever filled, and yet it embraced nineteen appointments. Here, as elsewhere, he labored incessantly, and won souls to Christ. His health, however, became too much enfeebled during the year for him to longer prosecute the high and holy calling to which he had so faithfully devoted six years of his life. It cost him a hard struggle to retire from the itinerant ranks. He located at the close of this year.

The Lewis Circuit increased from five hundred and five to seven hundred and forty-eight in the white membership, although there was a decrease of nine in the colored. Josiah Whitaker, who had charge of this circuit, not only labored with diligence and zeal, but he gathered the rich fruit of his toil in the hundreds who, under his ministry, were brought to Christ.

The work of grace which had begun in Newport, under the ministry of Robert Y. McReynolds the previous year, was still in progress. Wesley G. Montgomery, an educated and deeply pious young man, had been appointed to the station. As a preacher Mr. Montgomery did not take high rank, but as a pastor he excelled. During the winter thirty persons were added to the Church.

Robert Y. McReynolds was appointed to Covington. He was born in Allen county, Kentucky, January 20, 1809. He embraced religion September 17, 1826, and joined the Methodist Episcopal Church in the following November. On the 23d of December, 1827, he was licensed to exhort, and with no other authority he traveled the Christian Circuit, as the colleague of Blachley C. Wood, the remainder of the year. At a camp-meeting held in the neighborhood in which he was born and brought up, in August, 1828, he was licensed to preach and recommended to the Kentucky Conference for admission into the traveling connection.

The first appointment of Mr. McReynolds was to the Logan Circuit, as the junior preacher—John S. Barger being in charge. At the following Conference he was sent to the Cynthiana Circuit, with Josiah Whitaker. In 1830 his field of labor was the Livingston Circuit, and in 1831 the Henderson Circuit. At the Conference of 1832 we find him on the Hartford Circuit, in 1833 on the Taylorsville Circuit, and in 1834 on the Jefferson Circuit. He traveled the Breckinridge Circuit in 1835, and the Louisa Circuit in 1836. We follow him to the Franklin Circuit in 1837, to Newport in 1838, and from thence to Covington in 1839, where we now find him.

Possessed of a good mind, and entering the itinerant field when he was only a youth, and influenced by the single motive of doing good, but few young men gave signs of greater promise than Robert Y. McReynolds. Whether performing the duties of an itinerant preacher on circuits or in stations, he was instrumental in the accomplishment of good. Under his ministry sinners were awakened, penitents converted, and the Church established. We first met with him in 1835, while he was in attendance on the Conference at Shelbyville, and just after he had closed his year on the Breckinridge Circuit. During an evening he spent at our home we listened with pleasure to his conversation on the subject of the life of an itinerant preacher, on which we believed it our duty to enter. We then formed an attachment for him that increased through the passing years.

In Newport his ministry had been greatly blessed in the conversion of souls, but in Covington his work seemed to be confined to building up and strengthening the Church. In that charge he made many friends, and left behind him the savor of a good name.

The white membership in the Falmouth Circuit increased from five hundred and twenty-two to six hundred and thirty-eight, and the colored membership from thirty-two to forty. The preacher, William C. McMahon, was zealous and useful.

In the Cynthiana Circuit, under the ministry of George W. Merritt, the Church enjoyed great prosperity. At a quarterly-meeting held in Cynthiana, under the faithful preaching of John James, the Presiding Elder, and George W. Merritt, thirty persons witnessed a good profession and joined the Church. Mr. Maffitt reached Cynthiana while the meeting was in progress, and entered into the work with the zeal for which he had elsewhere been distinguished. The congregations, already large, were increased to overflowing, and the religious interest widened and spread all through the community. Two hundred persons professed to be converted, and joined the Church. The influence of the revival in Cynthiana extended to the adjacent country, and many were brought from darkness to light. It reached the Leesburg Circuit—the preacher in charge being George W. Simcoe—and more than one hundred souls turned away from a life of sin to a life of purity and holiness. In the Paris Circuit, where John C. Hardy preached the gospel, a deep religious feeling prevailed; while in the Sharpsburg Circuit Thomas Demoss received eighty-two persons into the Church.

While such displays of divine power were manifested in the Covington District, rejoicing and praise were heard in almost every portion of the Lexington District. In the city of Lexington the Church grew stronger, under the pastoral care of George W. Brush; while in the Winchester Circuit, under the ministry of Carlisle Babbitt, the membership was largely increased. In Frankfort, Peter Taylor had seasons of refreshing; and on the Georgetown Circuit, under the ministry of Hartwell J. Perry and Thomas R. Malone, the membership was nearly doubled. In the Burlington and Carrollton Circuits—the former served by Absalom Woolliscroft and Thomas Hall, and the latter by James C. Crow and James I. George—many were brought to Christ. No charge in the Lexington District was more greatly blessed than the Versailles Circuit. Under the ministry of Edwin Roberts, the zealous pastor, twenty-nine persons joined the Church at Nicholasville, where the first quarterly-meeting was held, and three hundred were added to the Church before the close of the year.

While the Mount Sterling Circuit reports a much smaller membership than it had the previous year, yet there were but few charges in the District that shared more largely in revival influence than this. John W. Riggin, a faithful and true man, was the preacher, and under his ministry many were brought from darkness to light.

The labors of Mr. Maffitt in Kentucky, which had extended through more than two years, and had been so signally blessed, were about to terminate. The last meeting at which he was present in the State was held in Mount Sterling, commencing August 1, 1840. Here, as everywhere else he had labored, sinners were awakened, penitents converted, and the Church revived. At the close of the meeting ninety-two persons had witnessed a good confession. A camp-meeting was held at Poynter's Camp-ground, immediately after the close of the meeting in Mount Sterling, at which William Gunn, Carlisle Babbitt, and Thomas Demoss, were present. Here thirty-two persons professed to find "the peace which passeth all understanding."

The question has often been asked, Why was it

that the labors of John Newland Maffitt were so blessed that everywhere he preached the gospel the work of God was revived?

Mr. Maffitt was a man of *one* work. The glory of God and the salvation of sinners occupied all his thoughts and controlled all his actions. He seemed to think of nothing else. We have very frequently known him, after preaching in the morning, to devote the afternoon to religious conversation with seekers of religion, and then preach again in the evening, and afterward spend hours at the altar, and then retire late—not yet to sleep, but to think of the best method of achieving success. We have known him to rise frequently during the night, to pen a thought that had occurred to his mind, or to kneel in prayer before God. His responsibilities to God and his duty to man absorbed every thought. Wherever he labored he not only expected, but *resolved, to succeed*, and his boldness and zeal inspired the confidence of the members of the Church, whom he expected and *required* to coöperate with him. He labored, too, with an energy that never flagged. He appeared never to grow weary. As long as a penitent sinner would remain at the altar Mr. Maffitt was willing to stay with him, and sing, and pray, and instruct him. He was no respecter of persons. Whether sin was to be found in high or in low places, in the most scathing manner he rebuked it. He divested it of all its covering, and exposed it in all its hideousness. He was faithful to God and earnest in saving the souls of his fellow-men.

It does not come within the scope of the present

volume to follow the career of Mr. Maffitt farther; yet it will not be improper to trace his history to the close of his life.

In 1841 he was elected Chaplain of the lower house of Congress. He discharged the duties of this position with great credit to himself and with benefit to his hearers. In the capital of the nation he lost none of the reputation he had won in the West.

After the close of the term for which he was elected he left Washington City, and visited Richmond, Virginia, and other cities in the North and East, where the same success crowned his ministry as in Lexington, Louisville, and other cities in Kentucky. "His residence was mainly in the Atlantic cities, until 1847. About this period he was married to Miss Pierce, of Brooklyn, New York, his first wife having died in Galveston, Texas. As some complaints were made against him, and his Church-relations falling into an informal state, he was considered as having withdrawn his membership from the Church in New York. Retiring to Arkansas, he joined the Methodist Episcopal Church, South, and was licensed to preach *de novo*." He remained in Arkansas about two years, when he left that State for the Gulf cities.

In the spring of 1850 we find him carrying on a religious meeting in a small chapel of a suburban village of Mobile, Alabama. This was the last meeting he conducted.

No man in the American ministry, so far as we have known, has ever been so relentlessly persecuted as John Newland Maffitt. We are not surprised at this. The Divine Master was persecuted before him. The bold and fearless attacks made on vice by Mr. Maffitt, if they failed to persuade the ungodly to abandon their evil habits, were well calculated to embitter and array them against him. His success, too, in the great work that occupied his life had a tendency to provoke the wrath of the enemies of the Church. Every thing that hate, and envy, and malice could invent, to impair his influence and to break his power, was said and done; yet, through more than thirty years in which he preached the gospel of Christ, he maintained an unsullied reputation as a Christian, not a single stain ever fastening itself on his escutcheon. Confiding too easily in pretended friendships, we are not surprised that he was often betrayed; yet no betrayal ever cast a blight on his fair name. Malignant, and bitter, and busy, as was the tongue of calumny, he cherished no malice against his enemies, but to all their charges his reply was, "God, forgive them!" Guileless in heart, and conscious of the rectitude of his intentions, he ought to have borne up under the heartless persecutions that were leveled against him to the last. No man knew the human heart—its depravity and corruption—better than he did, and he ought not to have allowed his spirit to be broken by the continued assaults of his persecutors. The attacks upon his reputation culminated in an article which appeared on Thursday before his death in a paper published in Mobile, copied from the *Police Gazette*, of New York. He had borne much, but his sensitive nature could bear no more. From the appearance of this article he was greatly disturbed, and never slept. His sister—Mrs. Ellen Ball, the wife of Dr. Ball, whom he was visiting—was boarding with Mrs. Ballasette, where Mr. Maffitt spent his time. Walking the floor of Mrs. Ball's room, he frequently pressed his heart, exclaiming, "O Ellen, they have broken my heart!" and again, "My poor heart is breaking!"

Upon the appearance of the article already referred to, Mr. Maffitt was advised to avenge himself. To this advice he replied that "such an act would be inconsistent with Christian life," and quoted, "Vengeance is mine; I will repay, saith the Lord." On Monday morning he went to Toulminville—a suburban village of Mobile—to the house of Major Reuben Chamberlain. "Napoleon's Grave" was his favorite piece of music. Between six and seven o'clock P.M., while Miss Chamberlain was playing this piece, Mr. Maffitt left the parlor and went out on the gallery, groaning heavily. He, however, immediately returned to the hall, and fell prostrate. He was lifted up and carried to a sofa. While lying there, Mrs. W—— said to him, "Your enemies will outdo you." He replied, "They will," and prayed, "Lord, have mercy on them, and forgive them!" Mrs. W—— asked him if he could forgive them. He replied, "Yes, from the bottom of my heart; for if I forgive not, how can I expect forgiveness?" Medical attention was procured without delay. Dr. E. P. Gaines administered an opiate, and forbade his talking. He spoke but little afterward, and died,

May 28, 1850, at fifteen minutes past two A.M., saying, "They have broken my heart!" He was buried in Magnolia Cemetery, where he still sleeps. No marble marks the spot. His grave is simply bricked over.

It might be thought that after the death of Mr. Maffitt the tongue of slander would be hushed. But, no; more busy than before, it continued to follow him, charging that he had died by his own hand—that poison had caused his death. This suspicion, which nothing but the most malignant hate could have suggested, soon found its way into the press, and spread throughout the country. It was due the reputation of the distinguished dead, and it was due the cause of the Master he had so faithfully served, that this slander should be arrested. After consulting with his sister, Mrs. Ball, Dr. Jefferson Hamilton and the Rev. W. H. Milburn, stationed preachers in the city of Mobile, determined that a *post mortem* examination should be had, under the ablest medical supervision. This examination silenced at once and forever the heartless calumny. It revealed a *broken heart.* On one side of it there were three holes; *the other side had literally burst.** *They had broken his heart.* Noble man! he has entered into the rest that "remaineth to the people of God," and to-day shares its bliss with the many thousands who were brought to Christ through his ministry. "Sleep on, and take thy rest." In thine own beautiful lan-

*Dr. Nott, who took out the heart, kept it for several weeks, and then sent it to the Medical Faculty, in New Orleans, for examination. It was returned and deposited in the grave.

guage: "The sorrowful bosom heaves no more, the tears are dried up in their fountain, the aching head is at rest, and the stormy waves of earthly tribulation roll unheeded over the place of graves. The voice of thunders shall not awake thee; the loud cry of the elements, the winds, the waves, nor even the giant tread of the earthquake, shall be able to cause an inquietude in the chambers where thou dost sleep." God watches thy dust, and will at last gather it unto himself.

The Louisville District had been blessed the year before to a greater extent than any other District in the Conference. The work of the Church for the present year looked to the care of the hundreds who had been brought into the fold rather than to new accessions. In several portions of the District, however, there were gracious revivals of religion, in which many were added to the Church.

Thomas N. Ralston, Henry N. Vandyke, and William Atherton, were sent to the Fourth-street Station, which included a small frame church on Eighth street. The health of Mr. Vandyke was feeble; indeed, he was rapidly hastening to the grave, and could not be relied on for any service. The membership of this charge amounted to seven hundred and five whites and seven hundred and six colored. The colored Churches, although under the supervision of the preachers appointed to Fourth-street, were supplied with preachers of their own color. This large membership, five hundred of whom were new members, having been brought into the Church under the ministry of Mr. Maffitt the previous year, required much care and attention. Mr. Ralston and Mr. Atherton were diligent in their work. Their labor during the winter was excessive. Revival influence existed all the time, while prayer or experience meetings were held nearly every evening. By the first of February thirty persons joined the Church. In the prosecution of their work they were assisted by a noble membership—Hasbrook, Howe, Glassford, Evans, Kendrick, Buckles, and old Sister New—while Dr. Bright and Dr. Pirtle, worthy local preachers, were always ready to lend a helping hand. The Brook-street Church had for their pastor Joseph Marsee, a good preacher and a true man. While no revival blessed his labors in this station, the Church, under his ministry, continued in a prosperous and healthy state.

In the Jefferson Circuit there were refreshing times. At a camp-meeting held at Hughes's Camp-ground, six miles below Louisville, commencing May 20, conducted by Moses Levi, the senior preacher, about forty persons "passed from death unto life." It was our privilege to be present at that meeting, and to witness the progress of the good work. The Newcastle Circuit, in which the year before several hundred persons had joined the Church under the ministry of James D. Holding and William H. Anderson, continued to increase in numbers and influence under the labors of James D. Holding, who was returned to this field, and William McD. Abbett, the junior preacher. While the Elizabethtown Circuit shows a decrease in the membership, when compared with the former year, yet the ministry of Gilby Kelly was greatly blessed. The apparent decrease in the membership was the result of a change in the circuit, by which some of the Societies were transferred to another charge. Besides these seasons of prosperity, seventy-three persons became members of the Church at a camp-meeting held at Cedar Creek, late in August, or early in September.

Gilby Kelly was born in Pulaski county, Kentucky, in 1812. His father and mother were distinguished for their fervent piety and devotion to the Methodist Church, of which they were zealous members. We do not know in what year he embraced religion, but when only twenty years of age he was admitted on trial by the Kentucky Conference, which held its session in Harrodsburg in 1832. His first appointment was to the Hinckstone Circuit, as the colleague of Daniel H. Tevis. In 1833 he was sent to the Big Sandy Circuit, with Thomas Hall, and in 1834 to Port William. His appointment in 1835 was to the Danville Circuit, and in 1836 to the Somerset Circuit, where he was brought up and began his ministry. At the Conference of 1837 he was appointed to the Hopkinsville Circuit, where he remained for two years; and in 1839 we find him on the Elizabethtown Circuit.

Being wholly uneducated at the time of entering the Conference, he resolved to acquire, by patient and untiring study, that which had been denied him in his childhood and youth. With an intellect far above mediocrity, he soon stored his mind with useful knowledge, and at an early age took rank, not only as a respectable scholar, but as an able minister, with the first preachers of his age in the Conference. Genial and warm-hearted, Gilby Kelly made friends in every circle in which he was thrown; and zealous and active in the work of the ministry, he was beloved and efficient in the several charges he filled. His devotion to books never inclined him to neglect his work; but, "instant in season, out of season," wherever duty called him, he was prompt to fulfill its requirements. As an example for young men who have entered the ministry without educational advantages, we point with pleasure to Gilby Kelly, to show what may be accomplished by industry and perseverance.

Albert H. Redford and Seraiah S. Deering were sent to the Yellow Banks Circuit. It was here that Daniel S. Barksdale and Richard Holding had accomplished so much good the year before. The circuit had been left in a healthy condition, and a deep religious feeling existed throughout its bounds.

Seraiah S. Deering, for so young a man, was an excellent preacher, as well as a good singer, and was powerful in exhortation. Throughout that large and interesting field he traveled, and prayed, and preached, and besought men to be reconciled to God. Sinners were everywhere impressed by the great truths he delivered, and in all portions of the circuit he won souls to Christ. In Owensboro, in Yelvington, in Hawesville, and throughout the country, he preached with a power that carried conviction to the hearts of the people. Catholic in spirit, deeply pious, and with a burning zeal, his soft and mellow voice, in touching and winning strains, sent forth its notes of warning and of comfort. Fifty persons joined the Church, chiefly under his ministry, before the first of February.

Between the Methodist and Baptist Churches in the town of Owensboro, during the previous year, there had been some difficulty, which resulted in an estrangement of feeling between these two Christian denominations, and the wound was not yet healed. Methodism was still rudely assailed, and its usages ridiculed. It was deemed proper, not only by the members of the Methodist Church, but by citizens of Owensboro, to invite Mr. Crouch, the Presiding Elder, to deliver a series of sermons on the subjects and mode of Christian Baptism. No man was better prepared for such a task than Benjamin T. Crouch. Familiar with this controversy, in all its ramifications, no opponent could successfully meet him in debate. He accepted the invitation. The third quarterly-meeting for the circuit was to be held in Owensboro in the month of May, and Mr. Crouch fixed on that occasion as a proper time to preach on Baptism.

On Saturday and Sunday he held his quarterly-meeting, and on Monday preached his first sermon on the points in controversy. Mr. John L. Waller,* an able debater, and the editor of the *Western Recorder*—the leading Baptist journal in the West—was in attendance, together with quite a number of

*Mr. Waller had not at this time been licensed to preach. He often delivered what he called "Lectures on Baptism," and was regarded as the ablest debater in that Church.

Baptist preachers. Never was a community more thoroughly aroused. Old men, who had seldom been seen at a house of worship, were present, and many came from a distance to listen to this gifted minister of Christ. For three successive days, and on each occasion for three full hours, he held the vast assembly in breathless silence, while he set before them the views he held on this question.

The reply of Mr. Waller was in language bitter, in argument tame.

The Methodist Church occupied, from this time, a more elevated plane in this lovely village.

Jonathan Stamper was still in charge of the Shelbyville District. The Shelbyville Station, under the ministry of Richard Tydings, continued to prosper. During the winter considerable interest was manifested on the subject of religion, and about fifty persons were received into the Church.

The Taylorsville Circuit, Andrew J. McLaughlin and Elkanah Johnson being in charge, was greatly blessed during this year. Never were two preachers more dissimilar than these, and no two men labored more in harmony to advance the cause of the Redeemer. If the former was more brilliant, the latter was more profound; if the one gained the affections and favor of the people sooner, the other held them longer; if Mr. McLaughlin was more successful in his appeals to sinners, Mr. Johnson was better qualified to build up and establish the Church. Side by side these two good men preached and labored, that sinners might be saved. Before the first of January fifty persons joined the Church; and at a meeting held in Mount Washington, in July, there were forty additions to the Society in that village.

William D. Matting and Andrew M. Bailey traveled the Salt River Circuit. Although Mr. Matting only entered the Conference in 1837, he had considerable experience as a preacher of the gospel. He came from the Cumberland Presbyterian Church, in which he had been a successful and popular preacher for several years. Mr. Bailey was quite a youth, being only eighteen years of age, without education and without experience. He had, however, been soundly converted to God, and could relate his Christian experience and recommend religion to others. The Salt River Circuit was one of the best in the Conference, and embraced several communities distinguished for their culture and refinement. While Mr. Matting preached sermons that charmed the crowded audiences that heard him, young Bailey exhorted, and wept over the people, and pleaded with them to turn to God. Success crowned their labors: nearly three hundred persons were converted and added to the Church. One hundred joined at a meeting held in June.

William M. Grubbs was stationed in Bardstown and Poplar Flat. At the latter place an interesting revival occurred in June, at which many were brought into the liberty of the children of God, while in Bardstown thirty had joined earlier in the year.

Robinson E. Sidebottom was returned to the Hodgenville Circuit, where he had spent a pleasant and profitable year, and where prosperity again followed him. Allen Sears, in the Litchfield Circuit, witnessed displays of divine power, and "good times" were reported in the Lebanon Circuit, by Richard I. Dungan and Lorenzo D. Harlan.

In the Harrodsburg District, the Irvine and Liberty Circuits are the only appointments in which an increase is reported in the white membership, and in these it is small; while Harrodsburg and Danville Station reports an increase only in the colored membership. At Harrodsburg, however, Richard Deering received sixty persons into the Church.

The Bowling Green District was more prosperous than the Harrodsburg. In the Columbia Circuit, William M. Crawford, a preacher of decided pulpit ability, received into the Church one hundred persons; while Robert Fisk, on the Burksville Circuit, was equally successful. The Greensburg Circuit, through the instrumentality of Thomas Waring, was greatly blessed; and in the Glasgow Circuit, under the ministry of Robert F. Turner and Aaron H. Rice, more than one hundred persons witnessed a good confession. The labors of Alanson C. Dewitt were blessed in the Scottsville Circuit.

In the Hopkinsville District, no charge enjoyed such prosperity as did the Princeton Circuit, under the labors of Robert G. Gardner and Samuel Turner. Early in the spring indications were favorable for a general revival. Before summer began the entire circuit was in a flame, and at the close of the year three hundred persons professed to be converted to God, and fully that number joined the Church.

Napoleon B. Lewis, who traveled the Greenville Circuit, had many seals to his ministry.

The Barboursville District was greatly favored this year. In the Kentucky Mission, "good times" were reported by William James, the pastor; and in the Mount Pleasant Mission, Nathanael H. Lee was eminently successful. A small increase was reported in the Williamsburg, the Prestonsburg, the Louisa, and the Manchester Circuits. The Barboursville Circuit, under the ministry of Jedidiah Foster, a good and useful preacher, enjoyed great prosperity. The white membership in that charge was nearly doubled, and there was also an increase in the colored.

The entire increase in the Conference was one thousand six hundred and eight white and six hundred and nineteen colored members.

Thomas Smith, who had before traveled the Paris District, succeeded Thomas Joyner, who had spent four years in this new and interesting field. James R. Walker was reäppointed to the Hickman Circuit, with Jonathan White as his colleague. This year was more prosperous than the year before; revivals crowned the labors of these faithful men.

John P. Stanfield entered the Tennessee Conference in 1836, and traveled the Sevierville Circuit as the colleague of William M. McFerrin. In 1837 he was the junior preacher on the Richland Circuit, and in 1838 was in charge of the Henderson Circuit. In 1839 we find him traveling the Paducah Circuit, where his ministry was greatly blessed: nearly three hundred persons were added to the Church.

The preacher on the Wadesboro Circuit was Daniel Mooney, who had just been admitted into the Conference. We are always glad to record the success of a young preacher, whose labors in the itinerant ranks have just begun. Mr. Mooney was instrumental in effecting much good: nearly two hundred persons joined the Church in his charge.

The net increase in Kentucky this year was *one thousand eight hundred and eighty-one* white and *six hundred* colored members.

CHAPTER IX.

FROM THE SESSION OF THE KENTUCKY CONFERENCE OF 1840 TO THE CONFERENCE OF 1841.

He shall come down like showers
  Upon the fruitful earth,
And love, joy, hope, like flowers,
  Spring in his path to birth:
Before him on the mountains
  Shall peace the herald go;
And righteousness in fountains
  From hill to valley flow.

BISHOP MORRIS presided at the session of the Kentucky Conference which met in Bardstown, October 14, 1841.

Thomas N. Ralston was elected Secretary, and William M. Crawford Assistant Secretary.

Jonathan Stamper, William M. Grubbs, and Hubbard H. Kavanaugh, were appointed a Committee on Public Worship.

Josiah Whitaker was appointed to take charge of the colored congregations.

John Christian Harrison, Daniel S. Barksdale, and William B. Landrum, were appointed Stewards of the Conference.

Robert Y. McReynolds, John Beatty, and Gilby

Kelly, were appointed a Committee on Necessitous Cases.

Hubbard H. Kavanaugh, Alanson C. Dewitt, and Peter Taylor, composed the Committee on the Book Concern in New York.

Hartwell J. Perry and William H. Anderson were appointed a Committee on Post-offices. It was made the duty of this committee to furnish the Book Agents at New York with a list of the post-offices of the preachers.

John Tevis and George W. Brush were appointed a Committee on Memoirs.

At the previous session of the Conference Henry B. Bascom was appointed by the Bishop to deliver, at this session, the annual address on Education; John James, on the Christian Ministry; and Richard Tydings, on Missions.

Immediately after the appointment of the several committees, Dr. Bascom offered the following resolution, which was adopted:

"*Resolved*, That the annual sermon, by appointment of this body, on the subject of the Christian Ministry, be preached on Sabbath next, at three o'clock P.M.; that the sermon on Missions be preached on Sabbath night; and that the address on Education be delivered on Tuesday next, at ten o'clock A.M.; and that such be the standing arrangement hereafter."

Benjamin T. Kavanaugh, of the Rock River Conference, Burr H. McCown, of the Ohio Conference, and Thomas Bottomley, who had but recently come to Kentucky, and had for several months filled a vacancy in the city of Louisville, were present, and were introduced to the Conference and invited to take seats within the bar.

A communication on the subject of Common-school Education, from Bishop Smith, of the Protestant Episcopal Church, Superintendent of Public Instruction for the State of Kentucky, was received and read. This communication was referred to a special committee, consisting of Dr. Bascom, Hubbard H. Kavanaugh, and Richard Tydings. On Friday morning, October 16, they made the following report, which was adopted:

"The committee, to whom was referred the communication from Bishop Smith, in relation to the subject of Common-school Instruction within the State of Kentucky, beg leave to report the following resolution for adoption by the Conference:

"*Resolved, by the Kentucky Annual Conference of the Methodist Episcopal Church*, That we highly approve the object and action of the Legislature of Kentucky, in its recent attempt to establish an effective system of common-school instruction within the limits of this commonwealth; and we respectfully recommend that all our ministers and people, in every part of the State, extend their countenance and encouragement to the furtherance of the object of the Legislature and people of Kentucky, in the successful establishment of the excellent common-school system now in course of organization throughout the State."

Benjamin T. Crouch, the Presiding Elder of the Louisville District, presented a resolution from the

Quarterly Conference of the Fourth-street Station, Louisville, in reference to Moses M. Henkle, a minister in the Methodist Protestant Church, recommending him to be received into the Methodist Episcopal Church, according to the provisions of the Discipline:

"Whereas, regular and satisfactory evidence has been presented to this Conference that Moses M. Henkle has been ordained a deacon in the Methodist Episcopal Church, and an elder in the Methodist Protestant Church, and that he is a regularly accredited elder of said Methodist Protestant Church, in good standing; and whereas, he has signified his wish to attach himself to the Methodist Episcopal Church, and his willingness to conform and submit to the regulations thereof; therefore,

"*Resolved*, That this Conference approve his reception by the proper authorities of the Methodist Episcopal Church, on his compliance with the requisitions of the Discipline, in such cases made and provided; and that we are prepared, on such compliance, to receive him with Christian confidence and affection as a minister of our Church.

"WILLIAM FARQUAR,
"WILLIAM N. MERIWETHER.

"The above preamble and resolution were unanimously adopted by the Quarterly Conference for Fourth-street Station, Louisville, Kentucky, October 5, 1840. B. T. CROUCH, *Presiding Elder*.

"WILLIAM KENDALL, *Recording Steward*."

Mr. Henkle had entered the itinerant ministry of the Methodist Episcopal Church in 1819, but located after traveling three years. At a later period he entered the Methodist Protestant Church, in which his commanding talents and fervent zeal soon made him a leader. No preacher in that Communion enjoyed the confidence of this branch of Methodism to a greater extent than did Mr. Henkle. Convinced, however, that he had made a mistake in the step he had taken, he resolved to retrace it and return to the fold whence he had gone out.

It was "moved that Brother Henkle have the right to exercise the office of an elder in the Methodist Episcopal Church"—which motion prevailed. It only remained for Mr. Henkle to take the vows of office, as prescribed in the Book of Discipline, which he immediately proceeded to do.

The following resolutions were offered by Messrs. Stamper and Tydings, and adopted:

"1. *Resolved*, That, with due respect, we accept the copyright of Brother M. Jamieson's book on Baptism, as a present offered to this Conference.

"2. *Resolved*, That this Conference present said copyright to the Western Book Concern, and request the Concern to publish the same."

From the time that Campbellism made its first appearance, Kentucky had been one of the most prominent fields in which it had operated. The Baptist Church—one of the largest and most influential denominations—was most affected by its teachings. In many instances Churches were divided, the larger number following the fortunes of Alexander Campbell, the founder and leader of the new order. Deriding experimental religion, and offering salvation on terms more congenial to human nature than those laid down in the Bible, it met with sympathy and favor in many communities. With truth enough in the system to conceal its errors, many persons had been persuaded to embrace it, and, accepting it as true, became its zealous defenders. Christians of all denominations regarded it with disfavor, because of its pernicious effects on vital Christianity. In the Kentucky Conference were several preachers who attacked this system with signal ability, among whom Edward Stevenson was prominent. No one, however, was so fearless in striking at its strongholds as Milton Jamieson. He was a preacher of extraordinary ability, and in the struggle with Campbellism he proved himself a giant. He challenged the ablest teachers of the Reformation (so-called) to a discussion of the doctrines they taught, and laid bare to public view the errors and dangerous tendencies of the system. Fully acquainted with every dogma they held, his sermons exerted an influence, in every community in which he preached, toward arresting the tide of error and in planting more firmly the cardinal truths of Christianity. In addition to the sermons he preached against Campbellism, Mr. Jamieson became the author of a small book on Baptism, generally known as the "*Blue Pill*,"* which was distributed largely throughout the State. It was an able exposure of the errors it attacked, as well as a potent defender of the truth. It was the copy-

*It was bound in blue muslin.

right of this book which he presented to the Conference.

The sermons on the Ministry and on Missions were preached on Sunday—the former, by John James, at three o'clock, and the latter, by Richard Tydings, at seven o'clock. Mr. James entertained a large audience and the members of the Conference with an able sermon on the character and responsibility of the Christian ministry. The sermon by Mr. Tydings, on the spread of the gospel and the final triumphs of the cross, was equally instructive to the large assembly which heard him.

The address on Education, delivered by Dr. Bascom on Tuesday at ten o'clock, was alike worthy of the distinguished preacher and the occasion.

During a session of the Conference, held in the afternoon of the same day, Hubbard H. Kavanaugh offered the following resolution, which was adopted by a rising vote:

"*Resolved*, That Brother H. B. Bascom be, and he is hereby, most respectfully requested to furnish this Conference with a copy of the very learned, able, and eloquent address on Education which he delivered before this Conference this morning."

At the previous session of the Conference a resoluion was adopted, requesting the members of the Church throughout the commonwealth of Kentucky to "memorialize the Legislature, asking for a change in the *License Law*, as it regards the sale of ardent spirits." From every part of the State memorials looking to the suppression of the evil of intemperance had been placed before the Legislature, and received the most careful consideration of that body.

At this session of the Conference Mr. Linn offered the following resolution, which was adopted:

"*Resolved*, That the very kind and respectful attention which was paid by the Legislature of this commonwealth to the memorials and petitions to procure the repeal of the License Law, as it regards the sale of ardent spirits, furnishes the friends of temperance grounds of encouragement, and calls most solemnly for a renewal of effort; and that we do more earnestly than ever recommend to the people within our respective charges the propriety and necessity of again memorializing the Legislature on this subject, praying a revision of the present License Law, and such a change in the whole system as no longer to permit tippling under sanction and countenance of law."

The amount of money reported at this Conference for missionary purposes was only *two thousand two hundred and eighty-five dollars and thirty-one cents*, against *four thousand five hundred and eighty-one dollars and eighty-five cents* the former year. The collection at the anniversary meeting, in Bardstown, was *five hundred dollars;* besides, the largest amount —*two hundred and ninety-four dollars and twenty-six cents*—was sent from the Fourth-street Station, Louisville. Several large and wealthy Churches made no report.

The Preachers' Aid Society was organized at this session of the Conference. The object of this Society was to render aid to superannuated preachers, and to the widows and orphans of preachers who had died in the work. The Society was placed under the supervision of a Board of Managers, consisting of Henry B. Bascom, Jonathan Stamper, Hubbard H. Kavanaugh, William Gunn, Isaac Collard, Richard Tydings, Benjamin T. Crouch, John Tevis, George W. Taylor, and Richard Corwine. The following persons were elected Lay, or Local, Managers: Lewis Parker, of Wayne county; John Armstrong, of Maysville; David Heran, of Louisville; F. A. Savage, of Minerva; Charles Campbell, of Hopkins county. The officers were: John Armstrong, President; Benjamin T. Crouch, First Vice-president; Jonathan Stamper, Second Vice-president; Henry B. Bascom, Treasurer; F. A. Savage, Secretary.

The preaching during the session of the Conference was good. William H. Anderson preached a sermon on Thursday afternoon, in the Methodist Church, from the text, "But grow in grace, and in the knowledge of our Lord and Saviour Jesus Christ,"* which was listened to with rapt attention by a large audience; and on Friday evening, in the same house, many hearts were touched while Edwin Roberts preached from the passage, "Even the mystery which hath been hid from ages and from generations, but now is made manifest to his saints: to whom God would make known what is the riches of the glory of this mystery among the Gentiles; which is Christ in you, the hope of glory."†

Nineteen preachers were admitted on trial at this session: Drummond Welburn, Francis M. English,

*2 Pet. iii. 18. †Col. i. 26, 27.

Fielding Bell, Henry F. Garey, John Atkinson, James E. Nix, James S. Woolls, Leroy C. Danley, Charles Hendrickson, George W. Crumbaugh, Zachariah M. Taylor, William Reed, William D. Trainer, William D. Minga, James I. Ferree, John Miller, William C. Atmore, William R. Price, and Thomas Bottomley.

Of those who entered the service the year before, the name of James J. Harrison is the only one that disappears from the roll.

George S. Gatewood, William B. Maxey, Daniel S. Barksdale, Robert F. Turner, Matthew N. Lasley, Solomon Pope, Henry E. Pilcher, John C. Hardy, and John Nevius, located.

Messrs. Gatewood, Maxey, Lasley, Pilcher, Hardy, and Nevius, reëntered the itinerant ranks at a later period—some of them in other Conferences. In the fields they had occupied their labors were greatly blessed, and many were added to the Church under their ministry. In a local sphere Messrs. Barksdale, Turner, and Pope, continued to labor efficiently and usefully.

George McNelly and Elijah M. Bosley died during the year—the former a veteran in the ranks, and the latter a young man who had not reached the meridian of life.

George McNelly was born in Sumner (then Davidson) county, Tennessee, February 1, 1793. We regret that we have no record of the time he professed religion and became a member of the Church. As early as 1814 we find his name among those who were admitted on trial into the Tennessee Conference, and traveling the Hartford and Breckinridge Circuit, as the colleague of William F. King, having the eccentric Peter Cartwright as his Presiding Elder. In 1815 his appointment was the Red River Circuit, lying partly in the State of Tennessee. His field of labor the following year was the Barren Circuit, which spread over a vast extent of territory. In 1817 he was sent to the Goose Creek Circuit, on which he remained for two years. At the Conference of 1819 he was again appointed to the Red River Circuit, on which he had formerly traveled.

The ministry of Mr. McNelly during the six years which closed with the Conference of 1820 had been spent on extensive fields. His circuits included from twenty-five to thirty-five appointments, which had to be filled every four weeks. Much of the country over which he passed was rough, and the travel difficult. Exposed to every variety of weather, and with a delicate constitution at best, we are not surprised that in 1820 he proposed to retire from the itinerant ranks, that he might repair his health and be better qualified to perform the duties of a traveling preacher. He remained in the local ranks, however, but a single year; for in 1821 we find him on the Fountain Head Circuit, in the Kentucky Conference, which was formed in 1820, prosecuting his ministry with fervor and zeal. The following year he travels the Red River Circuit, where he had previously labored, and in 1823 the Christian Circuit, where he remains for two years. At the Conference of 1825 his appointment was the Hartford Circuit, where he spent two years, and where he witnessed the fruits of his ministry. At the Conference of 1827 he was appointed to the Green River District, where he remained for four years. His labors on the Green River District so far impaired his health that in 1831 he requested a superannuated relation, which he continued to sustain until 1836. Believing his health was sufficiently restored to resume the active duties of the ministry, he once more reported himself as able to perform the work of a pastor, and was stationed at Danville and Harrodsburg. The pastoral work, however, was more than equal to his wasting strength, and the following year he was appointed Agent for Augusta College. In 1838 he was again placed on the superannuated list, where he remained until God called him home. He died on Tuesday, April 14, 1840.

Mr. McNelly was an acceptable preacher, a consistent Christian, and faithful in the discharge of his duties. His end was peaceful.

Elijah M. Bosley was born in Washington county, Kentucky, November 24, 1811. His parents were Gideon and Elizabeth Bosley, and to his mother, who was distinguished for her fervent piety and superior intellect, he was indebted, under God, for the position he occupied as a Christian and a preacher of the gospel. When only a child he gave his heart to God, and at a camp-meeting held at Pleasant Run Camp-ground, in Washington county, he realized a sense of the pardoning love of Christ. The change was so gradual that at first he only tasted the healing stream; but soon his heart was filled with unbounded joy and love. From the time of his conversion until God called him home, his confidence never wavered, and never for a moment did he lose sight of his inheritance in the skies. No son, perhaps, ever gladdened the hearts of parents more than did Elijah Madison Bosley. Obedient in all things, he devoted himself to their comfort, and studied, with true filial tenderness, their happiness in every act of his life.

Called of God to preach the gospel, he would have shrunk from so responsible a work; but the conviction that the path of duty lay in this direction continually followed him, whether engaged in prayer or in the ordinary pursuits of life.

In the summer of 1833 a camp-meeting was held at the Beech Fork Camp-ground, in Nelson county, at which Mr. Bosley was present. George W. Taylor was the Presiding Elder. "Brother Bosley, you must preach to-night," said the Presiding Elder. "I have no license," was the prompt reply of the young man. "I will give you a license," said Mr. Taylor, "and the laws of George W. Taylor change not in reference to this appointment." Never having attempted to preach, and remarkable for his diffidence, he would have declined the appointment if made by any authority less than that of George W. Taylor. What young preacher does not understand the strugglings of that hour? Retiring to the woods, alone with God, he knelt in prayer, and asked divine aid and comfort for the ordeal through which he was about to pass. His sermon was brief —too brief; it was a failure. Hardly had he left the stand, mortified and discouraged, when Mr.

Taylor said to him, "Well, Elijah, you must try again, to-morrow." His second effort was an improvement on the first. A few weeks later he was licensed to preach and recommended to the Annual Conference.

In 1833 he was admitted on trial into the Kentucky Conference, and appointed to the Somerset Circuit. In 1834 he was sent to the Glasgow Circuit, in 1835 to the Burksville Circuit, and in 1836 to the Wayne Circuit. At the Conference of 1837 his appointment was the Columbia Circuit, and in 1838 the Winchester Circuit. The last charge to which he was appointed was the Hardinsburg Circuit, in 1839.

During the seven years that he proclaimed the gospel hundreds were brought to Christ through his ministry. Wherever he traveled the people loved him. While he studied to show himself approved "a workman that needeth not to be ashamed," he carried his preparations for the pulpit from his study to his closet, and there, for hours together, with prayers and tears, would ask the benediction of Heaven on his efforts to win souls to Christ. When he would sing by himself the songs of Zion, as he often did, every heart would be touched, and every eye be filled with tears. On these occasions there was a melody in his voice such as we have seldom heard. A distinguished member of the Louisville Conference, referring to Mr. Bosley in a letter to his brother, the Rev. Thomas G. Bosley, says: "When I was in deepest agony, sinking in the mire, where there was no standing, your brother was by me, offering me the promises of the gospel; and when I was happily converted, he was singing,

'My brethren, I have found
A land that doth abound.'

I shall never forget," he adds, "the sweetness of that song, as sung by him; for he had a sweet voice, and he seemed to me more like an angel than a human being."*

He closed his year's work on the Hardinsburg Circuit, and was on a visit to the family of his wife, in Barren county, when he was attacked with pneumonia. It soon became evident that he could not survive. Looking back upon a well-spent life, and then contemplating the glories that awaited him, among his last words we find a message to his fellow-laborers: "Tell my brethren that the gospel I have preached to others sustains me while exchanging worlds, and that if I had a score of lives to spend all should be spent in preaching Christ crucified."

No purer man than Elijah M. Bosley was ever admitted into the Kentucky Conference, and none ever labored with greater earnestness and devotion than he did. His daily walk and conversation were such as became a minister of the gospel of Jesus Christ. No improper word ever fell from his lips, and no aberration from the path of virtue marked his life. He was in all things an example. During the seven years of his itinerancy he was the honored instrument in the hands of God in doing much

* Letter from the Rev. N. H. Lee, D.D.

good. In every charge he filled he not only left behind him the savor of a good name, but "living epistles, to be read and known of all men."

Our first acquaintance with Mr. Bosley was in April, 1840, only a short time previous to his death. It is true, we had seen him at one or two sessions of the Annual Conference, and were impressed with his small stature and his meekness and modesty; but nothing more than a formal introduction had passed between us. We had preceded him on the Hardinsburg Circuit, and were traveling on the Yellow Banks, an adjoining circuit, when he attended our quarterly-meeting in Owensboro, at the time we have mentioned. On Saturday evening he preached in the court-house to a large congregation, from the text, "Who then can be saved?"* With a soft and slightly suppressed voice he entered upon the investigation of his subject, his audience fearing that he might not be equal to the task before him. All apprehensions, however, were soon allayed. He showed himself to be "a workman that needed not to be ashamed." The sermon was not brilliant, but was pointed, clear, and forcible. There was in it no speculative theology, but it was replete with gospel truth, and carried conviction to many hearts. We never saw him afterward; but when we heard of his death we said, "We shall meet him again." He died in great peace, October 9, 1840.

Joseph Marsee, who had entered the Kentucky Conference in 1827, was transferred this year to the Indiana Conference. He had traveled in Kentucky

*Matt. xix. 25.

for thirteen years, and discharged the duties of his high and holy office with fidelity. His fields of labor during this period were the Little Sandy, the Lebanon, the Glasgow, the Elizabeth, the Newcastle Circuits, the Newport and Covington, and the Lexington Stations, the Georgetown and Germantown Circuits, and the Mount Sterling (two years) and Brook-street, Louisville, Stations. In these several charges he was beloved and useful, and in them his memory is tenderly cherished.

Thomas W. Chandler was transferred to the Illinois Conference. He entered the Conference at the same time with Mr. Marsee, and had traveled the Ohio, the Whitley, the Greenville, and the Wayne Circuits. At the Conference of 1831 he was stationed in Bowling Green, and in 1832 in Hopkinsville. We next find him on the Yellow Banks Circuit, and then stationed in Frankfort. In 1836 he was sent to the Barboursville District, where he remained two years. In 1837 his field of labor was the Augusta District, and the following year the Covington. The last year he spent in Kentucky was on the Millersburg Circuit. Whether laboring amid mountain fastnesses or in the valleys of Kentucky, whether performing the duties of an itinerant on circuit, station, or District, he was always true and faithful.

Andrew Peace, who was transferred this year to the Missouri Conference, became an itinerant in 1828. His first appointment was to the Greenville Circuit, as the colleague of Lewis Parker. In 1829 he was sent to the Yellow Banks Circuit, and in

1830 his appointment was the Big Sandy Circuit. At the Conference of 1831 he was transferred to the Missouri Conference, where he traveled until 1836, when he located. At the Kentucky Conference of 1837 he was reädmitted and appointed to the Barboursville Mission, and in 1838 to the Somerset Circuit, where he remained for two years. It is with pleasure that we bear testimony to the faithfulness with which Mr. Peace performed the duties assigned him. He was traveling on the Barboursville Mission when we first made his acquaintance. Our fields of labor adjoining, we were often thrown together. He was a true man, a good preacher, and zealous and useful wherever he labored.

Williams B. Kavanaugh and Robert Y. McReynolds were transferred to the Rock River Conference, but afterward returned to Kentucky.

A young preacher, who was present at this session of the Kentucky Conference, writes us the following interesting letter:

"On Tuesday night I sat for the first time in a Conference-congregation, and heard its hymns of lofty cheer, and the hearty Amens to its inspiring prayers. On Wednesday morning I was recognized by a few personal acquaintances, and with intense interest witnessed the gathering of about one hundred and twenty itinerant heroes—including elders, deacons, men on trial, and applicants for admission. Bishop Morris (then in the fullness of his strength) called the Conference to order, and, after religious worship, the roll was called by Thomas N. Ralston. Nearly one hundred answered to the roll-call, commencing with the name of James Ward, a veteran of the eighteenth century, then leaning on his staff in age and feebleness extreme, and ending with the class to which Albert H. Redford belonged; yet it was seen that even such paths of glory as these were traveling lead but to the grave; for George McNelly and Elijah M. Bosley had responded to the roll-call above. Of these two, after George W. Taylor had preached their funeral-sermon to a congregation glowing with religious ecstasy, William Holman said that 'though once, like their brethren, poor and homeless on earth, they now have homes near the Public Square in glory.'

"When the regular business commenced I ventured within the bar of the Conference, and troubled a friend with many questions in reference to the more prominent members.

"'Who is that tall, lean, Quaker-looking preacher, who has more to say than any one in the house, and who always replies to questions addressed to the whole body?' I asked.

"'That is Benjamin T. Crouch, of the Louisville District, one of the most laborious men in the State,' was the answer.

"'Who is that large old gentleman, with white hair and florid complexion? He speaks with great earnestness, although his sentences are not as clean-cut and clear as they might be.'

"'That is John James, of the Covington District.'

"'That large, coarse-featured man, with such straight hair, I know. He is William Gunn, my own Presiding Elder.'

"'Yes,' said the brother at my side; 'he is about to read your recommendation, and you had better leave the house as soon as possible.'

"Returning after a short period to the side of my friend, I listened to the Presiding Elder of the Louisville District, as he presented the recomendations of nine candidates for admission on trial into the Conference.

"Francis M. English is received without difficulty. There is no trouble with Fielding Bell; he is already an able minister. The next elicits considerable discussion; but he is brilliant and admired, and is triumphantly admitted. He is not a preacher now, nor a member of the Church; is a distinguished lawyer in an Eastern city, and fills a large space in public life—less happy, we think, than when he preached Jesus and persuaded sinners to be reconciled to God. The names of two others, long connected with the itinerancy, have passed under clouds, and are now local preachers in the Northern Church. Two others sweetly sleep in Jesus. The next case excited much discussion, and considerable opposition was expressed. Some one said that George W. Taylor, of the Harrodsburg District, knew something about this case. A plain farmer-looking man rose, with dignity, and, in a deliberate and emphatic manner, said, 'He will never make an itinerant Methodist preacher.' Said my friend, 'That settles it.' He was, however, received, and, after preaching two years, left the ministry of the Methodist Church, and became a Baptist minister. Only one man was recommended from the

Covington District. He was talented, useful, ambitious; moved to the North-west; became a candidate for Governor; took office at Washington; went to ruin. A sallow-complexioned, stoop-shouldered, delicate old gentleman, the Presiding Elder of the Augusta District, read the recommendation of William D. Minga. He was received, and was the first of our large class to escape to his heavenly home.

"Bishop Morris announced that the Ohio Conference was flooded with preachers, and that he had advised several brethren to come to Kentucky, not by transfer, but with recommendations. William C. Atmore, John Miller, and William R. Price, were thus received. William D. Trainer, a Virginian, and Thomas Bottomley, from the territory of the Baltimore Conference, were also admitted.

"Of the nineteen who then entered the Conference only three are now on the effective list in our Church. One is effective in the M. E. Church, North. Several are superannuated. Some have so lived as to give sad emphasis to the words, 'Blessed are the dead which die in the Lord,' which we pronounced at the graves of Minga, Miller, Trainer, Bell, and Danley.

"I see another Presiding Elder—pale, tall, delicate, and slow of speech. It is Richard Corwine, of the Hopkinsville District. Two years later he went in triumph from the Louisville District to his heavenly home.

"'Who is that, walking up the aisle? He is evidently a man of mark,' I said, as his keen eye and high forehead attracted my attention.

"'That is Jonathan Stamper, of the Shelbyville District, one of the truest men and one of the most powerful preachers in America.'

"Another sat before me, whose gray locks and benignant face attracted my attention. It was Richard D. Neale, the Presiding Elder on the Barboursville District, lying in the mountains of Kentucky. His energy and zeal know no bounds save his wasting strength. Several preachers, now prominent in the Conference, were brought into the Church and converted to God through his instrumentality. He is a grand old man. Everybody loves him. He looks every inch a soldier. He is a brave cavalier, and was born to command.

"Here, close by us, is James King, of the Bowling Green District. How modest he seems! See his keen black eyes, his fair, florid complexion, his well-knit frame. He is said to be an able preacher, a good disciplinarian, a dignified gentleman, and bids fair to do the Church much service before he goes up to reap his great reward. There is Dr. Bascom. I have heard him preach as no other man ever preached. He is tall, handsome, erect.

"'Where is Dr. Tomlinson?' I inquired. He was absent; sickness in his family detained him at home.

"'He is our most accomplished scholar and most classical orator,' said my friend. 'But, yonder is Professor McCown. He is here among the friends of his youth. Did you ever see a finer model of a man? And there is Hubbard H. Kavanaugh, the Agent of Augusta College, who often outpreaches any of them.'

"'Who is that venerable, graceful old man, who always wears a smile?'

"'That is Richard Tydings—every inch a gentleman. On both sides of the mountains he has won many souls to Christ.'

"'That one—a little man, with iron-gray hair? There seems to be nervous energy enough in him for half a score of men.'

"'Edward Stevenson is his name—now of Russellville. He is a very efficient man, and one of a large and influential family, devoted to Methodism since it first entered the State. Near him sits another, almost as gray. His name is William B. Landrum, and the Church has not in it a truer man. See that old man, with long face, large chin, thin, long hair, drawn up over an almost bald head—that is Josiah Whitaker. He is about to speak in reply to Stamper's philippic against local itinerants. Hear him: "I have never asked any favor of your Bishops; I have left old Sukey Honey* to scratch for the children, and have traveled a hundred or a hundred and fifty miles from home, to serve your roughest circuits, for almost nothing. These thirty years I have been serving the Church, and in all that time I have never complained. I have never located, nor stationated, nor supernumerated, nor superannuated, nor Presiding Elderated, and I have no favors to ask of any of you!" There sits by him his son-in-law, James C. Crow, a man of great worth and a perfect pattern of fidelity. But listen to what the old men are saying of one of the young

*The maiden name of his wife.

preachers. He has married before he is an elder. His brother defends him. He had traveled for two years under a Presiding Elder, and has been a probationer in the Conference for one year. George W. Brush is the next speaker. He says a deacon must be the husband of one wife; that, in this old usage against matrimony, we are imposing a yoke on our brethren which neither we nor our fathers were able to bear. The young man is acquitted. Others have a fair warning of what they may expect if in this respect they walk not according to the traditions of the elders.'

"'Please, tell me why I hear so little in this place from men in the prime, or morning, of life—men distinguished for their success in doing good among the people. There are Brush, Roberts, Deering, Babbitt, Linn, Crain, Lewis, Woolliscroft, Peter Taylor, Redford, Foster, Merritt, Abbett, Savage, Hardy, Harrison, Grubbs, Thompson, Perry, the Kellys, the Holdings, and others. I am disappointed in not hearing from them on the Conference-floor.'

"'You will hear many of them in the pulpit, and hear about them on the floor of the Conference. If all were to speak, too much time would be consumed; hence, those who are officially interested in the case in hand are the only persons who are generally expected to consume time upon it. Besides those you have named, there are others on our roll to whom the people gladly listen; and among those to be admitted into full connection, this year and next, there are several who have already distinguished themselves among the people, and will soon occupy places of prominence among their older brethren. There are Anderson, and Lee, and South. In the class of the present year, besides a number of young men who promise future usefulness, there are Bell, Atkinson, Miller, Atmore, and Bottomley, who are already able ministers.'"

It is always pleasant to review the labors of faithful men in the ministry, and to record the triumphs of the cross. In no State in the Union have the achievements of Methodism been more signal than in Kentucky. If the membership in the Church has not been so large at any one time as in some other States, it is not because fewer persons have worshiped at its altars, or been brought to Christ through its ministry. Successful at home, it has sent its blessings abroad, and planted the standard of Christianity in other fields.

In looking over the appointments for this year, we find no change in the Presiding Elderships.

In the Augusta District, Walter Shearer was returned to the Little Sandy Circuit.

In the Lexington District, George W. Brush was again sent to Lexington, Edwin Roberts to Versailles, Carlisle Babbitt to Winchester, John W. Riggin to Mount Sterling, and Hartwell J. Perry to Georgetown.

In the Louisville District, William McD. Abbett again travels on the Newcastle Circuit.

In the Shelbyville District, Richard Tydings, John F. South, A. J. McLaughlin, William M. Grubbs, and Richard I. Dungan, occupy the same fields in which they had labored faithfully and acceptably the previous year.

In the Harrodsburg District, Richard Deering was returned to Harrodsburg and Danville.

In the Hopkinsville District, we again find Robert G. Gardner on the Princeton Circuit, where his ministry had been greatly blessed.

In the Barboursville District, Nathanael H. Lee and William James were reäppointed to the same fields on which they had labored the year before—the former to the Mount Pleasant Mission, and the latter to the Kentucky Mission.

The year upon which we are now entering was replete with benedictions to the whole Church. The net increase of the membership was not so great as that of the previous year, yet there was scarcely a charge in the Conference that was not visited by a gracious revival of religion, while in many places the interest was of the most extraordinary character. Commencing with the Maysville District, the labors of Hubbard H. Kavanaugh were abundantly blessed, while in the Fleming Circuit, under the ministry of William M. Crawford and Henry F. Garey—the former an able preacher of several years' experience, and the latter a young man of promise—many were brought to Christ and added to the Church. The Germantown Circuit—under the pastoral care of Thomas R. Malone—enjoyed great prosperity; and in all the other charges in the District many were awakened and converted to God.

In the Covington District the displays of divine power were greater than in the Augusta District.

John James, the Presiding Elder, was untiring in his labors. He traveled his extensive District, sowing everywhere the seeds of truth, and gathering sinners into the fold of Christ. In the Covington Station, Calvin W. Lewis was eminently successful. He had scarcely entered upon his work when indications were favorable for a gracious outpouring of the Holy Spirit. The winter witnessed a signal triumph on the part of the Church, in a gracious revival in which many were brought to Christ. In the Newport Station, the ministry of Gilby Kelly was more successful. During the year both the white and the colored membership were more than doubled, and the Church reached an eminence it had not previously known.

Aaron Moore traveled the Leesburg Circuit. Although he descended from an aristocratic family in England, he was without education. His grandfather was a member of the British Parliament; yet when the grandson attained his majority he was unacquainted with the rudiments of an English education. Aaron Moore was born in Ohio, April 2, 1813. At twenty years of age he embraced religion and joined the Methodist Episcopal Church. He was admitted on trial into the Kentucky Conference in 1839, and was appointed to the Millersburg Circuit, as the colleague of Thomas W. Chandler. In 1840 he was appointed to the Leesburg Circuit alone, where we now find him. It was with considerable hesitation on the part of the Conference that he was received as a fellow-laborer. Without culture and without education, he seemed to promise but little to the Church. Only a short period elapsed before he evinced a superior intellect and a winning address. His fervent piety, his burning zeal, his uncompromising devotion to the cause of Christ, gave him an influence that but few men possessed. As a preacher he soon took rank with many of his more highly-favored brethren, while as an exhorter he had scarcely a peer in the Conference. More gifted in his public prayer than any preacher of our acquaintance, the most obdurate hearts were often melted while listening to petitions offered before the throne of grace in their behalf by this faithful servant of God. Mr. Moore had traveled but a few months until the people thronged to hear him preach. He had a clear head, a fertile imagination, a good voice, and was withal so humble. He had been soundly converted to God, and was well acquainted with the doctrines of the Church, and taught them with marked ability. On the Leesburg Circuit more than one hundred souls were brought to Christ through his ministry, and the Church was greatly revived under his labors.

George W. Merritt was appointed to the Paris Circuit. He was born in Fincastle, Botetourt county, Virginia, April 17, 1807. Losing his parents when he was quite young, he was placed under the care of an elder brother, who resided in Staunton, Virginia, where he was brought up and educated. In the autumn of 1827 he came to Kentucky, and settled in Winchester. During the same year, under the ministry of Henry McDaniel, a good and pure man, he was awakened to his condition as a sinner, and was received into the Church as a seeker of religion by Milton Jamieson. A short time afterward he found the pearl of great price. He was soon impressed with the conviction that it was his duty to proclaim the tidings of a Redeemer's love to perishing sinners, yet felt reluctant to enter upon so responsible a work. In the meantime he removed to Lexington, where, in 1833, he was licensed to preach by William Gunn, at that time the Presiding Elder on the Lexington District. In the spring of 1834 he was employed by William Adams, who succeeded Mr. Gunn as Presiding Elder, to travel on the Madison Circuit, with James Ward, until the next Conference should meet. He entered the Kentucky Conference in 1834, and was reäppointed to the Madison Circuit, with William B. Landrum. His next appointment was to the Shelby Circuit, as the colleague of Richard Holding. In 1836 he was placed in charge of the Mount Sterling Circuit, and of the Fleming Circuit in 1837. At the Conference of 1838 he was appointed to the Danville Circuit, with William D. Matting, who remained in the work but a short time, when Mr. Merritt was placed in charge, with Matthew N. Lasley, who was transferred from Pulaski Coal Mines, as his colleague. In 1839 he was sent to Cynthiana. In 1840 we find him on the Paris Circuit, one of the most pleasant charges in the Conference.

From his entrance into the ministry Mr. Merritt gave promise of great usefulness in the Church. His presence commanding, and popular in his address, he was well calculated to make friends in every circle in which he was thrown. Believing himself to be divinely called to preach the gospel of Christ, he prosecuted the work of the ministry with unswerving fidelity and zeal, and was instrumental in the accomplishment of much good. Acceptable as a preacher, and highly gifted in exhortation, his warm appeals were listened to with interest, while many were persuaded to abandon a life of sin and turn to God. On the Paris Circuit, where we find him this year, more than one hundred and fifty persons were converted, and the membership largely increased.

On the Millersburg Circuit, John C. Hardy was equally successful in winning souls to Christ. He was a warm and earnest preacher, and God honored his ministry.

In the Lexington District, several of the charges were favored with extraordinary revivals of religion. Under the ministry of John Christian Harrison, in Frankfort, many witnessed a good confession. The Versailles Circuit was in a blaze. Edwin Roberts, the zealous and indefatigable pastor, like a flaming fire, traveled through his circuit, urging the Church to greater fidelity, and pleading with sinners to be reconciled to God. As early in the Conference-year as November seventy-five persons were added to the Church, and the good work had only commenced. The preachers on the Winchester Circuit were Carlisle Babbitt and Drummond Welburn—the latter a young man who had just joined the Conference. Promptly entering upon their work, they prosecuted it with fidelity and zeal, and before the opening of spring about one hundred persons made a profession of religion.

John W. Riggin was in charge of the Mount Sterling Circuit. He was born in Maryland, August 26, 1794. When he was only eight years old his parents removed to Kentucky, and settled in Mason county. The country at that period was new and sparsely settled, and afforded him no facilities for acquiring an education. He grew up to manhood a stranger to God and indifferent to the claims of religion. In 1816, under the ministry of William Holman, he was awakened, converted, and joined the Church. Believing it to be his duty to preach the gospel, yet not prepared to enter the itinerant ranks, in 1823 he was licensed to preach, and for eleven years was active and useful in a local sphere. In 1833 he entered the Conference, and was appointed to the Fleming Circuit as junior preacher, and the following year to the same field as preacher in charge. At the Conference of 1835 we find him on the Germantown Circuit, and in 1836 on the Lewis Circuit. At the Conference of 1837 he was sent to Sharpsburg, where he remained for two years. In 1839 he was sent to the Mount Sterling Circuit, where we still find him in 1840. On the Mount Sterling Circuit, as in all the charges he had previously filled, the ministry of Mr. Riggin was greatly blessed. Revivals crowned the labors of this good man, and many souls were converted through his instrumentality.

The Louisville District was less prosperous this year than for several years preceding. Although the Fourth-street and Eighth-street Churches were two separate charges the greater portion of the year before, yet they were not formally separated until the Conference of 1840. John H. Linn was stationed at Fourth-street, and Thomas Bottomley at Eighth-street. The preachers in these two charges were useful and beloved. In the Fourth-street Church, Mr. Linn attracted large congregations, who listened to his warning voice and heard the words of life as they fell from his lips. From week to week was sown good seed, which soon bore fruit to the honor and glory of God. Crowded assemblies waited on the ministry of Mr. Bottomley, and many were brought into the Church through his unceasing labors. His preaching was very peculiar. His language was simple, and easy to be understood. The uneducated knew the meaning of his words, and the learned were interested and impressed with his plain, pure English. He but seldom preached what are technically styled doctrinal sermons, yet no one understood the doctrines of the Church better than he did. It is true, the theoretical teachings of Christ and the apostles were embodied in his sermons, in which were set forth the blessings of Christian experience and the practical duties of religious life. He made no effort at display, and yet he often ascended to the loftiest heights of oratory. He was calm and dispassionate in the investigation of his subject, and all the while there was a pathos and a power in his manner of presenting the great truths of the gospel by which the pulpit is but seldom distinguished. His exposition of the text was lucid and forcible, and his exhortations powerful and convincing. He wore a round-breasted coat—the old Methodist style—and looked every inch a Methodist preacher of the Wesleyan type. His quick perception and sound judgment, together with his consistent piety and burning zeal, pointed him out as a safe counsellor, and indicated the eminent position, in the affections and confidence of his brethren, which he would occupy in the coming years. Such was Thomas Bottomley when we first saw him, in 1840.

Mr. Bottomley is an Englishman by birth, having been born, June 2, 1805, at Cononley Woodside, near Skipton-on-Craven, West Riding, Yorkshire, England. On the 24th of December, 1817, when only twelve years of age, he joined the Wesleyan Methodist Society, and was converted December 24, 1819, just two years later, and preached his first sermon December 24, 1822, being then eighteen years of age. He was soon afterward licensed to preach. In 1827 he emigrated to America, landing in New York July 4 of that year. From this period until the spring of 1840 he exercised his gifts as a local preacher, when he was admitted on trial into the Baltimore Conference, and transferred to Arkansas. On his way to Arkansas he was detained in Louisville by the sickness of his wife. In the autumn of the same year he became a member of the Kentucky Conference, and was appointed to the Eighth-street Church, where we now find him.

William Holman was stationed at Brook-street. Although not gifted as a preacher, his persuasive powers could scarcely be excelled. In every portion of the State where he had preached the gospel of Christ there were seals to his ministry. He was first stationed in Louisville in 1833, and, with the exception of 1837 and 1838, had continued in that city. He was well known in the community, and much beloved by the people. Amongst the poorer classes, to whom he was especially attentive, he was a great favorite. He was a superior pastor, and it was in all probability his gifts in this department of ministerial work that contributed more than did any thing else to the power and influence he exercised in the city of Louisville. To him it made no difference whether his services were required in the palaces of wealth or in the garrets of the poor; it was always the same. Wherever affliction and sorrow, suffering and want, were found, like an angel of mercy he was present to administer a balm. The midnight watch often found him sitting at the bedside of sorrow-stricken ones, offering the consolations of religion, or kneeling and offering up earnest prayers in their behalf. The winds never blew so fiercely, the storms never howled so loudly, the rains never descended in such torrents, as to hinder him in his labor of love. Possessing a feeble constitution, he performed the work of a strong man, with an alacrity that surprised all who knew him. The Brook-street Church, the present year, continued to prosper under his care.

We have previously referred to the German population that was settling in Louisville. In 1839 the question of supplying them with the gospel was not only agitated, but the purpose was formed to furnish them with the means of grace. The establishment of a German Mission was contemplated; but, failing to secure a suitable preacher, the work was temporarily abandoned. In 1840 Peter Schmucker was appointed to this important field. It would have been difficult to find a man better adapted to the successful prosecution of this work than Mr. Schmucker. He entered upon his charge about the last of December, and on the 2d of March he writes from Louisville: "It is only about five weeks since I commenced forming a German Society here, and from five to ten have been received every Sabbath since, so that we now number fifty-six."* At the close of the year he reported ninety-three members.

In the Jefferson Circuit, under the ministry of Joseph D. Barnett and James S. Woolls, there was considerable prosperity, although there was a decrease in the colored membership.

Moses Levi traveled on the Elizabethtown Circuit, where his labors were greatly blessed; while Peter Taylor had charge of the Hardinsburg Circuit, in which there were extensive revivals.

In the Brandenburg Circuit, Alanson C. Dewitt and Francis M. English labored faithfully and with success. This was Mr. English's first circuit; but Mr. Dewitt had traveled as a preacher for several years. He was born in Bedford county, Virginia, July 23, 1809. He was converted September 1, 1824, when fifteen years of age. Believing that he was divinely called to the work of the ministry,

* Letter in *Western Christian Advocate.*

after many misgivings he yielded to the conviction, and was licensed to preach by George W. Taylor, May 25, 1833. In the autumn of 1834 he began his itinerant career, and for two years performed the duties of a traveling preacher under the appointment of the Presiding Elder. In 1836 he was admitted into the Kentucky Conference, and appointed to the Elizabeth Circuit, as the colleague of Joseph D. Barnett. In 1837 he was sent to the Glasgow Circuit, with James King, and in 1838 to the Bowling Green Circuit alone. At the Conference of 1839 his field of labor was the Scottsville Circuit, and in 1840 we find him on the Brandenburg Circuit. The preaching of Mr. Dewitt was calculated to build up the Church rather than to gather persons into its folds, yet in the charges he had filled many had been awakened and converted through his instrumentality. The Brandenburg Circuit was one of the most pleasant in the Conference. Methodism exerted a controlling influence within its bounds; but under the ministry of Alanson C. Dewitt the membership was considerably increased. Though as a preacher he was unostentatious and plain, yet in his sermons there was a clearness and strength that rendered them peculiarly impressive and attractive. Whether he defended the doctrines of Christianity or enforced the practical duties of religious life upon his hearers, his words were well chosen, and good was accomplished. Unassuming and modest, he yielded too readily to discouragements, and thus sometimes failed to win the prize that was within his grasp. With a large and growing family, and but poorly supported, he at times hesitated as to whether he should retire to the local ranks, and serve the Church in a more limited sphere, or prosecute the duties of the itinerant ministry, although confronted by difficulties. Believing that God had called him to devote his life to this service, he "chose rather to suffer affliction" and meet with trials than to turn away from the path of duty so obviously marked out.

In the Shelbyville District only two appointments report an increase—the Hodgenville and the Litchfield Circuits. Napoleon B. Lewis and James I. George traveled on the former, and James E. Nix on the latter. Both charges were blessed with revivals.

The Harrodsburg and Danville Station, the Danville and the Irvine Circuits, and the Mount Vernon Mission, in the Harrodsburg District, report each an increase in the membership this year. Richard Deering, who was reäppointed to Harrodsburg and Danville, labored with undiminished zeal, and the pleasure of the Lord continued to prosper in his hands. On the Danville Circuit, we find Robinson E. Sidebottom prosecuting his work with energy, and reaping the reward of his labors. Two revivals in the bounds of his work—one at Beech Grove, and the other at Joseph's Chapel—were the result, under the blessing of God, of his faithful ministry. At the former he had the assistance of Munford Pelley, who was traveling on the circuit with him, under the appointment of the Presiding Elder, and at the latter he was favored with the efficient services of Edwin Roberts. Peter Duncan had charge of the Irvine Circuit, where he preached with great success; while the Mount Vernon Mission, served by Thomas Hall, a good and pure man, enjoyed prosperity.

James King was the leader of the hosts in the Bowling Green District. But few men in the Conference attracted more attention in the pulpit, or preached with greater power, than did this plain and unostentatious minister of Christ. The influence he exerted for good was widely felt in the District over which he presided.

John C. C. Thompson, a burning and a shining light, had charge of the Greensburg Circuit. He had entered the itinerant ranks in 1835, and wherever he had preached his ministry was signally blessed. On the Glasgow Circuit, where his earliest trophies were won by the persuasive power of the truth as it fell warm from his lips, many were turned from darkness to light. As the colleague of the venerable John Denham on the Burksville Circuit, he had been eminently useful. He was reäppointed to the Burksville Circuit, but was removed, after a few weeks, to the Lebanon Circuit, to assist Matthew N. Lasley. In 1838 he was returned to the Lebanon Circuit, and in 1839 was appointed to Manchester, in the mountain region of the State, in both of which he continued to be useful. We meet with him the present year on the Greensburg Circuit, like a flaming fire, passing through his charge, comforting the people of God and exhorting sinners to repent. In the pulpit, in the altar, in the social circle, he recommended the religion of Jesus, and persuaded sinners to be reconciled to God. The sound of his Master's feet was heard behind him, and many were brought to Christ.

Matthew N. Lasley was the son of the Rev. Thomas Lasley, so distinguished in the history of Methodism in the West and South, and the grandson of the Rev. Manoah Lasley, to whose labors and zeal in the early settlement of Kentucky the Church is greatly indebted.

Matthew N. Lasley was born in Green county, Kentucky, December 2, 1812. Brought up under religious influence, he was early impressed with the importance of religion, and in the fifteenth year of his age he was converted, at Blowing Spring Campground, near Greensburg, while Abram Long was preaching on Sabbath night. His father a traveling preacher, and his father's house the home of the weary itinerant, in childhood he became familiar with the trials and sacrifices incident to the life of the faithful preacher of the gospel. The impression that the path of duty would lead him to the ministry greatly marred his happiness. With a proper conception of the sacredness of the office, and of his inadequacy for so responsible a work, he would gladly have shrunk from the task. It was not until he attained to manhood that he yielded to his convictions. On the 12th of July, 1834, he left his plow in the furrow, midway the field, and started to a quarterly-meeting held on the Glasgow Circuit, where he was licensed to preach by George W. Taylor, and placed by him on the Burksville Circuit, as the colleague of Thomas C. Davis.

At the following Conference he was admitted on trial, and appointed to the same circuit as junior preacher, Joseph D. Barnett being then in charge. Working in harmony, the labors of these faithful men were blessed. Vital Christianity, in this section of the State, was confronted at that period by the erroneous teachings of Campbellism, then in its full strength. The Church, however, prospered. A new camp-ground was established at Huffman's, in Monroe county, at which many were brought to Christ, and which became a great Methodist center, where hundreds have been converted. In that circuit the names of John and Obey Baker, with their excellent families, and those of James L. Greenup and Barton Harlan, worthy local preachers, deserve to be recorded.

On his way to the Conference held at Shelbyville in 1835, Mr. Lasley stopped at Beech Fork camp-meeting, in Nelson county, where he spent a few days pleasantly and profitably. From this Conference he was appointed to the Salt River Circuit, as the colleague of the venerable James Ward, with his estimable father in charge of the District, as Presiding Elder. The circuit was large in its territorial limits, and included thirty preaching-places. The year was pleasant and profitable to the young preacher, closing with an excellent camp-meeting at Beech Fork Camp-ground, at which Hubbard H. Kavanaugh and Dr. Bascom were present and preached with great ability and power. It was at this camp-meeting that Dr. Bascom preached, on Sabbath at eleven o'clock, from the text, "For the great day of his wrath is come; and who shall be able to stand?"* The sermon was powerful—overwhelming. As he portrayed the scenes of the judgment-day and repeated the words of the text, "For the great day of his wrath is come," five thousand people sprang to their feet, frantic with alarm.

From the Salt River Circuit we follow Mr. Lasley to the Lebanon Circuit, where he remained two years, and in which, under his ministry, hundreds were brought to Christ. His colleague the first year was William D. Matting, and the second year John C. C. Thompson, who was removed from the Burksville Circuit to aid Mr. Lasley—both of whom were burning and shining lights—while in the local ranks he was assisted by John Sandusky and James Cain, useful and gifted local preachers. The entire circuit was in a flame. Hundreds were converted. At a single meeting held at Pleasant Run, the first year—a place sacred in the annals of Kentucky Methodism—nearly a hundred passed from death unto life. At Spratt's Camp-ground, in Taylor county, the second year, a basket-meeting was held, whose fruitage will greatly augment the number of the saved in eternity; while at Pleasant Run a meeting was held, which, in power and in the number of conversions, exceeded that of the former year. Before leaving the circuit Mr. Lasley solicited a subscription to build a church in Lebanon, and then placed the house under contract.

It was at the Conference held in Danville, in 1838, that we remember to have first seen Mr. Lasley.

*Rev. vi. 17.

He was then in the prime of life, yet seemed enfeebled by the labors he had performed. His appointment was to the Pulaski Coal Banks, where he had hard work and meager support. He remained in this charge until spring, when the Presiding Elder sent him to Somerset, to rest and recuperate. While in Somerset he made arrangements to build a new church, but was called from this work to the Danville Circuit, a few weeks later, where he labored until Conference, with George W. Merritt, supplying the place of William D. Matting, who had retired from the circuit. In 1839 he was sent to the Prestonsburg Circuit, in the mountain region of the State, where he spent a delightful year.

During the period in which Mr. Lasley had been an itinerant no man in the Conference had labored with greater diligence and fidelity than he. A clear and forcible preacher, he was not only acceptable everywhere, but was greatly beloved by the people he served. Zealous and energetic, his feeble constitution was unequal to the heavy and constant drain made upon it, and at the Conference of 1840 he believed it to be his duty to retire and rest, that he might reënter the service with redoubled energy. He hoped that in a local sphere he might be able to accomplish something for the Master, and hence he located. He was, however, allowed to remain local but a few weeks. George W. Simcoe and Zachariah M. Taylor were appointed to the Glasgow Circuit. Mr. Simcoe failed to reach the circuit, and James King, the Presiding Elder, prevailed on Mr. Lasley to fill the vacancy. No appointment could have been more opportune; for he was well known on that charge, and highly esteemed as a minister of Christ.

Before he entered on the discharge of his duties on the Glasgow Circuit, meetings had been held at different points, resulting in much good. The interest, however, continued to increase, until the entire circuit was in a blaze. The revival continued through the year, and hundreds were awakened and converted to God.

Mr. Taylor was the son of a Methodist preacher, and had been brought up in the Church. His father, George W. Taylor, was one of the most able and influential members of the Conference. Under their ministry the Glasgow Circuit became one of the best in the Conference.

The Burksville, the Albany, the Wayne, and the Columbia Circuits, in the same District, were greatly blessed.

Joel Peak, a plain and faithful preacher, was traveling on the Burksville Circuit. He had entered the Conference in 1837, and had filled the Falmouth and the Madison Circuits—the latter two years. His appointment to the Burksville Circuit, in 1840, was pleasant to himself and gratifying to the people. Entering upon his work soon after the close of the Conference, he prosecuted his ministry with commendable zeal, and many, through his instrumentality, were brought into the Church. While Mr. Peak, in the Burksville Circuit, was winning souls to Christ, in the Wayne Circuit William D. Minga, who had been admitted on trial at the previous

Conference, was gathering many seals to his ministry. At the same time John C. Baskett was witnessing the fruit of his labors in the Albany Circuit; while on the Columbia Circuit James C. Crow received sixty members into the Church.

In the Hopkinsville District, there was an interesting revival of religion in Russellville, under the ministry of Edward Stevenson, and on the Elkton and Logan Circuit, where Wesley G. Montgomery and Warren M. Pitts—the latter a local preacher employed by the Presiding Elder—were dispensing the word of life. In the La Fayette Circuit, James I. Ferree, a sprightly and zealous young man, was the instrument of much good; while, in the Princeton Circuit, the ministry of Robert G. Gardner continued to be blessed. Thomas Demoss, on the Madisonville Circuit, and Jesse Cromwell, on the Greenville Circuit, witnessed the conversion of many souls.

In no part of the Conference, during this year, were such displays of divine power witnessed as in the Barboursville District. Richard D. Neale, the Presiding Elder, was one of the most zealous ministers in the Church. He traveled his extensive and rugged District, preaching, as he passed through it, on every occasion that offered. His sermons were attended with the demonstration of the Spirit, and with power, to the hearts of the people, and many turned to God.

On the Mount Pleasant Mission, Nathanael H. Lee, the faithful missionary, witnessed extraordinary outpourings of the Holy Spirit. From the center to the circumference of his charge sinners were awakened and penitents converted to God. In the Kentucky Mission, William James enjoyed interesting revivals of religion, and a large ingathering into the Church. The Prestonsburg Circuit was in a blaze. Allen Sears, one of the most indefatigable and industrious preachers we ever knew, labored with uncompromising zeal, and gathered much fruit to the Master. On the Louisa Circuit, under the ministry of Jedidiah Foster, the membership was nearly doubled; in the West Liberty Mission, Andrew M. Bailey almost trebled the membership; and on the Red Bird Mission, the preacher returned almost twice as many members as were reported the year before.

At the General Conference of 1840 the Tennessee Conference was divided—the western portion of it, embracing a part of Kentucky, to be called the Memphis Conference. The Hickman, the Paducah, and the Wadesboro Circuits were included in the new Conference. To the Hickman Circuit James M. Major and Daniel Mooney were appointed; to the Paducah Circuit, George E. Young and E. L. Ragland; and Benjamin Barham to the Wadesboro Circuit.

At a camp-meeting held in the Paducah Circuit, in July, thirty-five persons were converted, and about the same number were added to the Church. At the close of a camp-meeting held in the Wadesboro Circuit, the last of August, Daniel Mooney, in a letter to the editor of the *South-western Christian Advocate*, dated September 10, says: "The camp-meeting at Mount Pisgah is just over. The result was rather more glorious than we could have anticipated. The preachers preached in the spirit of their Divine Master; for, indeed, their words fell with all the weight of a prophet's fire on the congregation. Those who felt sensibly a declension of the work of grace in their own souls were greatly revived and strengthened; some who had been mourners for three or four years were happily and powerfully converted; and the gay and inconsiderate, and the gray-headed sinners, were smitten 'between the joints of the harness' by the arrows of the Almighty, which caused them to fall before God into the altar, like Dagon before the ark, and cry for mercy. The precise number converted is not yet known; but, from the best calculation, there were about sixty who found the gospel to be the power of God to their own salvation, and forty-seven attached themselves to the Methodist Episcopal Church, on probation."

On the Hickman Circuit, Mr. Mooney says: "At several of our appointments we have had a comfortable revival of God's work. At my week-day appointment, at Pleasant Hill, we had a most comfortable time with several mourners who came to the altar of prayer. On the next Sunday evening Brother Major had an appointment there, and five were converted. Brother Gentry, a local preacher, and myself held a two-days' meeting at New Hope, at which there were eight brightly and soundly converted. Some local brethren held a two-days' meeting at Walnut Grove, and I learn that five embraced religion there. Our camp-meeting at Mobley's was not as great as we anticipated, though there were thirty-five or forty who professed religion, if our calculation was correct. It is probable that there have been something over a hundred additions to the Church this year."

In the Kentucky Conference the increase this year was one thousand four hundred and seventy-nine white and four hundred and forty colored members; in Jackson's Purchase there was an increase of three hundred and ten in the white membership and a decrease of three in the colored.

The total increase in Kentucky was *one thousand seven hundred and eighty-nine* white and *four hundred and thirty-seven* colored.

CHAPTER X.

FROM THE SESSION OF THE KENTUCKY CONFERENCE OF 1841 TO THE CONFERENCE OF 1842.

The little cloud increases still,
  The heavens are big with rain;
We wait to catch the teeming shower,
  And all its moisture drain:
A rill, a stream, a torrent flows,
  But pour the mighty flood;
O sweep the nations, shake the earth,
  Till all proclaim thee God!

THE session of the Kentucky Conference of 1841 was held in Maysville, commencing September 15. There was no Bishop present, and Jonathan Stamper was called to the chair, and opened the Conference with reading the Scriptures and with prayer.

After the roll had been called, the Conference proceeded to elect a President. Upon balloting, Jonathan Stamper was duly elected.

Thomas N. Ralston was elected Secretary, and William M. Crawford Assistant Secretary.

Isaac Collard and Hubbard H. Kavanaugh were appointed the Committee on Public Worship.

John Christian Harrison, William B. Landrum,

and William H. Anderson, were appointed Stewards of the Conference.

Alanson C. Dewitt, John Beatty, and Albert H. Redford, were appointed the Committee on Books and Periodicals.

Burr H. McCown, John H. Linn, and Hubbard H. Kavanaugh, were appointed the Committee on Memoirs.

The following resolution, signed by Benjamin T. Crouch and George W. Brush, was presented and adopted:

"Whereas, there is much interest felt and manifested in our State, and especially in the northern part of it, on the subject of Temperance; and whereas, we regard the good already effected by the temperance reform as sufficient encouragement to all the friends of morality and religion to continue their exertions in its behalf; and whereas, we believe this Conference cannot acquit itself fully in the estimation of the public generally, and especially of the religious portion thereof, without a continuation of its usual coöperation in this great and good work by some distinctive action upon the subject, at its present session; therefore,

"*Resolved*, That a committee of three of the members of this body be appointed, to be styled the Committee on Temperance, whose duty it shall be to take this subject under consideration and advisement, and report thereon to the Conference as early as practicable."

The Kentucky Conference, at this period, was in full sympathy with the great temperance movement that was exerting so powerful an influence in the commonwealth; hence, we find that not only on the first day of the session, but in advance of any other question, the action of the Conference is invited to this subject. Hubbard H. Kavanaugh, George W. Brush, and Burr H. McCown, were appointed on this committee. A Committee on Necessitous Cases was also appointed, consisting of Jedidiah Foster and Carlisle Babbitt.

At the afternoon session of the first day a communication from Bishop Andrew was received and read before the Conference, presenting an account of the great affliction in his family as the cause of his absence, and expressing regret that he would not be able to be present. At the request of the Conference, the President appointed a committee of three to prepare a letter of condolence to Bishop Andrew. Edward Stevenson, Henry B. Bascom, and Burr H. McCown, composed the committee.

On the first day of the Conference, during the morning session, a resolution was passed, requesting that a committee of seven be appointed on the affairs of Augusta College; and during the afternoon of the same day Edward Stevenson, George W. Brush, John H. Linn, John Tevis, Napoleon B. Lewis, Peter Taylor, and John W. Riggin, were appointed as the committee.

On the second day of the session a plan for the improvement of ministerial qualification, in order to admission into the Kentucky Conference, was submitted in the following resolutions:

"Whereas, in the opinion of this Conference, the

aid of learning is deemed highly important to ministerial qualification; and whereas, in view of the vast and rapid advance of mental improvement throughout society, there is an imperious demand on us to elevate the standard of ministerial education, in order to maintain an influence in society, and to avail ourselves of all human as well as divine aid for increased usefulness,

"*Be it therefore resolved, by the Kentucky Annual Conference,* That after the session of —— we will require of all *unmarried* young men, who may present themselves for admission into the Conference, that they be examined, by a committee appointed by the Bishop or President of the Conference, upon the studies now prescribed for the first four years after admission upon trial; and if they are found deficient, that they be sent to Augusta College to pursue the said course, either in whole or in part, being furnished with a certificate, by the committee, showing their claims to the provisions of the plan, and prescribing the time to remain and the studies to be pursued.

"*Be it also resolved, by the Conference,* That we add to the above course the study of the original languages of the Bible, for at least one year.

"*By order of the Conference,* This plan shall take effect at the time prescribed: provided that against that time the Conference shall receive satisfactory assurance that provision has been made to meet the boarding expenses of such candidates for the ministry, during their course of instruction in the College."

These resolutions were signed by Burr H. McCown and Thomas N. Ralston, and were referred to the Committee on the Affairs of Augusta College.

While these resolutions contemplated more than was practicable at this period, yet we cannot but feel a pleasure in the effort the Conference was making to elevate the standard of ministerial qualification. Previous to this date the demand for preachers, together with the absence of facilities for acquiring an education, was an excuse for receiving men into the itinerant ministry whose mental culture had been limited to very few of the elementary branches of education. Circumstances, however, were changing—indeed, had changed—materially. The door to a liberal education had been opened to the people, and they were availing themselves of the advantages which were offered; and hence the ministers by whom they were to be taught would be expected to keep pace with those to whom they might minister.

On the third day of the session a resolution was offered, "that a committee of three be appointed to take into consideration the best methods of carrying into effect the objects of the 'Preachers' Aid Society;'" and Burr H. McCown, Carlisle Babbitt, and George W. Brush, constituted the committee.

The following resolutions, signed by Benjamin T. Crouch, John H. Linn, and William Gunn, were offered and adopted:

"Whereas, the Science Hill Female Academy, in Shelbyville, Kentucky, has long sustained itself as an institution of high literary and moral worth, justly entitled to the patronage and fostering countenance of an enlightened and Christian public; and whereas, this body is anxious, by all proper means and methods, to encourage and promote sound learning in general, and female education in particular; therefore,

"1. *Resolved*, That we will continue to extend our patronage to the Science Hill Female Academy, by presenting its character and claims to our people, and by such other means as may be suitable to recommend it to the public.

"2. *Resolved*, That the Presiding Elder of the Shelbyville District, and the preachers stationed in Shelbyville and in charge of the Shelby Circuit, from time to time, be a committee to attend the examinations of said Academy, and report its condition annually to this Conference."

The Science Hill Female Academy was founded by Mrs. Julia A. Tevis, the wife of John Tevis, in March, 1825. For more than sixteen years it had pursued its mission of good, and had proved itself worthy the confidence and patronage of the Conference, and was nobly sustained by the Church. However, it sometimes occurred, strange as it may seem, that Protestant, and even Methodist, parents, instead of sending their daughters to Science Hill, where they might receive a first-class education and become well prepared for the duties of life, patronized female colleges under the supervision of Romish priests, where only a superficial education might be acquired, while the mind of the pupil would become poisoned against the influence of home and the teachings of Christianity. The Kentucky Conference felt the dangerous tendency in this direction, and, not only by resolutions adopted on the floor of the house, but by active efforts during the year, did all that it could to arrest the evil.

The most of the session, previous to the Sabbath, was occupied in the examination of the character of the preachers and in considering the recommendations of local preachers to deacons' orders, and of local deacons to elders' orders.

On Monday morning an interesting report, in reference to the Preachers' Aid Society, was submitted by the committee appointed for that purpose, in which they say: "The object of this Society is one of vast and incalculable importance. It is to provide an assurance, a well-grounded confidence, that after the faithful minister has become oppressed with infirmities in the service of the Church, and has retired from effective labor, he shall still be cheered by the gratitude of the Church, and find a solace and support in some permanent provision made for his wants. All support, as yet provided, is insufficient and too precarious; and, humanely speaking, cheerless indeed must be the prospect of our ministers if, after decrepitude, infirmity, and pain have come upon them as the results of their laborious services in the Church, there is no sure relief, no certain and permanent provision for their wants, in the gloomiest condition of their existence. It must be seen that although the Society organized may afford some relief, it is only partial and entirely inadequate; and there are two difficulties connected with this very relief: one is that, in many instances, it is obtained from those who themselves are in want, and who in their generosity contributed the only money upon which they relied to bear their expenses to their appointments; the other is the impression that the Preachers' Aid Society having been established, the Church may in some measure withhold its customary aid, not to say that some of the preachers may become somewhat careless in lifting contributions; and thus, in all probability, we may forfeit as much as, or even more than, we gain by the organization. The committee have therefore concluded that if a fund be relied upon, our surest method is the appointment of a special agent, whose work shall be to collect a sufficient amount, the interest of which, when safely invested, shall relieve this portion of our wants and this source of our constant anxiety. Your committee do, therefore, recommend an agent for this special object."

This report was adopted.

The conception of a Society for the purpose of aiding in the support of superannuated preachers, and the widows and orphans of deceased preachers, was a noble one. Ministers with families were often induced to retire from the pastoral work that they might provide against the infirmities of age, while others, continuing at their posts, suffered from unpleasant misgivings in reference to the evening-time of life. Although the Preachers' Aid Society in Kentucky failed to accomplish what was intended and what was anticipated, yet it left its benedictions on the Church.

The following important resolution, offered by Thomas N. Ralston and John Christian Harrison, was adopted:

"*Resolved*, That it shall be the duty of each member of the Conference to furnish the Secretary, tomorrow morning, a written statement, over his own signature, of the date of his birth, conversion, admission on trial, and of his admission into full connection; and that the Secretary read the same, and arrange the order of names in the Conference-list so as to give precedence to seniority in full connection."

At this very Conference three preachers were reported as having died during the year, two of whom left no record as to the date of either their birth or conversion. The want of this information prevented the preparation of a suitable memoir, and hence the introduction of the resolution.

On Tuesday morning, at ten o'clock, the Conference adjourned to hear the address on Education, which was delivered by Thomas N. Ralston.

Business was resumed at the close of the address, when the following resolution was offered by Isaac Collard and Benjamin T. Crouch, and adopted by the Conference:

"*Resolved*, That the thanks of this Conference are due to Thomas N. Ralston for his address on Education, and that we request him to furnish a copy to the Book Agents, to be published in the *Western Christian Advocate*."

The committee to whom were referred the resolutions on the subject of ministerial qualification, to which we have already alluded, submitted the following:

"*Resolved, by the Kentucky Conference,* That the Trustees of Augusta College be, and they are hereby, respectfully requested to devise and adopt such ways and means as, in their judgment, may be deemed most proper for the procurement of a permanent fund, the annual proceeds of which shall be applied to the defraying of the boarding expenses of such candidates for admission on trial into the Kentucky Conference, and such sons of the itinerant ministers of the Conference above named, as may be recommended to the College by the aforesaid Conference: provided, nevertheless, that a plan embracing these desirable objects, now in the hands of a standing committee, shall ultimately receive the sanction of the body above named."

John H. Linn offered the following resolution, which was adopted:

"*Resolved,* That the Rev. H. B. Bascom be, and he is hereby, respectfully requested to deliver, at the next session of the Kentucky Annual Conference, to be held at Lexington, a series of lectures on Infidelity, at such times during the session as may suit his convenience."

A resolution signed by Henry B. Bascom and Benjamin T. Crouch, in reference to colonization, was offered and adopted. It reads as follows:

"*Resolved, by the Kentucky Annual Conference, in Conference assembled,* That, amid the varied and protracted discussion of the subject, we continue to cherish undiminished confidence in the wisdom, benevolence, and promise of African colonization, as projected and in course of accomplishment by the American Colonization Society."

Burr H. McCown and Thomas N. Ralston had been appointed a committee in reference to the publication of a book of memoirs, containing an account of the birth, conversion, ministerial labors, and death of members of the Conference. On Wednesday morning, the 22d, they made the following report, which was accepted:

"Inasmuch as the most important and interesting facts connected with the history of any people are as fading as the perishing forms of men, without transmission by immortal letters; and whereas, the history of the rise and progress of Methodism in Kentucky and the biographies of those holy and faithful men engaged in this great and glorious work are not before our Church in this State, in any distinct work; and it is considered exceedingly desirable to embody the history of Methodism, thus far and hereafter among us, with its most interesting facts and the biography of its most faithful servants, in a work particularly devoted to this special object; therefore,

"*Be it resolved, by the Kentucky Annual Conference,* That a committee of —— be appointed, to prepare materials for a work, to be entitled ———, which shall contain a clear and satisfactory account of the rise and progress of Methodism in this State, and a brief biography, preceded with engraved likenesses of the ministers of this Conference most distinguished for their zeal, faithfulness, and success in the work of God, which selection shall be made by a committee, or by a vote of the Conference.

"*And be it farther resolved*, That it shall be made the duty of the same committee to procure such a subscription as will amply justify this Conference in authorizing the publication of the said work."

It was farther suggested that the proceeds of the volume be appropriated to the Preachers' Aid Society.

The committee to provide materials, and to prepare the work, consisted of Burr H. McCown, Hubbard H. Kavanaugh, John Tevis, Edward Stevenson, and George W. Brush.

Fifty-five years had elapsed since James Haw and Benjamin Ogden first lifted the standard of the cross in Kentucky. During this period the Church had grown from a few scattered members to more than forty thousand communicants. Of all those who had confronted danger and encountered hardships in unfurling the crimsoned banner on the once "dark and bloody ground," but few remained. Their deeds of chivalry and noble daring, too, were passing rapidly into oblivion. To collect the scattered fragments of their lives and labors, and embody them in permanent form, that future generations might know how much it cost, of toil, and sacrifice, and suffering, to plant the standard of Christianity in the wilds of the West, was a grand and noble conception. It is to be regretted, however, that the volume never appeared, that only a few scanty materials were collected and preserved, and that so much of the early history of Methodism in the

West, in which there would have been so many incidents to interest and animate the Church in after ages, was thus lost forever.

It was announced on the floor of the Conference, on the afternoon of Wednesday, the 22d, by Dr. Bascom, that propositions had been received by him from a certain corporation, which he desired should be referred to a special committee of three. The committee, as appointed by the President, was composed of Henry B. Bascom, Benjamin T. Crouch, and Hubbard H. Kavanaugh. Joseph S. Tomlinson and Thomas N. Ralston were subsequently added to the committee.

On Thursday, the 23d, the following report was submitted, and unanimously adopted by a rising vote:

"The Trustees of Transylvania University having tendered the control and management of said University to the Methodist Episcopal Church, by the adoption of the following resolutions, bearing date September 21, 1841:

"'*Resolved*, That a tender of the control of Transylvania University, so far as the nomination of the Faculty in the College proper, the Principal of the Preparatory Department, together with the direction of the course of studies and internal government of said College, is concerned, be, and the same is hereby, made to the Methodist Episcopal Church, in the United States, and especially to said Church in Kentucky, upon such terms as shall be agreed upon between said Church and this Board.

"'*Resolved*, That S. Chipley be a committee to

confer with the Kentucky Conference on the subject of the above institution.

(Signed.) "'M. C. JOHNSON,
"'*Chairman Board T. T. U.*

"'Attest: D. S. VIGERS, *Sec. Board T. T. U.*'

"The special committee, to whom was referred the foregoing resolutions to consider and report upon, recommend the following resolutions, by the Kentucky Conference, in Conference assembled:

"*Resolved, by the Kentucky Annual Conference,* That, in behalf of the Methodist Episcopal Church, we will accept the proposition of the Trustees of Transylvania University, on the following conditions:

"*First.* The Board of Trustees of Transylvania University and the Church will unite to obtain any enactment of the Legislature that may be necessary in carrying out the design of the parties in the reorganization of said institution, as well as to give to the Church, through her constituted authorities, the right of electing three additional Trustees possessing the same powers possessed by other Trustees of Transylvania University.

"*Second.* The entire Faculty, as also the teachers in the Preparatory Department, in the reörganization of the University, as contemplated in the premises, shall be nominated by the Church, through her constituted authorities, and confirmed by the Trustees; and thereafter, when any of the chairs become vacated, by death or otherwise, the remaining members of the Faculty shall nominate, and the Trustees confirm, in order to fill such vacancy.

"*Third.* The control of the Collegiate and Preparatory Departments, the internal regulation of the College, the direction of the course of studies, the management of the Dormitory and Boarding-house, the superintendence and care of the buildings and grounds belonging to the University, shall be given to the Faculty.

"*Fourth.* The income arising from all the permanent funds now belonging to the University, and the income arising from all the College-funds now belonging to, or which may hereafter be raised by, said Church in Kentucky, as also the tuition fees, shall be appropriated for the support of the Faculty and teachers in the Preparatory Department, and for such incidental expenses as may be necessary to sustain such institution, when recommended by the Faculty; but the capital, etc., shall remain the separate property of the respective parties, each party controlling its separate interests.

"*Fifth.* It is expressly understood that the Church is not required to meet any of the present liabilities of said University.

"*Sixth.* The Kentucky Annual Conference shall, at each session, appoint a committee, whose duty it shall be to visit said institution, and report to the ensuing Conference its condition and prosperity, which report shall be disposed of by the Conference in such manner as they may think will best promote the interests of said institution, by publication or otherwise.

"*Seventh.* The Trustees shall at all times fix the salaries of the Professors: provided that the salaries shall not be less than is usually paid in similar institutions, unless at the instance of the Faculty.

"*Eighth.* The arrangements to carry out and complete the contemplated reörganization of said University, by the nomination and appointment of an able Faculty, teachers, etc., must be consummated by the end of the next collegiate year of said University, which will be in the autumn of 1842. In the meantime, should any of the chairs in said institution be vacated, and should it be thought necessary and be required by the Trustees, the Church, by her authorities, will endeavor to make suitable nominations for *pro tem.* appointments to fill such vacancies.

"*Ninth. Resolved,* That the Conference will, by a committee to be raised for that purpose, endeavor, as speedily as practicable, to get the Board of Commissioners appointed by the late General Conference of the Methodist Episcopal Church in the United States to take favorable action upon the subject, and to report the same to the next General Conference, in order to obtain, as far as possible, the influence and patronage of said General Conference in favor of said University.

(Signed.) "H. B. BASCOM,
"B. T. CROUCH,
"H. H. KAVANAUGH,
"T. N. RALSTON."

Thomas N. Ralston presented the following resolution, which was adopted:

"Whereas, we, as a Church, are now in negotiation with the Trustees of Transylvania University, in view of effecting a reörganization of the same, and having submitted the terms upon which we will accept the control of said institution; and inasmuch as it may be necessary for the consummation of this desirable object that farther negotiations with the Trustees be had; therefore,

"*Resolved*, That H. B. Bascom, B. T. Crouch, and H. H. Kavanaugh, be, and they are hereby, appointed a committee to carry out the views as expressed by this Conference, with power to do any other act that they may think will best promote the interest of the Church."

As early as 1790 the Methodist Church in Kentucky "fixed a plan for a school, and called it Bethel, and obtained a subscription of upward of three hundred pounds in land and money toward its establishment." In the important interest of education they were in advance of any other denomination in the State. Bethel Academy was located in Jessamine county, and stood on a high bluff on the Kentucky River. Notwithstanding our fathers failed in their efforts to sustain the Bethel Academy, yet the good this infant institution accomplished can scarcely be estimated. Their noble efforts were worthy of all praise.

The next attempt to establish an institution of learning was made in 1821. The project originated with the Ohio Conference, from which a committee was appointed to attend the Kentucky Conference, and propose the establishment of a college in the West, under the joint patronage of the two Conferences. The proposition of the Ohio Conference was received with favor by the Kentucky Conference, and a committee was appointed to confer with the committee from Ohio, and to take such measures as might be deemed proper to accomplish the contemplated object.

On the 15th of the following December the Commissioners visited Augusta, Kentucky, and held a conference with the Trustees of Bracken Academy, and laid before them the object of their appointment, and informed them that they had decided to locate the college in Augusta, provided they should receive proper aid from the Trustees of the Academy and the citizens in building a college-edifice. The proposition made by the Commissioners was accepted, and the college was chartered by the Legislature of Kentucky, December 22, 1822, and was soon in successful operation, under the presidency of John P. Finley.

For many years the Augusta College was a brilliant success. Its halls were crowded with young men destined to occupy a commanding eminence in the higher circles of life. Some of the first intellects of the age presided over its fortunes, and many of the brightest lights in the medical profession, at the bar, and in the pulpit, claimed Augusta College as their *alma mater*. Circumstances, however, for which the Kentucky Conference was not responsible, and over which it had no control, broke the power of this once popular institution. The agitation of the questions of slavery and abolition exerted an influence for harm upon its fortunes that no Faculty, however learned, could counteract. The Ohio Conference practically withdrew its patronage, because of its location in a slave-holding State, while the South, from whence a large proportion of its support had been received, declined to send her sons so near the border, or to have them educated in the same school with young men who held views, and so openly advocated them, adverse to an institution that was peculiarly Southern.

Before the proposition made by the Trustees of Transylvania University, the location of the college at Augusta was the subject of comment in Methodist circles throughout the State, and the opinion was commonly expressed that a removal to some more eligible point was requisite, if the Church desired to sustain an institution of learning of high grade. The proposition, therefore, to turn over Transylvania University to the Conference could not be deemed otherwise than opportune for the Church.

On Wednesday evening, September 22, Hubbard H. Kavanaugh and Benjamin T. Crouch offered the following resolutions, which were adopted:

"1. *Resolved*, That, in the judgment of this Conference, the objects of the American Bible Society are of unspeakable importance to our own nation and to many other and large portions of the world, and that we feel it to be our Christian duty cordially to coöperate with the Western Agent, or Agents, who may call upon us, in carrying out the designs of the Society.

"2. *Resolved*, That we regard the recent appointment of the Rev. E. W. Sehon, of the Ohio Conference, as General Agent of the American Bible

Society in the West as promising much to the sacred cause, and that we anticipate with pleasure his visits to our State in his official capacity, and trust that he may have the success that the importance of his agency deserves."

For several years Edmund W. Sehon had been prominent before the Church and the country as a preacher of the gospel. He was born in Moorefield, Virginia, April 14, 1808, and was converted and joined the M. E. Church September 20, 1824, at a camp-meeting near Clarksburg, Virginia. He was licensed to preach October 10, 1827, by William Stephens.

In 1828 he offered himself to the Pittsburgh Conference, which included in its territory that portion of Virginia in which he was born and brought up, and was accepted. Belonging to one of the best families in the State of Virginia, of fine personal appearance, with a mind highly cultivated, his manners polished, and distinguished for his eloquence, his burning zeal, his fervent piety, and his devotion to the cause of Christ, he promised great usefulness in the Church.

At the time he entered the Pittsburgh Conference Dr. Bascom was President of Madison College, an institution of learning in the bounds of that Conference. A strong attachment, on the part of Dr. Bascom, was formed for the young itinerant, which, on the part of Mr. Sehon, was fully reciprocated, and which grew into the warmest friendship in the hearts of both.

Mr. Sehon was appointed to Youngstown Circuit,

as the colleague of Billings O. Plumpton, and with Ira Eddy as his Presiding Elder, having traveled on the Lewis Circuit, and then on the Redstone Circuit, during the previous year, under the appointment of the Presiding Elder. His next appointment was to the Monongahela Circuit, as junior preacher. In 1831 he was transferred to the Ohio Conference, and appointed to the city of Cincinnati, where he remained two years. At the Conference of 1832 he was appointed Agent for the Colonization Society, in which position he remained but one year. In 1833 he was transferred to the Missouri Conference, and stationed in the city of St. Louis, but at the close of the year returned to Ohio, and was stationed in the city of Columbus, where he remained for two years. In 1836 we again find him in Cincinnati, in the Western Charge, with Cyrus Brooks as his colleague, and the following year, with David Womack, he preaches to the same congregation. In 1838 he was Agent for Augusta College, and in 1839 was returned to Cincinnati, and appointed to the Eastern Charge, where he remained two years.

During the thirteen years that Mr. Sehon had spent as an itinerant preacher he labored with uncompromising zeal and with extraordinary success. Whether he bore the banner of the cross, stained with Immanuel's blood, along the waters of the Monongahela, or proclaimed its hallowed story on the banks of the Mississippi, or in the Queen City of the West, hundreds sought repose and safety beneath its crimsoned folds. As Agent for the Colonization Society and for Augusta College, he had contributed much to the success of these enterprises. Six years of his pastoral life had been spent in the city of Cincinnati, where crowded audiences waited upon his ministry, and hundreds, through his instrumentality, were brought into the Church and converted to God.

At the session of the Ohio Conference of 1841 he received the appointment of General Agent of the American Bible Society for the West. It was this appointment that elicited the action of the Kentucky Conference which we have already stated.

At this Conference twenty-three preachers were admitted on trial—viz.: Samuel P. Cummins, Garret Davis, John B. Ewan, Charles B. Parsons, Munford Pelley, Mitchell Land, James N. Temple, Moses M. Henkle, William M. Humphrey, William Conway, William Lasley, James J. Williams, Samuel Glassford, John W. Fields, Josiah Godbey, Ransom Lancaster, William H. Kimberlin, Charles Duncan, Alexander B. Sollars, Samuel Kelly, Ajax H. Triplett, George Riach, and Marcus L. King.

Of those who had entered the Conference the previous year the names of Henry F. Garey and William D. Minga disappear from the list; the former was discontinued at his own request, and the latter had crossed over the last river and entered upon eternal life.

William D. Matting, Calvin W. Lewis, William C. McMahan, William S. Evans, Joseph G. Ward, and John Beatty, located.

Absalom Hunt, Alexander Robinson, Henry N.

Vandyke, and William D. Minga, had died during the year.

John H. Linn, by a resolution of the Conference, was requested to preach a sermon in memory of Alexander Robinson, Henry N. Vandyke, and William D. Minga; and Jonathan Stamper to preach a sermon in memory of Absalom Hunt.

Absalom Hunt was in the meridian of life when he entered the itinerancy. He was fortv-two years of age when his name first appeared on the Conference-roll. After traveling eight years he was placed on the list of the superannuated, where he remained, with the exception of four years, when he sustained the relation of supernumerary. He died in peace, February 21, 1841.*

We regret that we have no record of the date of either the birth or conversion of Alexander Robinson. He was a native of Kentucky, and was converted at a camp-meeting in Washington county. When he joined the Conference, in 1834, he was at the noontide of life. His first appointment was to the Wayne Circuit, as the colleague of William C. McMahan. In 1835 he was sent, with Jesse Sutton, to the Somerset Circuit, and in 1836 to the Manchester Mission. On this last field of labor we succeeded him, and listened with pleasure to the many tributes paid to his moral worth and unyielding devotion to the Church. Notwithstanding his feeble health, he performed with remarkable promptness the duties of this rugged and laborious charge, and

*A sketch of Absalom Hunt may be found in the "History of Methodism in Kentucky," vol. iii., pp. 346–352.

was the honored instrument in the hands of God in doing much good. At the Conference of 1837 he was appointed to the Mount Vernon Mission, with Walter Shearer as his colleague, where his health became too precarious for him to entertain a thought of continuing in the active service. In the autumn of 1838 he was placed on the list of the superannuated, from which he was never removed until called from labor to reward.

As a preacher, the talents of Mr. Robinson were only moderate; but his fervent piety and the luster of his life, together with the exhortations that came warm from his heart, won many souls to Christ. His end was peaceful.

Among the young men of promise in the Methodist ministry in Kentucky, with whom we first became acquainted, we mention with pleasure the name of Henry N. Vandyke. He became an itinerant preacher in 1834, and was sent to the Burlington Circuit. In his second year in the Conference he was appointed to Shelbyville and Brick Chapel—one of the most important charges in the State—as the colleague of Benjamin T. Crouch. When he came to Shelbyville he appeared to be about twenty-one years of age, and his appointment met with the hearty approval of the Church. It was here that we first knew him. For twelve months we enjoyed his companionship almost daily, and received instruction in the great work to which we expected to devote our life. We heard the gospel from his lips, from week to week, and never tired in listening to his earnest presentation of the great truths set forth in the Bible. During this period we never heard him speak unkindly of any one, nor utter a single word unbecoming the dignity of a minister of Jesus Christ. His daily walk and conversation shed a luster on the profession he made, while in his pastoral visits among the people he served he left behind him the savor of a good name. Although he was not brilliant as a preacher, yet his talents were of a very high order. He was a close thinker and an untiring student, and prepared his sermons with much care, and delivered them with great fluency and ease. He attracted large congregations to the house of God, and through his labors and zeal many were brought to Christ. We never knew a better man, nor one in whose life were more fully developed all the excellences of Christian character, nor one who was more universally beloved.

While stationed in Shelbyville Mr. Vandyke was married to Miss Marie Louisa Soule, daughter of Bishop Soule, who was at the time a teacher in Science Hill Female Academy.

He was stationed in Mount Sterling in 1836, in 1837 in Frankfort, and in 1838 in Cynthiana. In each of these charges he maintained the high reputation he had already won, and gathered into the Church many souls, who should deck the crown of his rejoicing in the hereafter.

From the time that Mr. Vandyke entered the ministry it was apprehended that his strength would not be equal to the duties of the office. For several years, however, he met its responsibilities and performed its labors with no indications of declining health. While stationed in Cynthiana, a cough—the hectic flush upon his pale cheek—told quite plainly that consumption had marked him as an early victim. In 1839 he was appointed to Fourth-street, Louisville, with Thomas N. Ralston and William Atherton, but was expected to render but little, if any, service. It was deemed advisable that he should winter in New Orleans. He continued in Louisiana during the year, and at the following Conference was placed on the list of superannuated preachers. Before the next Conference God called him home. His death-bed scene was full of triumph.

William D. Minga had just entered the ministry, and was appointed to the Wayne Circuit. His educational advantages were meager; but he gave great promise of usefulness to the Church. He, too, died with harness on. His end was triumphant.

The memorial-sermon preached by Mr. Linn was remarkably impressive. He gave a faithful delineation of the lives and labors of these holy men, and referred in touching language to the composure with which they met death, and the triumph with which their closing hours were replete. The last battle was fought, the last victory was won, and from the parapets of glory they were looking down on the vast assembly who were paying a tribute of respect and love to their memory. He read a letter from Mrs. Vandyke, in which she said, referring to the death of her husband, "It was I who died, not Mr. Vandyke."

The sermon preached by Mr. Stamper, on the death of Absalom Hunt, was such as might have been expected by all who knew the distinguished preacher. A brother had died; a comrade-in-arms had fallen at his post; a warrior had fought the good fight, and received his furlough; a Christian hero had conquered his last foe, and was wearing his crown, and his virtues and prowess were displayed as an incentive to those who had entered upon the labors of the noble dead.

The amount collected for missions, although not so large as had been reported on some previous occasions, greatly exceeded that of the former year: it reached the sum of three thousand seven hundred and twenty-eight dollars.

Jonathan Stamper and William M. Grubbs were this year transferred to the Illinois, and Henry E. Pilcher to the North Ohio, Conference.

Mr. Stamper had entered the itinerant ministry in 1811, and had for thirty years been a faithful, laborious, and useful minister of Jesus Christ. In the Church in Kentucky he occupied a commanding eminence, and in the Conference enjoyed a popularity that could be claimed by but few men. At this session of the Conference, as we have already seen, in the absence of the Bishop, he was chosen to preside over the deliberations of the body. He was a good and true man, and his transfer from Kentucky was greatly regretted by both the ministry and membership of the Church.*

William M. Grubbs was the son-in-law of Mr. Stamper. He was born in Franklin county, Ken-

*A sketch of Jonathan Stamper may be found in the "History of Methodism in Kentucky."

tucky, October 25, 1815. In 1820 his father removed to Logan county, and settled near Russellville. In 1830 he left his father's house and went to Russellville, where he was employed as a clerk in a dry-goods store. Impressed with the importance of religion, and awakened to the necessity of seeking it at once, in December, 1832, under the ministry of Henry J. Evans, he joined the Methodist Church, and sought and found Christ in the pardon of his sins.

From the time he "tasted the good word of God" he believed it to be his duty to preach the gospel. In May, 1834, he was licensed to exhort by Hooper Evans, and August 9, of the same year, he was licensed to preach by Isaac Collard, and recommended to the Kentucky Conference for admission on trial.

His first appointment was to the Lewis Circuit, with William Cundiff in charge. The following year he was sent, as junior preacher, to the Fleming Circuit, with Martin L. Eads. In 1836 his appointment was the Germantown Circuit, with Joseph Marsee. In 1837 he was placed in charge of the Salt River Circuit, where he continued two years, and the following two years he was stationed in Bardstown; he was transferred thence to the Illinois Conference.

The following letter from Mr. Grubbs will be read with interest:

"The revival at which I was converted and joined the Church was among the most powerful that have ever visited the old Methodist town of Russellville.

It began at the close of a quarterly-meeting held by the Rev. Isaac Collard, and almost swept the whole community. Hundreds were converted and joined the different Churches; but the old square brick meeting-house, with its heavy galleries and old-fashioned appointments—the work of Major Bibb, as he was then called, some fifteen years before, and located in the outskirts of the town—was the center of influence, and shared the largest harvest.

"Though reared in the Baptist faith, I readily entered into Methodist doctrines and usages, and received baptism, by pouring, at the old altar near which, about ten days before, I received the witness of pardon and adoption. I shall never forget the occasion when about fifty adults knelt and received the water of baptism from the hands of Brother Evans. It more nearly filled my conception of the scenes of Pentecost than any occasion I have ever witnessed. Several were so filled with the Spirit that they rejoiced aloud, and went through the crowded congregation exhorting their unconverted friends to turn to Christ, and the altar was speedily filled with penitents crying for mercy. It was a settler with me as to the better mode of administering that ordinance.

"My first four appointments filled the bill of old-fashioned four-weeks' circuits, both as to extent of territory and number of appointments. Lewis Circuit embraced the whole of Lewis county, with portions of Mason and Greenup, reaching from within three miles of Maysville to within a few miles of Portsmouth, Ohio, and numbered more than twenty preaching-places. Fleming Circuit embraced nearly all of Fleming county. Germantown Circuit took in the larger part of Mason county, with portions of Bracken and Harrison; while Salt River Circuit embraced Nelson county, with portions of Bullitt, Hardin, Marion, and Washington; and none of them numbered less than twenty appointments.

"My first colleague—the Rev. William Cundiff—was a holy man, of great zeal, and I profited much from his example and instructions. He was of singular *physique*—a short, stout frame, with ruddy face and bushy head, which seemed to rest squarely on his shoulders, almost without neck. He has long since passed from labor to reward. The people of that circuit were kind and appreciative, demonstrative in their religion, and we had a good year. At our last quarterly-meeting at Concord, while Brother Tydings was preaching on Sunday, I had a violent chill, sitting behind him in the pulpit. After a few days of severe suffering I recovered sufficiently to reach Mother Pelham's—that famous preachers' home—three miles above Maysville. Here I relapsed, and was sick for some two weeks, but was able to meet my colleague at our last appointment, for a two-days' meeting, at the mouth of Cabin Creek. I submitted to his request, and preached once on Sabbath; had another chill, and, returning to Mother Pelham's with a raging fever, received a good scolding for my imprudence. Under the kind nursing of that good family I was soon on my feet, and started for the Conference, which met that year (1835) at Shelbyville. It was there I first saw

Bishop Andrew, and subsequent years and events only served to increase my admiration for the man and the Bishop. Do you remember Bishop Andrew's sermon on 'Say not ye, There are yet four months, and then cometh harvest?' and how, under his powerful appeals and touching pathos, our old friend (the Rev. E. Stevenson) sitting in the altar became so excited that he sprang to his feet and shouted aloud, and we all wept and rejoiced together? It was there we heard our own Bascom preach the funeral-sermon of the Rev. William Adams. I shall never forget the old church, with its ascending seats, the imperial preacher, his grand sermon, and its wonderful effect on the Conference and crowded audience.

"My second colleague—the Rev. M. L. Eads—was stout in person, with strong voice and good elocution, and was regarded as an able and sound preacher. He lived in Harrison county, a day's ride from his work, and because of poverty, and family-wants, and small pay, was subject to frequent spells of 'the blues.' Several strong local preachers resided then in Fleming Circuit, and it was a great embarrassment for a timid young preacher to attempt to preach in their presence. Among them were the Rev. B. Northcott and the Rev. Joseph D. Farrow. At Father Hood's, whose only child, Farrow, had married after ten years of itinerancy, I found a good home and great kindness from all. Father Northcott was one of the magistrates of his county, and as his court-days in his neighborhood occurred on the Saturday of my appointment at old Locust

Church, he was seldom present. To compensate, however, he had me preach several times at his house at night. I well remember an exhortation he gave at the close of one of my efforts to preach. His voice was strong, his words came with authority, and his neighbors, to whom he had preached for forty years, listened as though they were hearing him for the first time. He had appointments of his own every Sabbath, and he preached more funeral-sermons, and officiated at more marriages, than did any other man in that county. He was a man of strong will, of single purpose and aim, and, whether presiding in the County Court or preaching to hundreds, he stood a head and shoulders above ordinary men, both in stature and influence for good. Though grace made him the antipodes of Wolsey, in all the essentials of moral character and intent, yet there was a similarity of bearing—

"Lofty and sour to them that loved him not,
But, to those men that sought him, sweet as summer.

"My third colleague—the Rev. Joseph Marsee—was in every respect a model man, a gentleman by nature, a saint by grace, and an effective, sweet-spirited gospel-preacher. His wife was the niece of the Rev. Marcus Lindsey. A few years afterward he removed to Indiana, and, after filling some of the best appointments, his health failed, and he died, in 1837, a superannuate of the South-eastern Indiana Conference. By judicious investments he became wealthy, and his family stand among the prominent Methodists of Indianapolis. We had a good year together, with two glorious revivals—one at Washington, the old county-seat of Mason, in the winter, and one at Salem Church, near Germantown, in August. The Rev. Hiram Baker was then, as now, an honored local preacher, living near Shannon Meeting-house. He was popular with the people, and magnified his office. The Rev. James Savage, of great wealth and marked character, was 'king' of the circuit. He was rather exacting in his demands of itinerants, but on the whole, at that day, was a man of influence and usefulness. I always thought he took a fancy to me, and I found a pleasant home in his family, at Germantown. We were greatly aided by the Faculty of Augusta College. Bascom, Trimble, and McCown, were magnates among the people, and the two latter, especially, were abundant in labors. Dr. Tomlinson seldom came into the country, as his health was poor; but he was in high reputation as a preacher. Dr. Bascom was a great favorite with the old Methodist families, who had known him from a boy. I well remember a visit he made to the Rees family, and his powerful sermon at Shannon Meeting-house, on a Sabbath in August, 1837. On Monday morning Mother Rees accompanied him to the gate. Her eyes followed him as he paced down the road, on his plump pony, and, wiping her eyes with her apron, she remarked to me: 'I always loved Henry Bascom. People say he is proud; but I know better. He is not above anybody that will behave and do right. He was a good son to his afflicted parents, has almost beggared himself to raise and educate his brothers and sisters, and he is to-day a good and great man.' A eulogy, that, as true as it was proper, from one who had known him all his life. George W. Brush was stationed that year in Maysville, and, as he had traveled our circuit a few years before, his frequent visits were greatly cherished by the people.

"Salt River Circuit contained at that day an intelligent and influential class of Methodists. Such men as Barnabas McHenry, Marcus Lindsey, John Fisk, and George W. Taylor, had left their stamp upon the people. It contained within its bounds the old Ferguson appointment—a favorite place of rest for Bishops Asbury and McKendree. The chief point of attraction was the old Beech Fork Camp-ground—an annual rallying-point for preachers and people from about the year 1820. I attended four camp-meetings there in succession, from 1838 to 1841, with the Rev. Jonathan Stamper in charge as Presiding Elder. At the meetings of 1838 and 1839 the people's favorites, Jonathan Stamper and Hubbard H. Kavanaugh, did the principal preaching. As these great camp-meeting preachers alternated from day to day, it was amusing as well as edifying to hear the comments and commendations of the older brethren. Now it was Stamper, and now Kavanaugh. Both were up to the mark all the time. The people had a feast of fat things, while they feasted us in return, in Old Kentucky style. As it was known in 1841 that Jonathan Stamper, who had served a term of four years on the District, was arranging to emigrate to Illinois, the people were wrought up to the highest point of interest and solicitude. He had been on the same District some fifteen years before, and the thought of parting was sad. As the thousands seemed unwilling that any one else should occupy the stand at the popular hour, he preached each day at eleven o'clock. As you know what he was in his prime, when fully harnessed for camp-meeting work, you can better imagine than I can describe the character of his daily efforts and their effect upon the vast audiences that crowded the encampment. As I write I see, in my mind's eye, the noble form of that great lawyer and good man, Governor Charles A. Wycliffe, as he appeared on that Sunday—now sitting, and now, through excited feeling, standing up beside a beech-tree, within a few feet of the stand. Hon. Ben. Hardin, who never failed to attend our meetings, and was always a Methodist in creed, was at the outskirts of the congregation when the Sunday sermon began, but at its close he was close up to the stand, and afterward, in his emphatic way, declared that an angel from heaven could not have excelled the effort of his favorite preacher. If the love and offers of help from old-time friends could have kept him in Kentucky, he had never left the State. One brother offered to deed him a rich farm of two hundred acres if he would stay."

William M. Grubbs was quite a young man when we first saw him; it was at the close of his second year in the Conference. He visited Shelbyville, and on Sabbath evening preached to a crowded audience, from Luke xxiv. 46, 47. We had never before heard so young a man attempt to preach. His keen black eye, his gentle countenance, his earnest manner, and his forcible presentation of the truth, attracted our attention and won our heart. From that hour we watched his progress and rejoiced in his success, whether the fields of his labor were in Kentucky or elsewhere.

Henry E. Pilcher entered the Ohio Conference in 1829, and in 1837 was transferred to the Kentucky Conference. His appointments were the Newport and Covington Station, Shelbyville Station, and Germantown Circuit. At the Conference of 1840 he located, but was reädmitted in 1841, and transferred to the North Ohio Conference.

For several years the Church in Kentucky had steadily advanced in influence and in numerical strength. Since the Conference of 1837 an increase in the membership had been reported annually; but the success which crowned the labors of the ministry in winning souls to Christ, during the year upon which the Church was now entering, had no parallel in the records of the past.

The Conference closed its session on the 23d of September, and only a few days elapsed until the preachers were at the posts to which they were assigned. Isaac Collard, John James, George W. Taylor, and James King, were returned to the Districts over which they had presided the year before. William Gunn was appointed to the Shelbyville District, made vacant by the transfer of Mr. Stamper to Illinois. Benjamin T. Crouch was placed in charge of the Lexington District, where Mr. Gunn had been the leader; and Richard Corwine succeeded Mr. Crouch on the Louisville District. Richard D. Neale, who had labored so faithfully for four years on the Barboursville District, was sent to the Hardinsburg District—a new field, just formed—while William B. Landrum follows him amid the mountain fastnesses. The warm-hearted Edward Stevenson succeeds Richard Corwine on the Hopkinsville District.

The Church in Kentucky has but seldom furnished so able and efficient a corps of Presiding Elders as those we have just named. They were preachers of marked ability and burning zeal, and under their leadership the happiest results were anticipated.

During the winter there were interesting revivals of religion in several portions of the State; but the grander conquests of the Church were to be seen and realized after the opening of the spring.

In the Augusta District there was a net increase of six hundred and forty white and thirty-four colored members. The Greenupsburg, Germantown, Fleming, Lewis, Little Sandy, Highland, and Shannon Circuits were all refreshed with showers of grace.

On the 23d of March* Walter Shearer writes, from the Greenupsburg Circuit, that "sixty or seventy" persons had joined the Church; and he adds: "The work is still going on and spreading." Although we have no farther announcement in reference to the progress of the work from the faithful pastor, yet the Minutes show a net increase in that

* *Western Christian Advocate,* April 22, 1842.

charge of two hundred and nine white and twenty-seven colored members.

Walter Shearer was one of the most laborious preachers in the Conference. He was born September 12, 1813, and embraced religion in 1832. At the session of the Kentucky Conference in 1837 he was admitted on trial, having previously traveled under the Presiding Elder. His first appointment, after he entered the Conference, was to the Mount Vernon Mission, as the colleague of Alexander Robertson. In 1838 he was sent to the Litchfield Mission, and in 1839 to the Little Sandy Circuit, to which he was returned in 1840. In all these fields he showed himself an approved workman, and won many souls to Christ. We find him this year on the Greenupsburg Circuit, prosecuting his work with untiring zeal and extraordinary success.

Jedidiah Foster had charge of the Flemingsburg Circuit, with William D. Trainer as his colleague. Under the ministry of these zealous preachers of the gospel, the net increase in this circuit was one hundred and forty-four white and twenty colored members.

In the Lewis Circuit, to which Allen Sears and William H. Kimberlin were sent, there was, during the year, a fine religious influence, although the increase in the membership was small.

The untiring William C. Atmore, who had charge of the Germantown Circuit, was greatly blessed. Mr. Atmore was born at Wednesbury, England, December 6, 1800, and was the son of the Rev. Charles Atmore, a distinguished preacher in the

British Conference. In a letter to the author, Mr. Atmore says:

"He who setteth the solitary in families caused my lot to fall in a godly household. The restraining grace of God was always upon and before me; but in private prayer, when but eight years of age, my heart was strangely warmed, and I made a covenant to try and serve God fully. I was baptized into the Church when an infant, and, when ten years old, ratified the act of my parents by personal connection with the Church, under the ministry of my reverend father. When eighteen years of age I was licensed to preach by the Quarterly Conference, at Salford, in Manchester, and in 1820 was recommended to the British Conference by the Rev. Jabez Bunting. I was married, November 14, 1822, to Miss Mary Wood, of Flixton, near Manchester, and now thank God for a union of near fifty-four years with her. In 1836 we came, with our three children, to America, bringing with me my certificate as a local preacher, from the Superintendent of the London Westminster District. We settled at New Richmond, Clermont county, Ohio, and I was recommended by the Quarterly Conference of that circuit to the Kentucky Conference, and received by that body, at Bardstown, in 1840.

"My father was born at Heasham, a village on the coast of Norfolk, in 1759, and joined the Wesleyan Society, under Mr. Pilmore, in 1779. In 1781 he was received by John Wesley, and appointed to the Grimsby Circuit, in Lincolnshire. On December 11, 1825, he preached his last sermon at Hackney, near

London, and on the 1st of July, 1826, he entered the paradise of God, in the sixty-seventh year of his age and the forty-fifth of his ministry.

"The light of my household God hath put out, and the few years I may remain from her I shall spend in the family of my dear son, praying that I may lead them and myself, by God's grace, to lay up treasure in heaven."

When Mr. Atmore came to Kentucky he was a preacher of much experience and decided ability. The Kentucky Conference received him gladly as a fellow-laborer in the Master's vineyard. His first appointment was to the Falmouth Circuit, where his ministry was owned of God in the salvation of souls. In 1841 he was appointed to the Germantown Circuit, where we have already met him. In this charge, as in the Falmouth Circuit, many were brought to Christ through his instrumentality. As a preacher he was clear and forcible. He understood the doctrines of the Bible, and defended them with signal ability. He was familiar with the practical duties of Christianity, and by precept and example enforced them on the people he served. Blessed with a sound experience, he made no compromise either with sin or a formal Christianity, but everywhere urged the Pauline—the Wesleyan—doctrine of the witness of the Spirit. Such was William C. Atmore when we first knew him. His excellent wife, to whom he makes such a beautiful and touching allusion in the letter we have quoted, was well worthy the place she occupied in the Church. We knew her well. Devoted to the Church, she willingly confronted any difficulty and submitted to any sacrifice to advance the cause of the Redeemer. No better, no purer woman than Mrs. Mary Atmore* ever lived.

The Little Sandy Circuit shared, to some extent, the religious influence with which the Augusta District was visited. At the second quarterly-meeting the pastor was assisted by Walter Shearer and several local preachers, under whose ministry a revival commenced, which continued during the remainder of the year, and in which many were brought to Christ. At the same time John P. Vance, a pious but eccentric preacher, was eminently useful in the Highland Circuit.

William M. Crawford traveled this year on the Shannon Circuit. He was born in Scott county, Kentucky, February 7, 1811. Although blessed with one of the best of mothers, he utterly disregarded her example and instructions until he had attained his majority. Participating in all the popular vices of the day, he wandered far from home and from God. Wherever he went he was followed by the Holy Spirit, while thoughts of home—his mother's prayers, to which he had so often listened, and her warm tears, with which his face had been baptized—rushing upon his memory, would make him resolve upon a better life. Again and again he formed the purpose to repent of his sins and return to God, but again and again the siren voice of the tempter would efface his resolutions and lead

*Mrs. Atmore died, in great peace, on the 17th of May, 1875, in La Grange, Oldham county, Kentucky.

him still farther from the paths of virtue. In the spring of 1834 he was powerfully awakened and happily converted. His conversion was sound and complete. Not a doubt entered his mind as to his acceptance with God. He was thoroughly changed. Simultaneously with his conversion he believed that God had called him to preach the gospel. Counting the cost, he resolved to enter upon the work. At the Conference of 1835 he was admitted on trial, and appointed to the Burlington Circuit, as the junior preacher. Handsome in person, his manners polished, his address popular, his talents of a high order, and with a zeal burning for the salvation of sinners, he entered upon the duties of his high and holy office, and performed the work assigned him with fidelity and success. In 1836 he was sent to the Hardinsburg Circuit, as the colleague of Joseph G. Ward, where he brought much fruitage to the Master. In 1837 he was appointed to the Mount Pleasant Mission, in the mountainous section of the State. From here we follow him to Bardstown, and thence to Columbia Circuit. In 1840 he traveled on the Fleming Circuit, with Henry F. Garey as his colleague. In all these fields he was exceedingly useful. His appointment to the Shannon Circuit, in 1841, was gratifying alike to himself and to the people. Several months elapsed, however—indeed, almost the entire year passed away—before he witnessed any favorable result from his labors in that charge. He had become discouraged, and writes: "The first three quarters of the year have passed away, and almost the fourth, and only thirty persons have joined the Church."* Grand and glorious results, however, were in reserve. About the first of August God visited his circuit in great mercy. At Mount Tabor, at Two Lick, and at Shannon, the work prevailed, and one hundred and eight persons passed from death unto life, and nearly that number were added to the Church. He was assisted at Mount Tabor by George S. Savage.

In the Minerva Circuit equal success attended the ministry of Gilby Kelly and Lorenzo D. Harlan. In Minerva, in Dover, in Augusta, and in other portions of the circuit, the religious influence was felt, and many were converted and added to the Church.

Although the Covington District does not record so great an increase as the Augusta District, yet, in reviewing the Church in that field, we find much to encourage us.

In the Covington Station, Andrew J. McLaughlin reported an increase of one hundred and five members. In the Sharpsburg Circuit an increase of fifty-five white and five colored members is reported by Lemuel Veach. In the Paris and Crittenden Circuits—the former under the faithful ministry of George W. Merritt, and the latter under that of Josiah Whitaker—many were added to the Church. At a meeting held at Mount Carmel Church, in the Paris Circuit, commencing August 13, "several were happily converted to God," and "thirty-two received on probation."

In summing up the work in the Covington District, John James, the Presiding Elder, writes: "I

* *Western Christian Advocate*, September 16, 1842.

may safely say it is in a state of general prosperity, and in some portions of it there are gracious refreshings. In the Crittenden Circuit there is a glorious work; forty-five joined on probation at our last quarterly-meeting, and we left the work on the advance. At Covington there is a fine state of things. During a meeting held by Brothers Hamline, Tomlinson, McCown, and others, some seven days previous to, and together with, the quarterly-meeting, twenty-six joined on probation. Covington is certainly in a far better condition than I have ever known it. At Newport we had a gracious meeting. About ten or twelve persons joined on probation, and the meeting closed most happily. At the Alexandria quarterly-meeting we had a good time." *

In the Lexington District, the displays of divine power can scarcely be described. The territorial limits it embraced had for several years been the stronghold of Campbellism in the State. To achieve success was the purpose of the noble men who occupied this field.

The following letter from Benjamin T. Crouch, written August 29, 1842, presents a fair view of the difficulties which confronted the Church and conspired to defeat its purposes:

"While the tide of revival intelligence has been teeming from every quarter, through the medium of the *Advocate*, and our hearts have been cheered with the success of our brethren in their various departments of the gospel work, there has been but little

* *Western Christian Advocate*, May 20, 1842.

communicated from the Lexington District to swell this stream of religious entertainment. The Conference-year opened upon us, in this division of the Christian field, under rather discouraging auspices; for the enemy truly came like a 'flood,' and it appeared for a time that we should have to submit to the *destructive immersion* of a second deluge, without any salvation from the threatening billows, by a baptismal entrance into the ark of safety. This, however, did not trouble us much; for we believed the preaching of the latter-day '*Noah*'—that 'our Heavenly Father will give the Holy Spirit to them that ask him'—and we 'prayed unto the Lord our God,' and he heard us, and sent forth the baptismal fire of his gracious Spirit in many places, and evaporated the suffocating floods with which the enemy attempted to overwhelm us, and our heads are still above the waves. Our prospects are evidently brightening, and have been for some months past, and the state of religious feeling is obviously rising in almost every part of the District. Most of the circuits have been recently blessed with very gracious revivals of the work of God, and the preachers have a favorable prospect of leaving their charges in an advancing condition when they go up to the approaching Conference. In some of those seasons of reviving the work was marked with much of the divine influence; convictions for sin were deep and pungent, conversions were clear and powerful, and additions encouragingly numerous. We have not been able, it is true, to vie with our brethren in some parts of the gospel-field, in extending the borders of our Zion and augmenting the hosts of Israel; but our most sanguine expectations have been greatly exceeded, and the Head of the Church is still going forth amongst his people in saving strength. The preachers are in the spirit of their work; they have applied themselves to the advancement of experimental religion, not only with a becoming zeal, but also with much doctrinal ability and ministerial discreetness. Amongst the subjects of our revivals have been numbered several persons who (according to the tenor of a recent gospel) had sought regeneration beneath the yielding wave; but as they did not come up therefrom 'as pure as an angel,' but deceived, disappointed, and unhappy, they presented themselves at the mercy-seat, and obtained, amidst the spiritual fires of the altar, the blessing of regenerating grace, which they had failed to obtain in the *grave of waters.* It is not, however, a matter of surprise that those should be disappointed who pervert the ancient order of things, and look for saving grace in that undevotional instrument of the divine displeasure by which the wicked antediluvians and the presumptuous Egyptians were destroyed, but which never was employed, by divine appointment, as the token of God's mercy. We are compelled to the opinion that it is the misleading voice of uninspired history, and not the 'sure word of prophecy,' that supports the immersionist superstructure. (Pardon the digression.)

"We are now closing up our year's work. The last quarterly-meeting is far advanced, and the state of things is delightful. Our thoughts are now turned toward the pleasant city of Lexington, where, in a few days, the laborious itinerants of Kentucky will assemble in Conference to make their reports; to devise plans and concert measures for the farther promotion of the cause of God; to receive their appointments for another year, and then away to their work again. The reported accessions to the thousands of our Israel, in the several circuits and stations of this Conference, will vary from a dozen or two up to several hundreds. Even in this District, where we had feared that we should not be able more than merely to hold our own, the Lord has been better to us than all our fears, and the numbers added to us will reach the cheering aggregate of twelve or fifteen hundred. And let no traducer of God's ministers say that the infants we baptize are comprised in these reported numbers. This envious imputation is being bandied over the land as one of the secrets of Methodist success, than which we know, and so does our Divine Master, nothing can be farther from the truth. We mark and foster the tender lambs, but reckon them not in the number of the laboring members of the flock. If selfishness and intolerance were turned out of the Church, there would be more room for brotherly love and Christian union. Let those whose liberality disposes them to hail the Christian in all who exhibit the spirit of Christ pray that the power of grace may correct the heads and improve the hearts of those whose only standard of piety, for themselves and everybody else, is the measure of their own opinions.

"Glory be to God for all his benefits toward us! for the good that is done upon the earth, the Lord doeth it." *

Every charge in this District was visited by showers of grace. The city of Lexington was favored with a blessed revival, under the ministry of Richard Deering; in Frankfort, William Atherton was eminently useful; Peter Taylor and John B. Ewan, the preachers on the Winchester Circuit, witnessed the conversion of hundreds. Peter Taylor had for several years been an itinerant, and was distinguished for his usefulness and zeal. Mr. Ewan had just entered the itinerant ranks, but was a young man of remarkable promise.

John Collins Hardy was the preacher on the Mount Sterling Circuit. He was born, October 1, 1809, in Ross county, near Chillicothe, Ohio. At a camp-meeting held at Brown's Camp-ground, in Ross county, in the autumn of 1825, he was powerfully converted, under the ministry of Francis Wilson, and joined the Church at the same time. In August, 1830, he was licensed to preach by John Collins, at the place where he first felt the pardoning love of Christ. At the session of the Ohio Conference of 1830 he was admitted on trial, and traveled two years, when, at his own request, he was discontinued. In a local sphere he was not happy. Believing it to be his duty to devote himself exclusively to the work of the ministry, he came to Kentucky, and offered himself to the Conference, in 1837. As the colleague of William C.

* *Western Christian Advocate*, September 9, 1842.

McMahan, he was appointed to the Lewis Circuit, and in 1838 to the Millersburg Circuit; thence we follow him to Paris, in 1839. At the Conference of 1840 he located. Mr. Hardy remained local but one year. He was reädmitted in 1841, and appointed to the Mount Sterling Circuit, where we now find him.

From the time Mr. Hardy entered the itinerant field in Kentucky, he took rank with the ablest preachers in the Conference. Retiring in his disposition, he placed upon his ministry a much lower estimate than was placed upon it by others. On the Mount Sterling Circuit, as in other charges, success crowned his labors. During the early part of the year indications were by no means favorable for a revival. On the first of May, however, he commenced a meeting in a remote portion of the circuit, which continued four days, and resulted in twenty-three additions to the Church and about half that number of conversions. On the 4th of June he began a meeting at Poynter's Chapel, which continued fourteen days, at which thirty-eight persons were added to the Church, and twenty professed religion. On the 12th of July a meeting was commenced in Slate, which lasted seven days, at which twenty persons were happily converted and thirty-three joined the Church. A camp-meeting held at Poynter's Camp-ground commenced August 18, at which one hundred and twenty persons joined the Church and eighty were converted to God. In this last meeting Mr. Hardy was assisted by Messrs. Veach, Wilson, Ewan, Taylor, and McMahan.

Drummond Welburn had charge of the Athens

Circuit. He was the son of Drummond and Mary Henderson Welburn, and was born in Accomack county, Virginia, October 22, 1818. His parents were devout Christians and earnest workers in the Methodist Church of which they were members. Two months before the birth of Drummond Welburn his father died, leaving the training of the son to the widowed mother. The influence of a religious home can scarcely be estimated. The teachings of his pious mother impressed his young heart, and led him, when only a child, to form resolutions for a better life. Attending Sunday-school when only seven years of age, he was awakened more powerfully than he had been before by reading the seventeenth verse of the third chapter of John's Gospel, printed on a ticket which had been given him. When twelve years of age he removed to the city of Philadelphia, where he remained until September, 1838. While in that city he attended the Methodist Sunday-school, occupying a portion of the time as teacher. In the autumn of 1838 he removed to Lexington, Kentucky. The first sermon he heard in the West was preached in Lexington by Bishop Waugh, the Sabbath after he reached that city—then on his way to the Kentucky Conference at Danville. Although surrounded by influences adverse to Methodism, the recollection of his mother's counsel and prayers led him to the Methodist Church, where he was a constant attendant.

On a pleasant Sabbath afternoon, April 14, 1839, while walking alone outside of Lexington, he was arrested by the Holy Spirit and impressed with the terrible thought that this call, if unheeded, would be the last. For a few weeks he endeavored to seek religion without revealing either his feelings or purposes to any one; but failing to realize the pardoning love of Christ, on the 8th of May he determined to ask the counsel and prayers of the people of God. That evening he went to the Methodist Church, and thence to two Presbyterian Churches, but found that there was no service at either of them. Unwilling to defer a question of such moment, he passed on to the Baptist Church, where he heard a sermon from the Rev. Mr. Hurley, of Missouri, and an exhortation from Dr. Burrows. At the close of the service, with several others, he presented himself for the prayers of the Church. On Thursday and Friday evenings he was still a penitent at the altar. After a conversation with Dr. Burrows on Friday night, he retired to his room and fervently pleaded for mercy. At eleven o'clock, while on his knees, reading the tenth chapter of Romans, he "was enabled by divine grace to believe with the heart unto righteousness." On the 26th day of the same month he joined the Methodist Episcopal Church.

Believing that he was divinely called to the work of the ministry, he was licensed to exhort December 19, 1839, by George W. Brush, and licensed to preach May 18, 1840, by William Gunn.

Several months elapsed from the time he was licensed to preach until the meeting of the Conference. These were spent on the Burlington Circuit, as junior preacher, Thomas Hall being in charge.

On this circuit he gave full proof of his ministry, and had the pleasure of witnessing the conversion of forty persons at a camp-meeting held in Kenton county.

Entering the Conference in 1840, he was sent, with Carlisle Babbitt, to the Winchester Circuit, where he was instrumental in winning souls to Christ. His appointment in 1841 was to the Athens Circuit —a new charge, without any membership. Within the bounds of his circuit there were thirty-one members of the Church, twelve of whom held their membership in Lexington, seventeen in the Winchester Circuit, and two in the Paris Circuit. Before the first day of the following April Mr. Welburn had organized five Societies and added forty-seven to the number already mentioned. The religious interest which had been awakened up to this time continued to widen and spread, until at the close of the year one hundred and eighty-six members were reported, most of whom had been powerfully converted.

It is but seldom that we are permitted to record such triumphs of grace under the ministry of a preacher so young and inexperienced as was Drummond Welburn. He was zealous, faithful, and gave great promise of usefulness to the Church.

Carlisle Babbitt and Moses Levi were the preachers on the Georgetown Circuit. Although the General Minutes report no change in the membership from the previous year, yet this circuit enjoyed much prosperity.

The ministry of James D. Holding, on the Burlington Circuit, was greatly blessed; while the Owenton Circuit, with Thomas Demoss and Marcus L. King, continued to prosper.

Thomas Demoss was born May 5, 1813, and was converted in 1830. In 1835 he was admitted on trial into the Kentucky Conference, and appointed to the Madison Circuit, as junior preacher. In 1836, with Thomas S. Davis, he was sent to the Salt River Circuit. It was during this year that we first saw Mr. Demoss. The Shelbyville Bible Society had employed us to distribute Testaments in Shelby, Anderson, and Spencer counties, to all the children under fifteen years of age who could read. While prosecuting this work in Spencer county we spent a night at the house of Isaac Miller, Esq., where we learned that Mr. Demoss would preach the following day. It was here that we met with him, and we still remember the words of advice and of cheer which we received from his lips.

At the Conference of 1837 his field of labor was the Germantown Circuit, as the colleague of Hiram Baker; in 1838 he was sent to the Leesburg Circuit alone, and in 1839 to the Sharpsburg Circuit. At the Conference of 1840 he was appointed to the Madisonville Circuit, and in 1841 to the Owenton Circuit, where we now find him.

In the several charges occupied by Mr. Demoss he was a faithful and successful preacher. In the Owenton Circuit, as early as the 6th of April, he writes that "upward of one hundred persons had joined the Church, forty of whom had become members at New Liberty, fifteen at Owenton, and the remainder in other portions of the circuit."* His colleague, Marcus L. King, was a young preacher of piety and zeal.

At Carrollton, success still attended the labors of Fielding Bell; while in the Versailles Circuit—whose preacher had fallen at his post in the early part of the year—under the ministry of Thomas Rankin, Richard Deering, and other brethren, who devoted as much time to that charge as could be spared from their own work, many were brought to Christ.

The total increase in the Lexington District was nine hundred and sixty-four white and four hundred and eighty-five colored.

The Louisville District shows, in the General Minutes, a decrease of seventeen hundred and seventy-five white and forty-one colored members. An examination of the appointments included within its territory, as compared with the former year, shows that the Elizabeth, Brandenburg, Hardinsburg, Hartford, and Yellow Banks Circuits had been taken from it, and constituted the larger portion of a new District, known as the Hardinsburg District. The actual increase in the Louisville District was nine hundred and twenty-six in the white and three hundred and forty-eight in the colored membership.

In the city of Louisville, from the Fourth-street Church the Fourth and Eighth-street charges had been formed. George C. Light was stationed at the former, and Thomas Bottomley at the latter. In

* *Western Christian Advocate*, May 6, 1842.

both of these charges there were extraordinary revivals of religion, in which many were brought to Christ. The Louisville and German Mission, under the oversight of Peter Shmucker, continued to advance in influence and in numbers.

Elkanah Johnson, with George Riach for his colleague, in the Newcastle Circuit, won many souls to Christ. The preachers on the La Grange Circuit were William James and James S. Woolls. Under their ministry a net increase of one hundred and seven white and sixteen colored members was reported.

The grandest achievements of grace were to be seen in the Jefferson Circuit. The preachers were Joseph D. Barnett and Charles B. Parsons. About three hundred persons joined the Church under their ministry, and about the same number were happily converted. It was under their administration that Dorsey's Camp-ground was established. The first camp-meeting held on that spot, consecrated by the conversion of hundreds, commenced about the middle of August, and continued six days. "About one hundred and twenty-five were converted to God, and ninety were added to the army of the Lord."*

The Hardinsburg District was a new field, formed by a division of the Louisville District, with the addition of the Litchfield Circuit and the Morganfield and Henderson Circuit—the former being taken from the Shelbyville District, and the latter from the Hopkinsville District. The energetic and zealous

* *Western Christian Advocate*, September 9, 1842.

Richard D. Neale was the leader of the hosts in this inviting field.

The Elizabethtown Circuit, under the pastoral care of Hartwell J. Perry, enjoyed much prosperity. Mr. Perry was born in Shelby county, Kentucky, November 1, 1806. His parents removed from Shelby to Henderson county in 1819. In the summer of 1825, while at work alone on his father's farm, the subjects of death, the judgment, and eternity, presented themselves to his mind, awakening serious reflections in reference to his responsibility to God. He promptly formed a resolution, from which he never swerved, to become a Christian. On the 16th day of April, 1826, in company with his excellent mother, he joined the Methodist Episcopal Church, and on the 30th of the same month he experienced that "peace of God, which passeth all understanding." In the autumn of 1829, at a camp-meeting in Livingston county, he realized the "fullness of the blessing of the gospel of Christ." Returning home, the altar was erected in his father's house, and morning and evening he led in family-prayer. Feeling that God required of him more than private membership in the Church, he frequently held meetings in the neighborhood, and endeavored to persuade his associates to seek religion. On the 13th of March, 1830, he was licensed to preach at Rawley's Meeting-house, in Henderson county, by George McNelly, and was employed by him to travel for the remainder of the year on the Henderson Circuit, with Clement L. Clifton. In this responsible position his labors were greatly blessed. His earnest appeals and warm exhortations persuaded many to abandon the path of sin and turn to God.

At the session of the Kentucky Conference of 1830 he was admitted on trial, and appointed to the Cumberland Circuit, with W. A. H. Spratt. This circuit embraced within its territory the counties of Knox, Harlan, Laurel, and Whitley, in Kentucky, and Campbell county, in Tennessee. Faithful in the performance of the duties assigned him, the young preacher was instrumental in winning many souls to Christ. After passing the winter in this rugged field, he was removed in the spring to the Somerset Circuit, to assist the zealous John Sandusky. From the Conference of 1831 he was sent to the Danville Circuit, with the earnest and indefatigable John James, where he spent "a pleasant and profitable year." His next appointment was the Green River Circuit, where success still crowned his faithful ministry. In the autumn of 1833 he was again sent to the Danville Circuit, where, after laboring a few months, his health failed, compelling him to retire from the work.

In 1835 he was sufficiently restored to enable him to return to the effective ranks, and we find him in the Newport and Covington Station, as the colleague of the gifted William Phillips, where many were converted and added to the Church. We next follow him to Cynthiana, where he remained two years, still making "full proof of his ministry."

In September, 1838, death came to his home and carried away its brightest jewel. She who for six years had followed his fortunes, amid privation, and toil, and sacrifice, was called to be the companion of the angels.

His subsequent appointments were Bowling Green, Georgetown, and Elizabethtown (where we find him in 1841). In these several charges his ministry was abundantly blessed. On the Georgetown Circuit, from the time he entered upon his work until he closed his labors in that interesting charge, at the expiration of two years, a deep religious influence pervaded the community. Among the stars that will deck the crown of his rejoicing, when God's jewels are gathered, will be found many of the Indian youths who at that time were students at the Choctaw Academy, located in Scott county. Invited to preach at the academy, he accepted the invitation. At first the gospel seemed to exert but a feeble influence upon the students, and the preacher entertained serious thoughts of surrendering the appointment. Unwilling to do so without a valid reason, on his third visit he proposed to all who desired an interest in his prayers, and wished to be saved, to give him their hand. The scene which followed gladdened the hearts of angels and sent a thrill of joy through the realms of bliss. More than sixty of these sons of the forest gave the preacher their hands, and, falling on their knees, cried out for mercy. Requested by the principal of the academy to preach in the afternoon, he did so, when the altar was crowded with anxious inquirers after the truth. Forty-two of them joined the Church at that time, and the good work progressed until one hundred Indians were added to the membership—among them

John Page, who became a preacher and entered the Kentucky Conference in 1842, and went as a missionary to his own nation.

Later in the year, at a camp-meeting held near Georgetown, one hundred and five persons were added to the Church, and twenty-four others within four days after the meeting closed.

On the Elizabeth Circuit, Mr. Perry continued to deliver his message with the same energy and success that had distinguished him elsewhere. Bold, fearless, energetic, true to his Master's cause, God crowned his labors with success.

The Big Spring and Hardinsburg Circuits—the former with Peter Duncan and Charles Hendrickson as the preachers, and the latter under the pastoral care of the sweet-spirited Seraiah S. Deering—enjoyed times of refreshing; while John Miller, on the Morganfield and Henderson Circuit, was eminently successful. The net increase in this District was three hundred and six white and forty-four colored members.

If any other District presented a larger increase during the year, none was favored with a more general revival of religion, than the Shelbyville. The good work commenced almost immediately after Conference closed, and before the winter had passed, upon every charge in the District, with a single exception, showers of grace had fallen, and many had been brought to Christ. With the opening of spring the work spread in every direction. Its influence was overwhelming. In the Shelby Circuit, under the ministry of Napoleon B. Lewis and John W. Fields, a meeting was held in Simpsonville, commencing early in March, at which there were thirty-eight accessions to the Church. At the close of this meeting Mr. Lewis returned to his home in Christiansburg, and during his stay concluded to preach a few sermons, under which a revival commenced; and there, also, thirty-eight persons cast in their lot with the people of God. The third quarterly-meeting commenced June 6, and was held at Pleasureville. Having no church-edifice there, the Methodists had been holding service in the Baptist Church; but the members closed their doors, and declined to allow the quarterly-meeting to be held in their house. The Presbyterian Church was situated about one mile from the village, and its use was kindly tendered to Mr. Lewis. The meeting was protracted nine days, during which time one hundred and nineteen persons were added to the Church. For the convenience of the neighborhood the meeting was transferred to Pleasant Grove Church, and thence to Christiansburg, and thirty persons were received in addition. Nor did the work stop here. More than three hundred persons had been converted and enrolled their names on the Church-book, when, in August, a camp-meeting was held at Crane's Camp-ground, in Henry county, which continued eight days, and thirty persons "passed from death unto life" and joined the Church. Two weeks later the fourth quarterly-meeting commenced at Cardwell's Camp-ground, when sixty more witnessed a good confession. The last meeting before Conference was held at Hebron, at which this zealous and faithful evangelist was unable to be present. The meeting was conducted by Messrs. Gunn, Ralston, Tevis, and Fields. Here more than twenty persons professed faith in Christ. The Minutes show a net increase of more than six hundred white and colored in this circuit.

On the Salt River Circuit, to which Richard I. Dungan and William R. Price were appointed, on the 22d of April a meeting commenced in the Chaplin neighborhood, which resulted in the conversion of forty persons. William Gunn, the Presiding Elder of the District, conducted the meeting, assisted by Robert Fisk, William D. Matting, and Jesse Bird.

In the Shelbyville Station, Thomas N. Ralston enjoyed a year of great prosperity; while in Bardstown Nathanael H. Lee was eminently useful.

Mr. Lee was born, in Campbell county, Virginia, April 29, 1816. When only a child he came, with his parents, to Kentucky, and settled in Monroe county. He was educated chiefly in Glasgow, Kentucky, meeting the expenses of his course by teaching school at intervals. Under the ministry of Clinton Kelly and John C. C. Thompson, in 1836, he was awakened to a sense of his condition as a sinner, professed religion, and joined the Methodist Church.

No sooner had Nathanael H. Lee realized the pardoning love of the Saviour than he believed it to be his duty to call sinners to repentance. To him the world had many charms, and, attracted by its tinsel and pageantry, he had dreamed of happiness in its pursuits. Endowed with a superior intellect and with untiring energy, he might have attained to eminence in any of the learned professions. The Church, however, had claims on him, and in entering its communion he brought all—talents, energy—to the foot of the cross. He was licensed to exhort in 1837, under the administration of James King, and licensed to preach, in 1838, by Jonathan Stamper. At the Kentucky Conference of 1838 he was admitted on trial and appointed, with Gilby Kelly, to the Hopkinsville Circuit. His second appointment was to the Mount Pleasant Mission, in the south-eastern portion of Kentucky. To this rugged field he was returned in 1840. In 1841 he was stationed in Bardstown.

From the admission of Mr. Lee into the Conference it was apparent to all who made his acquaintance that he was destined at an early day to occupy a commanding eminence in the Church. His uncompromising devotion, his fervent zeal, his self-sacrificing spirit, his love of the Church, and his superior intellect, qualified him as a leader among his brethren.

On the Hopkinsville Circuit, in his earliest ministry, he defended the peculiar doctrines of Methodism with an ability that has but seldom been equaled, while many were gathered into the fold of Christ who will be stars to deck the crown of his rejoicing in the hereafter.

His labors on the Mount Pleasant Mission were very arduous; but, ever faithful to the trust committed to him, he knew no sacrifice that he did not cheerfully make for the Master. For two years he was seen to thread the valleys of the Cumberland and to cross its rock-ribbed mountains, to preach the unsearchable riches of Christ. In the open forest, in the log school-house, in the cabins of the humble, he proclaimed the tidings of a Redeemer's love, and under his ministry hundreds gathered around the cross.

If the ministry of Mr. Lee was blessed in the lowlands and in the mountains of Kentucky, he was equally successful in the pleasant village of Bardstown. Among the many who were brought into the Church during his pastorate in this place was James B. Hardin, the second son of Hon. Ben. Hardin. In a letter to the author, Mr. Lee says:

"While at West Point, James B. Hardin was converted and joined the Methodist Episcopal Church. This was a short time before he graduated. On his return home he revealed the happy change to his mother, informed her that he had joined the Church, and believed himself divinely called to preach the gospel, and felt strongly impressed that he ought to become an itinerant preacher. Although Mr. Hardin and his family were Methodists in sentiment, and their house had been for many years the home of traveling preachers, yet none of them, up to that time, had become members of the Church.

"The family was among the most wealthy and influential in the State, Mr. Hardin having scarcely a peer as a lawyer. A handsome fortune had been spent in the education of their son. He had enjoyed all the advantages of educational training that could be afforded in the United States, and I am of the opinion that he spent some time at one of the universities in Europe. He was endowed with a princely intellect, and bade fair to be one of the most brilliant young men in the State. He was all that his parents could wish him to be. He was the idol of his family.

"It was very natural that they should oppose his entrance upon the life of a traveling preacher. Such a result would have contravened all the hopes they had entertained of him. In such a calling there could be no worldly honor, no glory, no wealth. It would necessarily, especially at that time, be a life of toil and hardship, spent mainly among the poor and obscure, who had no honor to confer, no emolument to bestow. They believed in and admired Methodism; they loved Methodist preachers, and delighted to afford them the noble hospitality of their comfortable home. They believed there was a necessity for Methodism; the wants of the world could not be met without it; it was their *beau ideal* of a Church; yet they could not consent that *their* son should become a Methodist preacher. Other people's sons might become such—this was all right. If their son had not been so brilliant, so well educated, so accomplished, it would not have been so hard. But their son was so gifted, and so well fitted to fill a large place in the eyes of the world, that they could not think of his consigning himself to the humble obscurity of an itinerant preacher. They were too successful in their opposition. He yielded, though against his convictions, to the worldly views of his family; but he never saw a happy hour afterward.

"He continued in the United States Army till the close of the Sac and Fox Indian war (where he acquitted himself well), when he resigned his commission in the army and entered upon the study of medicine, which, with his wonderful capacity for the acquisition of knowledge, he accomplished in an unusually short time—graduating at two medical colleges, with the highest distinction. He entered upon the practice of his profession under most favorable auspices, and soon had a good practice. In a year or two he abandoned the medical profession, and entered upon the study of the law. In a brief period of time he finished his course of study, and graduated, having no peer in his class. He entered upon the practice of his profession, and soon stood among the ablest advocates of the country. He had been but a few years engaged in the practice of law when he consented to become a candidate to represent Nelson county in the lower house of the State Legislature. He was elected by a large majority. He served his county in this capacity for several terms, and always with distinguished ability. He soon attained the reputation of the most promising young man in the State. In the meantime, he had been happily married to Miss Chinn, daughter of Major Chinn, of Harrodsburg, Kentucky, a distant relative.

"Without any premonition, as far as known, and with the most brilliant worldly prospects before him, while delivering a speech, he was suddenly attacked with a hemorrhage of the lungs. This attack being repeated, and growing more violent, and medical aid being of no avail, he determined to seek a tropical clime as a means of relief.

"Being appointed to the Bardstown Station in 1841, when I arrived I learned that, with his wife, he had gone to Cuba, seeking in that mild and salubrious climate a restoration of his health. But it all proved in vain: he constantly grew worse. Early in the spring he hastened home, anxious to breathe his last in his native land, in the midst of his kindred and friends, and to be buried with his ancestors.

"When, through the opposition of his family, Mr. Hardin had determined to give over entering upon the Christian ministry, he determined not to locate his membership in the Church; and though, during the dreary years from the time of his fatal decision in regard to the ministry to the time of his sickness, he had maintained an unimpeachable moral life, yet he had long been destitute of religious comfort, and, besides this, had become skeptical as to some of the fundamental truths of Christianity, thus illustrating the true saying that when we are destitute of the experience of religion we are in a fair way to reject its doctrines.

"In a short time after Mr. Hardin's return from Cuba, I was sent for to see him. I had heard much of his great ability and learning, and that he had given great attention to the study of the Bible and of theology; I had learned, also, that he had become very skeptical. Being young and inexperienced, I had great fear of approaching him on the subject of religion. When I called on him he seemed to appreciate my feelings, and sought at once to relieve me of my embarrassment and make me easy. In this he at once succeeded. In a very respectful manner he stated objections to some of the doctrines held by our Church, especially the vicarious atonement of Christ. Feeling that I was hardly competent to engage in a discussion on this subject, and thinking that such a discussion with a man in his condition would be out of place, I waived it, and said to him that, whatever objections to Christianity as we hold it might be raised, there was one thing that he would admit—that he could not reconcile it to his reason, or conscience, to substitute atheism, or deism, or Romanism, or Mohammedanism, or any form of heathen religion, in its place; that, with him, it was Christianity or no religion at all, and that no speculations about doctrines would now avail; that he must put the matter to a decisive personal test, and that very soon; that no time was to be lost. I shall always believe that I was divinely directed in making this reply. He never referred to his doubts as to the truth of Christianity any more, though I visited him, and read the Scriptures to him, and conversed and prayed with him, almost daily for several months. His concern for his soul rapidly increased, until finally the peace and joy which had thrilled his heart some years before were fully restored. In the meantime, he again united with the Church, before the congregation, on the holy Sabbath, being barely able to reach the church in his carriage, and give his hand, and receive the hand of fellowship from his Christian friends, and then return to his residence, not to be taken thence till the spirit was with God, and his mortal remains were borne to the grave to await the resurrection of the just.

"He survived until shortly after the close of my term at Bardstown, and then died in great peace and triumph, telling his mother, and wife, and the family, as he had perhaps told them before, that since the time at which he determined not to preach the gospel he had been a miserable man; that a fearful '*woe*' had pursued him and rested upon him all the time; that his constant restlessness, as the result, explained the fact that he had gone from one profession to another, vainly seeking relief from a consciousness of the divine displeasure, but failing to find it; that in this way he had lost his religious enjoyment, and had finally fallen into skepticism, which only increased his wretchedness. His mind had been overtasked with excessive study, and this, in connection with the conviction that he had disobeyed the divine call to preach the gospel, had worn down his physical constitution until it could bear no more; and thus the hemorrhage of the lungs and his untimely death. It was a matter of the keenest regret and self-reproach that his life had been a failure, as it had not been devoted according to the order of Divine Providence. The effect upon his family was wonderful. His wife was a devoted Christian and a Methodist when he married her. His venerable mother had joined the Church at a watch-meeting, the first day of the year 1842. During the same year his three sisters—Mrs. Helm, Mrs. Palmer, and

Mrs. Dixon—joined the Church; also, Col. Riley, his brother-in-law, whose wife had for some years been the only member of the family in the Church. Soon afterward his only brother, Rowan, became a member, and, some years after, his father joined the Church just before his death."

The Lebanon Circuit was served by John Sandusky and William M. Humphrey.

John Sandusky was born, January 11, 1798, in what was then called Jefferson (now Marion) county, Kentucky. As early as 1776 his parents emigrated to Kentucky, and settled on Pleasant Run, and established "Sandusky Station."

In 1817, before he attained his majority, he was awakened, converted, and joined the Methodist Church. We are not familiar with the circumstances that led to his conviction and conversion; but, from the time the great change was wrought, he was zealous and useful in the Church. We do not find his name in the list of itinerants until 1829, yet previous to that time he occupied a prominent position as a preacher of the gospel in the neighborhood in which he had been reared. His first appointment, after entering the Conference, was to the Green River Circuit, as the colleague of Nehemiah A. Cravens. In 1830 he was appointed to the Somerset Circuit, as the junior preacher, with the sweet-spirited James King. In 1831 his field of labor was the Green River Circuit, with Hooper Evans and Thomas Lasley. In 1832 he was placed in charge of the Lebanon Circuit, with Thomas Hall, and in 1833 he was the colleague of George W. Fagg, on the Salt River Circuit. At the Conference of 1834 he located.

No preacher in the Conference labored with greater fidelity than did John Sandusky. Enjoying in the highest degree the confidence of all who knew him, possessing talents of a high order, familiar with the doctrines of Christianity, forcible and zealous in the presentation of the great truths of religion, deeply pious, and devoted to the Church, no man in the itinerancy gave promise of greater usefulness. In the prime of his life he was compelled by feebleness of health to retire from the active duties of the itinerancy. For seven years he remained in the local ranks, often preaching beyond his strength, and evincing his devotion to the cause of his Divine Master by his abundant labors and uncompromising zeal. In 1841 he reëntered the Conference, and was appointed to the Lebanon Circuit, in which he was born and brought up, and had resided while local, and in which he was beloved by all who knew him. The wisdom of the appointment was fully vindicated in the success which this year distinguished his ministry. Hundreds were awakened and brought to Christ.

The Lawrenceburg Circuit, under the ministry of Robert Fisk, largely increased in membership.

The Harrodsburg District, under the leadership of George W. Taylor, shared largely in the religious influence that was sweeping over the commonwealth. In Harrodsburg and Danville Station there was a decrease in both the white and colored membership, but every other charge reported large accessions.

The circuit in the vicinity of Danville, which for several years had been known as the Danville Circuit, was divided, and formed the Stanford and Salvisa, and part of the Lancaster, Circuits. Clinton Kelly was sent to the Stanford Circuit and Munford Pelley to the Salvisa Circuit. In each of these charges there were gracious revivals of religion. The Lancaster Circuit, which included all the territory formerly embraced in the Mount Vernon Circuit, and of which Thomas Rankin had charge, also enjoyed refreshing times. Charles Duncan, on the Irvine Circuit, and Samuel P. Cummins, on the Hustonville Circuit, performed the duties assigned them with fidelity and success; while Aaron H. Rice, on the Liberty Circuit, was instrumental in bringing many souls to Christ.

Nowhere in the bounds of this District were such conquests made as in the Madison Circuit, under the ministry of Edwin Roberts and Robinson E. Sidebottom. Immediately after the Conference the circuit was divided, forming the Richmond Station, which was the field to be occupied by Mr. Roberts, while Mr. Sidebottom had charge of the circuit. Promptly entering upon their work, they prosecuted it with commendable zeal and extraordinary success. As true yoke-fellows, they worked together in harmony, and were instrumental in the accomplishment of great good. During the year, and in the midst of a career of usefulness, Edwin Roberts fell; but he fell at his post, "with sword in hand and armor on." However, the revival which commenced under his ministry did not abate. "Although God buried a master-workman, the work still went on. The preachers from Transylvania University, at Lexington; John H. Linn, from Danville; and Evan Stevenson, from Georgetown, came to Richmond, and many a precious gem was borne away from the dominions of death and hell."* The Madison Circuit was in a flame; every appointment was on fire! At Old Providence the revival was more extensive and powerful, perhaps, than at any other point.

The net increase in the District was seven hundred and twenty-five white and one hundred and eight colored members.

Although there was a decrease in the Bowling Green District, yet there was great cause for thanksgiving in several charges in that field. On the Greensburg Circuit, under the ministry of John C. C. Thompson, a holy and zealous preacher, many were brought from darkness to light; while on the Glasgow Circuit, to which John Atkinson and James I. George were appointed, many were converted and added to the Church, chiefly under the labors of the junior preacher—Mr. Atkinson having remained on the circuit but a short time.

The Scottsville Circuit had been divided, forming the Scottsville and Bowling Green Circuits. To these two charges Zachariah M. Taylor and Albert Kelly were appointed. At the same time Joel Peak was traveling the Burksville Circuit, and Elihu Green the Wayne Circuit. In all these charges there were "times of refreshing from the presence of the Lord," although there were no extensive re-

*Letter from Robinson E. Sidebottom.

vivals of religion. Wesley G. Montgomery, on the Columbia Circuit, witnessed the awakening and conversion of many souls.

In the Hopkinsville District, Edward Stevenson was the Presiding Elder. Although an itinerant preacher since 1825, this was his first appointment as a Presiding Elder. He brought to this important office not only a ripe experience, but talents of a high order and a burning zeal. Entering upon his work in the spirit of his Master, he traveled his extensive District, not only holding his quarterly-meetings, but preaching everywhere as he had opportunity. The gospel proclaimed by him was "the power of God unto salvation." Under his ministry sinners were awakened, penitents converted, and believers sanctified. The District was soon in a blaze. In Franklin, Russellville, Hopkinsville, Princeton, and other towns, during the winter, the displays of divine power were extraordinary. Hundreds were added to the Church.

In Russellville, one of the most pleasant and refined villages in Southern Kentucky, Eli B. Crain was stationed. Methodism had been planted in this community at an early day, and had grown and flourished under the auspices of the ablest men in the Conference. In no town in this portion of the State did it have such a hold upon the affections, or occupy so commanding an eminence in the confidence, of the people as in Russellville.

Eli B. Crain was born, in Mercer county, Kentucky, March 24, 1807. When quite a child he removed to Barren county, and was placed under the care of James Culp, a local preacher, in Glasgow. Under the teachings of this good man he was led to reflect seriously on the subject of religion, and on the 19th of September, 1824, at a camp-meeting held at Bethel, he was converted to God. His call to the work of the ministry was simultaneous with his conversion. Without the advantages of even an ordinary education, he was eager to warn sinners to flee the wrath to come, and availed himself of every opportunity to persuade his fellow-men to turn to God. Endowed with an intellect of a high order, and with an eloquence that was remarkably persuasive, and with a burning desire to save souls, he was anxious to enter the itinerant ranks and devote his life to the one work of doing good. With a constitution naturally delicate, and impaired by affliction, he hesitated to offer himself to the Conference, lest he might prove unequal to the life of sacrifice and toil incident to the work of the faithful itinerant. For nearly two years he traveled under the direction of George W. Taylor, a Presiding Elder; but, failing in health, he was obliged to quit the field.

Rallying his strength, in 1833 he offered himself to the Conference, and was accepted. His first appointment was, with Jesse Sutton, to the Glasgow Circuit, in which he had been brought up. In 1834 he was sent to the Newcastle Circuit, where he remained two years. In 1836 his appointment was to the Shelby Circuit, to which he was returned in 1837. In the several charges he had filled he was deservedly popular and eminently useful. As a preacher he occupied a commanding eminence, and as an exhorter he had but few peers among his brethren. Simple-hearted, good and true, he was universally beloved. It was while he had charge of the Shelby Circuit that we made his acquaintance. His family resided in Shelbyville, where we were living—then a youth, preparing to enter the ministry. Mr. Crain was sick; we visited him, and, at his request, attended several of his appointments in his circuit, rather to inform the people that he was sick than to occupy his place.* At the close of the year he was placed on the list of the superannuated. Unwilling to be idle, he returned to the effective ranks in 1839, and was sent to the Franklin Circuit, and in 1840 to the Georgetown Circuit. In both of these charges he made full proof of his ministry, winning many souls to Christ. We have already met with him in Russellville, where he was appointed in 1841. Only a few weeks elapsed after he had entered upon his work before there were indications of a revival of religion. Commencing with his first quarterly-meeting, the services were protracted from day to day, and then from week to week, until seventy-four persons were brought to Christ.

The preachers on the Elkton and Logan Circuit were John B. Perry and Albert H. Redford.

John B. Perry was born, in Belfast, Ireland, May 23, 1813. His father came to America in 1816, and settled in the city of Philadelphia. In 1830 John B. Perry joined the Methodist Episcopal Church, and soon afterward found "the pearl of great price."

* This was our first work as an itinerant preacher.

Before he was nineteen years old he was licensed to preach, and for a short time labored in the Philadelphia City Mission. In the autumn of 1836 he came to Kentucky, and was employed by William Gunn, the Presiding Elder, as junior preacher on the Newcastle Circuit, to assist Richard Deering. It was while he traveled on this circuit that we accepted an invitation to accompany him to several of his appointments. At the Conference of 1837 he was admitted on trial into the Kentucky Conference, and appointed to the Shelby Circuit. In 1838 his field of labor was the Barboursville Circuit, in the south-eastern portion of the State. At the Conference of 1839 he was sent to the Hartford Circuit, and in 1840 to the Hopkinsville Circuit. In 1841 he was appointed to the Elkton and Logan Circuit, with Albert H. Redford as his colleague.

Associated with Mr. Perry in the work of the ministry, we had every opportunity to form a proper estimate of his worth. Fully consecrated to the work to which he was divinely called, he devoted himself to it with a oneness of purpose worthy a true minister of Jesus Christ. In his character there was a child-like simplicity that attracted the attention and commanded the confidence of all who knew him. He was an Israelite indeed, in whom there was no guile. As a preacher, from the time we first heard him, he occupied a commanding eminence. He read but few books, but these were carefully selected, and were read well. With the Bible he was perfectly familiar, and from its sacred treasury drew "things new and old." His preaching was plain, his arguments supported by the word of God. Exemplary in his deportment, his life was a daily comment on the religion he professed and taught. In every sense an itinerant preacher, we never heard him express a preference for any appointment, nor an unwillingness to serve the Church in any field to which he might be assigned.

The Elkton and Logan Circuit embraced the fertile lands of Todd and Logan counties, and contained a community distinguished for their intelligence and culture. No circuit in the Conference was blessed to a greater degree with efficient local preachers than was this. Caleb N. Bell, John P. Moore, Jordan T. C. Moore, William S. Evans, and Warren M. Pitts, occupied prominent positions in the local ranks. Warren M. Pitts had served the circuit as a supply the previous year; indeed, although a local preacher in name, he was an itinerant in reality. With natural gifts of a high order, and with an anxiety to do good, he had filled several appointments under the direction of Presiding Elders. In 1835, soon after his conversion, he served the Bowling Green Circuit, and in 1836 the Logan Circuit. He traveled on the Greenville Circuit in 1837, on the Nashville Circuit in 1839, and in 1840 on the Elkton and Logan Circuit. In all these charges his ministry was honored and blessed in the conversion of souls.

In entering this interesting field, the preachers were confronted with many things to discourage them. Although portions of the circuit had from time to time been blessed with revivals, there had been no extensive ingathering into the Church for several years. Campbellism was at the height of its influence. With an energy which we have seldom seen displayed it was pushing its conquests, and, under able "evangelists," doing every thing in its power to make "disciples." Experimental religion was attacked from its pulpits, and the "mourners' bench" made the subject of ridicule. The proclaimers of this theory visited every neighborhood, and with great zeal endeavored to turn away from the truth the unwary and unsuspecting.

The Baptist Church, too, in this section, was not friendly to Methodism. The differences between these two denominations of Christians, in reference to their teachings on baptism, had been arrayed before the people. The Baptist Church was strong and influential. Baptist preachers of more than ordinary ability had boldly attacked the peculiar views of Methodism, as to "Who are the proper subjects for Christian baptism?" and "What is the scriptural mode?" In these attacks Campbellism, in perfect harmony with them on these questions, had joined. But little attention had been paid to these disputants—the Methodist Church deeming it better, for the peace of the Churches, to decline any participation in the controversy. It was under these circumstances that John B. Perry and Albert H. Redford commenced their labors on the circuit.

The winter passed with but little, if any, change. The congregations were small, and, with the exception of about twenty persons who had joined the Church, no special interest was manifested on the subject of religion. On the 12th of March the

20*

second quarterly-meeting commenced in the town of Elkton, and was protracted for seventeen days. The pulpit was filled, during the time, chiefly by Edward Stevenson, the Presiding Elder, and John B. Perry, the preacher in charge. About sixty persons were converted, and forty-eight joined the Methodist Episcopal Church. Among those who made a profession of religion and joined the Church were a gentleman in the eighty-fifth year of his age, his grandson and wife, and great-granddaughter.

During the progress of the meeting a prominent preacher in the Campbellite Church visited Elkton, and preached in the court-house at such hours as were not occupied by the Methodist Church. The revival did not please him; but his arguments and his ridicule were alike harmless.

The revival in Elkton was only the beginning of a rich harvest, in which many were brought to the knowledge of the truth. A religious influence went out in every direction, until hundreds were brought to Christ.

A few weeks later the junior preacher was requested by the Church to preach, in different parts of the circuit, sermons on the subjects and mode of Christian baptism. In compliance with this request, early in May, he preached a sermon in Keysburg, at the close of which he baptized seventeen children, the father of one of them being a Baptist, but the mother a member of the Methodist Church. His next appointment was announced for Pleasant Grove, to be filled on the third Sabbath in June; but, previous to this time, he was requested to preach on the same subject at Bell's Chapel, one of the most prominent appointments on the circuit.

The church was crowded to its utmost capacity, and many persons were standing at the doors and windows, outside the house. Soon after the announcement of the text a stranger walked into the church, seated himself in the altar, and, with paper and pencil, began to take notes of the sermon. It was Elder Robert Williams, of Harmony, Tennessee, an able polemic in the Baptist Church. At the close of the sermon he challenged the young preacher to discuss with him the points at issue, at Pleasant Grove. The challenge was accepted, and the 22d of June appointed as the time for the debate.

Several years had elapsed since the question of baptism had been openly discussed in this portion of the State, by a Pedobaptist preacher. Fifteen years before, John Johnson had met Jeremiah Vardeman, a celebrated Baptist preacher, in Hopkinsville and in other places, and compelled him, by the force of truth, to retire from Southern Kentucky. During this long period Methodism had reposed upon the laurels it had won.

No event had transpired in this community for many years that excited so much interest as did this discussion. The concourse that attended it was immense. The debate was to continue for several days; but, on the afternoon of the second day, Mr. Williams, without consulting his opponent, announced to the audience that, so far as he was concerned, the discussion would close on that day.

Remonstrance, argument, appeal, were alike unavailing to induce him to remain longer.

At the close of the year there was a net increase in the circuit of two hundred and two white and sixty-one colored members.

In other portions of the District there was a fine religious influence. The General Minutes show an increase in this District of ninety-eight white members and a decrease of one hundred and twenty-six colored members. The increase was much larger. The transfer of the Morganfield and Henderson Circuit to the Hardinsburg District makes a difference of several hundred.

In the Barboursville District the increase was two hundred and four white and thirty-five colored members. The Barboursville, Williamsburg, Prestonsburg, and Louisa Circuits, show an increase; in the other charges there are fewer members than were reported the previous year.

The entire increase in the Conference was five thousand two hundred and sixty-seven white and one thousand seven hundred and eighty-three colored members.

In that portion of Kentucky belonging to the Memphis Conference the religious awakening was equal to that in any other section of the State. The Paducah Circuit had been divided, and the flourishing town of Paducah made an independent charge. To this station James Young was appointed. At a meeting held in Paducah, early in December, twelve persons joined the Church and eight professed religion. During the winter there was considerable religious interest, from time to time. The quarterly-meeting which was held in February was a season of refreshing. Thomas Smith, the Presiding Elder, was present, and preached with great power. At this meeting twenty-four were added to the Church, and ten were happily converted. The Hickman, Paducah, and Wadesboro Circuits were in a continual blaze. John S. Williams and William E. Rogers, on the Hickman Circuit; James M. Major and John A. C. Manly, on the Paducah Circuit; and Alexander C. Chisholm and William H. Seat, on the Wadesboro Circuit, labored with diligence and success. In a letter to the *Southwestern Christian Advocate*, dated September 23, 1842, Thomas Smith, the Presiding Elder, writes: "We are now in the midst of the most glorious revival I have ever witnessed. In the bounds of this District there have been, the present year, about two thousand souls converted to God and added to the Methodist Episcopal Church. The aged and the young have been brought in. One man said to be one hundred and five years old was powerfully converted to God. The wise and sage philosopher, with the humble African, has found peace in believing, and the work is still increasing. We have but little opposition; all heads, hands, and hearts unite in carrying on the glorious work. It would delight you to witness the glorious work, as it moves on to victory—to see the wily politician, the crafty lawyer, the stern judge, the industrious planter, the busy merchant, the towering orator, the military chieftain, with the young men and maidens, all coming to Prince Immanuel, and passing on their way to the rest that remaineth to the people of God."

The net increase in this portion of Kentucky was nine hundred and seventy-nine white and twenty-three colored—making the total increase in the State *six thousand two hundred and forty-six* white and *one thousand eight hundred and six* colored.

CHAPTER XI.

FROM THE SESSION OF THE KENTUCKY CONFERENCE OF 1842 TO THE CONFERENCE OF 1843

Saw ye not the cloud arise,
  Little as a human hand?
Now it spreads along the skies,
  Hangs o'er all the thirsty land:
Lo! the promise of a shower
  Drops already from above;
But the Lord will shortly pour
  All the Spirit of his love.

THE Kentucky Annual Conference assembled in the Old Medical Hall, in the city of Lexington, on the morning of the 14th of September, 1842.

Bishop Waugh was present and presided during the session of the Conference.

Thomas N. Ralston was elected Secretary, and William M. Crawford Assistant Secretary.

Benjamin T. Crouch and George W. Brush were appointed the Committee on Public Worship.

John Christian Harrison, Hartwell J. Perry, and Nathanael H. Lee, were appointed Stewards of the Conference.

George W. Brush and James D. Holding were appointed the Committee on Memoirs.

John Tevis, George W. Brush, and Carlisle Babbitt, were appointed the Committee on Missions.

Hubbard H. Kavanaugh, Edward Stevenson, and Gilby Kelly, were appointed a committee to prepare a Pastoral Address "to the members and friends of the Church."

At this session of the Kentucky Conference, William C. Dandy, Samuel L. Robertson, George W. Smiley, Jas. H. Dennis, Hiram T. Downard, Samuel D. Baldwin, Isham R. Finley, Learner B. Davison, Henry M. Linney, George Hancock, James Kyle, John Bier, Thomas H. Lynch, Josiah L. Kemp, David Wells, William Ahrens, John Page, John Vanpelt, George Taylor, and Allen McLaughlin, were admitted on trial.

The Kentucky Conference has but seldom received on trial a class of preachers equal in talent to the present.

Of those who were admitted at the previous Conference, William M. Humphrey, William H. Kimberlin, Charles Duncan, Mitchell Land, William Conway, and James J. Williams, retired from the itinerant service, the most of them on account of ill health.

Albery L. Alderson and Absalom Woolliscroft located.

Thomas Waring, George W. Fagg, Stephen Harber, Zadok B. Thaxton, John Tevis, John Denham, James Ward, George S. Savage, Peter Taylor, and Wesley G. Montgomery, were placed on the list of the superannuated.

Albery L. Alderson, who located this year, was

one of the ablest preachers in the Conference. We have no record of the date of either his birth or conversion. He entered the itinerant ranks in 1833, and was appointed to the Wayne Circuit, with James King. In 1834 he was sent to Bowling Green Circuit, as the colleague of John Redman. In 1835 he was appointed to the Henderson Circuit, and in 1836 to the Madisonville Circuit. He located in 1837. He remained in a local sphere only one year, when he was reädmitted and appointed to the Elizabethtown Circuit. In 1839 he was placed on the list of supernumerary preachers, where he remained until he located, in 1842.

From the time Mr. Alderson entered the ministry he took rank with the first preachers in the Conference. An untiring student, without the advantages of more than an ordinary education in early life, he became not only a complete master in English literature, but a thorough Greek scholar. Familiar with the Bible—its doctrines, its duties, its experience—he unfolded its beauties, bringing from its sacred treasury "things new and old." As a polemic he had no superior among his brethren. In the field of religious disputation he was a giant. No opponent ever successfully met him in debate. With signal ability he wielded the weapon of truth, and exposed error and false doctrine, in whatever garb presented. We have heard him when, with a calmness as gentle and soft as the evening zephyr, he discussed his subject; and we have listened to him when, rising to the loftiest heights of oratory, he held spell-bound and entranced the vast assemblage that sat before him. Beneath his mighty appeals entire audiences were often moved, and many resolved upon a better life. In the pulpit he had but few equals. Endowed with an intellect of the highest order, with a fertile imagination and a mind richly stored with religious truth, thousands hung in breathless silence upon his lips while he delivered his message of life—of death. Under his faithful ministry hundreds were brought to Christ and made happy in a Saviour's love. It is to be regretted that such a man—warm-hearted, zealous, devoted to the noble work to which God had called him—should be compelled by any cause to retire from the active service. His health, however, was unequal to the duties of his high and holy office.

The name of George S. Savage appears this year on the list of superannuated preachers. He was born in Vanceburg, Lewis county, Kentucky, February 2, 1814. He was baptized in infancy by William McMahan, and joined the Methodist Episcopal Church, under the ministry of Samuel Veach, in Germantown, Kentucky, December 7, 1827, and on the 28th of May, 1828, in the same village, was happily and powerfully converted to God.

Believing it to be his duty to preach the gospel, he was licensed by William Adams, in Frankfort, Kentucky, September 5, 1835. At the Conference for that year, held in Shelbyville, he was admitted on trial. Before entering the Conference Mr. Savage had never attempted either to preach or to exhort. In becoming a preacher he met with opposition at home. His father, who was not a Christian, was unwilling that his son should enter the ministry, and especially to become a traveling preacher.*

Mr. Savage was appointed to the Versailles Circuit, as the colleague of the gifted Thomas N. Ralston. A serious attack of bilious fever prevented him from entering upon his work until near the last of October. His first sermon on the circuit, and the second he had attempted to preach, was delivered in Jessamine county, at the "Pocket." His text was "Pray without ceasing,"† and it was certainly an appropriate one. Mr. Savage expected to meet the preacher in charge, that evening, in Nicholasville. On his way thither he overtook a plainly-dressed countryman, who accosted him, and said:

"You are the young brother who preached for us to-day, at the 'Pocket?'"

"I preached there," was the modest reply of the young preacher.

"I think, my young brother, you had better go home. I do n't think you will ever make a preacher."

Feeling the responsibility of the work to which he had pledged his energies and his life, and conscious perhaps that he had failed to fulfill the expectations of those to whom he had ministered, the words of the stranger were calculated to dampen his ardor and impair his zeal. However, he met with Mr. Ralston that evening, who offered to him words of cheer, and encouraged him to prosecute the duties assigned him.

Although he occasionally met with discourage-

*Three years later George S. Savage received his father into the Church. †1 Thess. v. 17.

ments, yet the year was fruitful in experience and blessings. His journal contains the following record: "Traveled two thousand three hundred and twenty-three miles; preached two hundred and twenty-five sermons; received fifty into Society; read over fifteen thousand pages; obtained thirty-three subscribers for the *Advocate;* sold a good many books; did not miss an appointment, or experience an hour's confinement from sickness. To God be all the glory!"

His second appointment was to the Minerva Circuit, as the colleague of Martin L. Eads. The ministry of these zealous laborers was greatly blessed. Dover, a small village on the Ohio River, was distinguished for the wickedness of the community. Bishop Morris, then residing in Cincinnati, visited this village during the winter, and preached the gospel. The simplicity of his style, and his great earnestness, elicited the complimentary remark from a plain man, "Why, the Bishop is just like other men." At a meeting held at this place, in which John Collins—often called the St. John of Methodism—bore an active part, many were brought to Christ. The entire community was aroused, awakened sinners cried for mercy, and shouts of triumph from souls new-born to God went out upon the air. It was during this meeting that Campbellism, becoming alarmed, resolved to bring its forces to bear against the advances that Methodism was making. Under the leadership of two of their preachers, one hundred or more marched into the town and began a series of meetings. They remained, however, only a few days, and then left, after administering the ordinance of immersion to a few persons, in the Ohio River, having cut the ice to do so.

It was Sunday morning. A rough, uncouth man, distinguished for his profanity, who was engaged in hauling logs to the mill, while passing the place of worship made all the noise he could for the purpose of disturbing the service. The congregation was singing:

Nay, but I yield, I yield!
I can hold out no more:
I sink, by dying love compelled,
And own thee conqueror!

These words caught his ear, and rang like a funeral-knell; they may have been familiar to him. He could not rest, day nor night. At length, sad and uneasy, he came one evening to church, and, taking Mr. Savage aside, explained to him his feelings, and how he happened to become awakened. Words of comfort were whispered, and he was soon happily converted. A new house of worship was erected during the year, and one hundred and fifty-seven persons were added to the Church.

The two years of active service in the itinerant ministry had greatly impaired the health of Mr. Savage, and after his admission into full connection he requested and was granted a location. Besides, it was his purpose that the ministry should be the one great business of his life, and he desired to make a more thorough preparation for its arduous and responsible duties. He remained in a local sphere until the autumn of 1839, when he was reädmitted, and appointed to the Germantown Circuit, as junior preacher. The preacher in charge failing to come to the work, the entire duties of the pastorate devolved on Mr. Savage. The circuit was a large one, having nineteen appointments, to be filled every three weeks. With greatly impaired health, he prosecuted his labors. However, it was not until the winter and spring had passed that any extraordinary displays of divine power were realized.

On Sunday, June 7, 1840, Joseph M. Trimble, Professor of Languages in Augusta College, preached in the Shannon Church. The sermon was one of great power. Six persons joined the Church, and the meeting was protracted during the week. On the following Sabbath forty persons enlisted under the banner of the cross. "The power of God came down upon the congregation. If the baptism of the Holy Ghost was not visible, it was most sensibly felt. The faces of many shone as the faces of angels, and some could scarcely realize whether they were in the body or whether they were out of the body. The whole community was stirred on the subject of religion. During the meeting one hundred and fourteen persons, embracing all ages and classes, joined the Church."* Among those converted at this meeting was Joseph W. Ridgell, afterward a preacher of the gospel. The influence of this meeting extended to other portions of the circuit.† During

* Letter from the Rev. George S. Savage to the author.

† At the meeting at Shannon Mr. Savage was assisted by his uncles, James and Francis A. Savage, Samuel Veach, Calvin W. Lewis, and Joseph M. Trimble.

the year three hundred and seven persons joined the Church.

In 1840 his field of labor was the Shannon Circuit, being a portion of the circuit he had traveled the previous year. Although his health was still feeble, with untiring energy he toiled and labored to accomplish good.

In Sardis, a small village in his charge, there was a gracious revival of God's work. Such was the influence of this meeting, and such the manifestations of the Holy Spirit, that persons were converted in the class-room, in the prayer-meeting, during preaching, and on their way to and from the church. More than fifty persons found the "pearl of great price," and during the year one hundred and twenty-five persons enlisted in the service.

Unable longer to perform the active duties of an itinerant preacher, in 1841 he was placed on the list of the superannuated, where we find him in 1842.

We have reported for missions *one thousand four hundred and seventy-eight dollars and sixty-three cents,* less than half the amount collected the previous year, which was *three thousand seven hundred and twenty-eight dollars.*

Of those who had received appointments in 1841, two had fallen at their post. Peter O. Meeks and Edwin Roberts had answered the roll-call above.

Peter O. Meeks was born April 16, 1815. He embraced religion and joined the Methodist Episcopal Church in 1834. He spent several years as a student in Augusta College, where he graduated with great credit. In 1838 he was admitted on trial into the Kentucky Conference, and appointed to the Fleming Circuit, as the colleague of James Ward. In 1839 he was stationed, with Richard Deering, at Danville and Harrodsburg, and in 1840 was sent to the Barboursville Circuit. His last field of labor was the Versailles Circuit, where we find him in 1841.

But few young men in the ministry promised greater usefulness to the Church than did Peter O. Meeks. From the time he was converted he felt it to be his duty to devote himself to the ministry, and his years of toil and study in college had reference to this responsible work. In the fields he had occupied he was useful and beloved. In his intercourse with society he was kind and courteous, and as a Christian zealous and devoted. In the pulpit and in the performance of his pastoral duties he exhibited that singleness of purpose essential to success. Before he reached the meridian of life he was cut down. He died in the early part of the year, in hope of a blessed immortality.

Edwin Roberts was born, in Bedford county, Virginia, January 31, 1816. His parents were John and Mary Roberts. His mother was a member of the Methodist Episcopal Church, a woman of deep and consistent piety, who endeavored to instil into the mind of her son the principles of religion, while he was yet a child. Listening to the instructions of his pious mother, Edwin Roberts became impressed with the importance of religion, and at ten years of age reflected seriously in reference to his future state. From time to time, at intervals, he was awakened to a sense of his condition as a sinner, but refused to listen to the warning voice of the Holy Spirit, until he reached his twentieth year. In the meantime, his father had removed to Tennessee, and settled in Montgomery county, where he was converted July 6, 1835.

Brought up in the Methodist Church, Mr. Roberts identified his fortunes with that Communion; and believing it to be his duty to call sinners to repentance, he resolved to become an itinerant. His early education had been confined to the elementary branches, but by close study at home, and by teaching a small country-school, he had greatly improved his mind; yet such was his diffidence that he felt reluctant to enter upon a work involving such grave responsibilities. "Woe is unto me, if I preach not the gospel!" fully awakened him to a sense of duty, and in the autumn of 1836 he was admitted on trial into the Kentucky Conference.

His first appointment was to the Hopkinsville Circuit, as the colleague of James H. Brooking. In 1837 he was sent to the Morganfield Circuit, to which he was reäppointed in 1838. At the Conference of 1839 his field of labor was the Versailles Circuit, where he remained for two years. In 1841 he was sent to Richmond, where he closed his labors and his life.*

Few young men have preached the gospel who

* His appointment was to the Madison Circuit, with Robinson E. Sidebottom as his colleague. The Presiding Elder divided the circuit, and formed Richmond Station, in which he placed Mr. Roberts, while Mr. Sidebottom had charge of the circuit.

have achieved so much in so short a period as did Edwin Roberts. From the time he entered upon the work of the Christian ministry he devoted himself to it with uncompromising energy and untiring zeal. He had fully counted the cost, and, undaunted by sacrifice, privation, and suffering, resolved to meet the responsibilities incident to his calling, and to attain success. In his first field of labor crowds thronged to hear him preach and to catch the words of invitation as they fell from his burning lips. His calm, clear arguments, his earnest appeals, and the persuasive power of his eloquence, brought many to the altars of the Church and to Christ.

On the Morganfield Circuit, he was like a flaming fire. Wherever he preached the Church was aroused from its apathy, sinners were awakened, and penitents converted to God. For two years his strong and forcible sermons, his powerful exhortations, his earnest appeals, and his pure and holy life, were before the people of Union and Henderson counties, admonishing them of sin, and urging them to a better and brighter inheritance. From here we follow him to the Versailles Circuit, where for two years he preaches with a power and success that scarcely find a parallel in the annals of the past. During the first year in which he preached in that charge more than four hundred persons were brought to Christ through his ministry, while in the surrounding country he was the honored instrument in bringing hundreds from the paths of sin. He seldom preached a sermon, or made an appeal, but some wanderer came back to God. In labors abundant, he took no rest, knew no ease, but gave time, talent, energy, all to the glorious cause to which he was pledged. His journal, now before us, shows an amount of labor almost unequaled, and a devotion and zeal that no opposition could dampen. Day and night found him at his post. At every point where his Divine Master bade him assault, he resolved, with God's help, to conquer. Impediments and obstacles formed no part of his creed, but served only to nerve him for the contest. In all his efforts to advance the Redeemer's kingdom his piety shone with undiminished luster. In every department of ministerial work he excelled. Whether in the pulpit, in the altar, in the social circle, or mingling with the community, he recognized it as his chief business to persuade men to be reconciled to God.

He entered upon his work in Richmond in due time. We find the following entry in his journal:

"*Friday, October* 8.—Packed up and left. It was a time of sorrow with my wife and sisters. They had been left, when small, without a mother; had grown up together, and now they must part. Well, well, we all have to part in this life; but there is a place where we shall part no more."

The next evening found him in Richmond, and on Sunday, the 11th, a crowded audience assembled at the court-house to hear the words of life from this faithful evangelist. At night he preached in the Baptist Church.

From this period there was no abatement in his labors. In Richmond, at Bethel, at Centerville, at Bethlehem, at Providence, he lifted his warning voice, and many turned to God. He holds a meeting at Lancaster, where, assisted by John H. Linn and Richard Deering, of whom he speaks with great tenderness, forty-nine white and thirty colored persons unite with the Church. During the winter every moment is employed in study, in preaching, in exhorting, in pastoral visiting, or in something by which the cause of the Redeemer may be advanced. In his journal he makes frequent mention of Robinson E. Sidebottom, his fellow-laborer, to whom he was greatly attached.

On the first day of January, 1842, he makes the following entry in his journal:

"This is a new year; the old one is gone. I feel like commencing a new course of piety. I feel the importance of more love and humility, and that I may do better than I have done in my past life. May I be a better Christian and a better minister! Lord, give me grace!"

Every page of his journal shows his close communion with God and his oneness of purpose to achieve success. He says:

"*Friday, April* 8.—Left Nicholasville, and came to Richmond. Have felt rather unwell for some days. Left Mary behind.

"*Saturday, April* 9.—Went to Providence to quarterly-meeting, and preached at eleven. Brother Taylor, the Presiding Elder, preached at half-past four. I came to town in the evening; felt quite stupid and dull.

"*Sunday, April* 10.—At eleven preached in town, a searching sermon; at two met Bible-class; at night preached, with liberty, to a very attentive audience.

"*Monday, April* 11.—Rode to Providence, and preached at eleven, with some liberty.

"*Tuesday, April* 12.—Rode to town; wrote; read."

Here his journal closes.

He continued to preach with unabated zeal until about the first of May. His sermons were "in thoughts that breathe and words that burn." About the last of April he went to Centerville, in Madison county, eight or ten miles from Richmond, where he preached his last sermon. He complained very much during the day, and was soon confined to his bed. Through twenty-eight days of illness he was calm, patient, and serene as a summer evening. His disease was typhus fever. He slept a great deal, and seemed to suffer but little bodily pain. His colleague, Mr. Sidebottom, visited him a few days after his illness began, and asked him if he thought he would recover. He replied: "I do not know, but it makes no difference to me whether I live or die; for," said he, "'to live is Christ, but to die is gain.'" The Friday and Saturday before his death he rejoiced almost incessantly in the love of Christ. A short time before he breathed his last he was asked how he felt in reference to eternity. His reply was, "All is well." He asked for a drink of water, which was given him. After he had drank he recited the language of the Saviour to the Samaritan woman: "'Whosoever drinketh of the water that I shall give him shall never thirst; but the water that I shall give him shall be in him a well of water springing up into everlasting life.'" Upon being informed by his physician that his case was hopeless, he immediately requested all in the room to kneel down, when he called on a minister who was present to pray. During the prayer he rejoiced aloud, while his countenance was bright and angelic. On the 28th of May, 1842, he sweetly fell asleep in Jesus.

Although the revivals of religion were not so powerful nor so extensive this year as they were during the past, yet there was much to encourage the Church.

In the Maysville District there was a net increase of three hundred and twenty-five white and sixty-eight colored members. John Christian Harrison succeeded Isaac Collard on this District, and in every department of duty belonging to the responsible office of Presiding Elder he was a master and a workman. The only change made in the arrangement of the work was the formation of a German Mission, called Maysville and West Union, to which John Bier was appointed, and which, at the next Conference, reported sixty-eight members. At the close of the first round of quarterly-meetings, Mr. Harrison writes: "Several of the charges have enjoyed seasons of revival since Conference. As far as I can ascertain, near three hundred have been received on probation, in the bounds of the District, during the first quarter." *

On the 9th of March Isham R. Finley writes from Maysville: "There has been an accession to the Church here, since Conference, of between fifty and

* *Western Christian Advocate*, February 3, 1843.

sixty."* In the Germantown Circuit, Thomas Rankin held a meeting in Washington, commencing on the 9th and closing on the 19th of December, at which thirty-one persons joined the Church. The Little Sandy Circuit, under the ministry of Samuel P. Cummins, was greatly blessed. At the first quarterly-meeting, held at Mr. Buchanan's, on the Big Sandy Circuit, commencing December 24, nine persons joined the Church and several were converted; and at a watch-meeting, held a week later at the same place, "twenty-five or thirty persons presented themselves as seekers of religion, and at the close of the meeting six others joined the Church, making forty-one since Conference." In the Flemingsburg Circuit, William D. Trainer and William C. Dandy were pushing the battle to the gates of the enemy. Before the winter had passed more than one hundred persons joined the Church. In the Lewis Circuit, the eccentric and gifted Lorenzo D. Harlan witnessed very great prosperity. On the Highland Circuit, Edmund M. Johnson met with great success; and on the Shannon Circuit, Jedidiah Foster, gifted, popular, useful, and beloved, had "times of refreshing."

The Covington District was still under the leadership of John James. As early as the 31st of October George C. Light announced, through the columns of the *Western Christian Advocate*, that thirty-two persons had joined the Church in Covington. On the 27th of December he writes that "upward of two hundred and twenty have been added to the

* *Western Christian Advocate*, March 17, 1843.

Church since the commencement of the present Conference-year." On the 28th of January, 1843, he writes again: "The glorious work is still progressing in Covington, without any visible abatement. At least three hundred have been added to the Methodist Episcopal Church within the past four months, and at no former period have our prospects been brighter." This revival continued throughout the greater part of the year, dispensing its blessings on that community.*

On the 22d of November, only a few weeks after the close of the Conference, John Miller writes from Cynthiana, that "above forty persons have been received" into the Church. John Miller was an able and useful preacher of the gospel. He came from the State of Ohio to Kentucky in 1840. That year he was admitted on trial into the Kentucky Conference, and appointed to the Morganfield and Henderson Circuit, where he remained two years. In 1842 we find him on the Cynthiana Circuit. Before he entered the ministry he was distinguished as an able practitioner of medicine. But few men have risen more rapidly in the itinerant field than John Miller. From the time he entered the ministry he took rank with the most promising young preachers in the Conference. Zealous, active, enterprising, and deeply pious, he not only won a reputation for himself, as an able preacher, but was instrumental in the accomplishment of much good. On the Morganfield and Henderson Circuit he was greatly be-

* For a sketch of George C. Light, see "History of Methodism in Kentucky."

loved, and through his instrumentality many were brought to Christ. In the Cynthiana Circuit he was also useful and beloved.

On the Sharpsburg Circuit the labors of Josiah Whitaker were greatly blessed; and on the Millersburg Circuit John W. Riggin witnessed a gracious outpouring of the Holy Spirit. James C. Crow had charge of the Alexandria Circuit, where many were born to God.

In Newport, during the winter, under the ministry of John G. Bruce, there was considerable prosperity. On the 9th of February he writes to the *Western Christian Advocate:* "During the past few weeks we have received about thirty on probation, in this city." Mr. Bruce was transferred from the North Ohio to the Kentucky Conference in 1841, and was stationed in Newport, where we still find him the following year. Before he came to Kentucky he had spent several years in Ohio as a traveling preacher, where his ministry had been greatly blessed. In Kentucky, where he had been but a very short time, his labors had been crowned with success.

In the Crittenden Circuit, under the ministry of Samuel Veach, a good and true man, much good was accomplished.

In the Lexington District, which the year before was visited with such extraordinary displays of divine power, revivals still blessed the Church. In the city of Lexington, Richard Deering continued to attract large assemblies, while the membership of the Church constantly increased. During the year one hundred and ninety-five persons were brought into the Church.

A few weeks previous to the Conference the fourth quarterly-meeting for the Versailles Circuit was held in Nicholasville. Peter O. Meeks, the zealous pastor, had fallen at his post. Benjamin T. Crouch, the Presiding Elder, requested the assistance of Mr. Deering and William Atherton in conducting the meeting. "It was a time of great power and grace; many young men and young ladies joined the Church, and there were many clear and happy conversions." The meeting continued for more than a week, and sixty persons were added to the Church. Encouraged by what had been accomplished, the members of the Church proposed to hold a camp-meeting immediately after Conference, and requested Mr. Deering and the other brethren to be present. The session of the Annual Conference adjourned on Friday, the 23d of September, and on Saturday Mr. Deering was on the camp-ground, about four miles from Nicholasville. A large number of board tents had been erected, each provided with a stove, in case the weather should turn cold. The meeting was one of great power. Nearly one hundred persons were converted and joined the Church. The entire community was aroused. Under a single sermon preached by Mr. Deering, one evening, fully one hundred persons came to the altar and pleaded for mercy, and more than one-half of them were converted within a few hours.

William M. Crawford and George W. Smiley were appointed to this charge, and during the year one hundred and eighty persons became members of the Church.

In the Georgetown Circuit, the second quarterly-meeting, which commenced in Georgetown February 5, was a time of great power. Joseph D. Barnett, the faithful pastor, writes: "Twenty-three gave in their names as probationers, and we think more than that number testified that God hath power on earth to forgive sins."* On the 19th of February he wrote: "With a full soul, let me say to the friends of Zion that our protracted-meeting at Georgetown has just closed, and the number that offered for membership was seventy-four."† A few days later Evan Stevenson reported nine additional members. The Athens Circuit, too, was abundantly blessed. Drummond Welburn reported forty additions to the Church. Later in the year he reported an addition of seventy more, and ninety conversions. On the Burlington Circuit, there was a revival in almost every neighborhood, under the ministry of Fielding Bell; while Thomas Demoss and James H. Dennis, on the Owenton Circuit, were instrumental in bringing many to Christ.

The Louisville District shared largely in the riches of grace. On the 9th of March George W. Brush writes: "There is now a most powerful revival of religion in the three stations in Louisville, Kentucky." He, however, gives none of the particulars. An examination of the General Minutes shows a considerable increase in Brook, Fourth, and Eighth

* *Western Christian Advocate*, February 24, 1843. † *Western Christian Advocate*, March 16, 1843.

street Churches. Hubbard H. Kavanaugh was stationed at Brook-street, George W. Brush at Fourth-street, and William Holman at Eighth-street. The Clay-street German Charge, under the ministry of William Ahrens, was also greatly blessed.

The Jefferson Circuit was served by Charles B. Parsons and Andrew J. McLaughlin.

Charles B. Parsons was born, in Enfield, Connecticut, July 23, 1805. At an early period in life he chose the profession of the stage, and as an actor, before he was thirty years of age, he attained the highest reputation. Several influences combined to turn his thoughts to the all-important subject of religion. Reading religious books, the prayers in his behalf, offered by his brother, who was a Presbyterian minister, and the earnest appeals from the lips of John Newland Maffitt, were instrumental in leading him to Christ. He professed religion and joined the Methodist Episcopal Church in March, 1839. Before the period of his probation expired he was granted permission by the Presiding Elder to preach the gospel, to which high and holy office he believed himself to be called. After preaching a few sermons to admiring thousands, it is to be regretted that he withdrew from the Church and returned to the stage, to fulfill an engagement he had made previous to his admission into the Church. No act of the life of this distinguished man produced deeper sorrow, in his own heart and in the hearts of his friends, than this, and in after years he often referred to it with painful emotion. He remained out of the Church only a short time, when, with heartfelt contrition, he returned and asked for an humble place with the people of God. His tears and great sorrow for the wrong he had committed melted every heart, and with rejoicing they received the wanderer back. After the expiration of his probationary term he was regularly licensed to preach the gospel, and in the autumn of 1841 was admitted on trial into the Kentucky Conference.

Before he entered the Conference he preached in the several Methodist Churches in Louisville, where he had long resided, and throughout the surrounding country, and everywhere he proclaimed the tidings of a Redeemer's love listening multitudes caught with pleasure the burning words which fell from his lips. In him were combined all the requisites of the true orator—great emotion, passion, a correct judgment of human nature, genius, fancy, imagination, gesture, attitude, intonation, and countenance, with a commanding presence, all united in blended strength to accomplish the mighty purpose which moved his heart. He earnestly spoke the truth of God's holy word, relying on the divine arm for help. He preached as a dying man to dying men, as in the presence of God and the judgment-seat. He fearlessly pronounced the threatenings of the law, probed with a bold hand the sinner's heart, and in much assurance and with the power of the Holy Ghost declared the whole message of God.

His first appointment was to the Jefferson Circuit, as the colleague of Joseph D. Barnett. He entered upon his work in the spirit of the Master. Anxious crowds waited upon his ministry, sinners were awakened, penitents converted, and the Church established. At the close of the year three hundred persons had joined the Church under the labors of these zealous preachers. In 1842 he was returned to the same field. On the 12th of January following he writes from Middletown: "A revival is in progress in this village, which promises great good to the cause of religion. Fifty-six have been added to the Church, many of whom have been happily converted."* On the 2d of March he writes from Jeffersontown: "The time was when Methodism triumphed in this place, but years have fled since then, and her palmy days are almost forgotten. Thank God, the standard of the cross is again lifted amidst the ruins, and, phenix-like, our beloved Methodism has risen, thrice glorious, from her parent-ashes! The death of one of the few old saints of God, who, faithful to the last, have stood like monuments of by-gone days, perpetuating with gloomy grandeur the memory of other times, called our attention to the place, and we resolved once more to sound the battle-cry. Twelve old soldiers, the relics of a once large and flourishing Society, rallied around the standard, and the fight commenced. The God of battles was with us; union and communion was had with other branches of the family of Christ, and our meeting terminated with fifty-two additions to the Church and the re-collection of several who had strayed away and been well-nigh lost forever."† The work spread all around the

*Letter in *Western Christian Advocate* of February 3, 1843.

† *Western Christian Advocate,* March 17, 1843.

circuit, and hundreds believed and were brought to Christ.

The Shepherdsville Circuit, under the ministry of George W. Crumbaugh, was greatly revived, and more than sixty persons were added to the Church. In the La Grange Circuit, the revival was general. The zealous James D. Holding was in charge, with Samuel D. Baldwin as his colleague.

Mr. Baldwin was a young man. He was born, in Worthington, Ohio, November 24, 1818. His parents were Presbyterians. He had graduated with high honor in Woodward College, Cincinnati, standing in the first rank in the class of which Hon. George H. Pendleton and Hon. George E. Pugh were members. While at college he became concerned on the subject of religion, and was happily converted among the Methodists, and united with that branch of the Christian Church. The step that he had taken was a disappointment to his parents, who had hoped that he would become a minister in the Church of which they were members. Many efforts were made to persuade him to leave the Methodist Church, but they were unavailing. True to principle, for conscience' sake he forsook father, mother, brothers, and sisters, to serve God in that Church through whose instrumentality he was brought to Christ, and in which he might be most useful and happy. This severance from his family was to him a severe trial; but his judgment and conscience dictated and sustained him in this course, from which he never swerved. In his early life he had traveled in the Southern States. He admired the people and loved the manners and habits of Southerners, and hence he sought a place in the South. He had just entered the Conference, and his first circuit was the La Grange. Popular, gifted, eloquent, zealous, and devoted to his work, success crowned his labors.

The preachers on the Newcastle Circuit were Carlisle Babbitt and Samuel L. Robertson. Mr. Babbitt had been for several years a useful member of the Conference;* but Mr. Robertson had just been admitted on trial. He was a young man, and gave great promise of usefulness to the Church. He was born, in Bath county, Kentucky, February 6, 1818. In August, 1833, in Fleming county, Kentucky, he became a member of the Methodist Episcopal Church. Believing it to be his duty to preach, he nevertheless entered the ministry with much hesitation. After serious thought he decided to meet the obligations which confronted him, and on the 4th of June, 1842, was licensed to preach by Isaac Collard. On the Newcastle Circuit he performed the duties assigned him with earnestness and zeal, and with blessing to the people. At a meeting in Bedford, held in March, seventy-three persons joined the Church.

The Hardinsburg District enjoyed many refreshing seasons, although there was only a small increase in the membership. In the Big Spring, Hardinsburg, Hawesville, and Owensboro Circuits, there was much religious interest. Nathanael H. Lee and

*See sketch of Carlisle Babbitt, in the "History of Methodism in Kentucky."

George Hancock traveled on the Owensboro Circuit, and under their ministry many were added to the Church. On the 27th of March Mr. Lee reports a revival in Owensboro, at which fifteen were added to the Church. On the 11th of September he reports revivals at Burk's, in Ohio county, and at Pleasant Grove, in Daviess county. In these several revivals one hundred and forty persons were added to the Church. The Hardinsburg Circuit was served by Seraiah S. Deering and Learner B. Davison, true and faithful men, who were instrumental in bringing many to Christ. In other portions of the District there were seasons of refreshing.

Seraiah S. Deering was born, in Greenup county, Kentucky, April 10, 1816. Under the ministry of William P. McKnight he joined the Church, at Thomas Lawson's, in the same county, in February, 1831. He gave his hand to the Church as a seeker of religion, and after deep repentance and earnest supplication he was happily converted in the following June. He was alone in the woods when the great change occurred. The impression was not only on his mind that it was his duty to preach the gospel, but all who knew him entertained the same belief. In the summer of 1834 he was licensed to exhort, and in November of the same year to preach. In a previous chapter we referred to him as supplying, under the Presiding Elder, the Taylorsville and the Hartford Circuits, and to his zealous and useful labors on the Yellow Banks Circuit, after he entered the Conference in 1839. In 1840 he was again sent to the Hartford Circuit, where he had been eminently successful two years before. His appointment in 1841 was to the Hardinsburg Circuit, to which he was returned in 1842.

The membership in the Shelbyville District presents but little change from that of the previous year. In the Shelby Circuit, which, under the ministry of Napoleon B. Lewis, had enjoyed such great prosperity, the religious interest had not abated. Mr. Lewis was returned to the field in which he had already won so many trophies to the Redeemer.

Napoleon B. Lewis was born, in Russellville, Kentucky, September 25, 1809. His ancestors, on his father's side, were Virginians. They came to Kentucky at an early day, and settled in that beautiful plain which lies between the hills of Green River and the Cumberland. There two generations of them lie buried. Among the earliest Methodists in Logan county, Kentucky, was his maternal grandmother. For many years her house was not only the home of the weary itinerant, but the chapel for the neighborhood. At one time an effort was made to remove the Society, thinking it could not be longer maintained; but, in deference to Mrs. Stemmons,* the grandmother of Mr. Lewis, it was con-

*Mrs. Stemmons was richly rewarded for her devotion to the Church. Alexander H. Stemmons and Jacob M. Stemmons, her two sons, became Methodist preachers. One of her daughters married Herrington Stevens, a Methodist itinerant preacher. Napoleon B. Lewis was her grandson, and John W. Rhodes, a useful and popular preacher, married one of her granddaughters. James A. Lewis and John W. Lewis, at present members of the Louisville Conference, are her great-grandsons.

tinued at her house, and resulted in a strong Society, now removed to Keysburg. The father of Napoleon B. Lewis died, leaving his son, quite young, to the care of one of the best of mothers—wise, prudent, and self-reliant. She was afterward married to Robert Davis, a Presbyterian preacher, a godly man, who aided her in molding the character of her children, and in training them for heaven.

Mr. Lewis received the rudiments of a good English education under the instruction of his step-father, with whom he commenced the study of the languages, but was prevented by the death of Mr. Davis from realizing any farther benefit. The care of the family devolved on him, and as a true and affectionate son and brother he cheerfully fulfilled the responsible trust.

In May, 1830, he joined the Methodist Episcopal Church, as a seeker of religion, and a week later realized the pardoning love of Christ, in a class-meeting at Keysburg, Kentucky. It had been an abiding impression of his childhood that he would become a preacher. When but a boy he crawled beneath the pulpit of the old log church, and prayed the Lord that "*if he did make him a preacher, to make him a good one.*" Immediately after his conversion he erected the altar for family worship, from which, morning and evening, his prayers went up to God.

In the autumn of 1832 he was licensed to preach by Isaac Collard, and the following year was employed by him on the Livingston Circuit. At the Conference of 1834 he was admitted on trial into the Kentucky Conference, and was appointed to the

Cumberland Mission. In 1835 his field of labor was the Barboursville Mission. In 1836 he was sent to the Little Sandy Circuit, and in 1837 to Danville. In 1838 he was appointed to the Greenville Circuit, where he remained two years. From the Greenville Circuit we follow him to the Hodgenville, and thence to the Shelby Circuit, where we still find him in 1842, prosecuting his work with fidelity and zeal.

There were but few preachers in Kentucky whom we knew more intimately than we did Napoleon B. Lewis. He was an extraordinary man. From the time he entered the ministry he stood abreast with the ablest preachers in the State, and exerted an influence for good that but few young men could claim. God had called him to preach the unsearchable riches of Christ, and, whether the path of duty lay amid mountain fastnesses or in fertile valleys, he was ever found at his post. In the cabins of the humble poor and in the frescoed church alike he proclaimed "liberty to the captive and the opening of the prison-doors to those who are bound." His talents were of a high order. As a preacher he had but few equals, whether he discussed the cardinal doctrines of Christianity, or unfolded its practical duties, or dwelt on its blessed experience. In exhortation he was overpowering. We have listened to the appeals he made to sinners, when the tallest sons of vice fell before the power of truth as bends the forest before the raging storm. We have heard him when, rising with his theme, he carried his vast audiences with him to the loftiest heights, whence they might contemplate the scenes of felicity and of grandeur on which the disembodied spirit shall enter when it has dropped this earthly tabernacle in the dust. Influenced by a single motive—to do good and to save the souls of men—we are not surprised that thousands were brought to God through his instrumentality. Everywhere he preached crowded audiences waited on his ministry, and stars were gathered to deck the crown he wears to-day. On the Shelby Circuit he was eminently useful. Hundreds were brought into the Church and into the "peace of God, which passeth all understanding," through his labor of love; and at the close of his pastorate in that charge the Church blessed him for the good he had, under God, accomplished.

In the Taylorsville Circuit, William Atherton and Zachariah M. Taylor had prosperous times. In the Salt River Circuit, Richard I. Dungan and Garret Davis witnessed many conversions; while Leroy C. Danley and Allen McLaughlin had some success on the Hodgenville Circuit. In the Lebanon Circuit, William R. Price and John W. Fields labored with marked zeal and success; while Moses Levi, on the Lawrenceburg Circuit, successfully pointed sinners to the Shiloh.

In the Harrodsburg District there were also seasons of rejoicing. Before the first of April fifty persons had joined the Church, under the ministry of Moses M. Henkle.

In the Somerset Circuit, as early as the 4th of January, Ransom Lancaster writes: "On the 13th of December I commenced a meeting in Somerset, which continued until the 27th. The result was thirty-two accessions, making in all, since I came here, sixty-six additions to the Church." * On the 18th of February a meeting was commenced at Carson's Meeting-house, which resulted in twenty-one conversions and twenty-seven accessions.† On the 28th of May Mr. Lancaster writes again: "Up to this time I have received one hundred and eighteen, as probationers, into the Church." ‡

Ransom Lancaster was a young man of extraordinary zeal and uncompromising devotion to the Church. He was born, in Boonsboro, Madison county, Kentucky, April 15, 1818. He was converted at Pleasant Grove Camp-ground, in Daviess county, Kentucky, in August, 1839, and joined the Church at the same time.

In August, 1840, he was licensed to preach by Benjamin T. Crouch. For more than a year he served the Church as a local preacher, and in the autumn of 1841 he was admitted on trial into the Kentucky Conference. His first appointment was to the Barboursville Circuit, where his labors were greatly blessed. In 1842 we find him on the Somerset Circuit, prosecuting his work with fidelity and success.

In the Richmond Station, Gilby Kelly, the gifted and popular pastor, reports twenty conversions and thirty-eight additions to the Church, at the second quarterly-meeting, at which he was assisted by Drummond Welburn; while on the Madison Cir-

---

* *Western Christian Advocate,* January 20, 1843. † Letter from Stephen K. Vaught, in *Western Christian Advocate,* March 10, 1843. ‡ *Western Christian Advocate,* June 9, 1843.

cuit, the revival which commenced the previous year under the ministry of Edwin Roberts and Robinson E. Sidebottom was continued under the labors of the latter during all the present year.

The Conference had in it no man truer to the interests of the Church than Robinson E. Sidebottom. He was born, in Green county, Kentucky, April 12, 1809. He was converted in November or December, 1831, and in July, 1833, was received into the Methodist Episcopal Church by Hooper Crews, and was by him licensed to exhort. Early in the spring of 1834 he was employed to travel on the Livingston Circuit, in the place of Joseph D. Barnett, who had been removed to the Henderson Circuit. He preached until the fourth quarterly-meeting on the charge to which he was appointed, having license only to exhort. At this quarterly-meeting he was licensed to preach, and recommended to the Kentucky Conference for admission on trial.

In 1834 he was received into the Conference, and appointed to the Hinckstone Circuit, with Josiah Whitaker. His second appointment was to the Danville Circuit, with Gilby Kelly. Although the year had nearly passed away without any extraordinary outpouring of the Holy Spirit, yet toward its close, at the Durham Camp-ground, more than one hundred persons were happily converted to God. John Newland Maffitt and George McNelly were at the meeting, and rendered much service. At the following Conference he was returned to the same charge, with Milton Jamieson, who failed to reach the work, and the vacancy was supplied by Richard

I. Dungan. It was during this year that union meetings were held in that charge by the preachers of the different denominations, which resulted in the conversion of hundreds. In 1837 he was sent to the Burksville Circuit, where, although he labored with constancy and devotion, the total amount he received, for the support of himself, wife, and two children, was thirty-seven dollars and thirty-seven and one-half cents. His next field of labor was the Hodgenville Circuit, to which he was returned the following year, where his ministry was prosperous and successful. In 1840 we again meet with him on the Danville Circuit, after an absence of three years. In this charge extraordinary revivals crowned his labors, and many were brought to Christ. At Beech Grove and Joseph's Chapel sinners were awakened and penitents converted to God. On the Madison Circuit, in 1841 and in 1842, revivals blessed the labors of this good man wherever he delivered the message of life and salvation, and many were the seals to his ministry.

On the Stanford Circuit, Clinton Kelly persuaded many to be reconciled to God—the pleasure of the Lord prospered in his hands; while on the Lancaster Circuit, Thomas R. Malone was instrumental in doing much good.

The preacher on the Salvisa Circuit was Elkanah Johnson, one of the most remarkable men in the Conference. He was born, in Shelby county, Kentucky, May 5, 1811. In 1821, near Madison, Indiana, he joined the Methodist Episcopal Church, but was not converted until 1826. In 1838 he was licensed to preach by Benjamin T. Crouch, and entered the Kentucky Conference. His first appointment was to the Owenton Circuit. In 1839 he was sent to the Taylorsville Circuit, and in 1840 to the Shelby Circuit. At the Conference of 1841 he was appointed to the Newcastle Circuit, and in 1842 we find him on the Salvisa Circuit. In all these fields God blessed the ministry of this true man. His manner of preaching was peculiar. He imitated no one. His sermons were distinguished for their soundness, force, and power. He attracted attention wherever he ministered, and accomplished good.

In the Bowling Green District, there was an interesting revival of religion in the Bowling Green Station, under the ministry of Eli B. Crain. On the Scottsville Circuit, previous to the 15th of June, Munford Pelly reported more than one hundred additions to the Church. In the Glasgow Circuit, the ever-faithful Joel Peak witnessed seasons of great prosperity; while in the Burksville Circuit, Josiah Godbey was greatly encouraged by the success which crowned his labors. Albert Kelly, in the Wayne Circuit, and John C. C. Thompson, in the Columbia Circuit, were instrumental in doing much good.

In no District in the Conference were the displays of divine power more apparent than in the Hopkinsville. Edward Stevenson was still the leader—an indefatigable and zealous preacher of the gospel. The Conference adjourned on the 23d of September. On the 5th day of October a camp-meeting commenced at Ash Spring, in the Logan Circuit, to which Albert H. Redford was reäppointed. It continued until the 17th day of the month. At this meeting two hundred and eighty-one persons were happily converted, and one hundred and eighty-three joined the Methodist Church. The preachers who assisted the pastor were Robert Fisk, William Knowles, John F. South, and Mr. Brooks, a local preacher from Tennessee. Besides these, Edward Stevenson was present nearly all the time. This meeting was one of great power. In three days one hundred and five "persons passed from death unto life." At the close about one hundred adults were baptized by pouring. The revival spread throughout the circuit. On the 27th of January the pastor wrote: "The Lord is still reviving his work in this circuit. Since I last wrote, ninety have been added to the Church, making in all, since Conference, two hundred and seventy-three." * On the 4th of July he wrote again: "Three hundred and thirty-two persons have been added to the Church, and about the same number converted to God;" † and before the year closed more than four hundred persons had become members of the Church.

At Pleasant Grove—a Society which had been reduced to a few members, and where the debate on baptism, mentioned in the previous chapter, had occurred a few months before—the religious influence was overwhelming; nearly one hundred persons embraced religion and entered the Church. At Adairsville, one of the early battle-grounds for Methodism in Kentucky, the Society had been en-

---

* *Western Christian Advocate,* February 10, 1843. † *Western Christian Advocate,* July 14, 1843.

tirely blotted out; but a new organization, with forty-two members, again entered the same field. At Keysburg, Pleasant Run, Red Oak Grove, and Dry Fork, God blessed the labors of his servants, and souls were gathered into the Church. In Russellville, John F. South met with considerable success; and at Elkton, John B. Perry was instrumental in "turning many to righteousness." In the Hopkinsville Circuit, the plain, unostentatious Thomas Bottomley proclaimed the tidings of salvation to the hundreds who waited upon his ministry, and more than two hundred souls passed "into the liberty of the children of God." In the La Fayette Circuit, which included the delightful village of Cadiz, experimental religion triumphed over a formal Christianity, and Campbellism, mortified at its own defeats, for awhile stood aghast, and then retired from the struggle. At Smithland, James N. Temple was eminently useful; and on the Salem Circuit, William James and William Lasley rejoiced over the victories they had won. Robert Fisk, in the Princeton Circuit, and George Riach, in the Franklin Circuit, enjoyed refreshing seasons, and made full proof of their ministry.

In the Barboursville District, William B. Landrum reports revivals in Barboursville, in the Mount Pleasant Circuit, in Prestonsburg, in Louisa, and in almost every part of the District.

In Jackson's Purchase, the Hickman Circuit was divided, forming the Hickman and the Mayfield Circuits. While the several charges in this portion of Kentucky were blessed with interesting meetings during the year, there was a decrease of one hundred and twenty in the white and forty-seven in the colored membership.

The total increase in the State for this year was *two thousand seven hundred and ninety-one* white and *one thousand three hundred and sixty* colored members.

CHAPTER XII.

FROM THE SESSION OF THE KENTUCKY CONFERENCE OF 1843 TO THE CONFERENCE OF 1844.

Kings shall fall down before him,
  And gold and incense bring;
All nations shall adore him,
  His praise all people sing:
For he shall have dominion
  O'er river, sea, and shore,
Far as the eagle's pinion
  Or dove's light wing can soar.

THE Kentucky Annual Conference of 1843 met in the city of Louisville, on the 13th of September. Bishop Morris presided, and Thomas N. Ralston and William M. Crawford were elected Secretaries.

The appointment of the usual committees and the examination of the character of the preachers occupied the principal portion of the first three days of the session.

Several preachers of distinction, from other Conferences, were present—among them, Charles Elliott, D.D., editor of the *Western Christian Advocate;* Leonidas L. Hamline, editor of the *Ladies' Repository;* Leroy Swormstedt, Book Agent at Cincinnati; E.

W. Sehon, Agent for the American Bible Society; Messrs. Wood, Beck, Robinson, Daily, and Hays, of the Indiana Conference; Charles K. Marshall, of the Mississippi Conference; and Mr. Doring, of the Pittsburgh Conference.

On Friday morning Dr. Sehon addressed the Conference in behalf of the American Bible Society, and Dr. Elliott in behalf of the *Western Christian Advocate.*

At the close of Dr. Elliott's address, the following resolution was offered by Joseph S. Tomlinson and Thomas N. Ralston, and adopted:

"*Resolved, by the Kentucky Annual Conference,* That we have great confidence in the management of the Western branch of the Methodist Book Concern, and that we consider it of vast importance to the interests of our Church; and that we will use increased exertions to sustain and promote the usefulness of that institution, by a *prompt payment* of our liabilities to it, and by the circulation of the books and periodicals which from time to time emanate from that establishment."

A resolution of greater importance could scarcely have been submitted to an Annual Conference. The Western Book Concern had been established by the Church, that the demands of the West might be fully supplied. The Conferences whose benefit it was intended to subserve owed their *undivided* support toward its advancement and success. Not only was it their duty to circulate the books that emanated from it, but to place the *Advocate* in every family they served. The influence of a religious paper on the intelligence and piety of a household cannot be easily estimated. Another feature in the resolution looked to the payment of the debts due the Concern. With a laxity that can hardly be excused, they had filled orders for books without inquiring into the ability of persons to meet their obligations. Some of the preachers had been remiss in reference to their book accounts, and hence the suggestion of promptness in the resolution. It was at this Conference that a young preacher, who owed a large account to the Book Concern, offered his note at one year from date, which the Agent refused, and said: "*My young brother, you will pay me now, or I will report you to the Conference as a delinquent!*" The young man turned away, mortified, but borrowed the money and settled his account. To-day he remembers Mr. Swormstedt with feelings of gratitude for having taught him the virtue of promptness. Several others failed to pay what they owed, and the Agent submitted their names, with the amounts of their indebtedness, to the Conference, for such action as might be deemed proper. No preacher, and especially a young man, should allow himself to incur a debt to the amount of a dollar; but if he does, he should feel that his honor is imperiled if he fails to settle it at the close of the Conference-year.

A resolution from the New York Conference, memorializing the General Conference to restore Mr. Wesley's original rule on spirituous liquors, was concurred in, seventy-nine voting in the affirmative and one in the negative; also, a resolution from the same Conference, to request the General Conference to suspend the Restrictive Rules so far as to make the rule on slavery read as follows: "The buying or selling men, women, or children, with an intention to enslave them," was concurred in.

A resolution from the New Jersey Conference was submitted, recommending that the Discipline be so changed, on the subject of slavery, as to read: "The buying or selling of men, women, or children, with an intention to enslave them, or the holding them as slaves, in any State, Territory, or District, where the laws of such State, Territory, or District will admit of emancipation, and permit the liberated slave to enjoy freedom." The Conference unanimously voted non-concurrence.

Henry B. Bascom, William Gunn, Hubbard H. Kavanaugh, Edward Stevenson, Benjamin T. Crouch, and George W. Brush, were elected Delegates to the General Conference, and John Christian Harrison and George W. Taylor reserves.

A resolution was adopted, requesting Henry B. Bascom to collect materials for the history of the rise and progress of Methodism in Kentucky, and to write that history as soon as convenient.

It is to be regretted that Dr. Bascom did not perform this labor of love. He had entered the ministry in the heroic age of the Church, and was familiar with the men and had mingled with many of the scenes that would have invested such a work with thrilling interest. So far, however, as we are advised, no steps were taken in this direction by the distinguished preacher.

The following persons were admitted on trial: John Barth, Henry Coch, Larkin F. Price, John S. McGee, John N. Wright, James Penn, Edmund B. Buckner, Timothy C. Frogge, Warren M. Pitts, Geo. B. Poage, William J. Chenowith, Bartlett A. Basham, William Butt, Edward A. Martin, Alexander McCown, Milton G. Baker, Samuel P. Chandler, Stephen K. Vaught, Thomas J. Moore, Orson Long, George W. Burriss, Samuel D. Roberts, and William Neikirk.

James I. George and Alanson C. Dewitt located.

Thomas Hall, Thomas N. Ralston, Andrew J. McLaughlin, Peter Taylor, George S. Savage, James Ward, John Tevis, Zadok B. Thaxton, Stephen Harber, Thomas Waring, Abram Long, and John Vance, were placed on the list of the superannuated.

For the first time, the name of Thomas N. Ralston appears among the superannuated preachers. He was born, in Bourbon county, Kentucky, March 21, 1806. In November, 1826, he professed religion, and in May, 1827, at Greer's Creek Church, in Woodford county, Kentucky, he was received into the Church by William Adams, and by the same preacher was licensed to preach, the following August, at a District Conference, in Lexington, Kentucky. In 1827 Mr. Ralston was admitted on trial into the Kentucky Conference, and was appointed to the Mount Sterling Circuit, with Milton Jamieson in charge. In 1828 he was appointed to the Danville Circuit, with William Atherton. In 1829 he located, in consequence of feeble health, after having been admitted into full connection. He remained local four years, a portion of the time sustaining the relation of principal to the Bethel Academy, in Nicholasville, yet preaching as often as his health would permit.

In the meantime he removed to Illinois, where, in 1833, he reëntered the itinerant ranks in the Illinois Conference, and was appointed to the Rushville Circuit, having for his colleague the young, eloquent, and sainted Peter Bowen. In the spring of 1834 Rushville was detached from the circuit, and formed into a station, to which Mr. Ralston was returned in the autumn. In 1835 he was transferred to the Kentucky Conference, and appointed to the Versailles Circuit, having for his colleague George S. Savage. The next year we find him in Frankfort; thence we follow him to Maysville, where he remained two years. From Maysville he was sent to the city of Louisville, and stationed at Fourth-street, the oldest, and at that time the largest, church in the city. In 1840 he was appointed Agent for Augusta College, and in 1841 his field of labor was the Shelbyville Station, to which he was returned in 1842. In 1843 he was placed on the list of the superannuated, but took charge of the Lexington Female High-school.

From the time that Thomas N. Ralston entered the itinerant ranks he gave promise of great usefulness to the Church. Soundly converted and divinely called to the work of the ministry, he entered upon the discharge of his high and holy office with commendable zeal, and prosecuted its duties with energy and success. Endowed with an intellect of a high order, well improved by a liberal education and close study, as a preacher he attracted attention, while in the performance of his pastoral work he greatly endeared himself to the people he served.

In the Mount Sterling Circuit, where he won his earliest trophies, revivals, like a flaming fire, spread over the country, and more than six hundred persons were added to the Church. It is true, the zealous Milton Jamieson was in charge, and John Ray, Henry McDaniel, John Craig, William C. Stribling, John Sinclair, and Israel Lewis, in the ministry, and in the laity Caleb Caps, Isaac Redman, and Frank Owen, contributed their influence to the advancement and progress of the kingdom of the Redeemer; yet under the ministry of the young itinerant hundreds were brought to Christ. It was on this circuit, and during this year, that the good Joseph Sewell, one of the most useful local preachers in Kentucky, was licensed to preach. He had just entered the Church, and was impressed with the conviction that he ought to persuade sinners to be reconciled to God. Without education, he felt unwilling to enter on a work so responsible, until his agony became so intense that it was almost intolerable. Invited by Mr. Ralston, he accompanied him around the circuit. His exhortations were overpowering. Congregations were melted into tenderness under his warm appeals and earnest prayers.

On the Danville Circuit, the times were prosperous. At a camp-meeting near Perryville many were brought to Christ. William Holman was stationed in Danville and Harrodsburg, and the gifted Henry

S. Duke in Lancaster and Stanford, from whom he received valuable aid. The zealous Dr. Fleece, of Danville—a host in a revival—and the good Benjamin Durham and Carlin Padlock, in the country, held up his hands while he lifted "o'er the ranks the prophet's rod."

While traveling on the Danville Circuit, on one occasion he preached on the possibility of apostasy. A lady, who was a member of a sister Church, became offended at the sermon, and, passing from the church in company with another lady at whose house the young preacher was stopping, she was so excited that, while standing on a log by the side of her horse, preparatory to mounting him, just as she had repeated in a raised voice the words, "He says a Christian may fall and be lost; he preached a falsehood, for I know a Christian cannot fall," she made a spring for the saddle, but did so with such force that she fell to the ground on the opposite side of the horse—not hurt, however. "Now," said the Methodist lady, "that is to pay you for getting angry. I hope you will admit hereafter that a Christian may fall." The offended woman afterward became a Methodist, and with great humor often related the incident.

The excessive labors of two years had so impaired the health of Mr. Ralston that he was no longer able to perform the duties of an itinerant, and at the suggestion of brethren sought for rest in a local sphere. During the four years in which he was a local preacher he preached as often as his feeble health would permit, and often beyond his strength.

Entering the itinerant field in Illinois, in 1833, he had lost none of the zeal which had characterized his early ministry, but with untiring energy continued to persuade men to turn to God. In the town of Rushville a meeting, which was protracted through more than two months, resulted in the conversion of one hundred persons.*

---

*In Rushville there was residing, during this revival, a very reputable citizen—Dr. Cossett, an eminent physician—past middle age, and an avowed skeptic as to Christianity. He had been in the habit of indulging for many years in his daily drams, but never was known to be too much influenced thereby to attend to his professional calls. He had always been a regular attendant at church. His little daughter, perhaps eight or nine years old, professed conversion. She instantly rose from her seat, her countenance shining as did that of Stephen, and rushed to the bosom of her father. When the invitation for members was given, she came forward, among others, to join. As soon as the song closed, the doctor approached me, and asked the privilege of speaking. I replied, "Certainly," but feared he was desirous to explain his reasons for objecting to his daughter joining the Church. But no; I was mistaken. He spoke, with a trembling voice, substantially as follows: "I have been a skeptic all my life, till now. I know but little about the Bible. My little daughter, since she has been attending your Sunday-school, has taught me more about it than I ever knew before. I am now convinced that your religion is a reality. I know that my daughter is no hypocrite. I am resolved to change my life. I know not how to pray as these good brethren can pray. I ask you all to pray for me, and if you can receive such an old wretched sinner I wish to join the Church with my little daughter." The house was electrified; saint and sinner alike wept. He was admitted, and welcomed with universal acclamation. In about a month afterward he was taken severely ill. His physicians advised him to take some wine, brandy, or something to stimulate

On his return to Kentucky success still crowned his labors. On the Versailles Circuit he enjoyed a year of prosperity, in Frankfort he had seals to his ministry, and in Maysville many were converted and added to the Church.

He was appointed to Louisville in 1839, immediately after the most extraordinary revival that had ever occurred in that city. John Newland Maffitt had been eminently successful. A vast amount of work had necessarily to be performed in taking care of those who had entered the communion of the Church, and most faithfully did Mr. Ralston address himself to the task.

As Agent for Augusta College he traveled extensively, and labored faithfully to promote the interest confided to his care.

In Shelbyville, a gracious revival blessed the Church. Worn down by excessive labor, he yields to his wasting strength, and asks at the hands of his brethren a superannuated relation.

Richard Corwine, John Denham, and Elihu Green, had died. The two former were veterans,* the latter was in the morning of life.

Elihu Green was born, in Madison county, Kentucky, July 28, 1814. He was brought up under the

---

him. He replied: "*No.* I promised God when I joined the Church never to touch or taste it again. I am ready to die, but not to break my promise." He was resolutely firm. A few days afterward I sat by his bed, and saw him breathe his last in peaceful triumph.—*Letter from Dr. Ralston to the author.*

* For sketches of Richard Corwine and John Denham, see the "History of Methodism in Kentucky."

influence of a deeply pious mother. In 1837 he was converted to God, and soon felt inwardly moved to the work of the ministry. He was admitted on trial into the Kentucky Conference in 1838, and was appointed to the Mount Vernon Mission. He spent his second year on the West Liberty Mission. He subsequently traveled on the Lawrenceburg and Wayne Circuits. In these several charges he was useful and beloved. His last appointment was to the Bowling Green Circuit, in 1842, where, with the zeal which had distinguished him in other fields, he prosecuted his high and holy calling. He had just closed his year's work when arrested by the fever which terminated his useful life. When asked, in reference to his approaching change of worlds, if he was afraid to die, he replied, "No," and added:

"On Jordan's stormy banks I stand,
And cast a wishful eye
To Canaan's fair and happy land,
Where my possessions lie."

On the day before his death, arousing from a slumber, he sang the stanza of the hymn "Rock of Ages," beginning,

While I draw this fleeting breath,
When my eyes shall close in death,

and then remarked, "I am going straight to heaven." Sunday morning, September 10, 1843, his happy spirit left the earth in full prospect of that "rest that remaineth to the people of God."

The amount collected for missions was *two thousand eight hundred and thirty-nine dollars and eighty-one cents*, which was an improvement over the former year.

We meet with John Christian Harrison, again in charge of the Augusta District. He was born, in Mecklenburg county, North Carolina, October 1, 1809. He was the second son of Samuel Harrison, at that time and for many years after a member of the South Carolina Conference.* His mother, whose maiden name was Ann Rosser, was among the first fruits of Methodism in Roanoke county, Virginia. When John Christian Harrison was in his tenth year his excellent father, then in feeble health, located. The great West presenting an inviting field for emigration, in February, 1819, he left South Carolina, and set out in a small wagon, with his wife and children, to cross the mountains. The suffering and exposure of that journey made a deep impression on all the family, especially on John, the youngest child. The winter was an open, rainy one, with great variableness of the weather. The newly-opened territory of Indiana was the intended point of their destination. Reaching Franklin county, Kentucky, on the 6th of March, the jaded and worn-out condition of the horses rendered it impossible to prosecute their journey, and, after resting a few days, Mr. Harrison leased a farm in Mercer county. A short time afterward he purchased a farm in the same county, on which he passed the remainder of his life.

Brought up in the nurture and admonition of the Lord, and deeply concerned on the subject of re-

*For a sketch of Samuel Harrison, see the "History of Methodism in Kentucky."

ligion, John joined the Methodist Episcopal Church, August 29, 1827, at a camp-meeting held at Rockbridge, Shelby county, Kentucky. On the same day he was happily converted to God. Soon after his conversion he believed it to be his duty to preach the gospel, but shrank from the responsibility of the work, fearing that he was not suitably qualified to undertake it.

His refusal to enter the ministry cost him his religious comfort and many months of perplexity and doubt. Consenting at last to yield to the convictions of his heart, his "peace" again "flowed like a river," and all was happiness, and joy, and love. In August, 1828, he became the leader of a class, and commenced in earnest to exhort his classmates and others "to make their calling and election sure." September 7, 1829, he was licensed to exhort, and on the 18th of September, 1830, George W. Taylor licensed him to preach the gospel.

At the session of the Kentucky Conference, held in Danville the following October, he was admitted on trial, and appointed to the Mount Vernon Circuit, as the colleague of Thomas Wallace. The first fruits of his labors in the itinerant ministry were gathered at a meeting held near Mount Vernon, November 13 and 14, at which one or two persons professed religion and three joined the Church.

The Mount Vernon Circuit at this time embraced Rockcastle and Laurel counties, the larger portion of Clay, and extended into Pulaski and Lincoln. The country was mountainous and sparsely settled, with twenty-two regular appointments to be filled every four weeks, and occasional preaching at intervals. The winter was excessively cold, and the travel oftentimes attended with difficulties almost insuperable; yet, nothing daunted, this faithful preacher of the gospel met his appointments with remarkable promptness, carrying the tidings of a Redeemer's love to the cabins of the poor. In January Thomas Wallace, the preacher in charge, was compelled by feebleness of health to retire from the work, leaving the responsibility of its management with his young and inexperienced colleague. We have his journal before us, and as we follow him from place to place familiar names often occur, and we recount the difficulties through which we passed when a few years later, a beardless boy, we bore aloft the banner of the cross in much of the same territory. Notwithstanding the obstacles that impeded Mr. Harrison, he never faltered. His visit to his parents during the year is recorded with filial tenderness. In summing up his labors at the close of the year, he says: "I have traveled two thousand miles; have preached about two hundred times; have received from the Church for my support about fifty dollars; have suffered the extremes of heat and cold, of wet and drought; have been sick and have enjoyed health; have been on the mountain-top and in the valley low. I have read much, reflected much, prayed much. I have seen some few sinners turned from the error of their ways, but, upon the whole, have felt rather discouraged. I have not succeeded according to my hopes or wishes, and now feel more than ever my insufficiency for this great work."

Mr. Harrison did not attend the Conference that year, but remained at home to plant the small grain on the farm, while his father attended the Conference. On the return of his father he handed him the plan of the Mount Vernon Circuit, to which he was reäppointed, with the remark: "John, the Bishop has sent you back to do your work over again." The young man's reply was: "Another year in the mountains! I presume I shall get used to it."

Considerable prosperity continued to bless his labors. His journal contains an account of heart-searching examinations, of difficulties, of trials, and successes, and everywhere the spirit of entire consecration to the work to which he had pledged his energies and his life.

At the Conference of 1832 Mr. Harrison, not being fully satisfied as to the scriptural authority for infant baptism, submitted his difficulties to the Committee of Examination for the Undergraduates, and, at his own request, was continued another year on trial. From this Conference he was sent to the Somerset Circuit, with Thomas L. Davis as his colleague. This circuit covered a large territory, embracing the most of Pulaski, Russell, and Casey counties, with portions of Adair. Although not so mountainous as his former field of labor, yet the face of the country was rugged, contrasting well with the kind-hearted people he was appointed to serve. The year was one of marked prosperity: more than one hundred persons were added to the Church. He concluded his efficient labors in that charge at a camp-meeting held at Bethel, in Casey county.

At the Conference of 1833 he was admitted into full connection, having, after a thorough investigation of the subject, become fully satisfied that infant baptism is taught in God's word. He was appointed to the Green River Circuit, with Bluford Henry. Without the advantages of an ordinary education before he entered the ministry, Mr. Harrison had during the three years of his itinerant life been a close and untiring student. In the charges he had filled his facilities for study were by no means favorable, and yet his course of theological reading had been extensive, and he was now taking rank with the more prominent men of his age. An opportunity presented itself at this time for him to commence, under a suitable instructor, the study of the Greek language, and he promptly availed himself of the privilege. Professor Duke, of Green County Seminary, kindly offered to instruct him. In this department of study he made rapid improvement.

Good meetings during the year, and two successful camp-meetings—one at Breeding's, in Adair county, and the other at Hilliard's, in Green county—rejoiced the hearts of preachers and people.

At the ensuing Conference he was appointed to the Yellow Banks Circuit. After traveling one round he was summoned home by the death of his father, whose end was peaceful and happy. Unable to return to this charge because of its remoteness from his widowed mother, a change was effected between him and Robert F. Turner, who had been sent to the Taylorsville Circuit. Mr. Harrison entered upon the work in this charge about the middle of February, and at the following Conference was reäppointed to the same field, where he was eminently useful. At the Conference of 1835 he was elected a Reserve Delegate to the General Conference—a high compliment to so young a preacher.

We have seen that during the period of Mr. Harrison's ministry through which we have passed his fields of labor were extensive, and his support meager; yet he devoted himself to his work with the zeal of a true minister of Jesus Christ. Six years had elapsed since, with a feeling of insufficiency for the duties to which God had called him, he had left his father's house to preach the gospel of the grace of God. He was then a youth, timid and reserved. Step by step he had advanced, not rapidly but surely, until at the Conference of 1836 he takes his place in the front ranks among his brethren, a place he would occupy to the close of his life.

As the colleague of Benjamin T. Crouch he was sent to the city of Louisville, and stationed at the Fourth-street Church. From this time he occupied a large space in public thought as an able minister of the New Testament. He remained in Louisville for two years, faithfully and successfully performing the duties of an evangelist. A gracious revival blessed his ministry, and many turned to the Lord. Side by side with George W. Brush, who was stationed at Brook-street, he labored, never seeming to tire while sinners were coming back to God. Hundreds were brought to Christ.

From Louisville we follow him to Lexington, where he witnessed some prosperity. At the close of this year he was married to Miss Virginia J. Coke, daughter of Thomas Coke, of Anderson, one of the best women in the Church, and a member of one of the best Methodist families in Kentucky. His next appointment was to Russellville, where he was still useful. In 1840 he was sent to Frankfort, the capital of the State. A few months after he entered upon his work in Frankfort his aged and pious mother was called to heaven. On the 23d of December she exchanged the sorrows of the present life for a crown that will never fade away. In 1841 he was again sent to Louisville, and stationed at Brook-street, where he had a pleasant and successful year. At the Conference of 1842 he was appointed to the Augusta District, and became the gallant and faithful leader in that extensive field. In 1843 he sustained to us the responsibe relation of Presiding Elder, in charge of the same District to which he was appointed in 1842; and here we had every opportunity to know him well. Possessing fine executive powers, he filled the office with an ability that claimed the respect of all who knew him. With preaching-talents of a high order, he occupied a commanding eminence with the preachers and the people. Faithful in the discharge of the duties assigned him, and devoted to the Church, he enjoyed the confidence of all who knew him. Impartial in the administration of the affairs of the Church, he defied the criticism and challenged the admiration of all. Such was John Christian Harrison in 1843.

As the Presiding Elder on the Augusta District, he discharged every duty with fidelity, and by his ability in the pulpit, his spotless integrity, his earnest devotion, contributed to the advancement of the kingdom of the Redeemer.

This year we find the eloquent and zealous Napoleon B. Lewis in Maysville. Although the General Minutes show a small decrease in both the white and colored membership, yet his ministry was blessed with an interesting revival of religion. During a meeting held in the winter the altar of his Church was crowded with penitent sinners, inquiring for the way of life and salvation.

Albert H. Redford was placed in charge of the Minerva Circuit. His colleague was George B. Poage, a young man just admitted on trial.

Mr. Poage was born January 18, 1823, in Greenup county (now Boyd), Kentucky, one mile above where the town of Ashland now stands. His family was one of the most influential in that part of the State, and both his father and mother were pious members of the Presbyterian Church. Under the ministry of Jedidiah Foster he joined the Methodist Episcopal Church, in the town of Louisa, February 16, 1841, and was happily converted to God on the 25th of the next month. In December, 1842, he was licensed to preach by William B. Landrum, and was admitted on trial into the Kentucky Conference in 1843.

Entering upon the work of the ministry in the Minerva Circuit before he had reached his majority, with but a brief experience in the Church, we were surprised to find him so well prepared to perform the arduous duties of an itinerant. He filled his appointments for preaching, conducted prayer-meetings, met the classes, and visited among the people, as though he had been in the harness for several years. Not only beloved by the Church, but in the affections of many who were not members he soon won a warm place, while his fervent piety and burning zeal led many to the altars of the Church and to Christ.

The first meeting of special interest was commenced at Mount Zion on Christmas-day. For several days and nights the gospel preached had no apparent effect on the multitudes assembled at the place of worship. The Church entered into solemn covenant to pray to God to revive his work, and not to cease in their efforts until their prayers were answered. It was midnight, and the altar was crowded with penitents; but no voice of thanksgiving and praise had gone up to heaven. More than a year had passed since the shout of triumph from a soul new born to God had been heard within the walls of that church, consecrated by so many pleasant memories. One o'clock has come and passed, and tears of repentance are chasing each other down the cheek of sorrow for having sinned against God. A moment later, and a note of joy from the altar rings through the house. A soul has "passed from death unto life." Again and again the fetters fall, and souls regenerated give thanks to God. In a few moments six persons found the "pearl of great price." The meeting continued for several days.

Upward of sixty were converted, and seventy persons were added to the Church. About the middle of January a meeting was held at the Stone Church, a few miles below Maysville, at which twenty persons were enrolled as members.

Campbellism boasted a large organization at this time in Brooksville, an appointment in this circuit. A short time before a preacher of that persuasion had made an appointment to occupy the court-house (the only place for preaching in the town) at the same hour at which the preacher in charge of the circuit had an appointment. As the time approached an intense excitement prevailed in the community. The court-house was lighted by the Campbellites before sunset, and long before the hour for preaching every seat was occupied. A committee waited on the Methodist preacher, to inquire whether or not he expected to preach, and on receiving an affirmative reply, it was proposed that he have an interview with the Campbellite preacher, which he respectfully declined. The two preachers met in the court-house just as the hour arrived for the commencement of the service. An introduction passed, and then the Methodist preacher opened his hymn-book and was about to read his hymn, when the following conversation ensued:

Campbellite.—There is an unfortunate state of things here to-night.

Methodist.—If so, can you inform me who is responsible for it?

Campbellite.—Well, I hardly know.

Methodist.—Did you not preach in this house this

morning? and when you announced an appointment for this evening, were you not publicly informed that this hour belongs to the Methodist Church, and that I would occupy the house?

Campbellite.—Yes; but I thought we might arrange the affair peacefully, and I now propose that we both preach.

Methodist.—I cannot hinder you from preaching when I shall close my service, nor do I desire to do so; but you may feel assured that I regard your interference with my appointment as a violation of Christian courtesy.

The Methodist preacher occupied the stand, and at the close of the service dismissed the congregation, upon which they were requested to remain and hear another sermon. The text was, "But speak thou the things which become sound doctrine," and yet no doctrine whatever was presented and advocated by the preacher.

Early in February a meeting was held in Brooksville, where there had never been a conversion. A few persons had removed from other places, and formed a small Society. The meeting continued only one week. It was a time of great power. Eighty persons were converted, and sixty-seven joined the Church.

Among those who professed religion during the meeting at Brooksville were several who had passed three-score years. An incident occurred at this meeting, in which the power of grace was displayed, that ought not to be forgotten. Three young persons—a brother and two sisters—had joined the

Church, and the brother and one of the sisters had professed religion. Their only surviving parent was their father, who was an avowed Universalist. On learning that his children had joined the Methodist Church he became enraged, and declared that they should never return home. That evening he came into Brooksville, and, anxious to know the influence that had operated upon his children, attended the place of worship. At the close of the sermon, when penitents were invited to the altar, his daughter who had not been converted was among the first to present herself. As she knelt, her father, exasperated, approached the spot, and was bending over her to take her from the house, when his son and remaining daughter, observing him, and believing that he had gone forward to ask an interest in the prayers of the Church, rushed through the assembly, and, falling upon his neck and compelling him to kneel, shouted aloud the praises of God. Unable to extricate himself, he sent for one of the preachers, to whom he stated his dilemma (which had been discovered by the preacher), informing him that he had only come to take his daughter away, and that if he would get him out of the unpleasant position he was in his daughter might remain. The preacher suggested that he continue upon his knees until a public prayer should be offered, and at its close he could arise and leave without any disturbance. Among the members of the Church who were present was a pious woman named Lydia Hawes, a fine singer and remarkably gifted in prayer. The preacher called on Lydia Hawes to pray. The congregation knelt, and while on their knees, before praying, she sang, alone,

"Show pity, Lord, O Lord, forgive,
Let a repenting rebel live:
Are not thy mercies large and free?
May not a sinner trust in thee?"

She then offered up an earnest prayer to God, remembering her old friend and neighbor, and expressing gratitude that he had resolved to seek the salvation of his soul. The effect was wonderful. The prayer closed, and still he knelt.

"You can leave this place now," said the preacher.

"I would rather not. I feel that I am a sinner, exposed to almighty wrath, and wish an interest in the prayers of God's people," was the reply.

An hour later the court-house rang with the shout of triumph as the father and all his children, in each other's embrace, gave glory to God. The scene was grand beyond description.

On the 10th of February the second quarterly-meeting commenced in Augusta, and continued over two weeks, at which seventy-eight persons were added to the Church. At Minerva a meeting was held a few weeks later, which resulted in a gracious revival of religion. On Sunday evening of the meeting a lady was converted in the congregation, and, rising from her seat, pressed to the altar, praising God. Her husband was standing at the door of the church, surrounded by his companions, who, like himself, "cared for none of these things." A brief conversation with them ensued, and then he started down the aisle, determined to take his wife from the church. The members of the Church, observing him, and anticipating his purpose, gathered around her to prevent any interference. As he approached the altar, his lips white with rage, the preacher in charge said: "Mr. H——, your wife is converted. Stand out of the way, brethren, and let Mr. H—— shake hands with his wife." A benignant smile came over his face as he turned toward the preacher, and, offering his hand, exclaimed, "I will join your Church, too!" He made an excellent member.

At Dover there were times of refreshing, and before the first of April three hundred and fifteen persons joined the Church, in the circuit, and before the year closed more than five hundred cast in their lot with the people of God.

While this work of grace was progressing in the Minerva Circuit, there was an interesting revival of religion in the Germantown Circuit, which adjoined it, under the ministry of Thomas Rankin. The Shannon Circuit, too, with Jedidiah Foster in charge, enjoyed times of prosperity. At Nelson Asbury's, a meeting commenced on the 23d of August, and continued one week, at which fifty persons were converted, making a total during the year of one hundred and sixty-eight.

On the Little Sandy Circuit, Samuel Kelly made full proof of his ministry. In that rugged field he accomplished much good, and was instrumental in bringing many to Christ.

Gilby Kelly succeeded John James on the Covington District. This was the first experience of Mr. Kelly as a Presiding Elder. He was eminently qualified for the responsible trust, and performed the duties assigned him with signal ability. In the city of Covington, to which George C. Light had been appointed, a meeting was commenced in February, at which twenty-four were added to the Church; while at Newport the ministry of Fielding Bell was remarkably successful. In the Falmouth Circuit, Alexander B. Sollars reported thirty additions to the Church at Pisgah Meeting-house. On the Leesburg Circuit, "the pleasure of the Lord" prospered in the hands of William C. Atmore.

The name of Benjamin T. Crouch was still a tower of strength in the Lexington District. Since 1840 he had occupied this field, and as a Presiding Elder had but few peers. Under his leadership the Church improved in numbers and in influence. The Mount Sterling and Athens Circuits—the former in charge of Moses Levi, and the latter served by Joshua Wilson—and the Frankfort Station, whose pastor was Charles B. Parsons, increased in membership, while the remainder of the District reports a falling off. It is often true that a declension in numbers succeeds a large ingathering into the Church. For several years almost unparalleled success had followed the labors of faithful men in this section of the State, and a small decrease in the membership the present year affords no reason for discouragement.

The Transylvania University had reached the zenith of its glory. The eloquent and gifted Henry B. Bascom presided over its fortunes, while Burr H. McCown, William H. Anderson, R. T. P. Allen,

Josiah L. Kemp, and Thomas H. Lynch, composed the Faculty.

Burr H. McCown was born October 29, 1806, in Bardstown, Kentucky, and in 1818 was converted to God. In 1824 he joined the Presbyterian Church; but, believing the doctrines of the Methodist Episcopal Church to accord more fully with the teachings of the Bible, in 1826 he joined the Methodist Church, under the ministry of Hubbard H. Kavanaugh. He was educated at St. Joseph College, in Bardstown, and took the highest honors of his class in both the Latin and Greek languages.

From the time he became a member of the Presbyterian Church he had expected to enter the ministry in that denomination. We are not surprised, therefore, to find him in the Methodist ministry. He was licensed to preach by Marcus Lindsey, in 1826, and in 1827 was admitted on trial into the Kentucky Conference. His first appointment was to the Henry Circuit, as the colleague of William Atherton. In 1828 he was appointed, with John James, to the Jefferson Circuit. At the Conference of 1829 he was stationed in Russellville, and in 1830 in Louisville. In 1831 he was elected to a professorship in Augusta College, where he continued until 1842, when, with Henry B. Bascom, he removed to Lexington, and became a professor in Transylvania University.

During the four years that Mr. McCown was in the pastoral work he was useful and beloved. A superior preacher, with a sweet and gentle disposition, courteous to all, his address popular, and his personal appearance commanding, he exerted an influence for good that could be claimed by but few young men of his day. When we have seen him in the pulpit, and heard him preach the unsearchable riches of Christ, we have regretted that he was ever called from the pastoral work, in which he was so happy, and where he was so useful. In the halls of learning, however, he lost none of the zeal that had distinguished him as a pastor, and none of the love that had constrained him to enter the ministry. As a teacher he acquired an enviable reputation, and contributed much toward the formation of the character of hundreds of young men who, throughout the West and the South, adorn the learned professions.

William H. Anderson was born, in Wilmington, North Carolina, September 17, 1817. In 1827 his father removed from Wilmington to Richmond, Virginia. While a student at the Wesleyan University, in Middletown, Connecticut, in the autumn of 1833, he was happily converted to God. In 1835 his father removed from Richmond, Virginia, to Louisville, Kentucky; and in 1837, at the close of his classical course in the Wesleyan University, William H. Anderson followed his father to the West. Dedicated to God in baptism, in infancy, and brought up in a pious home, we are not surprised that in the dewy morn of life he gave his heart to God. Fully impressed with the conviction that he ought to preach the gospel, in the autumn of 1838 he received license from Benjamin T. Crouch, and entered the Conference the same autumn. His first appointment was to the Newcastle Circuit, as the colleague of the zealous James D. Holding. His second year he was sent to La Grange, with John Beatty. In 1840 he was appointed to Bowling Green, where we still find him in 1841. In 1842 he was appointed to the city of Frankfort, as pastor of the Church and as Agent for the Transylvania University. Before the close of the year he was called away from the pastoral work, where his ministry had been so greatly blessed, to fill the chair of English Literature in the Transylvania University, to which he was officially appointed in 1843.

No young man who had entered the itinerant ranks in Kentucky, for many years, had given greater promise of usefulness than did William H. Anderson. Descended from one of the most prominent and influential families, his education thorough, his piety uniform and consistent, his zeal uncompromising, his address winning, courteous in his manners, devoted to the Church, his style in the pulpit popular and attractive, and with a voice soft and sweet, his entrance into the ministry was looked to with more than ordinary interest. On the Newcastle Circuit, his first field of labor, under his burning words and warm appeals many hearts were touched, and fell in love with the Saviour. Wherever he preached crowds hung in breathless silence on his lips, and under his instrumentality hundreds were brought to Christ. On the La Grange Circuit the same success distinguished his labors, and many were the seals to his ministry. Before his appointment to the Bowling Green Station he had taken rank with the first preachers in the State. In that charge he continued to be eminently useful in winning souls to Christ. In the city of Frankfort, as a preacher, he occupied a commanding eminence, which he continued to maintain amid the classic halls of Transylvania.

In the Shelbyville District, the Lockport, Bloomfield, Springfield, and Lawrenceburg Circuits, and the Bardstown Station, show a small increase. William Gunn, the Presiding Elder, one of the truest men in the Church, labored with diligence, and the noble men associated with him discharged their duty with fidelity; yet the increase is small in the charges we have mentioned, while in the remainder the decrease is considerable.

The Louisville District shows a decrease of fifty-three in the white membership, and an increase of twenty-two in the colored. In several charges, in this District, however, there were gracious revivals of religion. In the city of Louisville, under the ministry of George W. Merritt, upward of one hundred persons were added to the Church; while in Upper Station (now Shelby-street) two hundred and four were received into the Church. In the other charges in the city there were times of refreshing, but no general revival.

In the Louisville Circuit, George W. Crumbaugh, a sweet-spirited preacher, was much beloved by the people. He was born, in Russellville, Kentucky, February 19, 1812, and in the same town was converted under the ministry of Peter Akers, in June, 1828, and at the same time joined the Methodist

Episcopal Church. In 1830 he was licensed to preach by Benjamin T. Crouch. For ten years he exercised his gifts as a local preacher, and in 1840 was admitted on trial into the Kentucky Conference. He was appointed to the Taylorsville Circuit, in the bounds of which he had resided previous to his entering the itinerant ranks, and where he remained for two years. In 1842 his field of labor was the Shepherdsville Circuit, and in 1843 the Louisville Circuit. He was a mild and pleasant preacher, and frequently preached with remarkable power. He was amongst the first ministers whom we knew, and through many years of intimate acquaintance we never heard him speak unkindly of any one.

We are gratified to find the name of George S. Gatewood in the list of appointments. He entered the traveling connection in 1836, and was appointed to the Madison Circuit, with Absalom Woolliscroft, both of whom were returned to the same charge the next year. In 1838 he was sent alone to the Williamsburg Circuit, and in 1839 to the Madisonville Circuit. In the itinerant ranks, but few men were more useful than George S. Gatewood. With a singleness of purpose he addressed himself to the arduous and responsible work of the ministry, and was successful. Hundreds were awakened and converted under his faithful labors. In 1840 he located. We regretted the step at the time, and rejoiced when he reëntered the Conference.

In the General Minutes, the Hardinsburg District shows a decrease in membership. Upon a careful examination, however, we find a more favorable exhibit. Several large and influential circuits were taken from it and placed in the Morganfield, a new District, just formed. In addition to this, the numbers in the Litchfield Circuit are entirely overlooked.

In the Hardinsburg Circuit, in the pleasant village of Hardinsburg, Richard D. Neale, the Presiding Elder, reported, on the 6th of June, an interesting meeting, at which there were several conversions and accessions. The preachers in this circuit were Bartlett A. Basham and Hiram T. Downard, men distinguished for their piety and zeal. On the 19th of August Mr. Neale reports fourteen conversions and sixteen accessions to the Church, at the fourth quarterly-meeting in the Hawesville Circuit, and at a meeting just held in the Owensboro Circuit an addition of six; while on the Hartford Circuit, at Bethel, at a meeting held July 20 and 21, there were "several conversions and ten additions." In the Big Spring Circuit, William McD. Abbett reports "an increase of fifty-nine members," and says: "At our late camp-meeting, although disappointed in the ministerial help we expected, we were not disappointed in the help and presence of the Holy One of Israel. His power was displayed in the conviction and conversion of about eighteen souls."* In the Brandenburg Station, Wesley G. Montgomery was beloved and useful. The Morgantown Circuit was greatly blessed; George W. Burriss, the preacher, was a young man of great zeal, and did much good. No charge in the District, however, enjoyed greater prosperity than did the Hartford Circuit, whose

* *Western Christian Advocate*, September 20, 1844.

preachers were Peter Duncan and Allen Sears, both energetic and laborious men in the ministry.

At this Conference the Morganfield District was formed, from portions of the Hardinsburg and Hopkinsville Districts, and the beloved Richard Tydings appointed to take charge of it. In this District there was an increase in the membership in every charge. The Henderson Station, under the ministry of James I. Ferree, continued to prosper, while the Henderson Circuit, with Learner B. Davison in charge, enjoyed many refreshing seasons.

Learner B. Davison was born May 3, 1813, in Grayson county, Kentucky. His parents were pious members of the Methodist Episcopal Church, and brought him up "in the nurture and admonition of the Lord." On the 7th of August, 1831, he embraced religion, and, during the first week in the following October, James L. Greenup received him into the Church. He believed himself to be divinely called to preach the gospel, but circumstances appeared unfavorable for him to enter fully upon the work. His duty to his parents required his attention to the affairs of home. Through several years his struggles were severe. However, he exercised his gifts as a class-leader, and often held prayer-meetings, where he endeavored to persuade sinners to be reconciled to God. On the 19th of March, 1842, he was licensed to preach by Richard D. Neale, and appointed to the Hardinsburg Circuit, with Seraiah S. Deering. At the Conference of 1843 he was sent to the Henderson Circuit, where we now find him laboring with apostolic zeal. He commenced a meeting at Hancock's School-house on Christmas-day, assisted by Messrs. Dutton and Fallin, two faithful local preachers, at which twenty-two persons were converted and twenty-eight joined the Church. On the 18th of March he writes: "Since my last correspondence I have received thirty-four probationers—in all, since Conference, sixty-six."* On the 5th of September he says: "God has poured out his Spirit, in a very powerful manner, at nearly every appointment. Since my last correspondence one hundred and fourteen persons have been admitted on trial—making, in all, this year, one hundred and eighty." In every department of his work Learner B. Davison was a faithful and acceptable minister of Christ, and promised great usefulness to the Church.

The Madisonville Circuit was served by Samuel Turner, and the Morganfield Circuit by Isham R. Finley, both of whom were useful preachers of the gospel.

Samuel L. Robertson and William J. Chenowith were appointed to the Salem Circuit.

In Smithland, under the ministry of Francis M. English, a zealous young preacher, assisted by Messrs. Taylor, Lancaster, and Robertson, there was an interesting revival of religion. Commencing with the quarterly-meeting, on the first Saturday in December, the good work resulted in "many conversions" and "sixty-seven additions to the Church." In Eddyville, twenty-seven persons were added to the Church, at the first quarterly-meeting, held in De-

* *Western Christian Advocate,* April 19, 1844.

cember. Ransom Lancaster, the efficient pastor, was at his post, and was assisted by Messrs. Taylor, English, and Baldwin. On the Princeton Circuit, Samuel D. Baldwin was instrumental in doing much good. Revivals crowned his labors, and many were happily converted.

In the Russellville District, there was almost a calm. In the Logan, the Elkton, and the Greenville Circuits, there was an increase of a few white members, but a decrease of the colored. Russellville and Hopkinsville show a decrease in the white and a small increase in the colored membership. In the other charges there was a decrease in both the white and colored membership. In the District, however, there were several interesting revivals of religion. The Church in Cadiz prospered greatly under the ministry of Zachariah M. Taylor.

The name of Robert Fisk—on the Franklin Circuit—has frequently appeared in these pages. He was the son of Henry and Martha Fisk, and was born, in Monroe county, Virginia, November 30, 1811. In 1816 his parents, who were distinguished for piety and devotion to the Church, removed to Kentucky, and settled in Montgomery county, and became members of the Grassy Lick Society. Blessed with religious instruction, Robert Fisk became awakened and fully convinced of sin when quite a child. He joined the Methodist Church in 1826, under the ministry of Isaac Collard, and soon afterward found "the peace of God, which passeth all understanding." Divinely called to the work of the ministry, he was licensed to exhort by Henry J. Evans, in the spring of 1834, and served as assistant preacher on the Danville Circuit, by the appointment of the Presiding Elder. At the ensuing Conference he was admitted on trial, and appointed to the Port William Circuit, as the colleague of Gilby Kelly. In 1835 he was sent to the Georgetown Circuit, with Joseph Marsee, and in 1836 to the Barboursville Mission. The field of his labor in 1837 was the Newcastle Circuit, with William Helm in charge, and in 1838 the Burksville Circuit, to which he was returned the following year. At the Conference of 1840 we find him in charge of the Scottsville Circuit, and in 1841 on the Lawrenceburg Circuit. In 1842 he was sent to the Princeton Circuit, and in 1843 he succeeded George Riach on the Franklin Circuit. Among the preachers of the Kentucky Conference, but few men have been more laborious than Robert Fisk. Reared in the lap of Methodism, connected with one of the best families in the State of Kentucky, converted in childhood, and entering the ministry in early life, he devoted himself to the duties of his high and holy calling with commendable zeal, and prosecuted his work with fidelity and success. In the several charges he had filled his labors were blessed, and many were brought to Christ.

The venerable George W. Taylor still presided over the Bowling Green District. Almost every portion of this extensive field exhibited signs of prosperity. In the Greensburg Circuit, to which Albert Kelly and Timothy C. Frogge were appointed, the showers of grace were frequent and refreshing. The preachers were both zealous and useful. Mr. Kelly had been a traveling preacher for several years, but his colleague had just entered the Conference.

Timothy C. Frogge was born, in Fentress county, Tennessee, April 21, 1821. He was happily converted to God in August, 1837, in Wayne county, Kentucky, and joined the Methodist Episcopal Church in September of the same year. In June, 1840, he was licensed to preach by James King. Brought up under religious influence, in the Methodist Church, the grandson of the faithful and zealous Timothy Carpenter, and knowing the Scriptures from a child, he bade fair to be useful in the ministry. In 1843 he was admitted on trial into the Kentucky Conference.

John S. Magee, a zealous and efficient young preacher, was appointed to the Barren Circuit. He was born, in Beavertown, Pennsylvania, December 9, 1819, but was brought up chiefly in Fayette county, Kentucky, spending, however, a short time in Butler county, Ohio. When nine years old he was converted, in Oxford, Ohio. In 1842 he joined the Church, in Salvisa, Kentucky, under the ministry of Richard Deering, and the same year was licensed to preach by James King. At the session of the Kentucky Conference of 1843 he was admitted on trial, and appointed to the Barren Circuit, where he was useful and beloved.

The Bowling Green Circuit enjoyed times of refreshing, under the labors of Robert G. Gardner. Mr. Gardner was an Englishman by birth. He was born, in Kent county, England, May 22, 1806, and joined the Wesleyan Methodists in August, 1822. In 1825 he was happily converted, and emigrated to America in 1830. In 1836 he entered the Kentucky Conference, as a traveling preacher. His first appointment was to the Shelby Circuit, as the colleague of Eli B. Crain. In 1837 he was sent to the Madisonville Circuit, where he remained two years. His field of labor for 1839 and 1840 was the Princeton Circuit, and in 1841 the Hodgenville Circuit. In 1842 he was sent to the Greensburg Circuit, and in 1843 to the Bowling Green Circuit, where we now find him. He was a most industrious and useful preacher.

The Scottsville and Albany Circuits—the former in charge of Munford Pelly, and the latter in charge of Joel Peak—increased in numbers; while the Wayne Circuit, with the sweet-spirited William Lasley, and the Columbia Circuit, with James Penn and Edward A. Martin as the preachers, had seasons of prosperity.

Occasional revivals crowned the labors of the preachers in the Harrodsburg District, yet there was no extraordinary display of divine power within its bounds, during the present year.

The Barboursville District was more prosperous. In the Barboursville Circuit, under the ministry of William P. Read and George Y. Taylor, the revivals were extensive and powerful; while on the Manchester Mission Allen McLaughlin was instrumental in the accomplishment of much good. The Louisa Circuit, under the pastoral care of Marcus L. King, increased largely in numbers and influence.

In Jackson's Purchase, we find Moses Brock in charge of the Paducah District. The Paducah Station shows a considerable decrease in membership, while in every other portion of the District there were large accessions to the Church. In the Hickman Circuit, in charge of Thomas Smith and Jesse F. Walsh, the work of revival was general. Commencing with the first of July, before the last of August two hundred and seventy-five souls were happily converted. The Mayfield Circuit was in a flame. Meredith H. Neal, the preacher, on the 9th of October, reported the revival influence throughout his charge. In the Paducah and the Wadesboro Circuits—the former served by William Lambden and William Higgins, and the latter by Daniel Mooney—the revivals were extensive, embracing hundreds in their influence.

Notwithstanding the revivals with which Kentucky was blessed, there was a decrease of *five hundred and twenty-nine* in the white and *five hundred and forty-eight* in the colored membership.

We have now passed through one of the most brilliant periods of the history of Methodism in Kentucky, embracing twelve years, replete with blessings to the Church and the State. When, in 1832—the date at which this volume opens—the Kentucky Conference assembled in Harrodsburg, there were enrolled in the Minutes the names of one hundred and fourteen preachers, including nineteen who were superannuated and five who were proclaiming the tidings of salvation in Jackson's Purchase, embraced in the Tennessee Conference. At that period there were in the Kentucky Conference six Districts, including fifty-one circuits and stations, besides two circuits in the Purchase. The membership of the Church in Kentucky amounted to *twenty-two thousand three hundred and eight* white and *four thousand six hundred and sixty-nine* colored. Of this number seven hundred and sixty-six white and eighteen colored members belonged to the Purchase. Twelve years have passed, and in Kentucky we find one hundred and seventy-four traveling preachers, including fourteen on the superannuated list and ten in the Paducah District, Memphis Conference. Instead of six Districts we have now eleven in the Kentucky Conference, and instead of fifty-one circuits and stations we have one hundred and sixteen; and instead of two circuits in Jackson's Purchase we have the Paducah District, with eight separate charges, six of which are in Kentucky.

During this period the membership in the Kentucky Conference increased from twenty-one thousand five hundred and forty-two white and four thousand six hundred and fifty-one colored to *thirty-nine thousand three hundred and seventy-seven* white and *nine thousand three hundred and sixty-two* colored members. In Jackson's Purchase, during the same period, the membership increased from seven hundred and sixty-six white and eighteen colored to *three thousand two hundred and thirty-one* white and *ninety-four* colored—making a total of *forty-two thousand six hundred and eight* white and *nine thousand four hundred and fifty-six* colored members. As we look at these results we thank God and take courage.

The History of Methodism in Kentucky.

BY THE REV. A. H. REDFORD, D.D.

IN THREE VOLUMES, WITH ENGRAVINGS — EMBRACING THE PERIOD FROM 1754 TO 1832.

PRICE PER SET: Muslin, $6; Muslin, Gilt, $9; Turkey Morocco, $12. Thirty per cent. discount to Preachers.

TESTIMONIALS OF EDITORS AND OTHERS.

THE portrait-gallery, through which the reader is led with sustained and increasing interest, is rich in original characters. How wide is the difference between Bascom and Axley, between Marcus Lindsey and Jonathan Stamper, Tevis and Holman! The natural diversities in genius and bent of intellect, which liberal training in the schools is apt to temper and shape into the same mold of character, here stand out in their original, sharply-defined features. To the general reader, as well as to the student of mind, this gives wonderful vivacity to the book. Many of these men rose, in sound judgment, acute observation, clearness and power of utterance, far above the average capacity of the human mind; yet each is himself; each possesses his distinguishing quality, his peculiar type of character. It is matter of profound gratification that the names of so many of these faithful, excellent men, over whose memories time was making haste to draw the veil of oblivion, have been rescued by the patient researches of our worthy historian.—*Bishop Wightman.*

It should be in every man's hand. Plain, unostentatious, it recounts the toils, sufferings, and successes of the noble men who planted Methodism in the "Dark and Bloody Ground" of Kentucky. The author is a splendid annalist. He has rescued from oblivion a vast mass of invaluable information, and grouped it into a form that will forever be attractive and useful. No one can get up from the reading of the book without being thrilled with new and holy resolves to emulate the glorious men whose names and deeds fill its pages.—*Rev. C. W. Miller.*

I have gone through "Methodism in Kentucky" again, and cannot say how much I enjoyed it. Dr. Redford has rendered a service of love to the memories of the dead, to whom the Church owes a lasting debt of gratitude, which entitles him to the thanks of the entire Methodist Church. He has rescued their names from oblivion, and has presented their characters in graphic briefness, yet with sufficient fullness to render them recognizable to the Church, as only the wielder of a facile and eloquent pen can do.—*Irish Correspondent.*

It affords me great pleasure to acknowledge the reception of both volumes of your "History of Methodism in Kentucky," the reading of which carried me back to other days, and to many of the men of other days, with a number of whom I was familiar, and of whom I have many fond recollections; and with the decided intelligence, honest independence, and perseverance of the preachers of Kentucky I have always been delighted. "The History of Methodism" is full of interest, not to Kentucky only, but to the Methodists and lovers of Christianity everywhere. Just think of the labor, the suffering, and success of those who introduced and planted Methodism in that State, and with united hearts let us give God all the glory! It affords me sincere pleasure to recommend your book to our people in Virginia, and all over the land, as the most interesting account of what God hath wrought, and by whom he hath wrought it, in that land.—*Bishop Early.*

The work before us is just such a record of the names and deeds of these men of God as I like to read. Dr. Redford has performed a good work for the Church in this publication. He has manifested a most indomitable spirit of patience and energy in the collection of these most important materials. This was a task of great difficulty, as but few could be found from whom important information could be obtained. But the work is obviously a labor of love, and right well has it been performed. The History should be in every family; and the preachers, especially, should read it and have their hearts warmed and their zeal rekindled by studying the self-sacrificing character of the men of God who planted and watered our glorious Methodism on the "Dark and Bloody Ground."—*Bishop Andrew.*

We admire this History because of its fairness and faithfulness. It tells of the good with pleasure, and of the evil from a sense of duty. It shuns not to meet the issues, and shrinks not from the task of disposing of them correctly. Highly as we prize the two volumes out, they would fall far short of meeting the expectations of this generation. It is true that many who were "burning and shining lights" in 1820 still live to bless the Church and link the past with the present, but the most of them have fallen asleep. And we are glad to have more than an intimation from the author that he intends to complete his work, which we sincerely hope he may do, with the same success and satisfaction that he has so far given.—*Christian Observer.*

The history of early Methodism in Kentucky is peculiarly interesting. The peculiarly romantic character of the pioneers of the "Dark and Bloody Ground" found one of its most marked developments in the first generation of Western Methodist itinerants, several of the chief of whom were either natives or foster-sons of Kentucky. Those early adventurers have been gathered up with great diligence and a good degree of success by the author of this work. He seems to write with conscientious fidelity and in good temper.—*Christian Advocate and Journal.*

One valuable trait is its biographical sketches. These are well-drawn pictures of persons whose memories are precious in the Church. We commend it to the Church as a valuable contribution to the history of Methodism in the days of trial that brought out the giants of our cause.—*Western Christian Advocate.*

The author has done a good work not only for Methodism in Kentucky, but for Methodism throughout the land. It is full of valuable information, is written in a pleasant style, and will furnish, when completed, a valuable addition to our historic literature.—*Rev. W. G. E. Cunnyngham, D.D.*

The second volume of this History, like the first, gives a graphic account of the pioneer work of Methodism on the "Dark and Bloody Ground," and interesting sketches of the lives and character of the workers. The work is well done and the material skillfully used. Such a sketch of the toils and triumphs of the pioneers of Methodism, amid hardships little known in modern days, ought to quicken the pulse of the Church and stimulate the ministry to a more ardent self-devotion. We commend it to all our readers.—*Southern Christian Advocate.*

The author, by the admirable style in which he has handled his subject, has invested the truth of religious history with all the interest of romance, and yet he has done it so beautifully that, while he portrays the scenes of a half century ago, we seem to live them over again. When he brings up the experiences of Wilkerson, and Axley, and others, who laid the foundation of the Church in the wilderness, he awakens recollections of the olden time that are dear as pearls to many who have not forgotten them.—*Knoxville Press and Herald.*

Redford's "History of Methodism in Kentucky" came out very opportunely, to tone up the sentiment of the Church by the romance of the early times, to stimulate modern zeal by the example of the fathers, to give fresh vitality and vigor to the denominational feeling by the glorious records of the past. I commend the book. Let it be widely diffused and read till the spirit of aggression once more animates the Church, and the great revival shall be no longer a marvel of history, but a living scene, a realized experience.—*Bishop Pierce.*

We hail the book with pleasure, and, from a few cursory glances, feel sure that we shall read it with much entertainment and profit. The ground over which the author takes us is classic in Methodist history. The noblest deeds of daring and self-denial, for the sake of preaching Christ on the "Dark and Bloody Ground," illustrate the pages of the work, and make the names of the pioneer preachers the precious ointment poured forth on the heads of their successors in the ministry.—*Richmond Christian Advocate.*

Mr. Redford has done good service in his Church and for the cause of Christ. He seems to have gathered up with great care, and narrated with beautiful simplicity, the story of the early trials and triumphs of Methodism in Kentucky. The spirit of his volume is eminently catholic, while yet thoroughly denominational—just the spirit which renders his story one of great interest to Christian people of all evangelical Churches.—*Free Christian Commonwealth* (Presbyterian).

I congratulate the Methodists of Kentucky and the community interested in their history on the signal success of the Rev. A. H. Redford, in writing "The History of Methodism in Kentucky." The style is historic, natural, and flowing. The language is easy, pertinent, and dignified, all telling on the subject in hand. The narrative so absorbs the attention and excites the interest of the reader that he is compelled to read this book.—*Bishop Kavanaugh.*

The friends of evangelical Methodism owe a debt of lasting gratitude to Dr. Redford for this admirable contribution to the literature of our Church. The second volume fully sustains the interest imparted by the first, and the entire work possesses all the fascination of a romance. It is singularly free from that ambitious sectarian and denominational cant which too frequently characterize such productions. —*Episcopal Methodist.*

Never in our life have we been so pleased and entertained by a book. No family should be without it.—*Texas Christian Advocate.*

The Methodists may well congratulate themselves upon having a competent historian to record their past. Dr. Redford's "History of Methodism," the second volume of which is upon our table, is exceedingly well prepared and arranged—in style attractive, natural, and flowing, graphic in description, and the talent, industry, and integrity of the author are guarantees of the reliability of the work as authentic. — *Western Recorder.*

Redford's History is not lacking in matter now for the first time published, but it is also valuable for that which is not new. From magazines and fugitive newspaper contributions—old, dusty, obscure, and out of date—he has rescued materials that were as good as lost, and collocated them into most readable pages, and into a form permanent and of easy reference.—*Bishop McTyeire.*

Showing wonderful industry and research, with very great success in gathering material and matter in a pleasant narrative style, clear, and vigorous, and well sustained, this volume abounds in facts and incidents of the greatest interest to religious readers, particularly to Methodists, not only in Kentucky, but everywhere throughout the country.—*Memphis Christian Advocate.*

All the pioneers of the Church, in the ministry and laity, who did so much to lay the foundations of Methodism in Kentucky, come before us in this work, invested with life-like interest, with all the charm of romance, and yet with all the trustiness of historic truth. The style is unambitious and popular, yet graceful and vigorous.—*Nashville Christian Advocate.*

It is one of the noblest contributions to our Methodist literature that has been made in the last decade. It possesses all the fascination of the most exciting romance and all the moral effect of religion in action. Such a feast as is afforded by these two noble volumes is rarely enjoyed, and hence they should be in every family.—*R. H. Rivers, D.D.*

The history of such a work of faith (Methodism) deserves to have been written. This has been done most faithfully and conscientiously by the Rev. A. H. Redford. The author purposes a continuation of this work, until the whole story is told. We hope to be able to follow him through all his charming narratives.—*Louisville Democrat.*

"Methodism in Kentucky" may be justly regarded as a valuable contribution to the history of our Church, especially in the West and South. It is well calculated to promote zeal and piety among our preachers and people. I read it with much interest.—*Bishop Paine.*

He has produced a contribution to the history of Methodism equal in value to any that has appeared in England or in this country, in romantic interest, stirring incident, and important record.—*New Orleans Christian Advocate.*

Resolved, That we most cheerfully indorse "The History of Methodism in Kentucky," and recommend it to all the friends and members of the Church.—*Louisville Conference.*

Methodists everywhere, and all lovers of the history of moral heroism, ought to purchase and read this excellent History.—*Rev. Lovick Pierce, D.D.*

We join our voice with thousands of others in thanking Dr. Redford for this book, so full of interest and instruction.—*Mrs. Jane T. H. Cross.*

It is the Iliad of our Church in Kentucky—a record of its heroes, their woes and their triumphs.—*Rev. H. A. M. Henderson, D.D.*

www.ingramcontent.com/pod-product-compliance
Lightning Source LLC
LaVergne TN
LVHW021258110826
845150LV00003B/418